Ulysses—En-Gende

CULTURAL FRAMES, FRAMING CULTURE
Robert Newman, Series Editor

Speaking in Hunger: Gender, Discourse, and Consumption in Richardson's Clarissa
Donalee Frega

Raids on Human Consciousness: Writing, Anarchism, and Violence
Arthur F. Redding

Ulysses*—En-Gendered Perspectives: Eighteen New Essays on the Episodes*
Kimberly J. Devlin and Marilyn Reizbaum, editors

Ulysses—En-Gendered Perspectives

Eighteen New Essays on the Episodes

Kimberly J. Devlin and
Marilyn Reizbaum, editors

University of South Carolina Press

Published in Columbia, South Carolina, by the
University of South Carolina Press

Manufactured in the United States of America

03 02 01 00 99 5 4 3 2 1

Library of Congress Cataloging-in-Publication Data

Ulysses en-gendered perspectives : eighteen new essays on the episodes /
Kimberly J. Devlin and Marilyn Reizbaum, editors.
p. cm.
Includes bibliographical references (p.) and index.

ISBN 1-57003-287-4 (cloth)
ISBN 1-57003-288-2 (pbk.)
1. Joyce, James, 1882–1941. Ulysses. 2. Gender identity in literature.
3. Masculinity in literature. 4. Femininity in literature. 5. Sex role in literature.
I. Devlin, Kimberly J., 1957– II. Reizbaum, Marilyn.
PR6019.O9 U7496 1999
823'.912—dc21 98-40221

to sister Cher
and beloved Bill
with gratitude

our thanks to the contributors
for this illumination

Contents

Series Editor's Preface

A commitment to relevance and to influence is the focus of this series of works on cultural studies. The series combines theoretical issues with practical applications so that abstract arguments are made accessible by framing them in terms of contemporary concerns of everyday life. The title of this series, "Cultural Frames, Framing Culture," indicates this intention. It highlights the mutual give-and-take between the way established culture frames our explanations and stories about contemporary affairs and the way these explanations and stories in turn produce the culture that frames them. The series will address a broad audience interested in reading contemporary culture—its images, messages, literature, and rhetoric—through fresh, provocative, and generally accessible approaches.

"Cultural Frames, Framing Culture" will encourage interdisciplinary studies. One of the potentially engaging facets of this series is that it offers books that combine a number of previously separated perspectives and also investigates why these separations have occurred. General topics of this series include pedagogical practices, representations of war, of the elderly or the infirm, religion and politics, constructions of race and gender, and the discourse of ecology.

ROBERT NEWMAN

Preface

The idea for this volume emerged during a workshop at the Zurich James Joyce Foundation in April 1993. The working title for the session, "The Maternal in Joyce," was inherently divided and divisive in its evocation of a specific position, function, and identity that has been variably defined and multiply configured. The approaches to mothers and maternity ranged from the Bahktinian to the Deleuzian to the Lacanian to the Kristevan—to others that defied theoretical conceptualization. By the end of the session, everyone—for better or for worse—was provoked.

At one point in the discussion, Fritz Senn asked if some of the issues raised during the workshop could not be fruitfully explored in a new multiauthored collection of chapter-by-chapter essays on *Ulysses*. Clive Hart and David Hayman developed this particular format over two decades ago in *James Joyce's "Ulysses": Critical Essays* (Berkeley: University of California Press, 1974). Discussing Senn's question several months after the workshop, we were attracted to reduplicating this format on account of its salient organizational features. Most basically, it preserves Joyce's own structural framework for his modernist epic, the eighteen episodes, each of which has a certain integrity within the larger design of *Ulysses.* Each essay in the Hart and Hayman volume captures some of the uniquenesses—the preoccupations, patterns, and developments—within these eighteen separate but integrated units. These sections of *Ulysses* are aligned with distinct critical voices: written by eighteen different Joyce scholars, with varying approaches and concerns, the volume produces an appropriate sense of parallactic vision (a preoccupation of Leopold Bloom and, of course, his creator).

Given the expansion and diversification of Joyce studies over time, we were simultaneously concerned that a parallactic approach to *Ulysses* in the 1990s might produce a very splintered view of the text. With the hope of generating at least one linking critical concern, we decided to formulate a cultural frame—a frame related but not limited to the topic of the Zurich session that led to the volume's inception. We chose to propose the concepts of gender and engenderings—hegemonic tropes in the larger ideological network that figurations of the maternal are enmeshed in. We then asked for participation from a range of Joyce scholars who, as a group, might help produce a new parallactic perspective on the novel.

The selection of our frame evolved from our sense that gender in *Ulysses* is a form of *overwriting,* a term that implies both excess and layering. Overwriting suggests a process of inscription that is profuse, that leaves discursive traces everywhere: gender markings in *Ulysses*—in widely variable forms—leave their imprint in every one of its chapters. Overwriting also suggests a palimpsestic process, a practice of writing over and on other entities, an imposition of a particular differential discourse on other cultural structures, an imprinting process that several essays in this volume document.

Karen Lawrence's contribution on "Lestrygonians," for instance, suggests that cultures often leave gender markings on eating habits, tastes, scents, and food preferences. Bloom's repulsion at the Burton restaurant during lunch hour is constructed as a recoil from a scene of manly eating, of masculinized cannibalistic consumption of dead meat; it is juxtaposed with an encounter with womanly aromas, which assail him before he enters the restaurant. Robert Spoo's essay probes the cultural (il)logic of gender overwriting in historiography, as it is dramatized in "Nestor": history is figured as a nightmare/night-mère, and historical causality is attributed to dangerous feminine initiators of cataclysmic events; yet historical agency remains a masculine domain in which women are consistently ghosted and repressed. Gender as an overwriting is vulnerable to reversal and self-contradiction: in his study of "Aeolus," Patrick McGee argues that subalternity is predominantly associated with femininity, but also, in other contexts, with hypermasculinity (the subjected native as Caliban). McGee further suggests that Joyce realized that revolutionary movements are productive of cultural transformations but are also often aligned with patriarchal authority and sometimes reproductive of imperialist hierarchies: this may be the engendered and anticolonialist logic behind *Ulysses*'s ambivalent, qualified nationalism.

We use the term *en-gendering* to describe a cultural process, often invisible in its workings, yet overly visible in its effects: a process of production (and reproduction) of meanings, that generates (and regenerates) the categories of "masculine" and "feminine" by aligning them with other differential forms and positions. This process inflects cultural perceptions and perceptual relations, as four of the contributions demonstrate. Margot Norris explores the political implications of the en-gendered categories of enchantress and enchanted through a discussion of the "Circe" myth in both Homer and Joyce. She argues that patriarchal culture's pornographical representation of the female as sexually powerful and contaminating, as a dangerous aphrodisiac effect, is in need of a critical moly or *pharmakos.* Joyce's Circean theatricality provides such a *pharmakos* by simultaneously constructing and deconstructing a specific engendered perception: it creates the illusion of the pornographical enchantress while exposing some of the disenchanting realities of the various women behind the discursive fantasy. En-gendered perception is also a concern of Vicki Mahaffey, who discusses the distortional lenses through which women in general and Molly in particular are refracted in masculinist vision. Alternately idealizing and gynephobic, these lenses in the "Ithaca" section transform the female into mysteriously remote and guiding lights but also into sources of fracturing, self-division, and loss. In an essay addressing the structures of spectacle and gazing in "Sirens," Jules Law examines interactive visual perception that disrupts traditional gender paradigms, through a represented female contempt for the male gaze and concomitant interest in dysfunctions of male sight. (Law also traces the frequent overwriting of gender onto nationalist issues, the imbrication of sexual and imperial politics, an imbrication also explored by McGee and Enda Duffy.) Christine Van Boheemen takes a critical stance on Joyce's own perceptions and constructions of the feminine in "Penelope": she emphasizes both the voyeurism and fetishism inherent in the chapter as well as its status as a "projection upon the screen of representation of the unconscious content of the masculine mind."

In this collection, the differentiations of "masculine" and "feminine," their definitions and elaborations, are negotiated in variable ways in variable contexts. In the opening piece on "Telemachus," Garry Leonard suggests that gender difference can be conceptualized as a contrast in levels of awareness of self-performativity and stylization. Feminine masquerade in modernity, he argues, is usually conscious of its constructedness, whereas masculine masquerade misrecognizes itself as something real and substantive—or, at minimum, aspires to the impossible status of the original copy. In Bloom's imagination, according to Maud Ellmann, gender is marked primarily through different occupancies of skin. Women are envisioned as having a precarious bodily integument, easily unbuttoned and shed, while men inhabit a securer physical wrapping, one that is safely—albeit phobically—buttoned up. This particular articulation of femininity, which Ellmann traces through "Lotus-Eaters" (and related parts of the text), may relate to Leonard's contention about the modern ontological alignment of womanliness with a theatrical envelope of sorts.

Our contributors' varying senses of gender differences are often connected to categories of experience. Bonnie Kime Scott's treatment of "Wandering Rocks" implies that the feminine emerges in spatial modes, in terms of marginality and indirect courses of progress; the figures of masculinized professional progress move, in contrast, along more direct and centralized routes. The difficulty of the episode, Scott argues, calls into question the possibilities of mastery, direction, and control, despite patriarchal culture's valorization of such desires. Cheryl Herr's reading of "Proteus" articulates genders through types and means of epistemology: it differentiates between "knowing that" and "knowing how," between male gynecology and female midwifery, and between patristic knowledge proper and marginalized old wives' tales. In a reinterpretation of "Nausicaa," the most overtly gender-divided episode of the text, John Bishop argues that the two halves are not so much en-gendered oppositions as they are sequential complements. The "feminine" and "masculine" parts of the chapter actually explore related and paired experiences: foreplay and the aftermath of coitus; the compensations of romance fiction and those of pornography; the idealizations of the eye and the de-idealizations of the nose; youthful premarital illusion and middle-aged postmarital burn out. "Nausicaa" finally emerges in this reading as an exploration, not of the gender divide but of the mysteries of en-gendered attraction and coupling.

Several of the contributors address Joycean representations of the maternal, returning to the focus of the Zurich workshop. Enda Duffy discusses the ways in which "Oxen of the Sun" participates in (but also parodies) a larger tendency of patriarchal culture: the production of both symbolic images of maternity and scientific discourses about maternal experience that are masculinist in their perspective, origin, and concerns. Such images and discourses elide the material realities of women's feelings and lives, as "Oxen" itself dramatizes by deliberately marginalizing Mina Purefoy's labor and birthing and by filtering the episode through the prose styles of male authors. Our own contributions on "Hades" (Devlin) and "Cyclops" (Reizbaum) engage the functions of maternality from other angles. Another version of female "labor," for instance, emerges in the marginalized toil of May Dedalus and other working women. In "Hades" and elsewhere, Joyce sets up the absent and ghostly mother as the double of Paddy Dignam, the absent and ghostly father, in order to en-gender death: that is, to mark the differences—both emotional and economical—that ensue when male and female parents leave the patriarchal family (through dying). In "Cyclops," we get perhaps the first attribution of motherhood to Bloom, not knowing "if he's a father or a mother" (12.1648). The feminizing blood libels against Bloom—his supposed experience of menstruation that renders him "one of those mixed middlings" (12.1658–59)—mediate and support the stereotypical construction of him as the Jewish outsider. "Cyclops" demonstrates the way in which gender hybridity is interpreted as a threatening ambiguity in cultures that valorize the distinctness of "masculine" and "feminine." In her discussion of "Calypso," Carol Shloss focuses on the maternal as an absence, tracing the lack of mothering experienced by Molly and Milly, and the consequences thereof. Realigning the standard parallels of *Ulysses* and *The Odyssey,* Shloss suggests that it is the Joycean daughter figure who, in fact, is positioned to suffer the Homeric father figure's trials: displaced from home and held captive by the nymph of traditional gender roles, Milly resorts to subtle forms of delinquency as her revisionary Odyssean strategy for survival.

Shloss foregrounds the mother-daughter plot because it is often ignored or submerged in most analyses of Joyce's works and in patriarchal culture in general. Another dimension of *Ulysses* that has received scant critical attention up until recently is the text's exploration of homosexuality, which Stephen Dedalus thinks of as a culturally muted desire, as "Wilde's love that dare not speak its name" (3.451). Two of the essays here continue the discussion of this issue that was initiated in a recent volume of the *James Joyce Quarterly*.[1] Colleen Lamos traces the dubious acknowledgments and anxious disavowals of homosexuality in "Eumaeus," with an emphasis on Bloom's knowing ignorance of male same-sex desire. Despite—and because of—Bloom's "queer" marriage to Stephen at the episode's close, homoeroticism is obliquely displaced onto his doubled "other," the vagrant D. B. Murphy, errant in both senses of the word. In a complementary discussion of Stephen in "Scylla and Charybdis," Joseph Valente argues that the aspiring artist's projection of heterosexual emasculation in his theory about Shakespeare holds at bay his homosexual panic. Stephen attempts to repress his fear of feminization—a consequence of his ambivalent relationship with his mother—but his phobic sense of gender inversion returns in symptomatic statements and thoughts. Even though "masculine" and "feminine" are overwritten onto many differences, Joyce implies that the "normalizing" cultural imperatives of both clear-cut gender identification and heterosexual desire always remain precarious.

The precariousness of en-gendered identity can also be analyzed in the context of an interesting schism in the psychic life of Bloom, Stephen's symbolic husband-wife-father-mother. In his conscious thoughts, Bloom tends to consolidate gender and sex, overwriting the former upon the latter, particularly through his musings about women. As several contributors note, women in the Bloomian mind are often generically labeled as "they" or "them," in a pronominal habit that reinforces their en-gendered uniformity while marking this essentialized category as other:

> Language of flowers. They like it because no-one can hear. (5.261–62)
>
> Extraordinary the interest they take in a corpse. Glad to see us go we give them such trouble coming. (6.14–15)
>
> Mirror there. Is that best side of her face? They always know. (11.1046–47)
>
> Of course they understand birds, animals, babies. In their line. (13.903–4)
>
> Never see them sit on a bench marked *Wet Paint*. Eyes all over them. (13.911–12)
>
> Colours affect women's characters, any they have. (15.2738)

This last meditation on "women" in "Circe" is followed by the concession, "This black makes me sad" (15.2738–39), suggesting that Bloom too—like the "opposite" sex—is susceptible to color moods: immediately after, Bella Cohen enters the room, triggering a fantasy in which Bloom occupies a feminized position (as he unconsciously understands one). Bloom's famous confrontation with Bella/Bello, on the surface, reads as a facile gender reversal which elaborates the protagonist's (degrading) notions of what it means to be "womanly"; but many details trouble this reading of the scene, indicating that it may, on a deeper level, be a fantasy of gender dissolution. After all, two of the most common gender markers—pronouns and names—are destabilized in the descriptions of Bloom. He is called "old son" (15.2868) and then a "good girly" (15.2884); he is constructed both as a female whore and as a "male prostitute"

(15.3177); and the pronouns that designate "his" positions in the fantasy shift between the masculine and feminine forms or transmogrify into discursive hermaphrodites ("Touch and examine shis points. Handle hrim" [15.3103]). Gender dissolution is accompanied by a disappearance of the unambiguously sexed body. In fantasy Bloom equips himself with testicles (15.2945) and then with a vulva (15.3089); at one point the body is written hermaphroditically as having "hegoat's udders" (15.2992). What is intriguing about the figure of Bello/Bella, moreover, is the way s/he is paradoxically constructed at points as a sort of gender enforcer: s/he commands Bloom to surrender his figurations of manliness for those of womanliness ("You will shed your male garments, you understand, Ruby Cohen?" [15.2965]), but then shortly afterward demands that he give up certain feminine positions for the masculine "norm" ("Do it standing, sir! I'll teach you to behave like a jinkleman!" [15.3023–24]). En-gendering emerges as one dimension of an elaborate disciplinary fantasy: Bloom appears within it, not as the idealized androgyne, but rather as a subject suffering from acute gender anxiety. One may wonder if Joyce is representing—through the juxtaposition of Bloom's waking ideas with this Circean fantasy—conscious gender essentialism as the reflexive defense against a profounder sense of gender undecidability, a psychic schism surely not unique to Leopold Bloom.

Historically, much of the feminist attention to *Ulysses* centered (at first) on the apprehension of the figure of Molly. Between Bonnie Kime Scott's *Joyce and Feminism* (Bloomington: Indiana University Press, 1984) and Margot Norris's *Joyce's Web* (Austin: University of Texas Press, 1992), there have been several influential texts that mark the development and expansion of feminism within Joyce studies. The titles of these two works provide a kind of critical march from initial interactions to complex integration.[2] Both recent and past overviews of the reception of Molly stop short of or move away from the essay of Father Robert Boyle, S.J., on "Penelope" in the Hart and Hayman volume. It demonstrably provides a threshold between one era and another in this criticism. At the panel presentations previewing this volume of essays during the James Joyce Symposium in Seville, Christine Van Boheemen, discussing the "Penelope" episode, mentioned Boyle's essay and commented on the ironic aptness of selecting a priest to act as critical redeemer of the figure of Molly. Indeed, Boyle's essay does seek to redeem Molly from the either/or vision of earth mother/whore, wife/adulterer, saint/villain. Yet one cannot get away from the sense that Boyle is also seeking to forgive her, or to provide her with absolution, treating her as a human subject: "She is, in general, somewhat self-centered and unable, apparently, to think of anyone else's good except in some relation to her own. But in this she is not different from most humans, I should judge. And granted this situation, her attitude toward her children appears healthy and even loving."[3] This treatment by Boyle seems particularly poignant because while it represented a radical view of Molly in 1974, as acceptably and problematically human, thereby releasing the figure from constraining archetypes, the figure also becomes essentially unliterary—all too human. Boyle's essay, then, provides not only a kind of segue between the previous collection and our own, but heralds the critical shifts from an "essential" focus on femaleness, or the feminine, to the larger issue of gender—from Molly Bloom, as "individual," to the countless figures and issues in *Ulysses* crossed by en-gendered markings.

In fixing upon the topic of gender and en-genderings, we were concerned about articulating one that would not be overly restrictive or proscriptive: one that would record within a particular cultural frame at least some of the diversity of Joyce studies in the 1990s and allow for the exploration of a variety of issues. The eighteen new essays on the episodes collected here do indeed have contrasting concerns and foci: their critical heterogeneity is reflected metonymically in the table of contents and, we hope, in the above brief overview. Finally, we set no theoretical mandates for the volume, but we did deliberately choose a frame that would enable contributors—if they so wished—to use their discussion of the episode, first of all, to represent the impact of feminist issues on Joyce studies and, secondly, to reflect related trends and discourses (such as historicism, psychoanalysis, postcoloniality, or culture critique) that have likewise left their marks on exegeses of the Joycean texts.

Abbreviations

All references to James Joyce's *Ulysses* are followed by chapter and line numbers in parentheses. We cite the paperback Gabler edition (New York: Vintage, 1986). References to the below works are followed by the designated abbreviations in parentheses with a page number.

JJ	Ellmann, Richard. *James Joyce*. New York: Oxford University Press, 1982.
CM	Joyce, James. *Chamber Music*. Edited by William York Tindall. New York: Columbia University Press, 1954.
CW	Joyce, James. *The Critical Writings of James Joyce*. Edited by Ellsworth Mason and Richard Ellmann. New York: Viking Press, 1959.
FW	Joyce, James. *Finnegans Wake*. New York: Penguin, 1984.
GJ	Joyce, James. *Giacomo Joyce*. Edited by Richard Ellmann. New York: Viking Press, 1968.
Letters I, II, or III	Joyce, James. *Letters of James Joyce*. Vol. 1, edited by Stuart Gilbert. New York: Viking Press, 1957 (reissued with corrections 1966). Vols. 2 and 3, edited by Richard Ellmann. New York: Viking Press, 1966.
P	Joyce, James. *A Portrait of the Artist as a Young Man*. New York: Penguin, 1983.
SL	Joyce, James. *Selected Letters of James Joyce*. Edited by Richard Ellmann. New York: Viking Press, 1975.
SH	Joyce, James. *Stephen Hero*. Edited by Theodore Spencer, John J. Slocum, and Herbert Cahoon. New York: New Directions, 1963.
U-G	Joyce, James. *Ulysses: The Critical and Synoptic Edition*. Edited by Hans Walter Gabler et al. New York and London: Garland, 1984.

Ulysses—En-Gendered Perspectives

1

"A Little Trouble about Those White Corpuscles"

Mockery, Heresy, and the Transubstantiation of Masculinity in "Telemachus"

GARRY LEONARD

> That the gendered body is performative suggests that it has no ontological status apart from the various acts which constitute its reality.
>
> Judith Butler, *Gender Trouble*

I

In *Portrait of the Artist as a Young Man,* Joyce shows Stephen Dedalus trying to "shore up" a self-image, and this process is figured as trying to build a wall to keep the sea at bay: "How foolish his aim had been! He had tried to build a breakwater of order and elegance against the sordid tide of life without him and to dam up, by rules of conduct and active interests and new filial relations, the powerful recurrence of the tides within him. Useless. From without as from within the water had flowed over his barriers: their tides began once more to jostle fiercely above the crumbled mole" (*P* 98). As this passage implies, Stephen's well-noted hydrophobia is both a fear of personal annihilation and a suspicion that the very psychological "barriers" which permit interiority, in fact offer no permanent or absolute protection from the exterior world they appear to exclude. However much he strives to experience the "tides" of the exterior world as the annihilating force of "otherness," he finds they are continuous with, and indicative of, the surges of emotion and desire within him.

If Stephen's fear of his identity being inundated is signified first by a fear of water in *Portrait,* in the "Telemachus" episode his continued hydrophobia is so pronounced it has become grist for Mulligan's humor mill: "Is this the day for your monthly wash, Kinch?" (1.473). We also see much more specific sources of this fear: his alarming dependence on Mulligan and the unwelcome ghost of his mother. But whether he is shivering at the thought of being inundated by cold water, or pleading with his mother to "let [him] live" (1.279), or fearing he will be altered somehow because he is wearing Mulligan's pants, or feeling he is not responsible for debts because all his molecules have shifted and rearranged themselves since he incurred them, the issue for Stephen is always the same one: how not to be reabsorbed into his surroundings, how to fortify his constantly crumbling walls of identity against an ever-present, ever-restless, *already interior* ocean of undifferentiated emotions and thought, which he tries desperately to misrecognize as an outside force seeking a way to enter.

Although this can be read as an existential crisis, I think Joyce figures it, in much more historical terms, as a crisis in masculinity peculiar to his particular social and historical reality. Indeed, modernism seems driven by radical and bewildering shifts in accepted notions about gender. Male modernist writers, as Peter Middleton notes, wrote about this crisis of modernity as though it were existential and universal: they "rarely acknowledge that their subject is men. . . . men's culture is simply assumed to be universal culture, men's issues simply human issues." Writers such as Virginia Woolf and Dorothy Richardson, however, are "much more flexible in their representation of self-consciousness . . . for the men there is a kind of all or nothing quality to it, either complete rational clarity or dark unconscious groping."[1] For the Stephen of *Portrait* and Gabriel Conroy of "The Dead," such "unconscious groping" is figured as a "swoon," a gesture which, in its connotations of a lady fainting under stress, suggests that the "swoon" concerns a crisis in masculinity, a crisis figured as a male character "falling" into a "feminine" space when his (imaginary) boundaries constituting his identity are breached.

More specifically, in my reading of "Telemachus" the construction of masculinity is like a tower built on the shore to resist a pounding surf; yet, unlike an actual tower—such as a Martello tower—this construct imagines it is one thing (a tower) and the surf is another (an invading force). The construction of the "tower" of masculinity requires one to deny, among other things, the original "sea" of a mother's womb, and, additionally, it requires countless rituals to maintain its (fictional) edifice against a sea of troubles. Rituals compulsively reenact definitive moments where the internal first took form and supposedly banished into outer darkness all threats to this newfound interiority. I refer specifically to the ritual of the Catholic Mass and, within it, transubstantiation. Viewed from a disinterested anthropological perspective (that is, with questions of sacredness and belief set to the side), this process of converting ordinary bread and wine into "body and blood" is a ritual that "makes" a man/God out of the disparate elements. At the Last Supper, Christ prepared his disciples for his impending disappearance by performing and explaining a ritual that would fetch him back from the invisible world whenever their doubts reached a point where they required such an act of affirmation.

Christ's ascension from the dead is, of course, miraculous in its own right, but also marvelous is the way his bodily integrity survives, throughout the process of crucifixion, despite being punctured by thorns, nails, and a lance. The assault on the boundaries of Christ's body, and its miraculous survival as a "self"-sufficient entity, is relentlessly documented in what we might call the "crucifiction": the story of a male body, in extremis for an extended period of time, and yet still intact at the end. This sort of "crucifiction" is also endemic to other "masculine" genres, such as Hollywood Westerns or Sylvester Stallone's *Rambo* series, where a character is shot, burned, hanged, deprived of food and water in the desert, and left for dead, only to rise again, in a triumph over pain and dissolution so miraculous that it renews men's faith in their "selves." Christ's ability to demonstrate that his body can survive hideously invasive wounds is presented as a key feature for instilling faith in others when he invites the apostle Thomas to insert his hand into these same wounds, thus proving to the doubter his own status as the Son of God. In this encounter, it is not just that he arose from the dead, but that, unlike Stephen's mother and Hamlet's father, he still has a body and it exhibits no sign of disintegration, despite having been nailed and slashed. The gesture that returns faith to Thomas would have no meaning except that the open wound in Christ's side, somehow, does not compromise the integrity of the flesh surrounding it.

Because, for merely mortal men, the edifice of masculinity (and the flesh that personifies it) is always crumbling, and because what a man can only imagine as excluded always seems, for this very reason, about to find a way back in, the ritual commemorating (that is, retelling) the "crucifiction" must be repeated endlessly. It is significant that Buck Mulligan, who appears to be a man's man (as the biography of Gogarty also attests), is shown parodying this ritual. As he does so he notes, "a little trouble about those white corpuscles" (1.22–23). The remark highlights the difficulty of constructing a culturally intelligible man from out of the undifferentiated elements of the world, what a fragile act of alchemy it is to "be a man."[2] Stephen is both fearful and scornful of Mulligan because, on the one hand, he envies the verve with which Mulligan attracts notice as a "real man," but, on the other hand, this very enthusiasm, and its evident success, makes it that much clearer to Stephen that masculinity is an effect of acting and performing rather than a result of being. With his constant physical twists and turns, his mercurial voice and expressions, and his staccato humor, Mulligan always seems to be on the verge of being torn apart, his own unruly white corpuscles spilled out onto the wind: "He capered before them . . . fluttering his winglike hands, leaping nimbly, Mercury's hat quivering in the fresh wind that bore back to them his brief birdsweet cries" (1.601–3). The "little trouble" with Christ's white corpuscles parallels the sense of Mulligan as something cohering and breaking apart—like the element mercury—with a rapidity that suggests some kind of imminent breakdown in the process of creating and sustaining "a man."

Mulligan's comment at the conclusion of his mock transubstantiation—"Switch off the current, will you?" (1.28–29)—aligns this process with another model of "making" a man, this one provided by Mary Shelley in *Frankenstein*. In Shelley's novel, and even more clearly in Boris Karloff's interpretation of the role of the monster in the film, the stitching together of the body is most prominent, betraying instantly to all onlookers that this is a man put together, assembled from spare parts, each of which has a separate origin and previous history. Curiously, in the parody of *Frankenstein* by Mel Brooks, the relationship between Dr. Frankenstein and the monster is similar to the one between Mulligan and Stephen. In an effort to civilize the monster (and thus get credit for his scientific genius), Dr. Frankenstein dresses him in a top hat and tails and puts him on stage. The monster proceeds to tap dance while giving a suave, urbane recital of "Putting on the Ritz." Mulligan dresses Stephen, urges him to show off for Haines, and insists on their special relationship: "I'm the only one that knows what you are" (1.160–61). Stephen, to say the least, refuses to tap dance, but this particular dimension of their relationship highlights, from yet another angle, the constant emphasis in this chapter on the question: "How are we to make a man?"

The pseudoscientific framework of Mulligan's joke about "the current" is relevant in an era of mass media and mass communication, where the central difficulty, especially early in the century, was "tuning" (in radio) and "focusing" (in cinema and photography). In the early days of radio, broadcast signals "broke up" with regularity, and the process of listening was one of constantly fiddling with the dial in a continuous effort to keep the signal whole and free from the ever-encroaching static (the aural equivalent of the watery inundation Stephen so devoutly fears). Likewise, keeping subjects in focus and negotiating depth of field were the central challenges and limitations of cinema in its early years. The construction of an image in photography and cinema, as well as the more modern sense of "image" as a composite of personal style, involves problems of projection and reception.

In the twentieth century, we tune our "personality" and focus our "style" to create the coordinates that allow our corpuscles to assemble themselves into a separate, apparently autonomous, "individual." Before modern mass production, "style" was a way to indicate where one stood in relation to a preexisting social hierarchy, but, with the advent of mass-produced images, clothes, and advertisements in the twentieth century, "style" became more personal, more a way to declare one's independence from the existing order. Whereas before one would have assumed a given style in order to "fix" oneself at a certain point in the social hierarchy, by the turn of the century, in a move pioneered by Oscar Wilde, attention to style indicated the exact opposite ambition: one's determination to move freely in and around, and up and down, a social hierarchy that had become unfixed. Such a use of style, as Wilde's career indicates, was of particular use for someone from a colonized country where "the natives" were white; their ability to mimic the imperialists, therefore, was unimpeded by the presence of easily stigmatized physical characteristics such as skin pigmentation. If Mulligan enjoyed traveling to England and merging his "self" with "oxy chaps" at Oxford, Stephen, with his "Latin quarter hat" (1.519), appears to have enjoyed being, while in Paris, a bohemian artist of no readily apparent origin.

The necessity to manufacture a *personal* style is relatively new to the modern production of "masculinity." Mulligan embraces the challenges and pitfalls with a reckless abandon that recalls Oscar Wilde, and urges Stephen to do the same: "Why don't you play them as I do? To hell with them all" (1.506). Stephen, on the other hand, with his "gloomy jesuit jibes" (1.500), has dropped his bohemian joie de vivre, and now sullenly maintains the earlier, quite outmoded style of his undergraduate days. Mulligan tries to package Stephen's performance as "authentic Irish genius" for Haines's benefit (and thus his own, for this will prompt Haines to buy the drinks), but Stephen is doing the same thing as Mulligan in the opposite way; whereas Mulligan has learned to copy the style of the educated British gentleman, Stephen first copies the single-minded British obsession with colonization and profit, and then reflects this back to Haines: when Haines tells him he intends "to make a collection of your sayings" (thus proposing to reap, back in England, the profits of a harvest grown in Ireland), Stephen replies, "Would I make any money by it?" (1.480, 490). Haines ought to understand this British way of speculating since, as Mulligan notes (in proper Oxonian slang), "His old fellow made his tin by selling jalap to Zulus or some bloody swindle or other" (1.156–57). But one purpose of the Oxford "style," in the halcyon days of British imperialism, is to obscure the various exploitive ways people "make their tin." The Oxford "manner" obscures this the way advertising discourse, in order to make a product more attractive to the consumer, obscures the labor that goes into producing a commodity. An Oxford education "packages" an individual the way an advertising campaign packages a product.

What is learned is how to present a "self" and how to critique other people's presentation of their "selves." To Haines, a manufactured Britisher, such a process feels like a natural and organic maturation, allowing him to use the royal "we" in casual conversation: "We feel in England that we have treated you rather unfairly" (1.648). In a further endorsement of his "self" as a natural result rather than an overdetermined product of unexamined ideology, he explains his emotions as, "naturally," the predetermined consequence of his nationality: "Of course I'm a Britisher, *Haines's voice said,* and I feel as one" (1.666, emphasis added). But this "of course" is so much not a matter of course that Stephen hears this pronouncement as no more than a voice *speaking through* Haines. In the uneasy trinity of Stephen, Mulligan, and Haines, one can see Mulligan showing off his prodigious ability to manufacture an image of his "self," Stephen, as would-be artist, struggling to resist, and Haines as the sort of unreflexive automaton that is produced when the foundational illusions about identity, gender, and nationality are so thoroughly naturalized that even what one presents as one's "feelings" are stock reactions manufactured elsewhere. To an Irishman like Mulligan (and also to Stephen, if we can judge by his fantasies about what Mulligan has told him of the experience), Oxford must seem a factory of image production, stamping out likenesses of Haines with a uniformity that masquerades as the art of individuality. It is this, more than anything else, Mulligan wishes to teach Stephen. Indeed, Mulligan is quite modern in his presentation of himself as a commodity, and Stephen is equally modern (albeit "gloomy") in his insistence upon recirculating the very economic and material reality Mulligan's projection of a given image is intended to obscure.

So Mulligan is not just a mocker, he is also a talented impersonator of a priest, a scholar, a poet, and, most importantly for my discussion of the chapter, a man. As Kimberly J. Devlin has observed, "It is worth noting how recurrently Joyce renders masculinity as an act, as something that is easily imitated."[3] Mulligan, at least from Stephen's perspective, is almost purely performative, except for brief, significant moments in between his unremitting mercurial transformations: "Buck Mulligan turned suddenly for an instant towards Stephen but did not speak. In the bright silent instant Stephen saw his own cheap dusty mourning between their gay attires" (1.569–71). In this "bright silent instant," Stephen sees both himself and Mulligan as costumed performers, briefly becoming aware, as he does so, of their scripted relationship as the "stage Irishman" and his comically morose sidekick, both performing for the dubious prize of Haines's befuddled appreciation.

II

My primary assertion about "Telemachus" is that it presents a detailed display of modern masculinity in crisis. What is "modern" about the crisis is that, if an increasing presentation of "self"-consciousness in modernism liberated many female modernists, it generated a corresponding crisis in male modernists for the same reason. Almost by definition, self-consciousness, or self-reflection, calls into question the originating of the self as a natural process, because such a process exposes as myth what has been relied upon by the "masculine" subject as pre-symbolic fact. Women were prepared to talk about masquerade, having lived it consciously for some time. But men, long having viewed masculinity as a universal and natural standard, were as unprepared to challenge that as they were to hear from women that much of what they counted on from women as proof of their male authenticity was neither spontaneous nor inevitable on their part. This, in a nutshell, is the gender and identity crisis that underlies much of modernism. More generally, my approach to the chapter is informed by the Lacanian assumption that there is no foundational basis to identity, an assumption I outlined in my book on *Dubliners:* "There is no organized 'self' serenely present behind the masque of 'meaning' and the mask of 'identity.' Instead, we perform masques because the alternative is to have no sense of destiny at all; we wear masks to keep intact the illusion that behind them we have a 'real' face that must be preserved."[4] In this essay, however, I focus on the masquerade of masculinity, a masquerade, as "Telemachus" makes clear, with traditions and paradoxes of its own, distinct from the more consciously playful masquerade of "femininity," and one that is undergoing—as modern sensibility, in all its vicissitudes, becomes more and more self-conscious—a historically specific period of crisis.

Masculinity is a performance that has multiple and diffuse points of origin, points which are derivative but culturally produced as "original." Accordingly, a performer of masculinity must step forth—wittingly or unwittingly—as the apparently inevitable effect of a singular, prediscursive ontological phenomenon: the self. Despite its overdetermined construction, and in distinct contrast to the "feminine" self, the "masculine" self must masquerade as an autonomous, authoritative, and substantive being. But univocal posturing as a substantive being is, as Judith Butler has argued, a fabricated unity based on a foundational illusion which depends upon a "performative invocation of a nonhistorical 'before.'"[5] The "masculine" self must appear timeless (as "reality") in a timely manner (or "style"). He must be, as advertisers like to say nowadays, "an instant classic." Although apparently produced for just a given moment, he must convey a sense of receiving his authority from a past that recedes beyond the scope of recorded history. He must cannibalize successful styles of masculinity from the past in order to nurture the illusion that he has somehow always been what he appears to be now. He calls himself into being through invocation and ritual, not unlike the ritual that causes Christ to appear as flesh and blood before the eyes of hopeful worshipers. It is just such an invocation—invocation understood as an appeal to something, through a public ceremony, that will offer support and justification in a particular circumstance—that is presented and subverted in the opening chapter of *Ulysses.*

While Mulligan tries to make mockery, parody, and burlesque the ever-shifting proofs and indicators of some foundation at the basis of his identity, he shows instead that his identity has no basis. As Lacan has pointed out, the paradox of performing "masculinity" is that any excessive projection of and insistence upon one's virility risks drawing attention to the usually obscured apparatus of its own production; in other words, a display of "masculinity" calls attention to its derivative status as an effect of performance, rather than, as it purports to be, an expression of a prediscursive, supposedly essential, "nature." Any virile presentation—that is to say, one too insistently coded as "masculine"—risks being perceived, at least by others, not only as a "fake" expression of manhood, but also, and at the same time, as an "authentic" expression of womanhood. In other words, if one overacts "masculine," one appears "feminine." In order for "masculinity" to be culturally intelligible, it must be performed, which means all presentations of the self, coded as "masculine," are potentially decodable as performative, and, therefore, "feminine." Masculinity, in other words, is always in crisis, crisis that must be denied even as it is being endured. This painful, bewildering paradox is perhaps hinted at in Lacan's description of a man as someone who must build a stage and a character out of a jumble of spare parts: "man has only to dream to see re-emerging before him that vast jumble, that lumber room he has to get by with."[6]

Typically, men are too busily (and anxiously) remaining unaware of the performative dimension of their "masculine identity" to notice or critique the masquerade of other men, and this is an important difference between the "masculine" masquerade and the "feminine" one. Since femininity is self-consciously performative, women critique other women, and, depending on how much is at stake, they do so passionately or dispassionately. Bloom notes this critique and thinks it is mean, while Molly sees it as a basic survival skill. Like so many theater critics, women assess the quality of a frankly admitted "feminine" masquerade. In contrast to this, men expect other men (and, even more importantly, women) to support the process by which the "masculine" masquerade is (apparently) naturalized, and regard it, in as unselfconscious a way as possible, as the simple, "commonsense" expression of universal rationality, and thus the antithesis of theatricality. The so-called "method acting" of Marlon Brando and James Dean, for example, which became a style of virility in America in the fifties, is the art of acting in such a way that everything one does—a shrug, a grimace, a smile—announces itself as completely unscripted and spontaneous; it is their feigned indifference to the camera that makes them photogenic, and their skill at acting disaffectedly that makes them such compelling models of "masculinity" for other men (and such attractive objects of desire for women).

The fact that a performance appears so "original" that it must be copied, in a manner that is respectful as well as parodic, is the essential tone of a "camp" performance. The other form of homage men make to other men's performances of "masculinity," more common and more secretive, is to copy in the hopes no one will notice, and will therefore mistake the projection of "originality" for the real thing. Mulligan's performance, of course, is of an earlier historical period, but nonetheless one influenced by the invention of photography, advertising, and perhaps early cinema. In performing the simple gesture of taking off his gown, Mulligan frames it as a parody of one of the Stations of the Cross: "He stood up, gravely ungirdled and disrobed himself of his gown, saying resignedly: /—Mulligan is stripped of his garments" (1.508–10). But this is also a cinematic moment, or "shot," in the sense that he strikes a pose, and then, as with early silent movies, says out loud the sort of framing narrative that would have been spelled out on a cue card in the silent movie.

This might be profitably compared to the sort of "camp," now known as "voguing," originally developed by the gay culture in Harlem, as depicted in the movie *Paris Is Burning,* then later mainstreamed by Madonna in her video "Vogue." The point is to strike a pose, or a discreet series of poses, so "in vogue," so exquisitely current and stylish, that the effect on the audience is to prove Wilde's thesis that life imitates art, and "reality" is an effect of performance and style. Mulligan's performance is so frenetic, changeable, and impulsively engaging that it appears as a "camp" performance of "masculinity." Viewed in cinematic terms, it appears to Stephen in the form of "jump cuts," or rapid changes of posture and performance that are hallmarks of "voguing." In more historical terms, the mercurial changes of expression and posture, combined with editing, are similar to those pioneered and perfected by Charlie Chaplin. Mulligan's response to a friend's remark about Milly, the photo girl—"Snapshot, eh? Brief exposure" (1.685)—indicates he already understands photography as a technological advance of the theatrical tableau ("snapshot").

The art of "voguing" makes it clear that all of us who dress are "in drag," although few of us convey to an audience that we know this (at which point, we would be moving into a "camp" performance). Joyce's astonishingly intricate fascination with "style" may be traced to his sense of it as an unmediated, unaltered configuration of power, only analyzable at a given moment in a given culture. Because gender can be understood as a stylization of the body, and because different styles have varying degrees of cultural intelligibility at any particular time, what is "in vogue" contains the blueprint of a historically specific superstructure of power built on the infrastructure of the body. Because gender is supposed to be natural, it is a regulatory fiction that only appears artificial when it falls out of style.

What is so unusual about Stephen, who is himself passively trying to pose as someone weary of poses (in this mode we can see him as playing an exhausted Dorian Gray to Mulligan's increasingly frenetic Lord Henry), is that he sees Buck Mulligan as nothing more than all the men he transforms himself into with his lightning-quick lateral imitations. For his part, Haines must work quite hard to defuse, for himself, the explosive deconstruction of masculinity offered by Mulligan's relentless, "self"-exposing paradoxical posture of virility: "He's rather blasphemous. . . . Still his gaiety takes the harm out of it somehow, doesn't it?" (1.605–7). On the contrary, it is precisely his gaiety that makes his performance so destabilizing. Of course, Haines's absurdly reductive sense of what "it must mean" to be Irish or British makes him the essentialist par excellence, and it is thus significant to my argument that his essentialist attitudes make him the most easily fooled, "self"-deluded character in all of *Ulysses*—so much so that even the merciless Stephen feels a bit mean-spirited about talking circles around him.

Stephen's critique of Mulligan's burlesque of masculinity is trenchant and exquisitely detailed. For example, he notes Mulligan's "sudden" shift—in terms of facial, vocal, and other mannerisms—from a man with "a finical sweet voice" to one who "growled in a hoarsened rasping voice" (1.378–80). I have suggested the influence of cinema on Mulligan's style of "camp," but there would also have been a readily available model for it in the popular theater and music hall. The term "camp" was in use, as slang, at least by 1907. According to Wayne R. Dynes, "it may have found its first artistic outlet in late-nineteenth-century music halls, vaudeville, and pantomime."[7] Camp seems a useful concept for understanding Mulligan's many and fleeting "impressions" of people; he does not simply recite, rather he "becomes" different people, but always in such a way as to call attention to his impersonation, in the best tradition of camp. Carole-Anne Tyler has remarked that camp, from a performative perspective, and not from the perspective of sexual orientation, is about "catching gender in the act—as an act—so as to demonstrate there is no natural, essential, biological basis to gender identity or sexual orientation."[8] While Mulligan does not, at first glance, seem as self-conscious as this description implies, his every gesture is announced in a way that calls attention to his preparation to go forth into the public as "a man."

When he is dressing, for instance, he literally speaks to his clothing, in a complex discourse that suggests a history of masculinity made manifest in the history of men's fashion: "And putting on his stiff collar and rebellious tie he spoke to them, chiding them, and to his dangling watchchain. His hands plunged and rummaged in his trunk while he called for a clean handkerchief. God, we'll simply have to dress the character. I want puce gloves and green boots" (1.513–16). This last, of course, is the stock description of a late-nineteenth-century dandy—a description that recalls the liberties Oscar Wilde took with men's fashion—but Mulligan is now "camping" *as* Oscar Wilde in order to imply he has gone *beyond* Wilde and developed his own style. When Haines asks if Stephen's theory of Hamlet is "some paradox," Mulligan replies, "Pooh! . . . *we have grown out of* Wilde and paradoxes" (1.553–54, emphasis added). The choice of metaphor figures something that no longer fits; Wilde's rhetorical style, like his sartorial splendor, had its moment, but it is no longer in vogue. Authenticity is a matter of performance and timing rather than substance. The problem is how to be a "character," how to signify presence with a persuasiveness that accumulates power, how to be the Dorian Gray of one's own time, without the clunky old-fashioned portrait in the attic.

And one answer to the problem in the twentieth century, as Susan Sontag has suggested, is camp: "Camp is the answer to the problem: how to be a dandy in age of mass culture."[9] When fashion is increasingly affordable, individual arrangements of mass-produced styles of presentation become the crucial distinguishing factor. When we watch Mulligan, we are watching a man in the process of reinventing "masculinity" so that it will be culturally intelligible for his time. Wilde did the same thing, or so people thought, and the acrimonious trial that sent him to jail demonstrates the rage of a heterosexual hegemonic community at anyone who successfully "fakes" masculinity. A possible cinematic equivalent for Wilde is Rock Hudson. His death from AIDS set off a similar convulsion/revulsion in the popular press. Because Wilde and Hudson each defined "masculinity" at very different times, they do not appear similar. But in both cases, their understanding of "masculinity" as a performance allowed them to create an image so apparently "natural" and "real," heterosexual men had to imitate it in order to be culturally intelligible to women.

By presenting "masculinity" as a historical construct, one with outmoded styles, preposterous styles, and "campy" composites of both, Joyce successfully fractures the presumed naturalness of gender roles and reveals the hidden labor of producing and maintaining a culturally intelligible image of masculinity. The labor of "femininity" has been exteriorized in the advertising of Joyce's time through makeup rituals and beauty tips, as evidenced in "Nausicaa," but "masculinity" still preserves the myth of a naturalness that is not the result of effort. The history of "masculinity" is implied throughout "Telemachus," in the presentation of what Andrew Ross calls "the historical production of the material conditions of taste," or "style," understood to include gesture, dialogue, and performance, as well as fashion. As he goes on to argue, "camp involves a rediscovery of history's waste."[10] Mulligan's many impersonations—through voice, gesture, and sartorial flair—which offer a temporal survey of ephemeral "style," make him a sort of scavenger picking over the waste dumps left behind the factory of meaning production, where the sort of conveniently blameful history (of which Haines is so fond) is "originally" manufactured.[11]

Mulligan's insistence on presenting the serious in a frivolous manner, and the frivolous in a serious manner, is the essence of camp, and Dynes's assertion that "camp is always presented with an invisible wink" suggests a much more nuanced approach to what, up until now, has been accepted as Mulligan's generic form of mockery, as if there were only one style of mockery.[12] As I have already shown, there are several "styles" of masculinity presented in this chapter, and Joyce suggests this through an implied history of men's "style," which is really a survey of ways to perform "masculinity." Because camp—by definition—scavenges outmoded styles once conceived of as "natural," the status of masculinity as a historically specific performative act is brought to the fore, and the cultural mechanism of its fabricated unity, quite literally, is dramatized. For Joyce, what is said is of less interest than observing the precise construction of the site from which it has been spoken. As a postcolonial subject, he wishes to delegitimize various sites (such as Oxford University) that bestow authority on a speaker but which are, by symbolic if not literal definition, closed to an Irishman, unless he chooses, like Wilde and Mulligan, to "camp" his way through; but it is equally clear that, regardless of how brilliantly Mulligan and Stephen parody the obtuse opinions of Haines, still those opinions bear the imprimatur of truth and "common sense."

Mulligan's style of mockery, when seen as "camp," operates as a parody of masculinity that highlights the extent to which masculinity—and thus all authority—is performative, not normative. As Judith Butler notes, "the replication of heterosexual constructs in non-heterosexual frames brings into relief the utterly constructed status of the so-called heterosexual original. . . . The parodic repetition of 'the original' . . . reveals the original to be nothing other than a parody of the idea of the natural and the original."[13] But crucial to my reading of "Telemachus" is my sense that "camp," especially at the turn of the century, is a "non-heterosexual frame" that is not necessarily "homosexual"; or, to put it another way, one's choice of sexual object does not, in itself, empower or disempower a "camp" performer. The fact that this appears to be so is more a historical development, one which indicates a regrettably successful marginalization of a form of presentation disturbing to a hegemonic discourse that insists upon the compulsive "nature" of heterosexuality. Put in performative terms, we should see "camp" as a framing device critical—through mockery—

of all constructs that pose as natural. "Being natural is a pose," Lord Henry begins, in an example of the "camp" pronouncement, "and it's the most irritating pose I know."[14]

III

If, as I am suggesting, "Telemachus" is a critique largely of the generation of "legitimated" versions of reality and "consecrated" versions of the truth through the creation and maintenance of an ontological structure that appears to be the bearer of various essential and nonessential attributes—what Butler calls "the metaphysics of substance"—then belief in the "self" becomes analogous to faith in "the church."[15] It is no coincidence that the Catholic faith is based so predominantly on recovering, maintaining, remembering, and worshiping the body of Jesus Christ. In a patriarchal culture that routinely fetishizes the female body, Catholic iconography is extraordinary in its fetishization of the tortured, comely body of Christ. Mulligan's morning ritual of washing and shaving is presented as analogous to a performance of the Catholic Mass—more specifically, the point in the Mass where bread and wine become the body and blood of Christ. The drama of the Mass—and Joyce often sees it in theatrical terms—is the daily drama of sustaining and maintaining masculinity as a natural state of being. Dressing up "in style," in this sense, can be seen as converting the available symbols of "masculinity" into the body and blood of "a man." Whereas women *transform* themselves into images of "Women" (that is, the feminine), men *transubstantiate* themselves into images of "Men" (that is, the masculine). "Femininity" converts into form, "masculinity" into substance. Another of several differences between the two actions is this: labor which produces "femininity" is coded as trivial and artificial, while labor which produces "masculinity" is coded as sacred and natural.

The unacknowledged issue at the base of the current discussion in the Catholic church about whether or not women should be priests is that the Mass is an ancient ritual by which *men* celebrate their ability to bestow "masculinity" (and, by extension, legitimacy and authority) upon *other men;* a woman on the altar, then, would be, no matter what she wore or did, a man in drag. Her every gesture, regardless of how reverential and traditional she felt about it personally, would register as "camp"—that is to say, as an imitation of gender revealing the imitative structure of gender itself. Mulligan secularizes the ritual of transforming bread and wine into body and blood by turning it into the equally important ritual of transforming the male body into a stylization of masculinity. As this ritual is performed by Mulligan, Stephen, to himself, runs over in his mind the long history of something that registers the changeable history of this presumably timeless act: heresy. Stephen's monologue on the subject should be read as an intersubjective dynamic: Mulligan parodies the ritual of transubstantiation, and the effect, on Stephen, is to make him question where the ritual originated and how it obtained its legitimacy as sacred and true.

The constant sense of denied crisis at the base of transubstantiation, reflected in the long history of the church's repression of heresy, mirrors the crisis at the basis of any substantiation of masculinity. Likewise, the perennially unstable "nature" of the Trinity of God/Christ/Holy Spirit—maintained in a sort of Hegelian equation as unity, heresy, reaffirmation, inevitably followed by a new heresy—is akin to the inherent instability of the only apparently stable construction of "masculinity": a construction which is, in turn, composed of a holy trinity of style/body/consciousness. Jesus himself, as it is recounted in Mulligan's "blasphemous" poem, sees himself as the unstable result of the unimaginable union between *"a jew"* and *"a bird,"* and, as a result, announces himself to be *"the queerest young fellow that ever you heard"* (1.584–85). Although masculinity must pose successfully as "natural," it is only perceivable to others if it is, in some way, performed. As a result, like the concept of transubstantiation in particular, or substantiation in general, the "masculine" subject is always in a state of imperfectly understood crisis, and dependent on faith (or suspended disbelief) in a way the "feminine" subject is not (where the assumption of performativity is already acknowledged); a heretic is nothing more or less than someone with an accurate understanding of this crisis, and a disturbing willingness to explore it.

It is Mulligan's bewildering and exhausting adoption of poses (he is the Robin Williams of *Ulysses*) that makes Stephen uncomfortably aware of his own existence as poseur: "I am another now and yet the same" (1.311–12). But is he really "the same"? All the many rituals enacted in this chapter (eating, dressing, shaving, praying) reveal the extent to which rituals manufacture a sense of continuity which is then misrecognized as the essence that makes the normative ideal of identity something in which the individual might believe. "A little trouble about those white corpuscles," Mulligan intones. Indeed. The transubstantiation Mulligan is parodying is about the process by which symbol becomes flesh and blood, and flesh and blood become symbol. The process is carefully monitored and contained in the ritual of the Catholic Mass, but not in Mulligan's parody of it: "Buck Mulligan peeped an instant under the mirror and then covered the bowl smartly. / —Back to the barracks! he said sternly" (1.17–19). The sudden intrusion of the military leader alludes to yet another institutionalized practice designed to "make men."

Buck Mulligan's performance of masculinity has been noticed by Kimberly Devlin ("Buck Mulligan illustrates the precariousness of the masculine gender act"[16]), but I would take this a step further and suggest that *Ulysses* takes as a central project all identity as an act. All is flux in this chapter and throughout the novel; experience is as protean as the ocean or, in the description of an item of Mulligan's attire, "Mercury's hat quivering in the fresh wind" (1.601–2). In addition to theorizing this perspective, however, we need to historicize it as well, because a crucial component in the late nineteenth century, one that points to a particular style of the performance of masculinity, is the actively debated issue of how "men" relate to other "men" in a manner that might permit the male bonding essential to the preservation of patriarchal power, while also preserving an ideology of compulsory heterosexuality that is equally essential for the formation of the bourgeois family unit. Buck Mulligan, for example, wishes to do something collaborative with Stephen: "God, Kinch, if you and I could only work together we might do something for the island. Hellenise it" (1.157–58). As Wayne Kostenbaum has noted, "Collaboration . . . became laden, delicately at the beginning of the 19th century, and ferociously at its end, with the struggle to define male bonds along a spectrum including lascivious criminality and sexless chumming."[17] Men such as Wilde, Pater, Swinburne, and Whitman, according to Richard Dellamora, "engaged in the production of revisionary masculine discourses . . . that attempt to enlarge masculine capacities for relationships while respecting the boundaries of conventional middle-class patterns of career, including marriage." Dellamora's project—a project built on the earlier work of Eve Kosofsky Sedgwick—is to historicize desire between men, not as "homosexual" or "heterosexual," but "as it figures in sexual-aesthetic discourse in England during the nineteenth century"; it is "a study of micropractices that show how individual subjects respond at the very moments when codes of sexuality are being induced and/or imposed."[18] Stephen's disengagement from, and disillusionment with, Mulligan can be seen as just such a "micropractice," where the homosocial relationship is being reconfigured along the lines of the more "modern" matrix of homosexual/heterosexual subject positions, with no apparent continuum connecting them.

Significantly, what Stephen becomes acutely aware of during this pronouncement about possible collaboration is that Mulligan is touching him: "Cranly's arm. His arm" (1.159). His reading of this touch as the repetition of an earlier touch, though of a different person, suggests a ritualistic sensitivity to moments such as these. What is constant is not who touches him, but how it makes him feel. This touch and the feeling it elicits supports his desire to be continuous as a substantive being in space and time—a desire expressed in his earlier, uneasy and unstable "self"-regard ("I am another now and yet the same"); yet Stephen disengages himself from this touch, just as he is disengaging himself also—less and less surreptitiously—from his friendship with Mulligan. None of this, however, is occurring in a historic vacuum, and readings of it as merely homophobic are too simplistic. Nor can it be very well understood strictly with reference to the "personalities" of Stephen and Buck. Their apparent disagreement about what Mulligan said about Stephen's mother, and who should be the most offended, is confusing, and, like so many disagreements, that is the purpose of the argument: to obscure an emotional dislocation too dangerous to be examined openly. This is evident by the fact that Buck's apology does nothing to resolve the tension. Furthermore, our understanding of the relationship between Stephen and Mulligan should not be polarized as "are they" or "are they not" attracted to each other. It is precisely this reductive polarizing matrix of homo/hetero desire that recent historians of sexuality have attempted to historicize. The idea that a man should have either no desire or a particular desire for other men, and the belief that such desire, or the lack of it, must be enacted in one way, but not another—all such considerations have a history and a cultural specificity.

Ways of being a man are as susceptible to shifts in fashion as the clothes which help make a given performance credible. As Lacan notes, "Style . . . is the man to whom one is speaking."[19] The relationship between Stephen and Buck recapitulates what Dellamora characterizes as "a debate about the meaning of masculinity that took place in papers, lectures, essays and poetry by men associated with Oxford University."[20] Sensing Stephen's unhappiness with him, Buck offers to give Haines "a ragging worse than they gave Clive Kempthorpe" (1.163–64). Scenes of Oxford promptly follow, in Stephen's mind, with men chasing men and shouting out their mirth in the voices of women: "O, I shall expire! . . . I shall die!" (1.166–67). This is a glimpse of a particular institution, in a particular historical framework, offering a particular "style" of masculinity, complete with a suggested script about how it should be performed, a script garnered from popular music and theater. For Dellamora, the men who established this particular fashion for masculinity were Pater, Wilde, Swinburne, Arnold, and (through his influence upon these men) Walt Whitman. There are repeated, direct, and important allusions to all these men in "Telemachus," and they are very much to the point of this essay, which is trying to theorize the problematics of masculine performance, as well as to historicize the intellectual and popular debates going on about the continuum of desire being negotiated between and among men. I wish to pursue this tack in deliberate resistance to the supposedly universal and a historical homosexual/heterosexual polarization. A critical maintaining of this matrix gives us no way to discuss ambivalence about masculine desire, an ambivalence that must be understood, in its own right, as something that is imposed by the larger culture, and not at all the "inevitable" effect of being confused about one's "proper" sexual orientation.

IV

Sedgwick, as Dellamora points out, "has proposed a persuasive case for viewing desire between men as part of the normal structure of gender relations. . . . [She] argues that masculine privilege was sustained by male friendships within institutions like the public schools, the older universities, the clubs, and the professions. Because of the importance of marriage in perpetuating the dominance of a bourgeois elite, however, desire between males needed to be curbed from the moment when men entered seriously upon their careers."[21] During the time depicted in "Telemachus," Joyce wrote a poem about his dwindling relationship with Gogarty, and in it the speaker is quite explicit that his rising passion for Nora will necessarily "curb" (to use Dellamora's term) the pseudo-Oxonian camaraderie that he apparently once indulged in with Gogarty: "Because your voice was at my side / I gave him pain, / Because within my hand I held / Your hand again. // There is no word nor any sign / Can make amend— / He is a stranger to me now / Who was my friend" (*CM* 141). Note the reason the former friend is unable to make amends of any kind: he has not done anything wrong (let alone done something unforgivable). Mulligan's confusion about what Stephen "has against [him] now" (1.180) seems quite credible to me. Indeed, the "now" makes it clear this is a recurring stalling point in their relationship, and one that he has never been able to get around successfully.

Stephen, we are told, before answering, "freed his arm quietly" (1.182); he then delivers his famous complaint about Buck's reference to his mother as *"beastly dead"* (1.198–99). Buck is visibly disconcerted upon hearing this, because the offense to Stephen's mother seems clear. But Stephen, after Mulligan apologizes for any offense to his mother, employs what I would describe as a sleight of hand, when he insists the offense is not to his mother, but to himself. Mulligan's rejoinder—"O, an impossible person" (1.222)—is one of his few sincere observations because he is frankly puzzled, as well he might be, by Stephen's incessant search for reasons why the friendship is over between them. All of these reasons, irrelevant in themselves, nonetheless have in common the vague implication that it is Mulligan who has poisoned the friendship. As in Joyce's poem—about the effect of his relationship with Nora on his relationship with Gogarty—"no word nor any sign / Can make amend." But the reason for this is not circumstantially motivated, it is historically and culturally contingent. The move away from Mulligan is a move away from a previously acceptable homosocial relationship, in preparation for one less ambivalently heterosexual.

Stephen's attitude, for no discernible reason, is that the damage to his and Mulligan's relationship is irreparable, and his evidence for this, absurdly enough, is a remark Mulligan made, which he cannot even recall having made, but for which, nonetheless, he has apologized. The contrast between the relative innocence of the offense, and Stephen's reaction to it, is better understood in a framework different than the one Stephen ponderously insists upon. The one I propose, instead, is the historical/cultural debate, endemic throughout the late nineteenth and early twentieth century, about how men should relate to one another. It is a debate that led to differing, not to say confused, styles of "masculinity." We need to remember that Mulligan rambles on all the time, often with the specific intent of being offensive, or least provocative, so the question should not be what is offensive about this particular remark, but why Stephen chooses this moment to be offended by one in an endless series of offensive remarks by Mulligan.

Throughout the "Telemachus" chapter, we see evidence that the question forcing itself on Mulligan is this: why does Stephen find nothing he performs or says funny anymore? In this sense, they seem like a couple on the verge of a breakup (precisely what they are, of course); everything Stephen once found attractive in Mulligan is now irritating to Stephen. Likewise, Stephen's exasperating reason for declining the offer of a good pair of pants ("I can't wear them if they are grey" [1.120]) may have less to do with codes of mourning and more to do with the homosocial statement Mulligan has made about enjoying the sight of Stephen in fashionable clothing: "You'll look spiffing in them. I'm not joking, Kinch. You look damn well when you're dressed" (1.118–19). Again, Mulligan telegraphs the sincerity of this remark by stating—very uncharacteristically—that he is "not joking." What is disconcerting to Stephen about Buck's remark is that it is evident to him Mulligan likes to dress him in such a way as to then admire how the clothes show off his body to some advantage.

Stephen needs to blame Mulligan for a headlong flight from the relationship he himself has initiated. This flight, which he will neither admit to, nor explain, nor permit discussion of, reflects a sudden shift in his attitude toward the homosocial continuum he and Mulligan have maintained to this point, a shift that makes him act in accordance to what he has been called: "an impossible person" (1.222). The critical perspective to be maintained in observing the relationship between Stephen and Mulligan should be one of fluidity, not polarity. The problem is not whether one or the other of them has homosexual inclinations, but rather what it means to be "masculine" at all. The visionary clarity and compression with which Stephen envisions the Oxford scene suggests that Mulligan has regaled him with tales of the homosocial atmosphere there, and these very stories may be another cause of Stephen's "panic" about their relationship.

We need to consider Victorian aestheticism as (among other things) a heavily coded debate about the "nature" of desire between and among men, and about the "proper" way to express it; "both Pater and Swinburne," according to Dellamora, "stand in marked contrast to Arnold. Although all three are polemical advocates of high culture, Arnold adopts a conventional line on sexual matters. And with reference specifically to desire between men, he takes care to bleach his favored cultural term, 'Hellenism,' free of sexual connotations."[22] Swinburne's poetry, of course, is Mulligan's most frequent source, apart from himself, for his impromptu recitals, and the tension between Pater/Swinburne on the one hand, and Arnold on the other, is reproduced in Stephen's vision of Oxford: "Shouts from the open window startling evening in the quadrangle. A deaf gardener, aproned, masked with Matthew Arnold's face, pushes his mower on the sombre lawn" (1.172–74). We see images of maintenance and enforced regularity (mowing the lawn), posed as "natural." The honest laborer has become a trope appropriated by Arnold to indicate an unselfconscious "masculinity," and yet the inherent artifice of this is reflected by Stephen's sense of this laborer as now "masked" (and thus effaced) by Arnold's face. This "manly" conceit is juxtaposed with the much more fluid, much less "bleached" performance of the young men of Oxford.

As Dynes notes in his discussion of Hellenism, "this ethos of aestheticism was grounded in part in the all-male public schools that combined the officially approved reading of Greek texts with a clandestine, but pervasive subculture of homosexuality."[23] Yet many young men—and Mulligan is a likely example (as was Gogarty)—participated in this "clandestine, but pervasive subculture" without defining themselves—in practice or in theory—as "homosexual." The question—to what extent should men desire, touch, or notice other men—is always a problem in any historical/social matrix, and it is one that is configured in a different discourse, at any particular juncture in place and time. It was especially an ongoing and shifting debate at the turn of the century, despite the tendency of Havelock Ellis and others (a tendency with its own historical and cultural underpinnings) to make the enigma of gender and identity a deceptively simple exercise in taxonomy. The artist Barbara Kruger implies the covert existence of a continuum of what we might call homosocial stylizations of masculinity that I find relevant to the two-step dance of intimacy and disavowal performed by Stephen and Buck Mulligan. She takes a photograph of a group of men tussling with one another, in evident goodwill, and emblazons across the photograph, in her trademark red ink, "You construct intricate rituals which allow you to touch the skin of other men."

This suggests that any ritual conducted as a prelude for men touching one another—a potential breach of their interiority—must take place within a framework that is "culturally intelligible" as masculine. For example, the catcher at the end of the World Series throws his legs around the pitcher and tumbles him onto the ground, but only after an exhausting season; or the football player pats the bottom of the man on the opposing team, but only after knocking him to the ground; or the gunslinger lifts another gunslinger's head and offers him a drink of water, but only after shooting him. In the absence of such ritual, touching by another man is experienced as a breach of one's bodily integrity—perhaps pleasurable, perhaps threatening, but always something that makes the supposedly impermeable boundaries of masculinity (and the interiority they protect) seem suddenly arbitrary. Stephen's shift away from Mulligan needs to be accounted for in relation to the cultural/historical "styles" of masculinity outlined in the work of Sedgwick and Dellamora, and in conjunction with the psychoanalytic approach to gender founded by Lacan, refined by Kristeva, Wittig, and others, and recently outlined by Butler.

Finally, Stephen's fascination with heretics—those who are accused of impersonating the truth, or what Lacan calls "the subject who is supposed to know"—is connected to his fascination/repulsion with Mulligan's impersonation of gender and identity. "Heresy" is any doctrine that shows, embedded in ritual, the very anxiety it is meant to dispel. Problems with the Trinity—three in one, three versions of one, or one version with three phases—mirror the problem of the "miracle" of masculine identity as "self"-sufficient entity, sustained through space and time. Transubstantiation of Christ's eroticized body is an extraordinary version of a peculiarly masculine masquerade, one that tries to resolve the paradox that a performance can somehow be essential, inevitable and natural, when in fact it is an act of faith, a fiction of the self, and something that can only appear to do the following: originate meanings, authenticate interpretations, and legitimize assumptions of power. Heretics, like impersonators, highlight the constitutive powers of structures that masquerade as original and inevitable. Heresies, like parodies, always mock the very notion of an original by exposing the mechanism by which they are constructed as "original." By presenting Mulligan's dressing ritual as a parody of transubstantiation, Joyce presents timeless ritual and cutting-edge style as the two fictional matrices upon which male subjects plot the specific point of their identities, thus giving credible (albeit temporary) form to their restless and troublesome white corpuscles.

2

Genders of History in "Nestor"

ROBERT SPOO

"What is a nightmare?"
"It's a name for a bad dream."
"Why is it a mare? Uncle Hartley said a mare is a mother horse. . . . Is it a night horse?"
"Well, no, I don't know, it's only a dream anyhow."
A nightmare is a mare in the night, it is a dream, it is something terrible with hooves rushing out to trample you to death. It is death.

H.D., *The Gift*

Ulysses begins with a stately, plump, lubber jester impersonating a priest at the altar and ends with a recumbent Dublin housewife become Penelope-Scheherazade become seed-heavy Gea-Tellus become the great spinning earth ball itself (to cite only the most adhesive of the symbolic labels that Joyce and his critics have assigned to Molly Bloom). Between these unlikely points, the category of history gets lost and found many times, then lost again, for good and all perhaps, as Molly, in the no-hour of "Penelope," under the sign of infinity, resolves all of the book's structures and languages into a pulsing idiom of restless, irreverent garrulity. By the time Leopold Bloom's consciousness drains off into the gaping dream-hole that puts *punkt* to male narratives at the end of "Ithaca," the idea of history has cycled through a Great Year of forms and meanings in the course of the novel, many of them invoking woman as motif, cause, or presiding muse, but none of them actually produced by a woman. In an almost all-male novel laid in the public sphere, it should come as no surprise that the nightmare of history is stabled with stallions and ridden by male jockeys, that it is a bad dream known to all men and confided in a round-robin of masculine hugger-mugger. Stephen Dedalus, recalling a phrase of William Blake's, muses that history is "fabled by the daughters of memory" (2.07), but in Joyce's picture of 1904 Dublin this is largely an honorary distinction. Female authorship of history—the actual events of history as well as their textualization—remains an abstract notion, a metaphor taken for the deed, as it is in Blake's impatient phrase.

History as process and text may not be engendered by Joyce's women, but it is consistently gendered *as* female in his fictions. What is denied women on the level of material and ideological production is restored to them, with uncanny surplus value, on the level of language and figuration. History is what hurts in *Ulysses,* as in Irish history generally, but it is also what haunts. The revenants that glide through the pages of the novel are refugees from historical conceptions that not only smother the reality of women but withhold authentic being and experience from everyone, male and female, citizen and artist. The various discourses of history in *Ulysses* are haunted at their core by a restless latent content that plaintively asserts a lost female principle, the "lost histereve" of *Finnegans Wake* (*FW* 214). Like the woman creeping behind the wallpaper's pattern in the story by Charlotte Perkins Gilman, the figure of the female in Joyce's text shakes the bars of its representational cage, causing the pattern to move perceptively.[1] Repressed female agency returns again and again in the form of uncanny metaphors, images, and allusions—faint reminders of women's reality in history as that reality has been shaped, deformed, and, as it were, ghosted by the intrinsic misogyny of Irish historical discourse at the turn of the century. "Here [is] great loveliness of ghosts," as Homer says of the female shades surging forward to drink from Odysseus's sacrifice.[2] But here is horror as well.

The "Nestor" episode formally introduces the theme of "History" into the dense web of meanings in *Ulysses.* It is an episode populated by male characters (Stephen Dedalus, the boys he teaches at the Dalkey school, the old headmaster Garrett Deasy) and devoid of women, who are also absent from the history lesson that Stephen wearily trots out to his distracted students. Yet the concepts of history that circulate heavily in "Nestor" like the stale smoky air in Mr. Deasy's study make insistent use of the figure of woman, notably by situating her as origin and chief cause of a fallen, sinful history, a history so fractured and contradictory that its meanings must be referred (and deferred) to the teleological unfolding of divine purpose, as the episode's ponderous philosopher, Mr. Deasy, loftily explains: "All human history moves towards one great goal, the manifestation of God" (2.380–81). Jacques Derrida has called such thinking "onto-theo-archeo-teleology," which, he says, "locks up, neutralizes, and finally cancels historicity."[3] The mock-cumbrousness of Derrida's term suggests the deadening artificiality and oppressiveness of teleological worldviews.

In Deasy's providentialist historiography, the revelation of God's will is the *telos,* the goal, of the temporal process, and women emerge as a recurrent monocause of history's ills:

> We have committed many errors and many sins. A woman brought sin into the world. For a woman who was no better than she should be, Helen, the runaway wife of Menelaus, ten years the Greeks made war on Troy. A faithless wife first brought the strangers to our shore here, MacMurrough's wife and her leman, O'Rourke, prince of Breffni. A woman too brought Parnell low. Many errors, many failures but not the one sin. (2.389–95)

For Deasy, woman gives birth to the twins, history and sin, in the same instant (the obstetric word "brought" echoes throughout the passage) and then retires from her malefactions; she is an unmoved mover who, once her labor is over, plays no part in the actual strife of history, the vast panorama of male aggression symbolized by the schoolboys' noisy hockey game in the playfield next to the schoolhouse. Despite the fact that so much real destructive power is attributed to her, woman's role is curiously titular, mythic, ahistorical; she vamps her male victims in an erotic ambush that is somehow outside time. Deasy acknowledges the fact of male collaboration in history ("We have committed many errors and many sins"), but with Miltonic logic this old Protestant Orangeman makes female seduction the first cause. Eve, Helen, Devorgilla, and Katherine O'Shea were all women who tempted world-historical men to their beds, conceived there in sin, gestated a dark history that would subvert the will of their lovers and of God, and brought forth the mortal condition—the Trojan War, the invasion of Ireland, the betrayal of home rule. In Deasy's philosophy, the march of civilization and the manifestation of God are held back and at the same time paradoxically driven forward by the monocausal temptress who corrupts male virtue. History is made and marred by the cunning of female unreason.

"Many errors, many failures but not the one sin" (2.394–95). Like the Englishman Haines, who in "Telemachus" singles out "German Jews" as "our national problem" (1.667–68), Deasy augments his cast of villains and complicates somewhat his theocentric historiography by naming the Jews and their sin "against the light" (2.361) as a special category of historical error. As punishment for denying Christ, the Jews are "wanderers on the earth to this day" (2.362–63); they have insinuated themselves into the fabric of the British Empire and are "already at their work of destruction. Old England is dying" (2.350–51). Stephen tries to counter Deasy's attack on "jew merchants" by throwing the emphasis on "*merchant* . . . one who buys cheap and sells dear, jew or gentile" (2.359–60, emphasis added), just as he does in the previous episode after Haines has indicted the Jews, though there the riposte remains unspoken, fleetingly implied in something Stephen's bored eye falls upon: "Two men stood at the verge of the cliff, watching: *businessman,* boatman" (1.669–70, emphasis added). Stephen's socialist-anarchist rejoinder is breezily ignored by Deasy, who sees in woman and the Jew, originary seductress and insidious vagrant, a solution to the problem of history. But Stephen silently pursues the argument by quoting Blake again to himself: *"The harlot's cry from street to street / Shall weave old England's windingsheet"* (2.355–56). Although this couplet forms part of his economic critique of Deasy's bigoted views, it too draws on the topos of the sinful female as root of historical evils.

The personification of history as female has had special appeal for Irishmen, whose nation has been variously symbolized as an old crone, a queen, a goddess, a young girl with the walk of a queen, and named Kathleen Ni Houlihan, the Shan Van Vocht, the Poor Old Woman.[4] (Deasy quips that Ireland never persecuted the Jews because "*she* never let them in" [2.442, emphasis added].)

W. B. Yeats, whose adoption of a cyclic view of time did little to calm his passion for apocalypse, searched myth and religion for examples of women whose sexuality, turbulent or passive, could figure historical crisis: Helen of Troy, Leda, Deirdre, the Virgin Mary. "For these red lips, with all their mournful pride . . . Troy passed away in one high funeral gleam."[5] His short poem "Lullaby," first published in 1931, combines eroticism and maternal care in lines spoken, possibly, by Mary to the infant Jesus. Lulling the child with a song about sleep after momentous exertion, she mentions in turn Paris and Helen, Tristram and Isolde, and Zeus and Leda, and notes that in each case a male found rest in the "protecting care" of a dazed sexual partner become nurturing mother figure. It is implied that this grateful sleep was merely a brief stay against destruction and slaughter to come, but direct reference to historical consequence is omitted from Yeats's lyrical meditation on the paradox of personal peace following ominous, God-fated intercourse. In "Lullaby," abduction and sexual violence give way to the symbiosis of mother and child, and the historiographic trope of dangerous female sexuality is balanced by images of maternal tenderness.[6]

Although he remains skeptically aloof as Deasy imparts his old wisdom, Stephen also tends to imagine woman as the origin of masculine history. Characteristically, he projects this origin as a maternal figure, a mother who is caring and self-sacrificing but in the end is trampled and discarded by the world-historical son she has reared. Stephen wonders if *amor matris* is alone "real" (2.144), the true ontological ground of masculine narratives, and then recalls the ruthless ambition of a medieval Irish missionary: "His mother's prostrate body the fiery Columbanus in holy zeal bestrode. She was no more" (2.143–45). Yet it was this selfless mother who kept the young boy safe from the crushing indifference of the world. Stephen gazes at the "ugly and futile" student named Sargent, in whom he recognizes his own insecure, awkward youth: "Yet someone had loved him, borne him in her arms and in her heart. But for her the race of the world would have trampled him underfoot, a squashed boneless snail" (2.140–42). The mother who shelters her weakling hobbledehoy from the march of history will herself be trodden under by that child when he steps forth into public life and historical being, or, to use Lacanian terms, into the realm of the symbolic. Pre-oedipal intimacy is superseded by the divisions and opportunities of the symbolic register, where identity and its meanings are to be found. The maternal ground of history is a stepping-stone for the male's heroic agency.[7]

Stephen himself feels remorse of conscience for using and abusing his mother, and in his guilty imagination May Dedalus becomes indistinguishable from the motherland (the Poor Old Woman) and from the personal and cultural past that he has repudiated, those nets of "nationality, language, religion" that he vowed to "try to fly by" in *A Portrait of the Artist as a Young Man* (*P* 203). During a student's recitation of Milton in "Nestor," Stephen recalls a jingle: *"Riddle me, riddle me, randy ro. / My father gave me seeds to sow"* (2.88–89). But buoyant confidence in a patrimony of vital seeds changes quickly into a ghastly image of the burial of the dead, and Stephen is indirectly describing himself when he challenges his students to solve a riddle about a "fox burying his grandmother under a holly bush" (2.115). A few lines later, this grandmother reappears in less displaced form as the revenant mother, the wasted corpse of May Dedalus with its "odour of rosewood and wetted ashes": "A poor soul gone to heaven: and on a heath beneath winking stars a fox, red reek of rapine in his fur, with merciless bright eyes scraped in the earth, listened, scraped up the earth, listened, scraped and scraped" (2.145–50). Stephen, the antihistorical artist who will settle for nothing less than total freedom, is the guilty, vigilant fox delving in the earth, attempting to bury the past but with his nails only digging it up again. The obsessive "scraped . . . scraped" of the passage hints at the act of writing, the simultaneous burying and unburying of meanings that artists and historians alike engage in.

As the denied content of his own past, Stephen's deceased mother makes horrific, ghoulish returns in his dreams and waking reveries: "Her eyes on me to strike me down. . . . No, mother! Let me be and let me live" (1.276–79). Later, in "Nestor," he addresses his now famous quip to Mr. Deasy, the self-appointed father who would give him sententious seeds to sow: "History, Stephen said, is a nightmare from which I am trying to awake" (2.377). Stephen's much-quoted remark is an oblique rumination on the son's relationship to history—or the night-*mère* of history—and suggests an isomorphism between the repressions necessitated by historical narrative and the son's self-engendering burial of the mother. The wasted maternal body always rises up out of the family plot to menace and strike down the denier, just as uncanny female figurations return to haunt the discourses of history in *Ulysses.*

History is haunted because it is a construct, an authoritative ousting of infinite possibilities in a language tempered to rationality, whether modestly described as "a kind of retrospective arrangement" (10.783) or confidently projected as "the manifestation of God" (2.381). As early as 1906, Joyce hinted at the repressed spectrality of history-writing in letters from Rome that read like early sketches for Stephen's fox riddle. In these letters, he persistently described the ancient ruins in terms of death and corpses: "Rome reminds me of a man who lives by exhibiting to travellers his grandmother's corpse" (*Letters II* 165). Back in Trieste he told his Berlitz class that "ancient Rome seems like a cemetery to me. The odor of its exquisite panorama clings to the Royal Palace: mortuary flowers, ruins, heaps of bones, and skeletons."[8] In this charnel perspective, historiography becomes a species of cemetery upkeep, and the historian begins to resemble a pallid, soft-spoken undertaker who lives by displaying the corpse of the past in the discreetly rouged, rationalized form of narrative. The night-*grandmère* of history, however, will not be so easily disposed of. The ingenuity of the guilty fox is not enough.

Between Stephen's history-as-nightmare and Deasy's history-as-manifestation-of-God there is a wide gulf of age and perspective. Deasy rehearses the teleological pieties of nineteenth-century culture, pieties that Joyce once characterized in lecture notes as "the idols of the market place . . . the succession of the ages, the spirit of the age, the mission of the race" (*CW* 185). Deasy's proud faith in the steady unfolding of Spirit in time is sharply contested by Stephen's antidevelopmental, counterteleological skepticism. The notion of a progressive spirit calls forth in him, as it did in Joyce, a counterdiscourse that figures history perversely as static, lifeless corporeality, that denies the temporal process a self-determining soul and points instead to its burdensome body, to the failure of providentialism as a shared cultural truth. Stephen's and Joyce's attitudes toward history partake of what I have elsewhere described as a "counterdiscourse of history" that gained currency in the nineteenth century.[9] Skeptical of dominant spiritual conceptions of historical process, writers and thinkers as diverse as Karl Marx, Henry Adams, George Eliot, Jules Laforgue, and Henrik Ibsen imaged history as an uncanny body, a specter or ghoul, a graveyard or tomb, a nightmare.[10]

Ibsen's *Ghosts* (1881), for example, asks disturbing questions about the seeds that fathers give their children to sow. The play is a savage inquest into the potent legal fiction of *amor patris* no less than the seeming reality of *amor matris.* Inherited history, both personal and cultural, comes to be seen as tainted, transmitting disease and idiocy instead of life-sustaining strength. In her famous speech, Mrs. Alving attempts to exorcize the "ghosts" that oppress her and her family: "It is not only what we have inherited from our father and mother that 'walks' in us. It is all sorts of dead ideas, and lifeless old beliefs, and so forth. They have no vitality, but they cling to us all the same, and we cannot shake them off."[11] Stephen Dedalus is no less stifled by the vampiric intimacy and tenacity of old ideas, by the nightmare that crouches on his bosom and causes him to tell Deasy that "I fear those big words . . . which make us so unhappy" (2.264). Both Stephen and Mrs. Alving reinterpret history against the grain of dominant discourses; instead of honoring the notion of spiritual inheritance, they complain of ghosts, corpses, and bad dreams.

I have argued elsewhere that Stephen Dedalus's use of the nightmare image was mediated by the rhetoric of despair that arose during the First World War, the period in which Joyce completed "Nestor" and the first part of *Ulysses.*[12] The word "nightmare" was routinely used to describe the war, most famously perhaps in the letters of Henry James, who, one day after the British declaration of war, referred to the situation as "a nightmare of the deepest dye" and two weeks later wrote Edith Wharton: "Life goes on after a fashion, but I find it a nightmare from which there is no waking save by sleep."[13] In Virginia Woolf's "The Mark on the Wall" (1917)—a story framed by references to the war—the female narrator likens her rebellion against "the masculinist point of view" and its brutal rituals to "waking from a midnight dream of horror."[14] The idea of history as a psychological or oneiric trauma becomes almost a reflex for modern writers. Stephen's nightmare metaphor, like James's and Woolf's, has a complex, overdetermined genealogy: nineteenth-century counterdiscourses of history provided a conditioning background (as they did for the nightmare tropes of Marx, Ibsen, and others), and the Great War acted as a catalyzing foreground.

I would like to consider briefly the other historical trajectory of the phrase "the nightmare of history": its role in Joyce criticism. It is remarkable how influential this received version of Stephen's quip has proven to be. Not surprisingly, it has served, both within and beyond Joyce criticism, as a trope of crisis or malaise, a convenient way of signaling a "bad" history, as in Terry Eagleton's claim that literature, for the English ruling class of the years following World War I, became "at once a solace and reaffirmation, a familiar ground on which Englishmen would regroup both to explore, and to find some alternative to, the nightmare of history."[15] Hayden White, teasing out one of the earlier meanings of "nightmare," has written of "the incubus of history," making this notion synonymous with his more Nietzschean formulation, "the burden of history."[16]

In Joyce criticism, "the nightmare of history" has had a wide and multivalent currency, even though it is a somewhat misleading version of the words actually spoken by Stephen. Until recently, the phrase has been, despite or perhaps because of its portentous vagueness, the attitude toward history most often ascribed to Joyce himself, or more sweepingly, to contemporary culture at large. From S. L. Goldberg's 1961 chapter, "Homer and the Nightmare of History," to F. L. Radford's 1978 article, "King, Pope, and Hero-Martyr: *Ulysses* and the Nightmare of Irish History," to W. J. McCormack's 1982 piece, "Nightmares of History: James Joyce and the Phenomenon of Anglo-Irish Literature," to Christine Froula's 1991 essay, "History's Nightmare, Fiction's Dream: Joyce and the Psychohistory of *Ulysses*," the phrase has served to advertise a problem, to deplore an intolerable condition, or to characterize a Joycean aesthetic strategy.

Comparing it to the phrase *amor matris,* McCormack notes (in one of the few close readings the phrase has received) that "it may point to a nightmare which history endures . . . or it may point to the enduring of history by X [some individual] in the manner of a nightmare."[17] Other critics have used it to name, not an objective reality or a subjective attitude, but something in between: history as reified construct, as fiction hardened into myth, or, in Derek Attridge's words, "a production of history . . . a narrative of exploitation, exclusion, and domination, of racial, national, gender and class hegemony."[18] The danger of such a seductive, elastic formulation as Stephen's is that it can easily be thought of as pointing to something definite, when in fact its referent, like history itself, is molten and mercurial, changing according to context and emplotment and perpetually being appropriated for diverse ends.

The routine use of this phrase for dramatic effect has had several consequences for Joyce criticism. One is that it has made it easy to figure history as a sort of abstract ground of potentiality, an unproblematic *terminus a quo,* a blank canvas, a thing to be fled by the modernist artist or, better, transformed by him or her into something of aesthetic permanence, as if history were sheer negativity or deficiency awaiting fulfillment in art. For S. L. Goldberg, *Ulysses* achieves a "transcendence of the nightmare of history" by virtue of "the imaginative truth, the poetic universality" latent in the naturalistic and symbolic detail of the text, detail which Joyce's art invests with "a fuller meaning."[19] Another critic, discussing *Finnegans Wake,* notes that "Joyce accepted history as the *condition humaine,* not obsession but salvation, not nightmare but vision."[20] Here, history is generalized as the artist's *prima materia,* the lump of clay from which a living work may be fashioned, an abstract origin not unlike Deasy's or Stephen's notion of the chaotic, dangerous female who, leaning out from the timeless bar of heaven, watches her opportunity to snare the God-sent hero and bring forth with him a monstrous history.

The picture of the fabulous artificer transmuting the base metal of history into the gold of art dominated Joyce criticism for several decades, bolstered by a range of theories including Joseph Frank's scheme for reading the modern novel against its diachronic grain and Mircea Eliade's powerful description of what he called the "terror of history" (a phrase reminiscent of the received version of Stephen's words), a terror he saw formally assuaged in the work of Joyce and T. S. Eliot, which he claimed was "saturated with nostalgia for the myth of eternal repetition and, in the last analysis, for the abolition of time."[21] For post-war critics who had welcomed Eliot's "mythical method" as a theory of reading, the idea of abolishing time and history in the novel's spatial form and mythic dimension was especially appealing. Modernism's encounter with history could be reduced to a kind of algebra in which history was solved, or at least made bearable, by art.

I am struck by the ways in which this neat, sanguine history/art dialectic persists, at least as a rhetorical gesture, in recent writing on Joyce, right across the critical spectrum. An especially common strategy offers the notion of "dream" as antithesis and sublation of its evil twin, "nightmare." Here are some examples: "through the imagination are history and the past conquered. History, no longer a nightmare, is a dream vision";[22] "it is by plunging into [the undifferentiated reality represented by Stephen's 'shout in the street'] that we can unmake the meanings imposed on us and awake from the nightmare of history into the dream of language";[23] "if history is a nightmare from which Stephen Dedalus is trying to awake, writing could be said to be the dream into which James Joyce awakened";[24] by the end of "Penelope," "history loses its nightmarish aspect. When it reawakens in the dream of *Finnegans Wake,* other voices will have taken over the tale of the tribe."[25]

Each of these critics has a more complex reading of history and textuality than these excerpts would suggest, yet the legacy of a confident, unreflective formalism is evident in the seductive ticktock of the nightmare/dream gesture. It betrays a residual temptation—resisted in other ways by these critics—to settle the relation of art to history without fully probing either category; perhaps it even reveals an unconscious nostalgia for a time when art could be seen as bringing order to the anarchy and futility of history rather than, as now, being an ideologically driven project always already fissured by the historical real. A more self-conscious approach to this question can be found in the work of Cheryl Herr, R. B. Kershner, Stephen Watt, and others who have approached the history/art dialectic through Joyce's use of popular culture.[26] Interestingly, these critics rarely use the "nightmare of history" tag, probably because Joycean cultural critique has focused on the bourgeois world of Leopold Bloom rather than on the historical imagination of Stephen Dedalus.

Stephen unquestionably suffers from the nightmare of history. It torments him as keenly as the related conundrum about how to translate *amor matris.* The dilemma of whether to love the mother or merely to accept her love confronts him with a painfully familiar choice between agency and passivity. Ernest Jones argued that the three cardinal features of nightmares are "agonizing dread," "a suffocating sense of oppression at the chest," and "a conviction of helpless paralysis."[27] That third element, the loss of free agency, characterizes much of Stephen's sense of himself and his relation to the world. As he listens to Mr. Deasy's fussy lecture about saving money, he realizes that he has heard the "same wisdom" three times now from the old man. "Three nooses round me here. Well? I can break them in this instant if I will" (2.233–35). But he does not yet possess the passionate Nietzschean will that, in a fierce act of forgetting, can burst through the stale repetitions of history to an exhilarating sense of authenticity. *Amor matris* tickles his brain with its Janus-like grammar, and the night-*mère* bears down on him in a contest of wills that reduces his earlier *non serviam* at his mother's deathbed to vain bullying, the harried delving of the wanted fox.

Deasy and Stephen both deny history, the former by wrapping it in Victorian metaphysics, the latter by spurning it in a Romantic quest for radical selfhood. Despite his resistance to the old man's maunderings, Stephen shares at times Deasy's sense of woman's role in history. The question he asks his student about the "end of Pyrrhus" (2.18) goes unanswered as classroom discipline breaks down, and the history lesson is abandoned in favor of puns, riddles, and poetry. But Stephen, a learner rather, answers his own question silently, recalling the tradition that the Greek general had "fallen by a beldam's hand in Argos" (2.48), unhorsed by a tile thrown from a housetop.[28] For Stephen, too, the *belle dame sans merci* lies in wait for the knight-at-arms, ready to oust the infinite possibilities of history in a moment of fatal seduction. The Shakespeare theory that he moodily rehearses in the library later in the day locates the origin of the bard's genius in a wound of sexual doubt inflicted by Anne Hathaway, the "boldfaced Stratford wench" who "tumble[d] in a cornfield a lover younger than herself" (9.259–60). Anne Hathaway is the female monocause of Shakespeare's personal history and oeuvre, the ground of his being and becoming. With Aristotelian certitude, Stephen defends her role as first artistic cause against the opinion of the Dublin Platonists, led by John Eglinton, that she "died, for literature at least, before she was born" (9.216). "She died," Stephen retorts, "sixtyseven years after she was born" (9.217). Her empirical historicity is essential to his claims.[29]

The nightmare that squats on the young artist's bosom, oppressing him and paralyzing his will, carries traditional associations of femaleness. Ernest Jones noted that "the original Teutonic word for horse = masculine 'mar,' feminine 'mare,' came to be used almost entirely in its feminine form, and . . . the same word was used to designate a whore or contemptible woman. A female horse was in the Middle Ages a despised horse."[30] Although it may be fanciful etymology to find equinity in "nightmare" or *"cauchemar,"* Joyce was fond of making just that popular connection. As early as *Chamber Music,* in the poem "I hear an army charging upon the land," a dreamer cries out against "the thunder of horses plunging, foam about their knees" and arrogant charioteers "in black armour," tossing their "long, green hair" (*CM* 179). This garish dreamscape, with its latent pun in the image of charging horses and its spectral charioteers out of some dim chronicle, can be read as an elaborate kenning for the "nightmare of history."[31]

In *Ulysses,* Garrett Deasy is an avatar of Homer's Nestor, the old tamer of horses, and the walls of his Dalkey study are covered with pictures of "vanished" racehorses owned by aristocrats. Stephen wearily contemplates these pictures, at one point quipping to himself, "What if that nightmare gave you a back kick?" (2.379). Much later, in "Circe," there is a phantom rerunning of the Ascot Gold Cup in which "skeleton horses" rush past and Deasy, outfitted as a jockey, brings up the rear on a broken-down nag, a struggler at the end of his days, reaching the one great goal dead last (15.3974–83). On the hallucinated stage of "Circe," history manifests, not God, but a dogged effort to finish the race and retire. In an early draft of the episode, the crowd shouts, "Throwaway and Even Money the Nightmare."[32] By the time of Joyce's final work, *Finnegans Wake,* any mention of "nightmare," "nightmale," "couchmare," "Coachmaher," or "Incubone" brings with it a gallop of horses and a whinny of equine allusions (*FW* 221, 485, 576, and 583).

"Nestor" inaugurates, and the rest of *Ulysses* sustains, this strange but telling inquiry into history-writing and historical thought, returning again and again to the uncanny female body, in particular the maternal body, to probe that gendered project. Joyce suggests that both traditional historiography (European as well as Irish) and masculine identity employ a dubious metaphysical strategy: the positing of the female, conceived of as wanton temptress or nurturing mother, as a vanishing cause, an origin that makes possible personal and historical narratives and then suffers burial at the claws of the cunning, storytelling fox. That the substance of woman, her body-in-history, will not remain in the earth for long is signaled by the implacable return of the cancer-wasted corpse of May Dedalus, the night-*mère* of history. Stephen will be visited by this night-hag, this bogey, this *Druckgeist,* until both history and *amor matris* take on a more tangible reality for his imagination, until the past ceases to seem a wasteland of ousted possibilities and becomes what is in some ways even more daunting, a field of actualities made vital by the potential they hold for the present and its purposes: "a movement then, an actuality of the possible as possible" (2.67). Neither flesh and blood nor raw head and bloody bones can reveal this movement to Stephen. It is a great goal to which he must move by chastened efforts of the will in his own time, in history.

3

Old Wives' Tales as Portals of Discovery in "Proteus"

CHERYL HERR

In her volume *The Second Voyage,* Eileán Ní Chuilleanáin addresses the famous Joycean mise-en-scène in the "Proteus" episode. In the poem "Site of Ambush" she writes:

> I am walking beside Sandymount strand,
> Not on it; the tide is nearly at the new wall.

Slightly apart from the beach, the poet notices its shifting signs and draws nearer:

> Four children are pushing back and forth
> A huge reel that has held electric cable
> They are knee deep in the water
> I come closer and see they have rubber boots on.
> The sand looks level but the water lies here and there
> Searching out valleys an inch deep.

Resisting the Joycean tidal pull toward abstractions, she speaks without the imposed binarisms of Stephen Dedalus's earlier thoughts inspired by Sandymount:

> . . . The old baths
> Loom square like a mirage.
> Light glances off water, wet sand and houses[1]

The strophe excerpted above is framed by the poet's readings of "the escaping tide" and of those who stand watching the sea, by the appearance of woman and child at the water's edge. For a Joycean accustomed to Stephen's ideological organization of the scene, it is notable that Ní Chuilleanáin attends to concrete details registered as sensory data and values the impressionistic over the portentously speculative; unlike Stephen, she does not interpret the scene in overt homage to Western philosophical tradition. Her response is to the strand and only obliquely to Joyce's portrayal of it.

Taking Ní Chuilleanáin's cue, this essay draws on the gains made in the past decade by feminist epistemologists (Vrinda Dalmiya, Linda Alcoff, Phyllis Rooney, and Luce Irigaray) and critiques Stephen's entrapment in male-identified, dichotomous philosophical discourses. The effects of the rationalist tradition's exclusion of what has been called women's knowledge—emblematized in the episode by reference to conception, gestation, and midwifery—can be discerned not only in the array of standard philosophical questions that interest Stephen but also in much of the existing criticism on "Proteus." That body of interpretation has tended to privilege the patriarchal metaphysical issues favored by Stephen, to neglect the crucial female agency in the Homeric background to the episode, and to sever the link between the Joycean text and Irish folklore in which women occupy center stage.

It is the male-identified allusions in "Proteus" that have occupied most Joyceans in the past. From the time of Robert Hurley's 1963 study of "Proteus," readers have sought to comprehend fully this most overtly philosophical and most binary of the chapters in *Ulysses,* and attention to this line of explication demonstrates the considerable gains that have been made.[2] It is well known that Stephen's topics of meditation on the strand in "Proteus" emerge from the consideration in "Telemachus" of consubstantiality, transubstantiality, and the church's handling of heretics. Here he wants to deploy reason—buttressed by considerable knowledge of philosophical and literary texts—in order to rehearse for himself some precepts about the nature of God, the relationships among various categories of things in the world (inanimate objects, plants, animals, human beings, deity), the interactions of corporeal and incorporeal substance in composing the scene before him, and the role of the senses in helping the aspiring artist in his apprehension and digestion of this abundant but less-than-fresh metaphysical feast. Much of what Stephen thinks about can be traced to the writings of Jacob Boehme, Giordano Bruno, Aristotle, and St. Thomas Aquinas—a pantheon of epistemological authorities. Indeed, Aristotle's focus in the *Metaphysics* on the substance of the universe, on the processes of generation and decay, and on the nature of God accounts for the broad structure of this episode and for Stephen's thoughts on the place that his soul occupies in the big scheme of things: recalling Dante on Aristotle, Stephen thinks fondly of the *maestro di color che sanno* (3.06–7, "master of those that know").

Mixing rather freely the elements of a realist epistemology with a desire for some form of intuition and even of potential "ontological promotion,"[3] Stephen begins the episode by posturing at the edge of the sea, proclaiming his classically masculine role: he is to read the writing that is the world, the "Signatures of all things" (3.02). He thinks oppositionally of spawn and wrack, diaphane and adiaphane, blindness and vision, time and space, *nacheinander* and *nebeneinander,* the now and the eternal, dead dog and live dog. The son of Si Dedalus strolls amidst the seaweed wrestling with dichotomies, and by reading this chapter it is possible to pin down some of Stephen's fundamental philosophical convictions—his adherence to the existence of external reality, his basic belief in divine being, his experience of himself as not only willed by God but as also consubstantial with the deity. We could easily argue that because he is fascinated by this highly traditional, patriarchal, and classically sanctioned theory of knowledge, Stephen goes only tentatively through the motions of testing and rethinking some fundamental tenets of Western rational philosophy.

Later, of course, both Stephen and Bloom consider the difficulties of proceeding from the known to the unknown. Movement from the language of the tribe to whatever void incertitude lies in the uncoded elsewhere brings into focus some notes that Joyce took when preparing the "Ithaca" episode:

> deal logically with the unknown
> working hypothesis
> reductio ad absurdum
> prod. elim. of some elements of complexity
>
> 1) state of ignorance
> 2) respect for the as yet unknown
> 3) never shirk absurd[4]

The reader has to grant Joyce as many degrees of irony in his notebooks as in his narratives, but it seems likely that at some level of the *Ulysses* experience, in one of its narrative registers, a patriarchal logic can be found struggling toward "the as yet unknown."

One reason that Stephen traces the philosophic history of the relation between reason and the irrational, form and matter, mind and sensation, male and female, formative subject and passive object, is that this dichotomized language came to him both ready-made and persistently, from all corners of the academic-philosophic-theological world. As Irish feminist philosopher Phyllis Rooney argues, binary distinctions of all kinds—from the beginnings of philosophical history—have been pointedly gendered, almost always to the disadvantageous representation of women, who are consistently excluded from the realm of reason.[5] That the Irish nation was characterized by their British colonial administrators as an essentially feminine race complicates the issue of assigned, gendered subject positions, whether in theories of history, theories of knowledge, theories of the relationship between humanity and nature, or theories of Joycean meaning. Obsessed with masculinist metaphors and only warily, ironically approaching a concern with the feminine, the Stephen of "Proteus" prompts us to meditate further on the role and functions of the episode's superficial affirmation of reason, speculation, and standardly gendered epistemological tropes.

Not that previous critics have entirely neglected to isolate in "Proteus" a role for women. An excellent feminist perspective is presented in Bonnie Kime Scott's two books on Joyce as well as her essay in *Approaches to Teaching "Ulysses."*[6] Scott explores the interassociation of the sea, matter, the moon, and woman to form a rhythmic reality to which Stephen's thoughts actively respond; she also attends to the variety of female figures that Stephen recognizes on the beach. Nonetheless, this chapter, which Joyce designated in his schemata as "male monologue," stops short of representing women as knowers. Rather than hearing women's discourses, Stephen watches women, longs for women, and ultimately reveals himself as terrorized by their apparent somatic access to Being. If anything, Stephen wants to turn all knowing, however tacit, however physical, into language; he grapples with language in order to dominate and control the stuff of Being.

So it is not to the usual portrayal of "Proteus," the structuralist's dreamtext of dichotomies and the logician's of syllogistic reasoning, that I want to point, but rather to the way that in the midst of what used to be called phallogocentric reasoning the processes of spawning come to the fore and mark as importantly problematic the interrelated conditions of birthing and of knowing (construed, if you will, beyond a binary logic) that preoccupy Stephen both directly and indirectly. On the beach at Sandymount, Stephen struggles with the forms of things only in order to approach the issue of materiality within, behind, beneath, and above the definitions of Being currently available to him. In fact, his multiplicitous grapplings organize the language of this chapter in at least two dimensions, each of them gendered, each directed toward radically different epistemological ends. What Stephen must come to terms with are categories heavily overcoded by a rationalist tradition, especially the cannily overlapping contrast between propositional knowledge and experiential knowledge, between what a male-biased tradition has claimed as knowledge proper and what has been marginalized as old wives' tales. And he must grapple while remaining unsure of his own engendering, the terms of his own identity and substance.

One instance of Stephen's probing this uncertainty is his imaginative projection of a visit to his Uncle Richie, the disparaged brother of Simon Dedalus's equally maligned wife. We find in Stephen signs of an ongoing effort—one that significantly fails—to tame his like-father-like-son looking down the nose at his maternal family ("O, weeping God, the things I married into!" [3.65]). Certainly, this learned negative attitude, seen as a thinly veiled gynophobia, is perfectly consistent with Stephen's crying out for *"Naked women!"* under the Howth tram and his only partly ironic internal rejoinder, "What else were they invented for?" (3.134–35). And yet Stephen does not finally distinguish between his maternal and paternal lines in terms of their current conditions: all are "Houses of decay" (3.105). Simply parroting Si Dedalus's denunciations does not direct Stephen toward a logic that will encompass and explain both bloodlines, their gendered differences, and their effects on Stephen's experience.

Similarly, Stephen's self-satirizing recollection of his reading program and epiphany recording allows him to attempt appropriating the power of language and thought against the constantly surfacing awareness of female power—an energy bound up with the making of a child. Some "she" must touch him, show him the way, connect the force of language to the immense force of the tide-drawing moon. The slippage that the episode's rhetoric creates between the female cockle picker and the vast sea, between any individual woman and the power of nature, suggests all that Stephen feels out of touch with:

> Across the sands of all the world, followed by the sun's flaming sword, to the west, trekking to evening lands. She trudges, schlepps, trains, drags, trascines her load. A tide westering, moondrawn, in her wake. Tides, myriadislanded, within her, blood not mine, *oinopa ponton,* a winedark sea. Behold the handmaid of the moon. In sleep the wet sign calls her hour, bids her rise. Bridebed, childbed, bed of death, ghostcandled. (3.391–96)

Until he comes to terms sensorily with the woman occupying these iconic beds, Stephen can only scribble pseudo- or proto-poems, meditate pompously, and keep himself sartorially on call to play the mourning son, Hamlet at grievous odds with his mother.

To a large extent, Stephen's lack is signaled in the Homeric precursor to the episode, a text in which we can locate an impetus toward a feminist epistemological inquiry that aims to know through the body and beyond patriarchal rationality. It is worth recalling here that although collectively Joyceans have tended to construe the Proteus story in remarkably gender-specific ways, Book IV of *The Odyssey* allows other interpretive possibilities to surface. Most Joycean commentators have focused on the heroic wrestling match between Menelaus and Proteus, seeing Stephen-Telemachus as a displaced version of the monarch, but it is important to emphasize that the daughter of Proteus, herself divine, is the god who tells Menelaus precisely how to achieve a victory. In fact, Menelaus certainly notices Eidothëe and boasts, "her heart I aroused especially." When he is "walking alone apart" from his fellow sailors, she falls into conversation with him. Proteus's daughter does not beat around the bush:

> "Are you a fool, stranger? Are you too slack of mind?
> Do you willingly let go and enjoy suffering pain?
> So long a time are you held back on the island and cannot
> Find a way out . . . ."[7]

In reply and because "the gods know all," Menelaus asks her which god has becalmed his ship and how he can safely extricate himself from this apparent punishment. It is here that Eidothëe tells Menelaus to hold fast to Proteus, first gaining proximity by dressing in the newly flayed skin of a seal. Such a narrative moment could have special meaning to the Celtic imagination, accustomed as it is to stories of selkies who shed their sealskins to live on land and give birth to human children. In Joyce's scenario, Stephen is the grappling king only at a considerable remove, his subject position being more that of remote observer, precisely the role of Telemachus hearing this story at a time well beyond that of the event. The answers that Stephen seeks are in the hands of a feminine being, an absent and unnamed Eidothëe, whom Joyce allows us to associate both with the "virgin at Hodges Figgis' window" (3.426–27) and with his mother, of whom Stephen famously asks, "What is that word known to all men?" (3.435). In phrasing his question toward androcentric agency, Stephen creates a closed circle structured to appropriate knowledge as language, without allowing the spheres of meaning that have come to stand for women's knowing to have a fair say in the process of discovery or in the metaphysical categories to which the history of philosophy has patriarchally directed us. So it is that the word Stephen seeks has to do directly with how to conquer *materia* without being consumed by the "old sow" that Mother Ireland represents to him.

In addition, the issues attendant on the politics of birthing recenter themselves in the reader's imagination as Stephen's thoughts circle from philosophy to memory, from concept to experience, from intellectual inquiry to the complex dialectics of emotional and somatic longing. Hence, when he extends his binary litany toward rehearsing the views of Arius toward divine substance, the question of who controls the processes of conception and birth cannot be overlooked. Turning to Aquinas's subtle thought to justify God's inability to will away the life of one willed into existence, Stephen finds himself drawn nonetheless into reflection on the pregnant tides, the cycles of the moon, an itinerant woman on the beach, and the "Frauenzimmer" (3.30). It is these women who lead us into the shadow world that Stephen must penetrate if he is to understand either father or mother, soul or substance, propositional knowledge or the alternative epistemological states that Vrinda Dalmiya and Linda Alcoff describe as the "experiential knowing" and "knowing how." In contrast with the conviction of "knowing that" which dominates Western philosophy and reason, Dalmiya and Alcoff discuss the kinds of knowledge they regard as common to women in preliterate spheres of occupation, such as midwifery before the twentieth century. They argue that "traditional women's beliefs—about childbearing and rearing, herbal medicines, the secrets of good cooking, and such—are generally characterized as 'old wives' tales.'" As such, they add, these practices "fail to get accorded the honorific status of knowledge."[8]

I would argue that it is by way of self-critique, then, that directly after Stephen's experiment in walking with his eyes closed (does Aristotle master this experience? does Berkeley?), the narrative turns to the *Frauenzimmer* walking flabbily by the sea. The first, whom Stephen immediately characterizes as one Mrs. Florence MacCabe, "swung lourdily her midwife's bag" (3.32). He adds, "One of her sisterhood lugged me squealing into life. Creation from nothing" (3.35). Stephen imagines that Mrs. MacCabe's bag has in it a "misbirth with a trailing navelcord, hushed in ruddy wool. The cords of all link back, strandentwining cable of all flesh" (3.36–37). Again, Stephen's subsequent speculations on life and death, on hypostasis and consubstantiality, have customarily been used by Joyce's readers to explore patristic doctrine: its authority and diversity; the efforts of the church fathers to control Christ's birth by surrounding it with fine-grained logical discriminations. But such meditations, reproducing the speculations of the church fathers, themselves merely underwrite the power of women as portrayed in this chapter. We are asked, for instance, to consider not only the intercabling of all flesh but also Eve's navel-free uniqueness, her original status.

Stephen's reflections on midwifery are part of a complex chain of allusions in *Ulysses.* On the one hand, we are surely asked to link these comments with Bloom's thoughts in "Wandering Rocks" about "Aristotle's *Masterpiece.* Crooked botched print. Plates: infants cuddled in a ball in bloodred wombs like livers of slaughtered cows" (10.586–87). Bloom's thoughts run to quantity ("Lots of them like that at this moment all over the world" [10.588]), but it is also important to note that the *Masterpiece* falsely attributed to Aristotle casts its questionable shadow on "Proteus" through the references to midwifery, the *Masterpiece* being subtitled *The Midwife's Vade-Mecum.* On the other hand, a philosopher sorting out true ideas from false would also inevitably think at this juncture of Plato's *Theaetetus,* in which Socrates explains that those who converse with him experience pain because they are bringing forth new ideas as a woman delivers a child: Socrates explains to Theaetetus that he is the son of "a fine strapping midwife called Phaenarete" and that he, Socrates, is also a practitioner of midwifery. Socrates adds that Artemis, herself childless, gave the power of delivering children only to those who had themselves borne children: "She didn't grant the gift of midwifery to barren women, because human nature is too weak to acquire skill in matters of which it has no experience." Although Socrates attends to men rather than to women, to intellects instead of bodies, he tropologically appropriates to his epistemological inquiries the skills and wisdom of the midwife's experiential knowing. It is the power to determine which child is deemed fit to live and which is allowed or encouraged to die that especially interests Socrates and supports his own role of sorting out the "genuine and true" from the misbirthed falsehood.[9] Against the predominantly Aristotelian cast of Stephen's mind, the "Proteus" episode reaches toward a crucial Platonic text that affirms women's knowing in the midst of Theaetetus's unsuccessful efforts to define knowledge and that works hard to co-opt that knowing by making the philosopher a midwife. That Stephen imagines a misbirth in Mrs. MacCabe's bag complicates our assessment of his own powers of perception and creation.

For all of the male bias of this chapter's metaphysical allusions, however, women's ways of knowing beyond the propositional can be discerned, however murkily, in the less patriarchal contexts that Stephen alludes to, Irish folklore on midwifery, in particular, can be helpful in interpreting "Proteus." For instance, in the most commonly cited folktales involving midwives, we are told of a night journey to the home of a woman whose child is about to be born. In what turns out to be a strangely sinister household, the midwife contaminates herself, either accidentally or by design, with a fairy substance. This tainting enables her to see the fairies—albeit with only one eye—when they mingle with ordinary folk at markets and fairs. Inevitably, when these supernatural beings realize that she assumed some of their sensory power, they take their revenge by putting out her clairvoyant eye. In midwife tales, then, we immediately encounter questions of visuality and knowledge similar to those that preoccupy Stephen on the strand. The mysteries of birthing coincide in these tales with the strangeness of the fairy world, both brought together in and through the body of the midwife.[10] Hence the midwife's occupation tutors her intuitively to see beyond the rational world of the here and now; her work enables her to occupy a threshold to the fairy world and its somatic power. But how is it, we might wonder, that fairies require the services of mortal birthers? One answer positions birth as a point of intersection between the otherworld and ordinary experience, the supernatural and the natural, whether the babe is mortal or changeling. A reader of "Proteus" might recall the figure of Agnes Sampson in Sam Hanna Bell's *December Bride* (1951). Agnes and her herbal display provoke some unease in the farming community where she and her husband reside, but she is also tolerated because of her skills in attending those who are being born and those who are dying. She is a wisdom woman whose magic is not entirely discountenanced by the community but is uneasily tolerated for the work she accomplishes.

We might return to the moment when "Heva, naked Eve" (3.41) comes to knowledge of good and evil as the moment producing the need for the midwife's skills; certainly Eve's sin and the divine curse of painful childbirth colored the medieval disparagement of Agnes Sampson's and Mrs. McCabe's historical sisterhood. Monitoring and facilitating those transitions from one state to another gave midwives the aura of supernatural knowledge, a woman's powerful cognition that the Middle Ages chose to malign and punish as well as utilize. Hence in the fourteenth century, the European medical establishment systematically expunged its connections to the "old wives" and their medicinal work; women and learning were mutually exclusive in this system. It was opined that midwife witches often murdered the children that they were delivering in order to provide fodder for satanic rituals.[11] And the biblical mythology that made painful childbirth a sign of God's displeasure cast, in the eyes of the church, an aura of sinful behavior over those women who chose to preside over birthing processes. Both state and church, then, Stephen's profound enemies, abjected midwifery to the status of nonknowledge.

Childbirth was not widely viewed as a situation demanding medical assistance until the nineteenth century, when male doctors across Europe took over the role of delivering babies. Patriarchal society systematically rebuffed the challenge to it that had always been exercized by women's control over the birth process. Because over the ages women could and did find ways to abort their offspring or to deliver them secretly, the midwife became anathema to the medical system and its masculinist bias. According to Irish sociologist Jo Murphy-Lawless, what is usually accepted as firm fact about women's experience, especially in disciplined sites such as Dublin's Rotunda, the first maternity hospital in the British Isles, has come to us entirely through the discourse of the male medical establishment and that preemptive category, the male midwife.[12] Eventually, even the process of giving birth was invaded by the clinician's way of knowing. Turning to Foucault and to Elisabeth Badinter's *The Myth of Motherhood* (1981), Murphy-Lawless marks the pivotal role of the Rotunda in the modern construction of motherhood under the watchful eye of interrogating male doctors and medical students. In particular, she deplores the positioning of pregnant women as passive and as "poor suffering women" in need of male help.[13] It is instructive to view Bloom's much-praised cross-gender sympathy with Mrs. Purefoy in this equivocal contextual light, as an ideofragment of the systematic reduction of female power within the hospital system. Given the birth and death of Rudy presided over, like the birth of Milly, by Mrs. Thornton (see 4.416–20), and given the irritation that Molly feels over her only recorded visit to a gynecologist, it is clear that in Joyce's Dublin two systems of medical professing still existed, occupying nonintersecting tracks. Neither Bloom nor Stephen fully assesses the binary cultural logic that separated putative fact from marginalized medical folklore.

When Joyce depicts the erudite, ribald doctorly discourse that saturates the atmosphere in the Holles Street maternity hospital, he crystallizes the history of many such gendered distinctions, both in action and in epistemological legitimacy.[14] In contrast to stately, plump medical students, the women Stephen has imaginatively designated midwives wander at the margins: the edge of the sea, the border between life and death, the periphery of social power, the raveled rim of the artist's perception, a few passages in a densely detailed and lengthy narrative. Again, it is a telling sign of this marginalization that when Stephen thinks he sees a midwife's bag he assumes the presence of a misbirth, propelling into his 1904 present the medieval connection with dead babies—potential knowers rendered merely material.

Brought center stage in the "Aeolus" chapter's "Parable of the Plums," the *Frauenzimmer* become more the residue in Stephen's idiom of pervasive male-bonding ribaldry than a conduit for social, political, economic, or gender-based understanding of his society's constitution of knowledge. Obviously, the power of the medical profession, as of church and state, is not uniform, either in history or in *Ulysses.* But it is significant that Stephen never allows his two women, for all of the detail lavished on their social circumstances and putative journey up Nelson's Pillar, to speak in their own voices. They remain passive figures amazed at the view at the pillar's peak.

Reading "Proteus" against that grain of philosophical bias enables us to destabilize the presumed opposition between the womanly folk knowledge that

Stephen denies and the Aristotelian orthodoxy that he tries to embrace. The universal exclusion of women's knowing from classical philosophy created the negative valuing of that knowing as it shows up in midwifery, labor and childbirth, and mothering. That said, a feminist philosopher who writes with awareness of the necessity for experiential voicing is Luce Irigaray, whose dialogue with Nietzschean thought intersects with Stephen's "Proteus" line of reasoning at remarkable junctures. The ideological echoes occur because both Joyce and Irigaray focus on Nietzschean categories and images. Nietzsche's fragmentary, unfinished, but intensive critique of Western metaphysics directed his vocabulary and considerations toward the issues of divinity, substance, selfhood, and reason that Stephen meditates on. In several senses, then, Stephen is "Toothless Kinch, the superman" (3.496). Like Irigaray, Stephen is not satisfied with Nietzsche's profound materialism and denial of a transcendental register in the "as yet unknown."

In tangential and wonderfully revealing contrast, a feminist epistemology helps to destabilize and reconceive this system into ever-more-fluid formulations. Consider Scott's statement about "Proteus," for instance, in her essay on feminist approaches to Joyce's text: "Part of what is protean in this difficult chapter is the assertion of fluidity and decomposition against the organizing forces of male philosophy. . . . Stephen sees midwives, cockle gatherers, dogs . . . all of which evade these classical systems and the attention of the male philosophers who have dominated his Jesuit training."[15] Irigaray's critique of Nietzsche stands as a logical extension of what Stephen can sense is needed but is unable to conceive within the metaphysical and categorical traditions at his disposal. Whereas the very issues that he focuses upon—particularly that of substance—never lead him toward anything other than replaying the gendering of that system, much of *Marine Lover* reads like a response to "Proteus" that goes far beyond the binary boundaries Stephen clings to. Irigaray attends from the outset to the nature of a female ground, which might be read as Stephen's protean *materia* valued at least as highly as form. The results of this ontological promotion are immense. For example, steeped in a masculinist philosophic tradition, when Stephen turns to poetry he can only box himself into an erotic situation in which he takes the role of "undead" exploiter of his own fantasmatic desire.

> On swift sail flaming
> From storm and south
> He comes, pale vampire,
> Mouth to my mouth. (7.522–25)

In Irigaray the decadent fin de siècle images that Stephen fetishizes have given way to a creative fluidity beyond difference. The Nietzschean superman, per se, is rejected by Irigaray in favor of an elsewhere not at the beck and call of the patriarchal philosopher. In place of the superman is put a multiple, open, dynamic subjectivity. Rather than being restricted to a vocabulary of "Monkswords" (3.387) and damning delectations, of discourses limited by church and state, Irigaray grounds words in an *autre* that cannot be recuperated.

In the lyrical first section of *Marine Lover* ("Speaking of Immemorial Waters"), while Irigaray fluidly disassembles Nietzschean logic, she sounds as though she were one of Stephen's fantasy women who has miraculously been given a voice in the extra-Joycean script of life; she also sounds a bit like Molly Bloom:

> had I never held back, never would you have remembered that something exists which has a language other than your own. . . . Yes, yes, yes . . . I hear you. And I do not hear you. I am your hearing. Between you and yourself, I ensure the vocal medium. A perpetual relay between your mouth and your ear. . . . How I should love you if to speak to you were possible.[16]

Irigaray's woman/muse/philosophy/truth is not satisfied with merely asserting her presence; she continues in words that would be appropriate to Stephen's phantasm, were he able to ring her up on the cosmic telephone ("Hello! Kinch here. Put me on to Edenville. Aleph, alpha: nought, nought, one" [3.39–40]):

> Let me go. Yes, let me go onward. Beyond the place of no return. Either you seize hold of me or you throw me away, but always according to your whim of the moment. I am good or bad according to your latest good or evil. Muse or fallen angel to suit the needs of your most recent notion.

Insisting on autonomy, she indicts Nietzsche for his "game: ceaselessly to bring the outside inwards. To have no outside that you have not put there yourself." To Zarathustra she adds a warning about forsaking the nurturing sea for the superman-run earth: "And when you say that the superman is the sea in whom your contempt is lost, that's fine. That is a will wider than man's own. But you never say: the superman has lived in the sea. That is how he survives." The adversarial relationships on which Nietzschean personae thrive point toward other configurations of relating when we occupy the metonymic chain that in "Proteus" and its cultural coordinates includes the sea, woman, and the material world as well as the desiccated word. An alternative ethos unfixable in the complex dialectic of the episode begins to be heard, one that, having suggested a warring between sea and earth, begins to subsume both within the role of a differential "foundation" that no longer is made to exclude principles of form, meaning, and language.[17] In contrast to the limits of knowledge that preoccupied Joyce, with the help of Irigaray's parallel text we discover in "Proteus" that illimitable and ineluctable processes of transgendered knowing reveal themselves even within Stephen's brine-drenched and metaphysics-drugged speculations.

Like Eidothëe strategizing her father's entanglement, Irigaray locates the

Achilles heel of the protean protagonists she accosts: "But this inert matter you exploit for your disguises, these props you use for your various character parts, are they not in fact a sign of your annihilation?" So in *Ulysses* Stephen begins to fade from our consciousness, and the "womanly man," Leopold Bloom, comes into view; so Stephen looks over his shoulder to note the shift in viewing position that will take us finally to Molly-Penelope. And beyond the Joycean narrative's ability to call forth, we may discern, as does Irigaray, another dimension of Being: "I want to disentangle myself from your appearances, unravel again and again the mirages conjured up by your seductiveness, and find where I begin once more." This "liquid ground" calls to Stephen even though he is not able to drink deeply from the wellspring; Aristotle, Aquinas, Boehme, Arius, and Nietzsche long ago set up shop there.[18] But textually speaking, the same sea that led Telemachus in search of his father and that forestalled Menelaus's travels seeps into the crevices between hard-edged metaphysical distinctions to assert a common and encompassing ground, immerses identity in a difference that is more properly something other, and elsewhere, than sameness.

Comparing Irigaray's text to the representative thoughts of Molly Bloom could be the basis of a demonstration that Irigaray cannot take us into the beyond that she detects and apostrophizes. It may no longer be enough for a reader to be assured, *à la l'écriture féminine,* that the feminine ground has no experiential or cognitive limits. But one can at least observe how Irigaray cues us to rescue the old wives' tales in "Proteus" and to treasure the traces of uncertainty in Stephen's thought. The pathway from the known to the unknown comes into focus not only through the lenses of Irish folklore but also in the purview of contemporary French feminism.

What Stephen Dedalus can know, then, becomes trivial in comparison to what he cannot conceive of as worth knowing. The relay that he seeks requires not only transforming his conceptions of the goals of knowing but also a reclaiming of women's knowledge as neither threatening black magic nor impotent folklore. Stephen's repeated entrapment by philosophy displays the struggle with Proteus as endless, shows that it is patriarchy and its traditions that have imagined into being the dead babes, vampire lovers, and corpsegas that infect Stephen's consciousness. Is it more fruitful to reach without words toward a liminal space, a traditional and negative space routinely claimed by the midwife? Joycean readers must place Stephen's thoughts within a larger epistemological context and somatic economy in order to recover the force of women's ways of knowing in *Ulysses.*

4

Milly, Molly, and the Mullingar Photo Shop

Developing Negatives in "Calypso"

CAROL SHLOSS

Suppose, now, you're with the army, leaving me at home, / And the slow months drag on, and you're still at Troy, / What thought do you imagine will occupy my heart, / When every chair I see will be empty of her, / Her bedroom empty, and I sit alone in tears / Mourning for her . . . ?

Clytemnestra in Euripedes, *Iphigenia at Aulis*

its as well he sent her where she is she was just getting out of bounds (18.1027)

Molly Bloom

The lady was placed on a chair before the camera, though at some distance from it. The gentleman leaned over the back of the chair . . . he was her oak and she the *nymph* who sat secure in his shade.

Charles Dickens (?), "Photography"[1]

Calypso's island in *The Odyssey* is an enclosure near the western edge of the world, and its name, Ogygia, Victor Berard tells us in *Les Pheniciens et l'Odyssée,* means "ocean."[2] Not only is it a mythic place of captivity, but it is a place identified by its surrounding form. Its land is named by the sea; that which is signified takes its signifier from the context of its occurrence, and, in meditating on this, we can see that the island itself can serve as a trope for Odysseus's predicament: held in thrall by the nymph, he can take the measure of his confinement only by observing the great stretches of water that keep him from Ithaca. There is no prison except the ocean, the very context of his life.

I have opened my essay in this way because the mythic predicament of

Homer's protagonist can alert us to some of the most pressing issues in the "Calypso" episode of Joyce's *Ulysses,* where the very mundanity of its subject might disguise the intricacies of its design, and where its focus on the home, an island of domesticity, might discourage us from seeing how domestic rituals depend for their meaning, at least in part, on the ocean of assumptions about the public order in which they are embedded. Dwelling, moving about, speaking, reading, shopping, and cooking—the activities that tell us that Leopold and Molly Bloom are most "at home," most privately themselves, in 7 Eccles Street and in their neighborhood—are marked by the very world that these behaviors have been designed to exclude.

Michel Foucault would identify these strategies of living as "subjugated knowledges," which remain beneath the notice of the technical apparatus of the state;[3] and Michel de Certeau, extending Foucault's work, speaks of behavior in such interior spaces as a kind of "remainder"—a way of operating which has no legitimacy with respect to rational productivity—and which, because it has been left behind by "ethnological colonization," "acquires the status of a 'private' activity [that is] charged with symbolic investments. . . . it becomes . . . the legendary and at the same time active memory of what remains on the margins or in the interstices of scientific or cultural . . . praxis."[4]

The connection of these cultural theories to Odysseus's languishing sojourn on Ogygia is made through the concept of captivity and through the question of our ability to maneuver within or against it. In Joyce's version of the myth, we can ask, "to what are the Blooms 'enthralled' in the Dublin of their lifetime and to what degree can they free themselves from the normative pressures of the social, economic and cultural institutions which surround them?" De Certeau asserts that even the most ordinary people have the means to subvert, evade, or invert the economy which seemingly contains them: "Beneath . . . the 'monotheistic' privilege that panoptic apparatus have won for themselves, a polytheism of scattered practices survives, dominated but not erased by the triumphal success of one of their number."[5] I wish to extend his work and to ask how the practice of everyday life can respond to the pressures of gender formation and to consider how the seeming trivialities of private behavior can be considered tactics of evasion that challenge the captivities of normative gender roles. The "nymph" in this reading of Joyce's work is neither a woman nor a girl, neither a wife nor a daughter, but the very procedures of identity formation that condemn us to repeat gendered cultural scripts without alternative. "[T]hey all look at her like me when I was her age of course" (18.1036), Molly remarks of Milly. "A wild piece of goods. Her slim legs running up the staircase," Bloom thinks, "Destiny" (4.429–30), and we remember that his most careful and fond plan for her is to be an apprentice in a photo shop in Mullingar, where she will learn to develop negatives. The voice at the end of "Oxen of the Sun" identifies Bloom as "Photos Papli" (14.1535–36)—the progenitor of images, alerting us to further issues of reproduction, as if Milly Bloom's fate were already known to be a repetition of the same.[6]

How is it that an unformed girl can be perceived so certainly as the "same thing [as her mother] watered down" (6.87)? One way to answer that question is to explore the logic of her fictional career and to follow the configuration of human possibilities suggested to us by the trope of photography; Milly, in the opening of *Ulysses,* is absent from home, sent out to Mullingar by her father to work as a photographer's assistant. Her mother, apparently without say in the matter ("its as well he sent her where she is she was just getting out of bounds" [18.1027]), does not really understand why Bloom preferred sending her to a camera shop rather than to a clerking position in Dublin; but contemporary readers can see that photography, certainly the modern world's most insistent device for the multiplication of images, has a particular aptness in describing the configuration of Edwardian mothers and daughters that we find in this novel.

From Walter Benjamin, we know the disturbances of culture that can ensue from the photograph's ability to exist in unwonted contexts, proliferating, invading, and denying the previously singular and irreplaceable nature of works of "high" art.[7] By 1904, photographs were to be found everywhere in Ireland, even in small towns on the outskirts of Dublin, even in the hands of people like the Blooms, whose bedroom wall is adorned with a picture of a nymph, torn from *Photo Bits,* framed and recirculated so that Molly, in her nighttime musings, wonders if she more resembles such a long-haired, nubile creature or her husband's Spanish photo of a "dirty bitch" (18.564). For Milly, too, the photograph as an artifact is a way of broadcasting her prettiness: she plans to send to "Dearest Papli" the one "Mr Coghlan took . . . of me" (4.401), little realizing that her everyday gesture can serve as the figure of her more general position in a male economy of desire and exchange—imaged and circulated as decisively as any "photo bit" posted through the mail.[8] Like Molly she recognizes her affiliation with the image rather than the image maker, and though her mother is puzzled by Bloom's insistence on this particular vocation for his daughter, it, too, points to her lack of agency in the world: neither maker of the symbolic order nor its master, she is instead the manipulator of the print, bringing to light what is latent in someone else's film. She is functional, instrumental, but always, like her own untold story, hidden away in the darkroom of culture.

In pursuing the logic of this aspect of a metaphor, we are led to see that in bringing the daughter's story to light, we are violating the narrative consciousness of Joyce's text, where, to use a phrase from Marianne Hirsch, the "mother/daughter plot" remains submerged.[9] Like the photograph, it is imprinted in such a way that its very power emerges from darkness, the unconscious nature of the behavior in no way interfering with its repeatability.

If we were to move away from the photo as an artifact, and what it can tell us about the gendered creation of culture, we would come to some other and more disturbing implications of the "negative makings" of Joyce's photo girl. For, as much as anything, "Calypso" reveals that Milly and Molly are reproducing a negative pattern, first in the sense of repeating or reproducing the life of a disempowered mother, and, further, in the sense of developing manners that are negative or counter to the accepted life of families, where heterosexuality, monogamy, and reproductive sex are as imperative as the allegiance of daughters to the system of inheritance that will eventually exclude them. In the first case, we are presented with the constant reiteration of something regrettable; in the second, we can begin to see de Certeau's sense of the delinquency which can serve as a site of resistance to the overwhelming cultural scripts which hold us enthralled to normative gender roles. In thinking about the patterns of reproduction that are signaled in "Calypso," I would like to foreground both the ways gendered character and behavior are reproduced and also the nature of the bond that is assumed to exist between Molly and Milly, holding their lives in a reiterative pattern.

When Nancy Chodorow began in 1978 to ask why women mother, she was working against the grain of contemporary explanations, which tended to posit answers based either on biology or on role socialization.[10] Dissatisfied with both theories, she herself drew on the object relations work of Melanie Klein and D. W. Winnicott, which emphasizes the connection between intrapsychic structure and relational capacities.[11] "Elements of social structure," she decided, "especially as transmitted through the organization of parenting as well as the features of individual families, are appropriated and transformed internally through unconscious processes and come to influence affective life." All adults, she claimed, have internalized what has happened to them *in relation to* others, and since these configurations persist long after the original relationship that set them in motion, one's very ability to love can be affected by conditions one no longer remembers. "Adults unconsciously look to recreate, and are often unable to avoid recreating aspects of their early relationships, especially to the extent that these relationships were unresolved, ambivalent, and repressed." In this system of thinking, early caretakers who have problems with their charges are referred to as "bad objects," and the effects of their distress careen out into the future of the child who may come to experience him- or herself as rejected or as someone who drives love away. Mothering is, of course, the experience of every infant regardless of gender, but Chodorow accorded extraordinary importance to the fact that the child's earliest relationship is with a woman. "That women mother and men do not is projected back by the child after gender comes to count."[12]

Without going too much further into the complexities of Chodorow's theory, I think it is now possible to project the line of reasoning that follows from the metaphoric associations of this essay and to see that "Calypso" provides us with an interesting case study not only in the generation of images of women but also in the reproduction of mothering. As Nancy Chodorow reminds us, "the sexual division of labor [in families] both produces gender differences and is in turn reproduced by them." "Women are prepared psychologically for mothering," she continues, "through the developmental situation in which they grow up and in which women have mothered them"—a situation that is profoundly and without exception influenced by their own participation in a social system already in place. "Her mothering, then, is informed by her relationship to her husband, her experience of financial dependence, her expectations of marital inequality and her expectations about gender roles."[13]

Looked at in this light, Joyce's configuration of the Bloom family is interesting both for what we can infer about Molly's assumptions about motherhood—assumptions that Chodorow tells us will have been internalized by Milly in her infancy—and as a study in absences; many of the women of this book have been torn from one another by death, by marriage, by economic necessity, or by psychological preoccupation.

As I begin to tease out of the text the assumptions about gender that would have engendered Milly, I am struck by what I don't know and have no way of ever discovering. Was Molly a good mother? Did Bloom participate in rearing his daughter? Were their lives made happy by Milly's birth? Of all the things that can be reconstructed about Dublin 1904 by reading *Ulysses,* motherhood is not one of them.[14] In a very general way, Molly sees that men have no way of understanding maternity—"they don't know what it is to be a woman and a mother how could they" (18.1441)—but her own memories disclose more annoyance than affection. Milly is remembered primarily for the trouble she has caused: "what I went through with Milly nobody would believe cutting her teeth" (18.158–59); "I had a great breast of milk with Milly . . . hurt me they used to weaning her" (18.570–75); "she didnt even want me to kiss her at the Broadstone . . . she had the mumps" (18.1047–49); "when she was a child . . . she had worms" (18.1167–68). And while Molly recognizes her life as circumscribed by the domestic—"what between clothing and cooking and children" (18.1130)—her mind sees only those characteristics in her daughter that remind her of her own sexuality: "like Millys little ones now when she runs up the stairs" (18.850–51); "shes restless knowing shes pretty . . . I was too" (18.1065–66). The only heritage that counts in this private libidinal economy is beauty, and it is a short-lived inheritance: "as for being a woman as soon as youre old they might as well throw you out in the bottom of the ashpit" (18.746–47).

On this day, June 16, the Blooms have received a letter and a card from their daughter. To her mother, Milly sends thanks for her birthday gifts; to her father, a more extended communication. This letter is the only representation of the voice of the daughter in the whole of *Ulysses,* and in it, Milly apologizes for her bad writing. In doing this, she unwittingly aligns herself with her maternal grandmother, whose only foray into the symbolic—the naming of her daughter—has been similarly disparaged. And we must also notice the irony or the discordance of the letter itself: in writing, she narrates her own story, but the story she has to tell is of her own lack of agency.[15] That is, what she narrates is her reduction to image, to "photo girl": "Mr Coghlan took one of me and Mrs. Will send when developed" (4.401–2). Bearing a stamp, her letter reaches its desired destination, but the stamp itself reminds us of her grandfather, Major Tweedy, who collected stamps of value but whose collection left nothing to his own daughter: "I rose from the ranks, sir, and I'm proud of it. Still he had brains enough to make that corner in stamps. Now that was farseeing" (4.63–65). Bloom gives Milly as well his stamp of approval. In reading her words, he reflects on the coincidence of her being fifteen on the fifteenth of the month, and then articulates what is to become a persistent subtext of *Ulysses:* the separation of generations of women and their eclipse by male heirs. Even in death, Rudy is able to dislodge the memory of the living daughter from his father's mind: "Her first birthday away from home. Separation. Remember the summer morning she was born, running to knock up Mrs Thornton in Denzille street. Jolly old woman. Lots of babies she must have helped into the world. She knew from the first poor little Rudy wouldn't live. . . . He would be eleven now if he had lived" (4.415–20).

If we use the reflections of Adrienne Rich as our guide, what is absent in Joyce's rendering of the interior of family life in Eccles Street is as significant as what he does record; and, in fact, we might imagine books like *Ulysses* to have led to her comments about the limited repertoire of stories in Western culture:

> This cathexis between mother and daughter—essential, distorted, misused—is the great unwritten story. Probably there is nothing in human nature more resonant with charges than the flow of energy between two biologically alike bodies, one of which has lain in amniotic bliss inside the other, one of which has labored to give birth to the other. The materials are there for the deepest mutuality and the most painful estrangement. . . . Yet this relationship has been minimized and trivialized in the annals of patriarchy.[16]

In Joyce's hands, the daughter is "silly Milly" (4.284) and a "pert little piece" (4.295). Her father at least imagines visiting her in August at the banker's holiday; but her mother's eyes rove over her postcard on the way to the letter that is of more pressing concern to her, the note from Blazes Boylan confirming their assignation.

We can see, even from this brief incident, that Molly's primary role in this text is in a heterosexual drama involving the men of her own generation. Like Jocasta of the Sophoclean drama, she is encoded primarily as a lover rather than a mother; and like Antigone, Milly experiences herself as without maternal protection and as someone who must live beyond the walls of the city. Mullingar might as well be Thebes.

If Molly's legacy to her daughter is problematic, it is also understandable, for she herself was unmothered. Bloom may have intervened in sending his daughter away to Mullingar, breaking the mother/daughter dyad and interrupting any further story between Molly and Milly, but death itself intervened in the plot between Molly and her Gibraltar mother. "[W]here would they all of them be if they hadnt all a mother to look after them what I never had" (18.1441–42) is Molly's self-reflection. When she thinks about Stephen Dedalus, she associates his ungoverned behavior with the loss of his mother (18.1441–42), but having made this connection, she remains blind to the effects her own mother's death might have had on her own choices in life and on the life of her child. Milly is a "wild piece of goods" (4.429–30).[17] Is wildness the legacy of all unmothered children? Molly knows only that she has inherited her "mothers eyes and figure" (18.890–91), knowledge that she could only have gleaned from a photograph, a circumstance that expands Walter Benjamin's reflection on the cultural effects of the circulation of photographs, showing us that images, whatever their original context, not only disrupt the symbolic order but bring us to the margins of that order to confront us with death.[18] "[M]y mother," Molly says, "whoever she was" (18.846–47). Originally cast as Jocasta, she too resembles Antigone, whose life is emplotted around that irremediable absence. Lunita Laredo's single legacy to her child, her isolated entry into the symbolic, was naming it; and even here, we find estrangement and breach of affection, for Molly dislikes the only cultural inscription her mother was able to make: "my mother . . . might have given me a nicer name the Lord knows after the lovely one she had Lunita Laredo" (18.846–48).

Death may have torn Lunita and her daughter apart, but we can judge Milly's similar perception of the emotional unavailability of her mother by the "slip" in her letter to Bloom, when she catches herself associating Molly with the lover the daughter presumably should not know about: "Give my love to mummy and to yourself a big kiss and thanks. . . . There is a young student comes here some evenings named Bannon his cousins or something are big swells and he sings Boylan's (I was on the pop of writing Blazes Boylan's) song about those seaside girls" (4.404–9). Without claiming that either of these women has the self-reflection to understand the effect of this lack of cathexis, we can observe that they recognize the reiterative nature of their experiences as women: "her tongue is a bit too long for my taste," Molly admits, "your blouse is open too low she says to me the pan calling the kettle black . . . they all look at her like me when I was her age" (18.1033–36).

Without being overly general, I would like to suggest that the troubled relation of these three generations can serve as a paradigm for the relation of women, each to the other, in the text of *Ulysses* at large. Rarely do we find women of any generation bonding in this book; rarely do we find continuity between generations of women or between women of the same generation. Dilly, Maggy, Katey, and Boody Dedalus are as motherless as Milly; Gerty MacDowell's outing with Edy Boardman and Cissy Caffrey is interrupted by a fantasy about a man who is a stranger to her; we do not even have to look beyond the first page of Molly's soliloquy to discover the friction between herself and other women: "that old faggot Mrs Riordan . . . no man would look at her twice I hope Ill never be like her" (18.04–12). With hindsight we can see that the disparagement of other women is a defense against having a plotless life: since women experience themselves only as markers in male cultural narratives, they measure themselves according to their success in being chosen, allaying their anxiety by naming their own superior attractiveness ("I knew more about men and life when I was 15 than theyll all know at 50" [18.886–87]). For the Molly

Blooms of Joyce's Dublin, isolation, argument, and competition are experiences that appear to be normative.

What can grow on this site of loss?

It is here that I would like to return to de Certeau's theoretical frame and to assert that even in an ocean of cultural assumptions, assumptions that have infiltrated the homes that were designed expressly to keep them "at bay," emancipatory practices are still possible. Speaking of an entirely different cultural situation, but one that is applicable to the Bloom family, de Certeau notices "the countless ways [ordinary people have] of refusing to accord the established order the status of a law"; "without leaving the place where [s]he has no choice but to live and which lays down its law for [her], [s]he establishes within it a degree of plurality and creativity . . . metaphorizing . . . the dominant order . . . mak[ing] it function in another register." He asks us to consider how, in everyday practice, it is possible to "subvert from within—not by rejecting . . . or by transforming . . . but by many different ways of using[—] . . . customs or convictions [which are] foreign to the colonization they could not escape." He adds that "there are clever tricks of the 'weak' within the order established by the 'strong,' an art of putting one over on the adversary on his own turf."[19]

I think de Certeau's method of analysis of everyday practice lets us see that in "Calypso" there is an additional, entirely different libidinal economy at work, one that, at the least, is manifest to us in the circulation of illicit letters,[20] in the hiding of intentions, in walking, in daydreaming, and in one of the other major undercurrents of the episode—the anticipation of transgressive sex.[21] Milly uses her body much as her mother does, as a vehicle to express her revolt against structures, putting the physical at the service of political intentions.[22] Her mother is annoyed, claiming that Bloom sent the girl away at just the right time: "its as well he sent her where she is she was just getting out of bounds" (18.1027). Molly remembers one transgression after another: "I had to tell her not to cock her legs up like that on show on the windowsill before all the people passing" (18.1034–36). She broke a small "statue with her roughness and carelessness before she left" (18.1014–15); she was sly; she flirted (18.1023); she smoked cigarettes in secret (18.1028); she helped herself to her mother's face powder (18.1064); she received secret letters from "Conny Connolly writing to her in white ink on black paper sealed with sealing wax" (18.1052–53). An obstreperous child. A "saucebox" (4.423).

But I would like to suggest that Milly's delinquency may well be her most hopeful aspect. Born into a culture that will systematically slight her, into a home where the highest ambition for her is expressed as a choice between Skerry's Academy (where she would learn typing) or the Mullingar photo shop, and into a family where the mother's main concern at the time of her departure is the need to always lock the door against her ("I couldnt turn round with her in the place lately unless I bolted the door first gave me the fidgets" [18.1009–10]), Milly will need every kind of subversive tactic she can envision. In a world where even the memory of one's birth is eclipsed by regret over a dead brother, the nymphs of engendered roles have indeed cast a strong spell. She is a young girl with a long journey ahead of her, a child with affinities to Homer's protagonist on Ogygia at the beginning of *The Odyssey.* We might revise that great master of the oceans of Western culture whom Milly may have to confront in her struggle to find a home for herself: "[her] I saw on an island, shedding plenteous tears in the halls . . . [who is held] there perforce so that [s]he may not come to [her] own country, for [s]he has no ships with oars and no companions to send [her] on [her] way."[23]

5

Skinscapes in "Lotus-Eaters"

MAUD ELLMANN

We might say indeed that modern man has an epidermis rather than a soul.

James Joyce, "The Universal Literary Influence of the Renaissance"[1]

I

Of all the adventures of Odysseus, the story of the lotus-eaters is perhaps the most retold, relived, redreamed—the most susceptible to mythic reimaginings. The fantasy of a society lulled into tranquillity, oblivious to enterprise and strife, resurfaces in culture, high and low: ranging from William Blake's false heaven, Beulah, where benumbed innocence masquerades as beatitude, to the sci-fi series *Star Trek,* where the officers of the Enterprise beam down to a laid-back planet, not dissimilar to California, and even the robotic Mr. Spock, under the influence of a narcotic flower, falls idiotically in love. Although the details of Homer's story are often forgotten, the moral quandary continues to assert itself, for lotus-eating is the archetypal cop-out. Time and again, our cultural heroes have to teach us to avoid the lotus flower's easy satisfactions in favor of the dubious rewards of struggle. Yet why should we resist the artificial paradise induced by drugs, when we know no other paradises more reliable?

Considering the richness of its echoes and associations, Homer's version of the episode is curiously perfunctory: it is as if the poet, like the hero, could not get his men out of the lotus-eaters' clutches fast enough. Within a few lines, Odysseus has seen enough of the effects of lotus-eating on his crew to drag them weeping back into the ships, "for fear / someone else might taste of the lotus and forget the way home."[2] Odysseus fears the lotus because it makes his men forget their home and everything that home entails about their obligations to their origins. "Home is where one starts from," in Eliot's deceptively transparent phrase: home stands for all the bonds to place, to persons, to the past, that determine our identity within society. By forgetting home, the lotus-eater is liable to forget *himself:* forget his origins, his name, his race, his gender. Most perilous of all, he may forget the rules of narrative, forget to bring the story to its end. . . .

In Joyce's "Lotus-Eaters," Bloom forgets his latchkey, which is one way of forgetting home. Another way is by discarding his previous identity—his name and address—for he adopts the pseudonym of Henry Flower to undertake a postal odyssey to his erotic pen pal, Martha Clifford:

> Henry Flower Esq,
> c/o P.O. Westland Row,
> City. (5.62–64)

This is one of many transformations of Bloom's name, which undertakes an independent journey through the pages of *Ulysses* in the guise of synonyms, misspellings, puns, and anagrams. In this episode, the name Flower, a synonym for Bloom, aligns the hero with the lotus flower and suggests that Henry Flower is himself the foreign substance, the forgetful drug, that circulates around the postal and commercial arteries of Dublin. Flowers, together with the drugs procured from them, are known to be the dominant motifs of "Lotus-Eaters." Both, for instance, are encoded in the opening sentences, when Bloom catches sight of "a boy for the skins" (a rubbish scavenger) smoking a chewed fagbutt—a disenchanted version of the lotus flower. "Tell him if he smokes he won't grow," thinks Bloom, but then decides against the interference: "O let him! His life isn't such a bed of roses" (5.05–8). From this point onward flowers multiply: Martha Clifford sends a "yellow flower with flattened petals" (5.239) to the man she knows as Henry Flower, perhaps in honor of the "boom in yellow" typical of Decadence (Buck Mulligan also sports a yellow dressing gown).[3] Her "language of flowers" is one of many secret codes that Bloom attributes to the female sex: "Language of flowers. They like it because no-one can hear" (5.261–62). Later, when he drops into the church, Bloom imbibes the heady scents of flowers and incense, which, together with the "stupefying" influence of Latin, make religion the lotus of the people: "Good idea the Latin. Stupefies them first. . . . Lulls all pain. . . . Flowers, incense, candles melting" (5.350–51, 5.367–78, 5.431–32). Later still, when Bloom visits the chemist's shop, the drugs in the alabaster pots remind him of his father, Virag, who killed himself with an overdose of aconite, a drug derived from the flower of the same name (17.624). Virag means flower in Hungarian, and thus the flowers that bedeck the text could be interpreted as traces of the father, who, like the ghost of Hamlet's father, demands to be remembered by his son.

The chapter ends with Bloom imagining the "languid floating flower" of his penis in the bath—"limp father of thousands" (5.571–72). It would be hasty, however, to conclude that the flower is as simple as a phallic symbol. Although Joyce named the "Genitals" the organ of the episode in the Gilbert schema, he did not specify that these were masculine or feminine, and the image of the flower functions as a switchpoint between the sexes.[4] For one thing, "flowers" is a term for menstruation, much relished by the Earl of Rochester; and Bloom himself attributes Martha's headache to her "roses" in the "Lotus-Eaters" episode: "Such a bad headache. Has her roses probably" (5.285). In courtship, it is customary for the man to offer flowers to the woman (a convention reversed by Martha Clifford); yet it is the woman whom we speak of as "deflowered," as if she sacrificed her flowers in return for his. In dreams analyzed by Freud, flowers often stand for "an exchange of sexual gifts"; in one example, carnations symbolize the "carnal" transaction of the marriage bed, in which the dreamer receives the flower of her husband's penis in compensation for her defloration.[5]

Thus flowers, rather than differentiating genders, circulate between them in a phantasmic borderland where either may transform itself into the other. Under the influence of flowers, "Lotus-Eaters" is an episode of gender-benders. Bloom experiments with drag, impersonating the young woman he encounters in "Calypso" in the butcher's shop:

> How did she walk with her sausages? Like that something. As he walked he took the folded *Freeman* from his sidepocket, unfolded it, rolled it lengthwise in a baton and tapped it at each sauntering step against his trouserleg. Careless air: just drop in to see. (5.47–51)

In this comic gender reversal, Bloom makes a baton of his newspaper to emulate the woman's "sausages," as if he had to pretend to be a woman in order to reclaim the phallus. Yet his baton scarcely protects him from the threats of phallic females and castrated males that pursue him through the episode: "eunuchs" and "castration," in addition to the "genitals," are named by Joyce as correspondences for "Lotus-Eaters."[6] Bloom encounters gelded horses, "a stump of guttapercha wagging limp between their haunches" (5.218); and he ruminates about castrati in church choirs: "Suppose they wouldn't feel anything after. Kind of a placid. No worry. Fall into flesh, don't they? Gluttons, tall, long legs. Who knows? Eunuch. One way out of it" (5.410–12). If men in "Lotus-Eaters" are castrated, however, it is women who assume the phallic role: the young woman with her swinging sausages is one example; Martha Clifford, with her promises of punishment, another: "Remember . . . I will punish you. . . . you naughty boy, if you do not wrote" (5.251–53). Similarly, the actress Mrs. Bandman Palmer, who played Hamlet in Dublin on the evening of June 15, 1904, is described by Bloom as a "Male impersonator." Her transvestism provokes him to wonder whether Hamlet was himself a woman and if this was why Ophelia committed suicide (5.195–97); such speculations are the Bloomian alternative to Stephen's equally improbable interpretation of the tragedy.[7]

Amidst these threats of emasculation, bombarding Bloom from every side, the sheer proliferation of the flower image could be seen as a defense against castration. Freud argues that "the language of dreams is fond of representing castration by a doubling or multiplication of a genital symbol," one of the most common of these symbols being the flower.[8] In "Lotus-Eaters," however, there is something pestilential in the way that flowers spread and multiply themselves, and this rhetorical contagion is mirrored by images of vermin and disease which also pullulate throughout the episode—for flowers are bestrewn across the surface of the text in the same way that spots and blotches are bestrewn across the pallid countenances of its characters. Most of the infections of the episode manifest themselves upon the skin, which was the organ Joyce assigned to "Lotus-Eaters" in the Linati schema. Most of the references to skin seem to have been afterthoughts added to the page proofs of the text in 1921. Yet it is appropriate that skin should represent at once the hidden kernel and the palimpsestic overlayer of the episode: for skin itself is both exposed and hidden, both superficial and profound; it is associated with both the deceptive surface and the shivering, defenseless nakedness of truth.[9]

"Lotus-Eaters" opens with a reference to skin disease, the "scars of eczema" disfiguring an urchin's face (5.06); later pages refer to smallpox, dandruff, freckles, warts, bunions, pimples, barber's itch, and worst of all, to the unfortunate Lord Ardilaun, who reputedly was forced to change his shirt four times a day because his skin bred lice and vermin. Bloom's mission in "Lotus-Eaters" (which he fails to accomplish) is to combat skin disease by purchasing "Skinfood" (5.497) for Molly at the chemist's: sweet almond oil, tincture of benzoin, orange-flower water, and white wax, which make "her skin so delicate white like wax" (5.490–93). Longing for the softness of her Spanish skin, her *"Peau d'Espagne"* (5.500), Bloom concludes the chapter imagining his own wet flesh stretched out before him in the bath, "oiled by scented soap, softly laved" (5.568); and he regrets he has no time for a massage to stimulate the surface of his skin (5.505).

At the chemist's, Bloom's thoughts turn to Prince Leopold, one of the sons of Queen Victoria, who suffered from hemophilia, an affliction attributed by popular belief to his having "only one skin": "Three we have," Bloom reassures himself (5.498–99). Throughout the chapter, Bloom ruminates about the depth, both metaphorical and literal, of skin. When he visits the church, he imagines women revealing their "lovely shame" to their confessors, and reflects that their repentance is only "skindeep" (5.430–31). How deep is skin? Paul Valéry once wrote, *"Ce qu'il y a de plus profound dans l'homme, c'est la peau."*[10] To understand the prevalence of skin disease in "Lotus-Eaters," we must begin by exploring the profundities of skin.

II

What is skin? This organ, which covers the entire surface of the body, constituting 17.8 percent of its weight and giving rise to all its sense organs, is often overlooked, as if its sheer ubiquity had rendered it invisible. Yet of all the sense organs, skin is the most vital: we can live without sight, hearing, taste, or smell, but we die if the greater portion of our skin is not intact. And skin is more than just a sense organ: it breathes, perspires, absorbs, expels, and also stimulates respiration, circulation, and digestion.[11] Sex is basically the meeting of two skins—or more. Our metaphors reveal the centrality of skin to our ideas of self and other: we speak of being "in touch" or "in contact" with our friends, of "rubbing" people the wrong way, or of "handling" them with kid gloves. If we are "thick skinned" insults bounce off us; if we are "touchy," they get "under our skin." The truths we hold to be self-evident are "palpable" or "tangible," whether we are "tactful" or "tactless" in expressing them. We "jump out of our skin"; we escape "by the skin of our teeth"; and we "save our skin" when we let others take the rap.

Social groups are differentiated by the texture, age, and pigmentation of their skin, some of the most terrible injustices of history being based on skin color. Individuals, by contrast, tend to be identified by peculiarities of skin, such as moles or scars or the intricate cartography of fingerprints. We recognize those closest to us by the odor of their skin, which can be enhanced by perfume, another flower product prevalent in "Lotus-Eaters." And perfume, in "Nausicaa," is envisaged as a second skin woven over women's bodies: "It's like a fine fine veil or web they have all over the skin, fine like what do you call it gossamer, and they're always spinning it out of them, fine as anything, like rainbow colours without knowing it. Clings to everything she takes off" (13.1019–22).

In spite of the importance of skin, however, Western culture is so preoccupied with depths that it is difficult to credit surfaces: we overlook the outside for the inside, the container for that which is contained. Value is attributed only to profundity: to be described as "superficial" is an insult; as "deep," a tribute. That beauty is skin deep is a truth that painters celebrate, but poets fear, valuing the skin only as the soul shines through it. Since the Renaissance, Western painting has been fascinated by the color, texture, and ductility of women's skin; but poets tend to notice skin only when it blushes, darkens, or grows pale, and thus reveals the inner workings of the soul.

Valéry mocks this prejudice, proposing instead that the inner depths are merely fabrications of the surface. *"Et puis, moelle, cerveau, tout ce qu'il faut pour sentir, pâtir, penser . . . ce sont des inventions de la* ***peau****. . . .* Nous avons beau creuser, docteur, nous sommes . . . ectoderme."[12] There is some biological evidence for Valéry's assertion that the inside is the invention of the outside, the cortex of the brain, for instance, being formed by the introversion and reticulation of the surface of the embryo. Didier Anzieu, in a psychoanalytic study of the "skin ego," observes that the internal organs develop, in utero, through a folding-up process technically known as "invagination," which creates the endlessly complicated array of folds, creases, envelopes, tubes, caps, fans, and pockets of which the body is composed.[13] In other words, the inside of our bodies is composed of skin turned outside in: the core is created by the husk, the kernel by the shell.

Anzieu's central insight is that skin is a double-sided entity: one side faces inward, enveloping the contents of the body and registering its sensations, needs, and drives; the other faces outward, shielding the interior but also filtering exchange between the body and the world. This traffic, mediated by the skin, forms the basis of the ego, which is itself a kind of envelope designed to mediate between the psyche and the stimuli impinging on it from without and from within. The same kind of traffic occurs in Bloom's interior monologue, which registers impressions from the outside world while embedding each new message into the connective tissue of his memory. Indeed it is worth considering whether thinking—especially in the case of Bloom—is merely a refinement of the operations of the skin.

Anzieu's conception of the ego was anticipated by Freud, who argued in 1923 that the "ego is first and foremost a bodily ego; it is not merely a surface entity, but is itself the projection of a surface."[14] In other words, the ego develops out of the surface of the body as the phantasmic counterpart of the skin, containing mental life in the same way that the skin contains the entrails. Being formed by the sensations of the skin, the ego represents a kind of monument to early cutaneous experience: its well-being depends upon the way in which the infant's skin is held, thus defining the boundaries of the body. Ashley Montagu, in a study of touching, shows how newborn bears are literally "licked into shape" by their mother's tongues, which outline every curve and crevice of their bodies, nudging their internal organs into action. In human beings, he argues, this licking is replaced by the prolonged contractions of a human labor (a questionable advance of evolution), which provide the newborn baby with an all-over body massage, stimulating respiratory and digestive functions.[15] In any case, the body simply does not work unless the skin is touched: we must be licked or squeezed or tickled into life. In the same way, the self is called into existence by the touch of others: a dramatic instance is Helen Keller, whose mind was literally created by the stimulation of her skin.[16]

Skin and ego, however, do not always coincide. Anorectics who see themselves as fat, or amputees who suffer pain in phantom limbs, reveal that the mental image of the body often differs drastically from its physical reality. Even in the case of "normal" people, it is unlikely that body image ever corresponds to the exact dimensions of the skin. This is because the body's envelope is molded by the touch of others: a containing sac and a protective shield, the skin is also a receptive surface on which the marks of others are inscribed. "Their smiles catch into my skin, little smiling hooks," writes Sylvia Plath, in a macabre image of this process of inscription.[17] Similarly, Samuel Beckett's strange work *How It Is* (1961/1964) presents a world of nameless beings crawling in primeval slime, each of which is compelled to torture another into speech by carving questions on its skin. The implication is that speech and consciousness begin with the inscription of the other on the skin, a mutilation that establishes the social order. A more familiar example may be found in Kafka's story of the penal colony, in which the sentences of the condemned are stabbed into their skin by the needles of a monstrous typewriter. These parables imply that the individual is assumed into the social order by means of a lacerating script tattooed upon the skin, symbolizing the dependence of the subject on the other.

Anzieu postulates that the infant originally shares its mother's skin, imagined as a single indivisible integument. The emergence of the ego, however, necessitates the rupture of this membrane. There are many ways in which this separation may be thwarted: sometimes the skin becomes too tight and suffocates the ego, an experience reflected in mythology by poisoned garments. The shirt of Nessus, given by Daianera as an aphrodisiac to Heracles, consumes the hero's flesh, driving him to flay himself alive; a poisoned veil destroys Medea's rival, Glauca. Yet if the skin may prove too tight, it may also prove too porous, allowing the contents of the self to leak away. In a case discussed by Anzieu, a little girl suffers from amnesia because she imagines her head as full of holes; in another case, an anorectic patient dreams her skin has turned into a sieve through which her entrails seep into the outer darkness.[18] In Sylvia Plath's poetry, the speaker veers between the terrors of constriction and porosity, feeling at times suffocated by her skin, at other times excoriated by it. "Skin doesn't have any roots," she writes, "it peels away as easy as paper."[19]

While psychoanalytic studies of the skin tend to focus on its meanings for the individual, anthropological studies emphasize its social implications. For the outer surface of the body functions as a boundary between the individual and the surrounding world, symbolizing their cooperation as well as their antagonism. The reason that shame manifests itself upon the skin, whether in the form of blushes (in Western culture) or hot sweats (in Papua New Guinea), is that shame is social: it is experienced when other people see us, find us out, and is opposed to guilt, which gnaws at us invisibly.[20] Thus the crime of Cain is branded on his forehead; the improprieties of women crimsoned on their cheeks. In the myth of Genesis, shame originates in the recognition of the nakedness of skin and its exposure to the gaze of others; and shame produces the compulsion to clothe or decorate the body, which is fundamental to the social order. "Society," wrote Thomas Carlyle, "is founded upon Cloth"; man is "bound by invisible bonds to All Men," and his clothes are "the visible emblems of that fact."[21] Recent anthropological research supports Carlyle's insight: Terence Turner, in an essay on "The Social Skin," argues that "the imposition of a standardised symbolic form upon the body, as a symbol or 'objective correlative' of the social self, invariably becomes a serious business for all societies."[22] Shame, however, harks back to a more primitive relation to the other: for shame takes refuge in the unclothed face, in the blushes that reveal a nakedness beyond the nakedness of skin, the nakedness of capillaries, muscles, viscera. The philosopher Emmanuel Levinas has argued that the "skin of the face is that which stays most naked, most destitute; there is an essential poverty in the face; the proof of this is that one tries to mask this poverty by putting on poses, by taking on a countenance." According to Levinas, the primal relation to the other is neither one of mastery nor even one of recognition, but rather one of shame, exposure, and passivity. The skin, naked and exposed to wounds and outrage, but also to caresses and eroticism, embodies this essential passivity or "passion" of being.[23]

If skin gives us away, however, it also conceals us, for skin, like clothing, is traditionally regarded as an inessential husk disguising the authentic core of subjectivity. Hence our inveterate distrust of makeup, which adds a further surface to the surface, a second skin more specious than the first. The beautification of the body, undertaken to enhance the self, paradoxically erases individuality: the person, as we say, becomes a "sex object," deprived of personhood. Thus cosmetics, which adorn the surface of the body, are condemned for belying its interior.[24] Yet other cultures overturn this prejudice: the highlanders of Papua New Guinea, for example, conceive of body decoration as revealing, rather than concealing, the true self. To decorate the body is to bring the inside outside, to expose the hidden riches of the self to public view. In certain parts of Polynesia, the entire surface of the body is covered in tattoos, symbolizing the inscription of the individual in the community. Here the self is seen as indissociable from the skin: there is no conception of a hidden or intrinsic self to be defrauded by its ornamental surface. Alfred Gell explains: "This reasoning runs: the skin is on the outside of the body; the outside of the body is that part which is public and which comes into contact with other people; people are the sum total of their relations with other people; the person is his/her skin."[25]

III

Why is skin disease so rife in "Lotus-Eaters"? The simplest reason is historical: in 1904, Dublin was riddled with diseases, many of whose symptoms presented themselves on the skin. Stories in the *Lancet* at the turn of the century speak of the "barbaric uncleanliness" of the city, citing among other horrors an ill-regulated private slaughterhouse on Townsend Street, where hundreds of children at a local school were forced to breathe "the effluvia wafted to them from the hideous quagmire of blood and offal."[26] It was not until 1906 that the main drainage system began to deposit sewage out beyond the harbor; and Oliver St. John Gogarty, when he escaped execution during the Civil War by swimming across the Liffey, described the escapade (mindful of the sewage bobbing around his head) as "going through the motions."[27] Amid such filth, a "cloacal obsession" (such as H. G. Wells detected in Joyce) might well be cultivated as an antidote to nausea.[28]

In 1899 the death rate in Dublin was higher than in any big city in Europe or America (33.6 per thousand living), the figures swollen by a fierce onslaught of measles that caused nearly 650 deaths in the city alone. The 1904 smallpox scare in Belfast, mentioned by Bloom ("I hope that smallpox up there doesn't get worse" [5.188–89]), was preceded by an outbreak in Dublin in 1903, in which 34 out of more than 250 cases resulted in death. Tuberculosis, known in this period as the "Irish disease," peaked in 1902, attacking not only lungs, intestines, spine, and bones, but also skin, in which it took the form of lupus. Peculiar eruptions on the skin were also caused by typhus, which was rife among the overcrowded poor in Dublin. Syphilis, too, was epidemic, especially among the British army stationed in Dublin, which Arthur Griffith reviled as the most immoral army in Europe, and Bloom describes in "Lotus-Eaters" as "an army rotten with venereal disease" (5.72).[29] Syphilis had the effect of darkening the skin: in "Circe," Bloom is accused of being "bronzed with infamy" (15.1757), a euphemism for a syphilitic rash; elsewhere, *"a dark mercurialised face"* (15.748) reveals the cutaneous effects of mercury, the kill-or-cure remedy for syphilis.

Before the widespread use of X ray, ultrasound, SPECT, and other imaging techniques, many diseases could be identified only once they had erupted on the skin. Joyce's inventory of skin diseases in "Lotus-Eaters" might be compared to the cabinet of cutaneous horrors in the Hospital Saint-Louis in Paris, which contains lifelike simulacra of every form of skin disease encountered on the European urban street before our era. These surgical casts, designed by Jules-Pierre-François Baretta (1834–1923) between 1867 and 1914, reveal the evolution and often fatal course of infantile syphilis, scarlatina, measles, mumps, leprosy, scurvy, scrofula, lupus, smallpox, ringworm, and impetigo, along with countless and nameless disfiguring spots, ulcerated scabs, fungous infections, and running sores.[30] Theorists of degeneration in the nineteenth century, such as Cesare Lombroso and B. A. Morel, regarded skin deformities as the stigmata of moral and physical decline. Even tattoos, according to Lombroso, were evidence of atavism, the traces of a "primitive" language disfiguring the bodies of the "lower orders." Perhaps Joyce shared Lombroso's prejudice: the mendacious sailor in "Eumaeus," D. B. Murphy, is tattooed with the number sixteen, signaling his homosexuality and hence (according to Lombroso) his degeneracy. In literature, Lombroso argued, degeneration manifested itself in such idiosyncrasies (dear to readers of Joyce) as "a tendency to puns and plays on words," "an excessive fondness of systems," "an exaggerated minuteness of detail," and "an extreme predilection for the rhythm and assonances of verse in prose writing."[31] If the race is to regenerate itself, Lombroso intimated, the blemished page, like the disfigured skin, must be wiped clean of the marks of its polluted heritage. Similarly, Max Nordau, author of *Degeneration* (1892/1895), argued that the "outer crust" of humanity was cracking into "cold, vitrified scoria"; while in the arts, "impressionists," "stipplers," "mosaists," "pappilloteurs," "quiverers," and "roaring" colorists were busily degrading literature and painting in crazed dermatologies of spots and blotches.[32]

Joyce's sensitivity to skin disease may be attributed in part to his short-lived training as a doctor, although he abandoned his degree in medicine in 1904 (a decision which no doubt saved many lives). Yet Bloom reads the lineaments of disease on the bodies of the crowd with the discernment of a medical student.[33] Like the speaker in Blake's "London," he roams the streets of Dublin seeing "marks of weakness, marks of woe" inscribed on the faces he encounters. Blakean, too, is his interest in blemishes, for Blake defended such "Peculiar marks" against Joshua Reynolds's neoclassical distaste for them. Where Reynolds wrote the "Peculiarities in the work of art, are like those in the human figure. . . . They are always so many blemishes," Blake retorted angrily: "Infernal Falsehood! Peculiar marks are the only merit."[34] Stephen Dedalus also champions peculiar marks: in "Scylla and Charybdis," he asserts his mole as evidence of his unique and continuous identity. Although his molecules all change, he says, his mole regenerates itself incessantly: "the mole on my right breast is where it was when I was born, though all my body has been woven of new stuff time after time" (9.378–80).[35] According to Barbara Maria Stafford, this obsession with a "quirky and thus personalized integument and with a broken or suffering veneer" belongs to a Romantic outlook. She argues that the science of dermatology, invented by Jean-Louis Alibert (1766–1837) in the early nineteenth century, resembled divisionist chiaroscuro in painting insofar as both expressed a Romantic fascination with the "externalisation of idiosyncrasy."[36]

If the interest in spots is distinctively Romantic, however, the interest in skin is commonly associated with the realist novelists. Indeed some critics have attacked the realists not only for describing skin disease but for propagating a literary form of it themselves. Barbey d'Aurevilly complained that Balzac had made description "a skin disease of the realists."[37] Similarly, the American critic William Thayer, in an 1894 article, condemned the "new Realists," such as James and Zola, for mistaking the surface for the depths. He dubbed them the "Epidermists":

> The camera sees only the outside; the Realist sees no more, and so it would be more appropriate to call him "Epidermist," one who investigates only the surface, the cuticle of life,—usually with a preference for very dirty skin. . . . They have mistaken the dead actual for reality, the show of the moment for the essence, the letter for the spirit.

Thayer went on to argue that the "heaping up of minute details," characteristic of the writings of the "Epidermists," had been smuggled illegitimately into literature from the sciences.[38] His strictures resemble Nordau's invective against the Impressionists, whose paintings were composed of excremental splotches in defiance of a classical conception of the whole. No one, of course, was fonder of heaping up details than Joyce, nor more aware of the cloacal pleasure of the exercise. For Thayer, however, such heaps were nothing but the "dirty skin," the carbuncular exterior, concealing the profundity of human life.

In different ways, both naturalism and aestheticism attempted to revalorize the surface, so long disparaged in favor of the depths, and Joyce's writing shows allegiances to both these schools. The naturalist Zola, through the minute registration of empirica, asserted the importance of external forces in determining the character of individuals. In his novels, the surface of the body, rather than expressing individuality, bears the scars of labor and the cruel impingements of the outer world. In *Germinal* (1885), Maheu's skin appears "white as that of an anaemic girl," indicating the degeneration of his racial stock; but his pallor is "tattooed with scratches and grazes made by the coal—grafts, the miners called them." Similarly, his daughter Catherine's complexion has been "ruined" by her labor in the mine, and Etienne, watching her undress, is disturbed by the contrast between "the pale whiteness" of her hidden flesh and "the ravaged skin of her hands and face." For Zola, who believed the individual to be determined by hereditary factors on the one hand, and environmental factors on the other, Catherine's skin reveals the influence of both determinisms, its pallor signifying her genetic enervation, its scars the imprint of her merciless environment.[39]

Meanwhile, aestheticists from Baudelaire to Beerbohm defended the artificiality of surfaces against the customary predilection for the depths. In his famous defense of cosmetics (1863), Baudelaire argued that "the use of rice-powder, so stupidly anathematized by our Arcadian philosophers, is successfully designed to rid the complexion of those blemishes that Nature has outrageously strewn there, and thus to create an abstract unity in the colour and texture of the skin, a unity, which, like the tights of a dancer, immediately approximates the human being to the statue, that is to something superior and divine."[40] Max Beerbohm, in his "Defence of Cosmetics" of 1894, suggested that we have become suspicious of the surface because we have reduced it to a token of the depths. "Too long has the face been degraded from its rank as a thing of beauty to a mere vulgar index of character or emotion." With the full renaissance of cosmetics, he argued, "surface will finally be severed from soul," and a woman's face will no longer be read as a "barometer" of character, but admired as an artifact, "beautiful and without meaning."[41]

IV

If skin stands for a modernist celebration of the surface, as opposed to a Romantic fascination with the depths, the trope of skin disease complicates this facile schematism: for boils, pustules, warts, and pimples represent the depths erupting on the surface—the inside on the outside of the flesh—and violating the interiority of subjectivity. This is how skin disease functions in F. Scott Fitzgerald's novel *Tender Is the Night* (1934), in which a minor character dies of eczema, her illness being blamed on her refusal to divulge her "secret." Since she does not *know* her secret, she can only *show* it in the pustular abrasions of her skin: her secret secretes, her inner self "breaks out" into a rash that devours the surface of her flesh.[42] In "Lotus-Eaters," however, skin disease expresses neither personality, as in the Romantics; nor the ravages of labor, as in Zola; nor degeneration, as in Nordau; nor hysteria, as in Fitzgerald. Bloom's sensitivity to skin disease is one symptom of a far-reaching anxiety about the security of the bodily envelope. This anxiety is largely projected onto women, whose outer coverings of clothes and skin are perceived by Bloom as dangerously detachable. In the church, for instance, Bloom discovers that his waistcoat is unbuttoned and imagines women gloating over his embarrassment: "Women enjoy it. Never tell you" (5.453). He takes revenge on these imaginary women, punishing them for their castrating gaze, by picturing their skirts unfastened, "placket unhooked," exposing "glimpses of the moon" (5.454–55). Thus Bloom, disconcerted by his own unbuttoning, projects his shame onto the "plackets" of the other sex.

This pattern of projection recurs throughout the chapter. When Bloom is "fingering" Martha Clifford's letter, with its innuendoes of castration ("Remember . . . I will punish you. . . . you naughty boy"), he draws a pin out of the pocket in which it is concealed:

> Fingering still the letter in his pocket he drew the pin out of it. Common pin, eh? He threw it on the road. Out of her clothes somewhere: pinned together. Queer the number of pins they always have. No roses without thorns. (5.275–78)

Thus Bloom responds to the threat of castration, implicit in the letter as well as in the pin, by imagining the female body as a garment loosely "pinned together" and about to split apart. By fetishistic logic, he transfers his own anxiety about dismemberment onto women's detachable parts, especially their underclothes, which are neither clothes nor skin but represent precisely the ambiguity between the two. Indeed Bloom's next association is to undergarments, the subject of a ditty sung by two prostitutes he met in Coombe:

> *O, Mairy lost the pin of her drawers.*
> *She didn't know what to do*
> *To keep it up,*
> *To keep it up.* (5.281–84)

In this ditty, which recurs at the opening of "Circe," the woman Mairy, having lost her "pin," has also been divested of her "drawers" or her second skin: only the pin can "keep it up." Bloom is puzzled by "it," since "drawers" are plural: "It? Them," he thinks (5.285). The job of a prostitute, of course, is "to keep it up"; but Bloom, somewhat naively, misses the innuendo of erection. His next gesture is to tear up Martha's envelope, which is analogous to tearing off her clothes or skin.

This chain of thought, like many others, suggests that Bloom's fears about his penis are a decoy, deflecting his (and our) attention from a vast unnamable anxiety extending over the entire surface of his flesh. In his imagination, the penis, like the pin, is that which "keeps it up," prevents the skin from falling off. Molly describes the penis as a "button" in "Penelope": "I made him blush a little when I got over him that way when I unbuttoned him and took his out and drew back the skin it had a kind of eye in it theyre all Buttons men down the middle on the wrong side of them" (18.814–17). The fantasy that men's bodies, like their feelings, are "buttoned up," whereas women are forever "unbuttoning" themselves, exposing both their secrets and their flesh, seems widespread in our culture. For Bloom, the penis is the button that keeps his skin securely fastened to his flesh; women, on the contrary, must substitute the "pin," which is forever dropping off, leaving them unhooked, unpeeled, unskinned.

In "Hades," Bloom remembers the day when Molly, wearing a cream gown "with the rip she never stitched," and aroused by the sight of two dogs copulating, begged him for a "touch": "Give us a touch, Poldy. God, I'm dying for it." It was from this touch that Rudy was conceived: "How life begins" (6.78–81). The ripped gown, "never stitched," represents the female body, torn asunder, breeding death in life and life in death: for the "rip" is the vagina, where "life begins," but also represents the grave where Rudy lies (R.I.P.). Back in the present, Bloom reflects that Molly's body is "getting a bit softy," and wonders if "the skin can't contract quickly enough when the flesh falls off" (6.204–5). Once again, the female skin is imagined as a loose and flimsy garment liable to detach itself and drop away. The only man (apart from himself) whom Bloom imagines "unpinned" is a priest:

> He saw the priest stow the communion cup away, well in, and kneel an instant before it, showing a large grey bootsole from under the lace affair he had on. Suppose he lost the pin of his. He wouldn't know what to do to. Bald spot behind. Letters on his back: I.N.R.I? No: I.H.S. Molly told me one time I asked her. I have sinned: or no: I have suffered, it is. And the other one? Iron nails ran in. (5.369–74)

According to the psychoanalyst Ernest Jones, the function of the Catholic priest is to bear the onus of castration, represented by such symbols as the shaved head, the women's robes, and the prohibition against sexual relations.[43] The priest in "Lotus-Eaters" also represents imperiled masculinity: like a woman, he is "pinned together," revealing a "bald spot behind," where his hair or his genitals should be. His large grey bootsole is absurdly masculine, peeking out from underneath his campy "lace affair." His robes are inscribed with the initials "I.H.S.," misread by Bloom as "I.N.R.I.," both of these being acronyms for Christ. But Bloom, following Molly, misinterprets them hilariously, reading "I.H.S." as "I have suffered," and "I.N.R.I." as "Iron nails ran in." It is significant that both misreadings emphasize the sadomasochistic side of Christianity. The letters themselves—which are notably described as "on his back," not on his clothes—become metonymies for wounds inflicted on the flesh of Christ. In Bloom's imagination, then, the priest's back becomes the surface for punishing inscriptions nailed into his skin, like the sentences of the condemned in Kafka's penal colony.

Thus skin is seen by Bloom as a fragile membrane, liable to be stretched, loosened, ripped, peeled, flayed, nailed, scarified, and crucified. Yet skin is also conceived of as a writing surface, as in *Finnegans Wake,* where Shem the Penman writes with his own excrement on "the only foolscap available," his own skin (*FW* 185). Reading the skin is a central activity of "Lotus-Eaters": it occurs, for example, in the melodrama *Leah, the Forsaken* (1862), which was performed in Dublin on June 16, 1904. In this play the villain, Nathan, an apostate Jew masquerading as an anti-Semite, is recognized by the blind patriarch Abraham, who reads his skin: "With my fingers I read thy dead father's face, for with my fingers I closed his eyes, and nailed down his coffin! Thou art a Jew!"[44] This extraordinary scene, in which Abraham reads the father in the features of the son, alludes to the famous story of misrecognition in the Old Testament, in which the blind Isaac mistakes his "smooth" son Jacob, disguised in a goat's skin, for his "hairy" son Esau, and thereby deprives the latter of his birthright, bestowing it instead upon the younger son. In both these stories, the skin of the son is envisaged as a text in which the father's legacy is enigmatically inscribed.[45] The father, on the other hand, is associated in *Ulysses* with self-skinning: in "Circe" Virag appears as a disheveled bird of paradise, *"sloughing his skins, his multitudinous plumage moulting"* (15.2622).

Surrounded by these threats to skin, Bloom shrinks from any form of penetration of the body's surface. Molly tells us that he "knows a lot of mixedup things especially about the body and the inside" (18.179–80); but he prefers to fantasize about the inner organs than to break the skin, welcoming the X ray, invented by Wilhelm Roentgen in 1895, as a preferable diagnostic method. Although Bloom's hand possesses the "operative surgical quality," he is "reluctant to shed human blood even when the end justified the means, preferring, in their natural order, heliotherapy, psychophysicotherapeutics, osteopathic surgery" (17.293–95). With Roentgen rays, he speculates, one could watch food metamorphose as it journeyed through the alimentary canal. Similarly, if a fellow were to swallow a pin, one could trace its odyssey through all the body's secret passageways. Sometimes such objects "come out of the ribs years after, tour round the body changing biliary duct spleen squirting liver gastric juice coils of intestines like pipes. But the poor buffer would have to stand all the time with his insides entrails on show. Science" (8.1047–50). Here Bloom might have been thinking of a case reported in the *Lancet* of February 20, 1904, in which a child was subjected to Roentgen rays for the purpose of searching for a needle supposed to have entered his body through the knee. The machine having been held too close, the boy was burnt, and his parents were suing for damages.[46]

It is his reluctance to break skin that inhibits Bloom from sexual intercourse, for the act of penetration represents to him a rupture of the bodily envelope. Andrea Dworkin might applaud his squeamishness, but in the context of *Ulysses,* the fear of penetration represents a torturing anxiety about the continence of skin. It is also to avoid penetration that Bloom chooses writing over voice, for writing is associated with surface, and voice with immersion in the depths. In the "Sirens" episode, when Simon Dedalus and his mates are competing for machismo in a singing contest, Bloom writes a secret letter to Martha Clifford: a lady he never intends to meet, let alone to penetrate. In this chapter, the voice is figured as a penis invading the virgin sanctuary of the ear: "Sure, you'd burst the tympanum of her ear, man . . . with an organ like yours" (11.536–37). By contrast, Bloom sees woman not as an ear to be penetrated, but rather as a surface to be written on. Ogling the barmaid he thinks, "Blank face. Virgin should say: or fingered only. Write something on it: page" (11.1086–87). His fantasy materializes when the gilded letters of the bar mirror are superimposed on the reflection of her face: "her skin askance in the barmirror gildlettered where hock and claret glasses shimmered" (11.118–19). These images hark back to "Proteus," where Stephen envisages Eve's "belly without blemish" (without a navel) as a "buckler of taut vellum"—an unwritten page (3.42). Similarly, Bloom conceives of women's skin as a surface to be written on, but not to be broken: having foresworn intercourse ever since the death of Rudy, his fantasy of writing on the body has replaced the act of penetration.

V

Bloom's task in "Lotus-Eaters" is to save his skin, threatened by wounding from without, by leakage from within, as well as by the skin diseases that befuddle this distinction. Images of skin disease, so copious in "Lotus-Eaters," may be understood in part as a symptom of contemporary fears about degeneration; but they also bring to light the existential insecurity of skin, its susceptibility to wounding, penetration, desquamation. The psychoanalyst Dinora Pines attributes skin disease to a failure of the skin's containing function. Infants, she argues, develop eczema to inveigle inattentive mothers into touching them, this cutaneous contact being necessary for the integration of the self. Without this contact, the infant fails to learn where its skin begins and ends, which produces a terror of the loss of self and an intense desire to be merged in the maternal envelope.[47] Bloom is overcome by this desire at the end of the "Lotus-Eaters" episode, when he dreams about his bath, that "womb of warmth" in which he will submerge his skin to make it whole again, after its exposure to the broken skins of Dublin: "This is my body" (5.566).

Bloom ends the chapter proleptically admiring his penis in the bath: "limp father of thousands" (5.571). Yet other flowers float in these imaginary waters which compete with the penis for priority. In particular, Bloom contemplates "his navel, bud of flesh" (5.570), which is the mark of his maternal, rather than paternal origin. Even Bloom's penis is sexually ambiguous, since the phrase "limp father of thousands" alludes to "mother of thousands": the common name of *Saxifraga stolonifera,* a flower that spreads by runners, like the branches of an endless navelcord.[48] In *Ulysses,* the navel, or *omphalos* in Greek, is associated with the home that lotus-eaters are so prone to forget: both Bloom and Stephen dwell in *omphalos* symbols; and Stephen in "Proteus" imagines the umbilical cord as a vast telephonic switchboard connecting all humanity to our first home in "Edenville" (3.37–40). The word *omphalos* further complicates the question of gender, for it derives from Omphale, the name of the queen who held Heracles captive, forcing him to dress in women's clothes. According to Robert Graves, the *omphalos* was traditionally seen as "the seat of female desire," and Heracles as slave to a domineering woman. In earlier interpretations of the myth, however, his cross-dressing was understood as a ritual practice in which Heracles, as Omphale's deputy, assumed her garments in order to assume her powers.[49] As we have seen, this topos of transvestism resurfaces throughout the "Lotus-Eaters" episode.

Bloom's navel gazing also testifies to his cutaneous anxieties, because the navel marks the point of rupture with the original maternal skin in which he longs to be reenveloped. At the same time, the navel is the "belly button" which, like the button of the penis, holds the epidermis in one piece. Joyce's most terrifying epiphany concerns the death of his brother Georgie, whose navel splits apart, unleashing the contents of his body.

> MRS JOYCE—(*crimson, trembling, appears at the parlour door*) . . . Jim!
> JOYCE—(*at the piano*) . . . Yes?
> MRS JOYCE—Do you know anything about the body? . . . What ought I to do? . . . There's some matter coming away from the hole in Georgie's stomach. . . . Did you ever hear of that happening?
> JOYCE—(*surprised*) . . . I don't know. . . .
> MRS JOYCE—Ought I send for the doctor, do you think?
> JOYCE—I don't know. . . . . . What hole?
> MRS JOYCE—(*impatient*). . . The hole we all have. . . . . here (*points*)
> JOYCE—(*stands up*)[50]

Both "hole" and "button," both wound and seam, the navel certifies our individuality, sealing our bodies in our private skins; but it also marks the spot at which identity dissolves into an infinite entanglement of navel cords. In theoretical terms, it is clear that the psychoanalytic theory of castration cannot account for phobias extending over the entire bodily envelope, whose focal point is not so much the penis as the navel. In Joyce, the phallus is supplanted by the *omphalos.*

6

Visible Shades and Shades of Visibility

The En-Gendering of Death in "Hades"

KIMBERLY J. DEVLIN

Odysseus's memory of his journey to the underworld in Book XI of *The Odyssey* unfolds as a parade of specters. After the visitations of Elpenor, Tiresias, and Anticleia, Odysseus is witness to a procession of visible female shades:

> "anon Proserpine sent up the ghosts of the wives and daughters of all the most famous men. . . . So they came up one after the other. . . . The first I saw was Tyro. . . . Next to her I saw Antiope. . . . Then I saw Alcmena. . . . I also saw fair Epicaste. . . . Then I saw Chloris. . . . And I saw Leda. . . . After her I saw Iphimedeia. . . . Then I saw Phaedra and Procris, and fair Ariadne. . . . I also saw Maera and Clymene and hateful Eriphyle."

Odysseus eventually tires of his own epic recall of the dead ("'But it would take me all night if I were to name every single one of the wives and daughters of the heroes whom I saw'") and ceases speaking; but he ultimately indulges Alcinous's request to hear more and produces another round of narrative that enumerates the male spirits. The two-part structure of the episode hints that the Homeric netherworld is gendered, as if the house of Hades has two portals: one marked with the sign of "Ladies" or—more accurately—with the familial and relational appellation of "wives and daughters"; the other marked with the sign of "Gentlemen" or—more accurately—with the public and autonomous appellation of "heroes." In the second segment of the chapter, Odysseus recounts his unexpected sighting of the shade of Agamemnon ("'and I too wept and pitied him as I *beheld* him'"). The betrayed hero reports a specific and painful visual deprivation, consequent of Clytemnestra's murder of him: "'my wife did not even allow me the happiness of *looking upon* my son.'" After an assurance to Achilles of his son's nobility and renown, followed by a snub from the resentful Ajax, Odysseus catches glimpses of other spectral male spectacles: "'then I saw

Minos. . . . And after him I saw huge Orion. . . . And I saw Tityus. . . . I saw also the dreadful fate of Tantalu . . . . and I saw Sisyphus. . . . And after him I saw mighty Hercules.'" The parade of apparitions in the underworld is a transient one, with one vision receding behind the next. Initially, however, when Odysseus sees his mother, Anticleia, he is tricked into mistaking this temporary sight for material palpability: "'Thrice I sprang towards her and tried to clasp her in my arms, but each time she flitted from my embrace as [if] it were a dream or phantom.'"[1] This book of *The Odyssey* generates two binaries: its narrative organization separates female and male while one of its thematics distinguishes between visual presence and substantial absence, implying that opticality is no guarantee of physical actuality.

In his delineation of the parallels between the classical underworld and "Hades," R. M. Adams suggests that the modern counterparts to the Homeric shades of the famous dead in Joyce's text are provided, most specifically, by the numerous statues Bloom sees as the funeral procession moves through Dublin.[2] We might generalize the shades to include the countless visible objects that shimmer across the narrative ken, allowing the reader to experience vicariously the phenomenon of visual ephemerality—the defining sensation of the land of the dead, as Odysseus recalls it:

> A tiny coffin flashed by. (6.322)
>
> Gloomy gardens then went by: one by one: gloomy houses. (6.467)
>
> The high railings of Prospect rippled past their gaze. Dark poplars, rare white forms. Forms more frequent, white shapes thronged amid the trees, white forms and fragments streaming by mutely, sustaining vain gestures on the air. (6.486–89)

The visible shades figured in the mortuary statues here are "mute," unlike their Homeric antecedents, which are rendered temporarily articulate by the drinking of blood; but as the gestural dimension of the "white forms and fragments" implies, the visible in and of itself—independently of any recourse to audibility—always aspires to a language of its own. This essay in its first two parts attempts to read in "Hades" a pervasive discourse of ocularity, which I believe is Joyce's elaboration of the predominant sensory axis of the Homeric episode. This discourse includes structural references to seeing and being seen; Bloom's explicitly en*vision*ing thoughts; numerous allusions to visibility and invisibility; as well as a narrative adumbration of a spectrum of "shades" in between these last two specular polarities. In the third section I turn to "Hades" in its larger context—*Ulysses* as a whole and, ultimately, several of Joyce's other fictions—with an eye toward what the author allows us to see about what I will call "engendered death."

PASSING

In his reanimation of the evanescent Homeric shades in the circumambient urban world of the visible, Joyce cannot resist a repeated double entendre:

> The blinds of the avenue passed and number nine with its craped knocker, door ajar. (6.26–27)

> From the door of the Red Bank the white disc of a straw hat flashed reply: spruce figure: passed. (6.198–99)

> Mr Power gazed at the passing houses with rueful apprehension. (6.310)

> A divided drove of branded cattle passed the windows, lowing, slouching by on padded hoofs, whisking their tails slowly on their clotted bony croups. (6.385–87)

> Crowded on the spit of land silent shapes appeared, white, sorrowful, holding out calm hands, knelt in grief, pointing. Fragments of shapes, hewn. In white silence: appealing. The best obtainable. Thos. H. Dennany, monumental builder and sculptor.
>
> Passed. (6.459–63)

> They looked. Murderer's ground. It passed darkly. (6.476)

> A team of horses passed from Finglas with toiling plodding tread, dragging through the funereal silence a creaking waggon on which lay a granite block. (6.507–8)

The emphatic repetition of the verb *passed*—with its deathly residue, later explicitly recalled by Bloom ("Who passed away. Who departed this life" [6.936])—imbues the spectacle of the city and its environs with a tinge of mortality: like Homer, Joyce reanimates his visible shades only to slay them by underscoring their impermanence. The more obvious meaning of "to pass" in these contexts—"to go by or move past," to stream by a specific visual locus—creates an optical illusion of sorts, an impression of a motile urban landscape. Although many of the "passing" visible signs are indeed advancing at varying speeds, many others are stationary. It is, of course, the funeral procession that is "passing" as it winds its way toward Paddy Dignam's grave, as other usages of the verb emphasize:

> they had turned and were passing along the tramtracks. (6.29–30)

> The carriage, passing the open drains and mounds of ripped up roadway. . . . (6.45–46)

> They passed under the hugecloaked Liberator's form. (6.249)

> the carriage passed Gray's statue. (6.258)

In the first half of "Hades," Joyce creates a doubly transient narrative, with the physical movement of the centered carriage generating the visual sensation of flowing scenery at the periphery.

It is not simply the procession that is "passing," but also its participants: the "Hades" episode reminds us in a scattering of details that the men attending the funeral—as well as their relatives and acquaintances—are not immune to the signifiers of decline that time inflicts on mortal relationships and bodies. The marriages of Martin Cunningham, Bloom, and Jack Power are either moribund or only precariously intact, while Simon Dedalus has been a widower for almost a year. Bloom recalls the middle-age "spread" visible in Molly's figure: "Body getting a bit softy. I would notice that: from remembering. What causes that? I suppose the skin can't contract quickly enough when the flesh falls off" (6.204–6). Richie Goulding suffers from chronic backache, Mr. Power's hair has turned "greyish over the ears" (6.242–43), John O'Connell's beard is turning a similar shade, and a mutual friend of Ned Lambert and Simon has gone bald. Most obviously, of course, a familiar of several of these men has quite suddenly died.

The perspective of the first half of "Hades" is consistently "centered" within the passing carriage (and often, of course, within Bloom's thoughts in particular), moving back and forth from the visually proximate to the visually marginal. Yet numerous details in both fields remind us that the carriage—the locus of sight, so to speak—is itself highly visible and that an ocular "center" is always random. "That's a fine old custom," Simon remarks toward the opening of the episode, "I am glad to see it has not died out" (6.36): he refers to the tradition of the procession taking a route through the center of the city that enables maximum visibility, so that onlookers may "pay their last respects,"[3] as many in the episode's peripheries indeed proceed to do: "All watched awhile through their windows caps and hats lifted by passers" (6.37–38); "The jarvies raised their hats" (6.173–74); the bargeman "lifted his brown straw hat, saluting Paddy Dignam" (6.451–52); "The waggoner marching at their head saluted" (6.509); "A portly man, ambushed among the grasses, raised his hat in homage" (6.708–9). Simon's brief comment and the noted gestures of respect adumbrate the fact that "Hades" is organized around a public spectacle (foreshadowing, on a small scale perhaps, the viceregal cavalcade, situated in extreme visual prominence in "Wandering Rocks"). The occupants of the carriage register their awareness of being seen through gestures or statements that betray a residual self-consciousness. Laughing in the midst of a supposed solemnity, Mr. Power "shaded his face from the window" (6.257), for instance, and his second outburst causes Mr. Cunningham to remark, "—We had better look a little serious" (6.295).

As I explained in opening, Book XI of *The Odyssey* is organized around binaries, splitting most notably spectacle and substance as well as male and female specters. The classical myth also neatly divides the seeing perspective of the living from the passing simulacra of the dead, in part through a paradoxical binary of stasis and movement: with the exception of the attempted embrace of the mother, Odysseus is emphatically inert, while the visible shades shimmer by. In his rendition of "Hades," Joyce takes measures to unsettle this stable division in the Homeric scene. On one level, the maximum visibility characteristic of spectacle attempts to produce a magnetic centering of looks, a peripatetic visual focus; but this Joycean spectacle simultaneously decenters point of view in the very reminders that the watching mourners are powerfully watched, that a visual center is necessarily an optical illusion. In other words, Joyce destabilizes Homeric categories by marking the procession of the living as a visible parade in itself and as "passing" in both senses of the word. The structure of "Hades" might be conceptualized as a concession to marginal visibility, to a "shade" in between utter spectacle and visual absence: it notes that the visual peripheries contain "other" points of view, and points of view, moreover, that impinge upon the necessarily arbitrary visual "focus." Marginal visibility will emerge as a crucial hue in Joyce's representational spectrum: for what is remotely seen and acknowledged can account for more discernible sights.

VISUAL REPRESENTATION, MISREPRESENTATION, AND NONREPRESENTATION

As Paddy Dignam passes out of the visual field—"the coffin dived out of sight" (6.833)—Bloom recalls two textual artifacts, a picture and an opera, which reveal some of the valences he attaches to both spectacle and vision: "Devil in that picture of sinner's death showing him a woman. Dying to embrace her in his shirt. Last act of *Lucia. Shall I nevermore behold thee?*" (6.851–53). Spectacle here is a potential source of temptation: according to Bloom, it is the organ of sight that constitutes the sinner, that betrays human errancy.[4] In his faulty recall of the operatic song, Bloom revealingly locates the agony of death in visual deprivation, in the loss of the ability to see a beloved being—Joyce may be alluding to Agamemnon's lament about the son of whom he feels visually bereft. In the actual line of the aria from *Lucia di Lammermoor*—"Yet once more shall I behold thee" in the afterlife—death is quixotically affirmed as visual repossession of lost ones:[5] Bloom's parapraxis, with its distinctly visual nostalgia, hints at how much he values the visible realm and the penetrative eye that enables him to explore it. Bloom's ocular curiosity is not even deterred by death itself, as evidenced in his imaginative attempts to see beyond the surfaces of the cemetery. He does not flinch from visualizing the underside of Glasnevin ("All honeycombed the ground must be: oblong cells"

[6.766–67]), including the various organs scattered beneath his feet ("Lots of them lying around here: lungs, hearts, livers" [6.675–76]). If Homer desubstantiates the visible shades, Joyce graphically resubstantiates them, when Bloom pictures in detail rotting corpses, envisioned in his mind as merely "changing shades": "Turning green and pink decomposing. . . . Then begin to get black, black treacle oozing out of them" (6.777–79).

Salient shades of the dead are everywhere apparent in Joyce's indirect documentation of the technologies of remembrance extant in 1904, technologies which share a specular dimension: the erection of public statues and monuments, the publication of obituaries, the construction of grave markers, the chiseling of epitaphs, the taking of photographs—all these commemorative projects appeal to visibility. The one exception to this pattern is a technology of audibility, but Bloom immediately likens its memorial product to a visual image: he imagines a gramophone that would allow him to "put on poor old greatgrandfather. . . . Remind you of the voice like the photograph reminds you of the face" (6.964–67). These memorial technologies are often presented in "Hades" in ways that emphasize their distortional power: Joyce insistently highlights the gap between the representational shade and the real it purports to memorialize. The punch line of John O'Connell's joke, for instance, hinges on the patent visual discrepancy between the late Mulcahy and the statue of Christ that marks his grave: *"Not a bloody bit like the man,* says he. *That's not Mulcahy,* says he, *whoever done it"* (6.731–32). Bloom is critical of a statue of Christ on other grounds, noting the minimal visual mimeticism in images of the Sacred Heart: "The Sacred Heart that is: showing it. Heart on his sleeve. Ought to be sideways and red it should be painted like a real heart" (6.954–55). Epitaphs undergo a related critique when Bloom notes their misrepresentation of the usual human resistance to death ("Who passed away. Who departed this life. As if they did it of their own accord. Got the shove, all of them"); proposes a less euphemistic formulaic phrase ("Who kicked the bucket"); and then imagines an alternative iconography that conveys more accurately the material realities of the deceased subject's life ("More interesting if they told you what they were. So and So, wheelwright. I travelled for cork lino. I paid five shillings in the pound. Or a woman's with her saucepan. I cooked good Irish stew" [6.936–40]). Paul van Caspel points out that Bloom here "may have been thinking of certain Jewish burial customs. In Jewish cemeteries, the gravestones—simple enough in themselves—frequently carry long-winded inscriptions, full of praise and usually mentioning the deceased's profession or function in the community."[6] Joyce may also be alluding once again to Book XI of *The Odyssey,* to the moment when the shade of Elpenor requests that his grave be marked with a metonymic artifact patently symbolizing his role and identity: "'plant over my grave the oar I used to row with when I was yet alive and with my messmates.'"[7] Like Elpenor's marker and those in Jewish cemeteries, Bloom's fantasized epitaphs register a desire for some sort of individuating representation. Ever the realist, he realizes with wry humor that this alternative iconography might not necessarily be flattering, as in Dublin it would necessarily (and frequently) record not only employment but also occupational failure and debts ("I paid five shillings in the pound").

The prototype for the sort of misnomering individuals are subject to upon their disappearance is provided, of course, by the case of the transient mystery man, reduced to the style of coat he is wearing ("Macintosh" [6.894]), and further compacted in Hynes's transcription ("M'Intosh" [6.895]). In its exploration of substitutional shades, "Hades" symptomatizes a common human anxiety, a fear that representation is inevitably misrepresentation. The phobic realization that likeness is never lifeness, that visible signifiers ultimately fail us, is the psychic subtext of Odysseus's futile embrace of the maternal specter. Joyce provides versions of this delusive Homeric shade, so visually present it almost passes for its referent, when Bloom briefly contemplates two types of imaging that aspire to absolute mimetic accuracy, two forms that aim to trick the eye into mistaking the artifactual for the real (at least temporarily). Upon seeing a motionless bird, Bloom is reminded of a taxidermic gift—"Like stuffed. Like the wedding present alderman Hooper gave us" (6.949–50). Moments later, after envisioning a realistic heart in place of the Sacred Heart on the statue of Christ, he recalls a fabled *trompe l'oeil* painting: "Would birds come then and peck like the boy with the basket of fruit[?]" (6.957–58). In both instances Bloom ultimately acknowledges the inviolable difference between the living real and the dead record of it. Answering his own query, he remembers that the authentic-looking basket of fruit in the painting was negated by the inauthentic visual simulacrum of the boy ("but he said no because they ought to have been afraid of the boy" [6.958]). Similarly, he knows the bird in the cemetery resembling his taxidermic owl can readily be reanimated by the sling of a catapult. Both optical illusions fail, with transient and motile reality stubbornly insisting on its distance from surrogate shades.

The very motility of the real generates a further anxiety rooted in the specular: a fear, not of misrepresentation but of nonrepresentation, a fear symptomatized in vanishing and hence ultimately absent presences. The shades of visibility recorded in "Hades" can be set up as a spectrum: the utterly visible (the spectacle of the procession), the marginally visible (the numerous figures in the peripheries), the spuriously visible (the representational shades of the dead), the transiently visible (numerous disappearing objects), and finally the invisible (the buried Paddy). Like Homer's pretext, "Hades" explores the precarious status of the visible, through recurrent references to vanishing acts. "Where is that child's funeral disappeared to?" (6.506), Bloom wonders as he approaches the gates of the cemetery. The question anticipates the equally puzzling appearance and disappearance of "M'Intosh": "Where has he disappeared to? Not a sign. Well of all the. Has anybody here seen? Kay ee double ell. Become invisible" (6.899–900). In response to Jack Power's inquiry about Fogarty, Simon Dedalus remarks in a related vein, "Better ask Tom Kernan. . . . Though lost to sight . . . to memory dear" (6.455–57)—a wry description, I assume, of Kernan's concerted efforts to make himself invisible to an indulgent creditor. Bloom's marked sensitivity to opticality forces him to recognize recurrently its vulnerability. He imagines that the recently published obituaries recording Paddy's death are already undergoing visual erasure ("Inked characters fast fading on the frayed breaking page" [6.160]), and later notes that commemorative tributes in forms that are invulnerable to visual contraction belie the reality of death as disappearance: "Rusty wreaths hung on knobs, garlands of bronzefoil. Better value for the money. Still, the flowers are more poetical. The other gets rather tiresome, never withering. Expresses nothing. Immortelles" (6.945–48).

As Bloom watches the clay fall during Paddy's burial, he silently observes to himself, "Begin to be forgotten. Out of sight, out of mind" (6.872). The spectacle of the procession becomes, in a sense, the dead's final public visual appeal, his last command over the attention of others, the antithesis of his imminent invisibility and possible loss of intersubjective recognition. En route to Paddy's grave, Bloom also notes to himself, "Only man buries. No, ants too. First thing strikes anybody. Bury the dead" (6.809–10). Bloom characterizes death as an inevitability that humans usually want to invisibilize both physically and psychically: they attempt to put it "out of sight" through ritual burial and to put it "out of mind" through ritual denial ("Can't believe it at first. Mistake must be: someone else. Try the house opposite" [6.844–45]). The gesture of burying in *Ulysses* often works as a metaphor for attempted repression.[8] Bloom's anatomy of human responses to mortality is insightful, and his envisioning of dying and death is matter-of-fact and nonsuperstitious; but he concedes at the end of the chapter that the cemetery nevertheless gives him a touch of "the creeps" (6.999–1000) and that the dead can have a certain power over the living after their supposed vanishing: "I will *appear* to you after death. You will *see* my ghost after death. My ghost will haunt you after death" (6.1000–1001, emphasis added). These threats of haunting simulacra are explicitly marked as visual assertions, as refusals of the deceased to accept their specular erasure. As returns of the repressed, ghosts can materialize in varying shades, some psychically dim and "light" in their visual affects, others psychically intense and "dark" (a point I will return to later).

Bloom's interest in shades-as-simulacra in "Hades" is part of a larger pattern in his perceptual mode throughout the novel: he recurrently notices visual likenesses or similarities. Martin Cunningham's visage looks "like Shakespeare's face" (6.345); Molly resembles the model in the photo of the *Bath of the Nymph* ("Not unlike her with her hair down: slimmer" [4.371]); the back of "whatdoyoucallhim" is "like that Norwegian captain's" (4.214–15); William Brayden's appearance reminds him of Mario the tenor (see 7.52–54); and the well-dressed woman he spies on in "Lotus-Eaters" reminds him of Mrs. Dandrade ("That one at the Grosvenor this morning. . . . Who is this she was like? O yes! Mrs Miriam Dandrade that sold me her old wraps and black underclothes in the Shelbourne hotel" [8.347–51]). Bloom is also optically attuned to familial likenesses. John Howard Parnell, for example, is perceived as the double of his famous brother, as the equivalent of the nationalist hero's perduring visible shade ("There he is: the brother. Image of him. Haunting face" [10.502]). Bloom notes Dilly's inheritance of Mr. Dedalus's eyes ("Knew her eyes at once from the father" [8.29]), Stephen's resemblance to both sister and father through the same physical trait ("the eyes more especially reminding him forcibly of father and sister" [16.1181–82]), and his visual evocation, in profile, of his dead mother ("He looked sideways in a friendly fashion at the sideface of Stephen, image of his mother" [16.1803–4]). Bloom's sensitivity to visual simulacra may be symptomatic of an imagined psychic lack, hinted at in his thoughts of Rudy toward the opening of "Hades": "If little Rudy had lived. See him grow up. Hear his voice in the house. Walking beside Molly in an Eton suit. My son. *Me in his eyes.* Strange feeling it would be. From me" (6.75–77, emphasis added). Like Agamemnon, Bloom has been deprived of the happiness of looking upon his son—he can only fantasize wishful imagoes, as he does here. The thought "me in his eyes" suggests the father's desired visual imprint of himself in the facial region of vision itself; it also conveys a desire for recognition from the son, an insistent need for paternal self-reflection in the offspring's look—the explicitly visual acknowledgment that the phantasmic Rudy of "Circe" refuses to grant to Bloom: the mirage of the lost child *"gazes, unseeing, into Bloom's eyes and goes on reading, kissing, smiling"* (15.4964).

If one introduces gender into this visual thematic, one can speculate as to why Bloom desires this visual trace, and also as to why he is not psychically satisfied with the physical shade of himself that does exist—his living daughter, Milly. Bloom's imagined psychic lack, I suspect, is the by-product of an oppressive patriarchal logic whereby daughters do not count for much[9]—a patriarchal logic very much in evidence in Book XI of *The Odyssey.* In the Homeric underworld, the female specters are granted visibility only because they are "the wives and daughters *of all the most famous men,*" and they are consistently defined in terms of their relationships with male heroes (as their offspring, lovers, or spouses). Dead fathers such as Achilles, moreover, need accomplished sons to guarantee their own worth; the clear heir to this tradition in "Hades" is Simon Dedalus, worried about Stephen's entanglement in "a lowdown crowd" (6.62) and characterized with residual envy by Bloom as "full of his son. He is right. Something to hand on" (6.74–75). In a strange but not uncommon en-gendering of progeny, Bloom tends to see the lost Rudy as *his* child ("My son inside her" [6.82], he revealingly thinks, as opposed to "our child inside her") and, in turn, repeatedly thinks of the surviving Milly as Molly's. His sense of connection to Rudy is so strong that, in another parapraxis, Bloom thinks he may have indeed left a visual imprint on his male offspring—not the positive trace of visual perdurance, but rather the negative stigmata of guilt. Recalling the Childs murder case (with its implicit verbal overtones of infanticide), Bloom dwells briefly on the superstition about visual fingerprints being left on the retinas of the dead: "The murderer's image in the eye of the murdered" (6.478), he thinks to himself. The thought is patently connected to his earlier fantasy of "Me in his eyes," albeit in phobically inverted form:[10] it may record Bloom's illogical but lingering sense of responsibility for his son's failure to survive. In an elaboration of this patriarchal gender logic, the daughter becomes a diluted version of the mother—"Molly. Milly. Same thing watered down" (6.87)—whereas a son, in marked contrast, is conceptualized as "the substance" (6.552), as an untainted preservative residue, "the substance" Bloom fears he lacks. In "Circe," Bloom's desire for a male heir turns him—in a *wishful* phantasm—into "the new womanly man" (15.1798), productive of compensatory male octuplets; however, one cannot help but wonder if his lack of the phallic male child is not in part responsible for his more *anxious* feminine identifications as well. A detail in the questions and answers of "Ithaca" suggests that Milly bears a partial resemblance to the father (see 17.871–74); but despite this evidence and the affection he feels for her, Bloom's dominant psychic impulse is to invisibilize Milly as his visual trace, by focusing on her blonde hair, her maternal resemblances ("Very same teeth she has" [13.1195]), or the likenesses in female mannerisms or habits ("Handed down from father to, mother to daughter, I mean" [13.917–18]). The implicit image of Molly and Milly as horses in "Oxen of the Sun" underlines—through the multiple meaning of "follows" ("goes behind," "succeeds," "is lead by," "copies," *or* "resembles")—the often perceived link between mother and daughter: "*She follows her mother* with ungainly steps, a mare leading her fillyfoal" (14.1082–83, emphasis added).

Bloom's sense of Milly as a diluted version of Molly represents the daughter as the attenuated shade of the mother. At other junctures he sees females as a group as inherently identical shades, as evidenced in his grammatical equation of Molly with her entire sex: "Is there anything more in him that they she sees?" (6.201). Due in part to his experience with advertising, Bloom is perceptually discerning about representational forms and their power to transform their referents. As representations in themselves, of course, Bloom's thoughts also have distortional tendencies, nowhere more so, perhaps, than in his speculations about the monolithic nature of women:

> Extraordinary the interest they take in a corpse. Glad to see us go we give them such trouble coming. (6.14–15)

> They sometimes feel what a person is. Instinct. (6.202–3)

> Where old Mrs Riordan died. They look terrible the women. (6.378–79)

> Must be careful about women. Catch them once with their pants down. Never forgive you after. (6.484–85)

> Want to keep her mind off it to conceive at all. Women especially are so touchy. (6.753–54)

It is not always easy to gauge how seriously Bloom believes these essentializing assumptions. Some of them are obviously speculative self-amusement, as one can see in his en-genderings of the tastes of the dead: "The dead themselves the men anyhow would like to hear an odd joke or the women to know what's in fashion" (6.789–90). Bloom's own interest in fashion facilely undermines his tidy representational categories: witness in "Hades" his critical evaluation of Ned Lambert's suit ("Nice soft tweed Ned Lambert has in that suit. Tinge of purple. . . . Dressy fellow he was once" [6.828–30]) or his sartorial approval of the caretaker's "wellcut frockcoat" (6.842). But Bloom's reflexive overwriting of gender onto mortality—a patently transgendered fact—may indicate that the masculine/feminine divide structures his cognition just as sharply as it does the Homeric house of Hades. Bloom's representational en-genderings also pose a subtle danger to their referents—the absent women they purport to describe. For gender assumptions can turn into a figurative form of taxidermy, substitutional shades all too readily misrecognized as the real. Under these simulacra, the complexity of the actual vanishes; women are rendered spuriously visible and effectively invisible, perduring only in their inert taxidermic likenesses. This phenomenon is interesting to consider in the context of "Hades," where invisibility is coded as a form of disempowerment, and visibility as its opposite.[11]

As I explained earlier, however, the perspectival organization of "Hades" adumbrates a shade of marginal visibility through its repeated focus on the visual peripheries. Somewhat similar to the underworld in *The Odyssey,* Joyce's episode splits along gender lines: if the Homeric epic delineates two distinct groups of shades, contrastive in the origins of their fame, the modernist revision maps out an equally asymmetrical structure—a masculine center and a decentered zone, where actual women are remotely espied. An old woman watches the passing carriages in the street from an adjacent dwelling ("One [blind] dragged aside: an old woman peeping. Nose whiteflattened against the pane" [6.12–13]); Mrs. Dignam mourns, presumably, within "number nine with its craped knocker, door ajar" (6.27); and an anonymous woman and girl silently pass Paddy's mourners on their departure from an earlier funeral (6.517–20). The marginal feminine position in "Hades" and in the larger androcentric culture the chapter metonymically documents is figured in the game of bowls at Mat Dillon's that Bloom recalls at the episode's close: "Yes, Menton. Got his rag out that evening on the bowlinggreen because I sailed inside him. Pure fluke of mine: the bias. Why he took such a rooted dislike to me. Hate at first sight. Molly and Floey Dillon linked under the lilactree, laughing. Fellow always like that, mortified if women are by" (6.1010–14). Menton and Bloom enter the spectaclized arena of male athletic competition, while Molly and Floey look on from the sidelines—they are literally and figuratively in the shade. It is worth noting the paradoxical structure of the tableau: the women are relegated to its visual margins, and yet their shaded presence exerts pressure on its center, has an effect on its dynamics, here as the audience that the men aim to impress through their play.

This image of female leisure is not representative of the dominant figuration of women liminally visible in "Hades." Rather, the thematic of their envisionings in Bloom's mind is labor, in every sense of the word. Suggestively, one of his earliest thoughts about women juxtaposes childbirthing and physical toil: "Glad to see us go we give them such trouble coming. Job seems to suit them. Huggermugger in corners. Slop about in slipperslappers for fear he'd wake. Then getting it ready. Laying it out. Molly and Mrs Fleming making the bed. Pull it more to your side" (6.14–18). Elsewhere in the episode, women are represented tending to ravaged male bodies ("Out on the rampage all night. Beginning to tell on him now: that backache of his, I fear. Wife ironing his back" [6.59–61]), mending clothes ("But I wish Mrs Fleming had darned these socks better" [6.106]), cleaning domiciles ("Mrs Fleming is in to clean" [6.237]), keeping garments presentable ("His wife I forgot he's not married or his landlady ought to have picked out those threads for him" [6.831–32]), and cooking meals ("Or a woman's with her saucepan. I cooked good Irish stew" [6.939–40]). We are reminded at several junctures in "Hades" that Molly is a professional singer, that her meeting with Boylan—for all its erotic cathectings elsewhere—has a practical function as well, and that her singing tours are a source of family income ("You see the idea is to tour the chief towns. What you lose on one you can make up on the other" [6.217–18]). As is often the case, in Molly's past, one form of imminent labor interferes with another: "Got big then. Had to refuse the Greystones concert. My son inside her" (6.82–83). In Ned Lambert's response to John Henry Menton's query, it is clear that Molly's career has given her some professional renown in Dublin, so that Bloom is defined through his spouse before she is labeled in relation to him: "Who is that chap behind with Tom Kernan? . . . Bloom, [Ned] said, Madame Marion Tweedy that was, is, I mean, the soprano. She's his wife" (6.690–94). The issue of working women, visible in the peripheries of "Hades," is crucial to understanding a likely function of this episode: I will return to female labor in the subsequent section of my essay, where I situate the episode in the larger context of the novel and other Joycean texts.

THE DEDALUSES AND THE DIGNAMS

The literal funeral procession to and away from Paddy's burial site—the most patently visible plot of "Hades"—is traversed by a funereal procession of a different sort: an allusive train of decedents, formed as characters recall bygone family, friends, and historical leaders. Although Joyce's "Hades" focuses on one particular death, it is textually haunted by a throng of shades, as varied as the one encountered in its original Homeric locus.[12] Homer's narrative exploration of the land of the dead finds its emotional center in the death of the mother Anticleia; Joyce's corresponding episode, in contrast, decenters maternal loss, temporarily banishing the insistently returning shade of May Dedalus to its margins. She traverses the text of "Hades" only twice, symbolically through the mourning garb of the briefly espied Stephen, later through her commemorative visual trace, when Simon points out her grave to Jack Power. But despite the tenuousness of her presence in the chapter, I believe May is crucial to an understanding of why "Hades" was probably included in *Ulysses* to begin with, and how Dignam and his family—created by the episode, in a sense—function rhetorically within the novel as a whole. For Joyce establishes Paddy Dignam as May Dedalus's counterpart, as the other prominent ghost in the text, as the other recently deceased parent survived by spouse and numerous offspring. In doing so, he simultaneously sets up the Dignam family as the double of the Dedalus family, albeit with a crucial gender difference: the former is marked by a masculine absence, while the latter is marked by a feminine one. The "Hades" episode and its residues elsewhere in *Ulysses* allow Joyce to explore the aftereffects of a familial death as indeed en-gendered. The novel, in other words, elaborately contrasts the consequences of paternal death in turn-of-the-century Dublin (through the figurative "wake" of Paddy) with those of maternal death (through the figurative "wake" of May). The differences in the emotional wakes of these two shades are clearly visible and fairly predictable, given the typical structure of the patriarchal family; the differences in the economic wakes are discernible but more surprising. A speculative examination of the causalities of the discrepant financial plights suggests that the material bedrock of this familial structure is, in some circumstances, not patriarchal at all.

The doubling of the two families is made most explicit in "Wandering Rocks," where Joyce situates their two eldest sons in front of similar pieces of visual textuality: Stephen looks at "in Clohissey's window a faded 1860 print of Heenan boxing Sayers" (10.831–32), while Patsy sees in "the window of Madame Doyle" the more contemporary advertising poster of the Keogh-Bennett "pucking match" (10.1130–35). The parallel scenes highlight the pronounced differences in the emotional responses of the heirs to the deaths of their respective parents. Stephen's ruminations are interrupted by the appearance of Dilly Dedalus, and the pathos of her situation—ultimately figured as a drowning (see 10.875–77)—reminds him of his mother's demise, earlier fantasized as death by water ("A drowning man. His human eyes scream to me out of the horror of his death. I . . . With him together down. . . . I could not save *her.* Waters: bitter death: lost" [3.328–30, emphasis added]). Nearly a year after this demise, he is stung once again by the "Agenbite of inwit. Inwit's agenbite" (10.879), which in its compulsive and repetitive returns has all the markings of a neurotic symptom. The death of Patsy's father is temporally fresh in its occurrence a mere three days ago on the "ides . . . of June" (6.803). Measured against Stephen's, his response to parental loss is psychologically vacuous, utterly flat in its emotional affects:

> Death, that is. Pa is dead. My father is dead. He told me to be a good son to

> ma. I couldn't hear the other things he said but I saw his tongue and his teeth trying to say it better. Poor pa. That was Mr Dignam, my father. I hope he's in purgatory now because he went to confession to Father Conroy on Saturday night. (10.1170–74)

Patsy's void of feeling here hints at the potential accuracy of Simon's earlier prediction to Dilly about how paternal death is greeted by surviving offspring: father tells daughter, "Wouldn't care if I was stretched out stiff. He's dead. The man upstairs is dead" (10.684–85).[13] Joyce implies here that within rigidly defined patriarchal families, where paternal bonding with children is minimal, fathers may render themselves emotionally dispensable; if fathers are only marginally visible in their offsprings' lives, then their ultimate disappearance may be scarcely noticed.

The differences in the emotive legacies of the two deceased parents are also registered in their contrasting representational modes. Joyce inflects the engendered parental shades with literary genres provoking contrasting readerly responses: these responses resonate with characterological affects within the text itself. In "Cyclops" Paddy's shade materializes as a theosophical joke; in "Circe" it returns "by metempsychoses" as a howling hybrid dog-man, a mutating incarnation of "Spooks" (15.1226). Paddy becomes a bathetic and tamed Cerberus, a hellhound with a bark but no bite, whose parameters are shaped by the canine advertising trademark of Victrola phonographs ("My master's voice," Paddy cries to John O'Connell, Joyce's modern prototype of the god of the underworld [15.1247]).[14] In anticipation of his comic genre, the solemnities of Paddy's funeral rites are relentlessly punctuated by humor, both in the conversations of his mourners and in the internal monologues of Bloom. The penultimate spectacle he presents to his son is a mildly ludicrous one, leaving it unlikely that Patsy will be visually tormented by the image: "The last night pa was boosed he was standing on the landing there bawling out for his boots to go out to Tunney's for to boose more and he looked butty and short in his shirt." Realizing that he will "never see him again" (10.1167–69), Patsy anticipates Paddy's visual disappearance without much regret. The son accords the fading memorial vision of the father here the sort of utterly minimalist recognition that later characterizes Stephen's response to the name of the father ("—You know Simon Dedalus? [the sailor] asked at length. / —I've heard of him, Stephen said" [16.378–79]). If Bloom's desire for filial recognition is a common paternal feeling, disappointed in the Circean phantasm of Rudy, then Simon and Paddy are subjected to similar failures of acknowledgment.

From the specter of his mother, Stephen receives something in excess of a gaze of recognition—a gaze of accusation, indictment, and punishment ("Her glazing eyes, staring out of death, to shake and bend my soul. On me alone. . . . Her eyes on me to strike me down" [1.273–76]). Stephen's fantasies of May foreground her odor and, increasingly, her relentless vision: when she materializes as an eyeless corpse in "Circe," the mother is nevertheless coded by Stephen as sheer gaze, as a "Lemur" (15.4176), a large-eyed animal that can see in nocturnal darkness. Although *Ulysses* foregrounds filial guilt, the gruesome details of the maternal dying and death which provoke it are visible enough within Stephen's memories. In contrast to that of father Dignam, the shade of mother Dedalus provides no occasion for amusement. Stephen's mother wanders amid all the comedy of *Ulysses* as a markedly nonfunny figure, draped in the representational figures of tragedy: premature demise, extreme physical deterioration, and excruciating pain, aggravated by the requisite attitudinizing offspring.[15]

The genre of the maternal shade in *Ulysses* is also increasingly gothic, particularly in the transformative association of May Dedalus with vampirism. Discussing Stephen's fantasy in "Proteus" of a pale vampire kissing/biting his mother (see 3.395–400), Vincent J. Cheng writes, "Who is the vampire? Not May Dedalus, surely, who seems here to be the vampire-corpsechewer's victim"; he later notes, however, that in Stephen's nightmare-vision in "Circe," the vampire-corpsechewer image is clearly attached to the mother herself.[16] I would add to this interpretation that Stephen may be figuring, through random but revealing gothic imagery, the way that death-as-vampire has transformed his mother, in turn, into a vampire: for in death she has a lethal potency in the son's psyche which, I believe, in life she never possesses (given her characterization in both *A Portrait of the Artist* and *Stephen Hero*). When her shade materializes before Stephen's eyes in "Circe," her metamorphosis into a vampire figure is suggested by the crab claws she sticks deep in her son's heart (see 15.4220–21)—an imagistic variant of the vampiric fangs penetrating the victim's neck. In sharp contrast to the harmless Circean hellhound of Paddy Dignam, May Dedalus is a ghoul who preys ultimately upon nearly every sensory register of the son: she haunts as a perduring vision and gaze, as a noxious smell, as a minatory voice, and as a deadly vampiric touch.[17]

Less visible and dramatic than the discrepancies in the emotional wakes of May and Paddy are the differences in the material plights of their respective children. These plights are briefly marked in minor details: while the Dignams will dine on pork steaks from Mangan's, the Dedalus daughters must be satisfied with pea soup from a charity kitchen. Katey Dedalus in "Wandering Rocks" is seen hungrily "lift[ing] to her mouth random crumbs" (10.286–87). The economic futures of the two sets of offspring are likewise implicitly contrasted. The Dedalus daughters, one can speculate, will continue to attempt to survive on the unreliable resources provided by the auction room and the pawnshop; the financial fortunes of the Dignam children look considerably less bleak, as Ned Lambert informs Simon in "Hades" that Martin Cunningham is getting up "a whip for the youngsters. . . . A few bob a skull. Just to keep them going till the insurance is cleared up" (6.564–66). Paddy Dignam's insurance policy appears initially as a potential source of financial uncertainty for his survivors: Bloom is informed earlier in the episode that it "was heavily mortgaged" (6.536) and later finds out that the insurance company has not been notified of this fact. In "Cyclops," however, when Bloom apprises Joe Hynes of the situation, the latter has a good laugh at the expense of Paddy's moneylender, confident that Dignam's widow will come out "top dog" and that "old Shylock" will in turn be "landed" (12.765–66). The fate of Dignam's heavily mortgaged insurance policy cannot be resolved on June 16, due to the legal ambiguities involved in such cases;[18] but the reader is left with the assurance that a network of Paddy's friends is actively intervening on behalf of his family's economic security and that the reliable Bloom plans to visit the insurance company in the very near future. Fortuitously for the Dignams, Bloom's numerous employment experiences include a stint at Drimmie's, a life insurance agency ("—What is this he is? Isn't he in the insurance line? / —He's out of that long ago, Nosey Flynn said. He does canvassing for the *Freeman*" [8.939–41]).

Bloom reminds himself of his promise to visit Paddy's insurer toward the end of "Nausicaa," where he also contemplates the en-gendered implications of the company's name: "But Dignam's put the boots on it. Houses of mourning so depressing because you never know. Anyhow she wants the money. Must call to those Scottish Widows as I promised. Strange name. Takes it for granted we're going to pop off first" (13.1225–28). Bloom's insight here is limited, only partial, as the selected appellation of the Scottish Widows' Fund contains another gender assumption as well: specifically, that only male lives are worth insuring, that a Scottish Widow*ers'* Fund is unnecessary because wives are economically marginal. The name of the company indirectly posits that a female spouse is not a support of the family and that, as a result, no planned material compensation is needed in the event of her death. This implicit gender assumption raises two obvious questions: is a turn-of-the-century Dublin wife—Stephen's mother, for instance—indeed inevitably economically marginal? And if this particular figure is so, how is it that the material plight of her family seems even more precarious in *Ulysses,* where she exists only as a visible shade, than it is at the end of *A Portrait of the Artist,* where she still has ontological substance?

I believe that the various texts in which she appears, taken as a unit, suggest in their margins that May Dedalus is not economically marginal at all. First of all, *Portrait* briefly hints that she is a source of domestic economy: when Stephen wins academic prize money and immediately proposes to take his family out to dinner, despite their strained finances, her first response is that the restaurant at least be "Some place that's not too dear." What Stephen sees in this scene—his mother "thinly clad" in a "keen October wind"—may help explain what motivates her frugality (*P* 97). Secondly, when she reappears at the opening of chapter 5, a vaguely specified labor is taking place in the family kitchen, and one brief line hints that the female members of the household are doing laundry. Seamus Deane glosses Boody's statement that she is "going for blue" as meaning that she is going out to get laundry detergent.[19] We are not allowed to see what is in the sink where Stephen must wash, but Boody's remark may point to invisibilized dirty clothes. This laundering appears with greater visibility in *Stephen Hero,* the remnant early draft of *Portrait,* although it is still subordinated to the intellectual preoccupations of the son: "His mother had not asked to see the manuscript: she had continued to iron the clothes on the kitchen-table without the least suspicion of the agitation in the mind of her son." When Stephen asks his mother "point-blank would she like him to read out his essay," she responds, "O, yes, Stephen—if you don't mind my ironing a few things"; as the young artist expounds his theories, Mrs. Dedalus folds a handkerchief and presses a petticoat, willing audience to her son's intellectual labor but not at the expense of her own material tasks (*SH* 83–85). There is nothing particularly unusual in this, until another barely visible and subordinated textual detail hints that the kitchen is perhaps being transformed into a permanent laundry, that a particular bowl for food has assumed an official labor-related status, as if eating has become secondary to washing clothes: "the mere sound of [Whelan's] speech reminded [Stephen] of the noise Nurse Sarah used to make when she mashed Isabel's bread-and-milk in the blue bowl which his mother now used to hold starch" (*SH* 101). When the three Dedalus daughters briefly glimpsed in chapter 5 of *Portrait* resurface in "Wandering Rocks," they are plainly doing laundry in the kitchen once again. Until recently, I always assumed that the female members of the Dedalus household were washing the family's clothes—until, that is, I noticed a visual oddity in the shoddy shape of the daughters' attire: Katey's skirt is "stained" (10.275), while Dilly's dress is "in flitters" (8.41), according to Bloom, and "shabby" (10.851), according to Stephen. In Circean phantasmagoria, Dilly is identified with a working-class girl—the "factory lass" of "My Girl's a Yorkshire Girl"—precisely through her dowdy attire *("Dilly with snowcake no fancy clothes"* [15.4147–48]). The minor incongruity between this incessant attention to presentable clothing and this personal sartorial disarray leads me to speculate that Joyce implies, through a "shade" of figurative visual marginalia, that May and her daughters, in their turn, run an unofficial laundry service for others out of their kitchen.

This speculation is supported by *Finnegans Wake,* which, I have argued elsewhere, is an uncanny text, a dreambook where elements of Joyce's earlier fictions—particularly repressed elements—return in forms at once strange and remotely familiar. May Dedalus, for instance, resurfaces in various configurations of the maternal ALP.[20] One section of ALP's chapter (I.8) finally foregrounds the mother's labor, previously only dimly visible, as well as her economic dependency on the dirty clothes of the privileged. Her song may echo an employment inquiry of the overworked Dedalus matriarch, given the hints of relentless laundering in the family kitchens: *"Is there irwell a lord of the manor or a knight of the shire at strike, I wonder, that'd dip me a dace or two in cash for washing and darning his worshipful socks for him now we're run out of horsebrose and milk?"* (*FW* 201). Like the various working females discernible in the background of Bloom's thoughts in "Hades," the Dedalus women labor in the peripheries of three "waking" Joycean fictions, only to be accorded recognition of their toils in the Wakean dream: their marginalized toil may well subtly effect familial economics, as surely as Molly and Floey's marginalized gaze effects the dynamics of Menton and Bloom's game of bowls.[21]

If my speculations are correct, then upon May Dedalus's death, the family loses one of the few members of the household who labors on behalf of that entity as a whole—which could account for its material plight being even more dire in *Ulysses* than at the close of *Portrait*. Given the possibility that Simon's spouse is a minimally paid but nonetheless crucial economic support of the family—the counterweight of his own heavily consumptive behavior—he would not have been unwise to challenge the gender bias inherent in the title of the Scottish Widows' Fund and to insure his wife's life. In its familial doubling, *Ulysses* implicitly contrasts widower Dedalus, attempting to survive by means of occupational sponging, and widow Dignam, securing the contested insurance policy at least in Circean fantasy (see 15.3842). The contrast suggests that this particular gender bias in insurance practices—the bias rooted in an assumption of female economic negligibility—ultimately, of course, works against men. Ideology is, in a sense, invisible in its immateriality, but visible in the reified practices of a particular culture: an ideological contradiction operant in turn-of-the-century Dublin—that culture's dependency on women's work and its simultaneous negligence in insuring female lives—comes into crucial visual focus, I believe, in the "Hades" episode and the Dignam/Dedalus subtext that ensues.

Bloom's ruminations in "Nausicaa" on the aftermath of spousal deaths record an additional gender bias, insofar as widowers receive the bulk of his sympathies. This asymmetry may be a function of the fact that he thinks first of the surviving wife with "her widow's mite," in the form of an insurance settlement (13.1230), a material asset which, as the text insinuates, widowers are not assured of receiving, due to a contradictory gender ideology. But the deprivation Bloom envisions, in the case of the widower, is more explicitly emotional than economic: "Widower I hate to see. Looks so forlorn. Poor man O'Connor wife and five children poisoned by mussels here. The sewage. Hopeless. Some good matronly woman in a porkpie hat to mother him. Take him in tow, platter face and a large apron" (13.1232–35). Bloom's thoughts here on the fate of the widower—on his need upon the occasion of his spouse's demise—are revealing: the widower rebonds with another woman because he wants not another wife but another mother. The envisioned aftermath of the wife's death betrays her actual status as a parent rather than a partner and the husband's childlike dependency on her. May Dedalus's premature death makes clear, of course, that this wifely role—in fact maternal in its contours—is not physically kind on those who must occupy it. Bloom has recalled earlier *Simon's* fifteen offspring ("Fifteen children he had. Birth almost year" [8.31]), but the count for *May's* brood might more accurately be sixteen, as it is tempting to include Simon himself.[22] In the phantasmagoria of "Circe," Bloom brings his conscious thoughts on spousal death to their logical conclusion: if a husband can function in a family as an adult dependent, as a child who refuses to grow up despite his age, then widowhood can be decidedly nontragic, Bloom figuring it in comic fantasy as a potential source of felicitous rejuvenation. When he is called upon, in his role as the do-gooder Lord Mayor of Dublin, to *"console a widow,"* Bloom does so by reassuring her that "Absence makes the heart grow younger" (15.1605–6).

One of the many paradoxes of *Ulysses* can be located in the way that this sort of light comedy is mixed with darker tones: the novel's playfulness, wit, and sparkle are persistently shaded by death. "Hades" is the episode that foregrounds "passing" and its aftermaths, reminding us that the world of the living is as ephemeral as Homer's parade of visible shades. "Hades" also contains the most elaborate Homeric scaffolding: in the Linati schema of the episode, for instance, the list of Homeric "persons" for whom Joyce created modern equivalents is the longest in the entire outline.[23] What I have tried to convey here, however, is my sense that this episode is much more than an ingenious and obsessive modernizing of the earlier myth, my sense that Joyce uses it to introduce an engendered political issue through the doubling-with-a-difference of the Dignams and the Dedaluses. Molly's monologue, most visibly, suggests that when families end up economically "on the rocks," they often rely on a bedrock of low-paying female labor ("when he said I could pose for a picture naked to some rich fellow in Holles street when he lost the job in Helys and I was selling the clothes and strumming in the coffee palace" [18.560–62]). Prior to his construction of this elaborate female point of view, Joyce hints at this economic situation in the visible peripheries of his text. In the representational field created by his writerly enterprise, Joyce may relegate female labor to the shade, so to speak—but not without making it implicit, through the plight of the Dedalus family, that such a positioning has real material consequences. Up until *Finnegans Wake,* Joyce's works may imitate cultural praxis insofar as they tend to marginalize female work—particularly feminized work such as laundering; yet he records simultaneously the palpable economic effects of this problematic patriarchal devaluation.

7

Machines, Empire, and the Wise Virgins

Cultural Revolution in "Aeolus"

PATRICK MCGEE

Near the end of the "Aeolus" episode, as Stephen Dedalus and the other men who have congregated in the offices of the *Evening Telegraph* head toward Mooney's pub, the narrator of *Ulysses* notes, "They made ready to cross O'Connell street" (7.1041). According to Gabler's synoptic text (*U*-G 310.15), this line was written in 1918 and underwent no later revisions before the publication of the book in 1922. Yet the name of the street that Stephen and company cross in 1904 is Sackville and not O'Connell Street. In fact, it remained Sackville Street until 1924, two years after the publication of *Ulysses*.[1]

There are probably several explanations for this anachronism, and the most obvious would be that Dubliners referred to Sackville Street as O'Connell Street long before it was officially renamed. Such a gesture could be interpreted as a subtle form of resistance to the rule of British authority, which named the street after an eighteenth-century Irish viceroy. Surely, in the summer of 1918, when Joyce probably wrote the line, it carried a special significance: only two years had passed since the Easter Rising and the rejuvenated party of Arthur Griffith, Sinn Féin, was becoming the dominant political force in Ireland under the leadership of Éamon De Valéra. During this period, the British "resorted to the old policy of pinpricking coercion," which only consolidated the support of Sinn Féin and guaranteed its victory in the general elections of 1918.[2] Joyce could not have ignored these developments and must have been pleased by the change of attitude in a man he had once admired (despite Griffith's anti-Semitism). Though in 1904 Griffith had expressed contempt for O'Connell and indifference to Parnell, in 1917–18 "he asserted that 'The election of O'Connell for Clare was the first Sinn Féin election in Ireland,' and agreed that Parnell had forced 'the clear issue between Provincialism and Nationalism.'"[3]

This reference to O'Connell Street also occurs at a telling point in "Aeolus." Stephen Dedalus has just finished his story about two Dublin vestals who visit Nelson's pillar on Sackville Street. The headline to the section reads, "SOPHIST WALLOPS HAUGHTY HELEN SQUARE / ON PROBOSCIS. SPARTANS GNASH MOLARS. / ITHACANS VOW PEN IS CHAMP" (7.1032). These words introduce the segment in which Professor MacHugh compares Stephen with Antisthenes, "a disciple of Gorgias, the sophist." He was "the son of a noble and a bondwoman. And he wrote a book in which he took away the palm of beauty from Argive Helen and handed it to poor Penelope" (7.1935–39). The professor, who may be more insightful than most readers have thought, recognizes that Stephen, in telling his story, has aligned himself with the figure of the subaltern, the bondwoman. He has chosen one of the two identities that would seem to be available to the colonized Irish subject in *Ulysses.* The one he associates with his dead mother, and the other with his father, who has pretensions to class; along with Mulligan and the other Irish intellectuals, his father has also assimilated the culture of imperialism (even though these figures may support nationalist politics). By transferring his loyalty from Helen to Penelope, that is, from the feminine object of masculine desire and imperialist power to the woman who labors, Stephen emphatically responds to the call of an Irish elite, represented by Mulligan, to hellenize the island.

Of course, Penelope, who was herself a royal, makes a curious figure for the subaltern; but in this context Joyce suggests that subalternity is partially a gendered condition or is at least associated with the feminine. As Virginia Woolf believed, women like herself, who occupy a social position in the privileged classes of society, do not necessarily wield a corresponding amount of social power: "we are," she stressed, "weaker than the women of the working class" because "we have no weapon with which to enforce our will."[4] Woolf's cultural and economic logic here is probably open to question, but she does accurately point to the feminization of the subaltern position that led to British representations of the Irish as a feminine race.[5] Penelope embodies this situation since she is the archetype of the woman who is imprisoned in her own home—and, to some extent, by her class position. In a sense, the only thing that truly belongs to her in this house is her labor, which becomes the basis of her strategy for survival as she weaves and unweaves. She refuses to be what Helen has become, the symptom of masculine desire. In *Ulysses,* the condition of Helen's beauty is Penelope's labor; the condition of aesthetic idealism is material exploitation. Strictly speaking, of course, Professor MacHugh's interpretation may not be Stephen's conscious intention. In response to the professor, Stephen thinks, "Poor Penelope. Penelope Rich" (7.1040). But even Penelope Rich, the Stella of Sidney's *Astrophel and Stella,* was forced into marriage against her will,[6] just as Ireland was forced into a union with Britain. Whatever Stephen intends, the political unconscious of this text speaks through the substitution of the name "O'Connell street" for Sackville Street and through the headline. The Spartan-like British militarists will gnash their teeth when they realize that Pen, or Penelope the subaltern subject, is champ. The Irish Ithacans, by contrast, will eventually celebrate her victory when they realize that the pen, or writing (and I would suggest that this must be understood as general writing, which refers to the iterability or performativity of the cultural signifier itself), is also the necessary instrument/condition of social liberation.

I am not suggesting, as has been suggested so often, that Joyce was a pacifist and simply rejected the Irish revolution as "absurd," the word Dominic Manganiello uses to characterize Joyce's view of the Rising.[7] On this account, I would have to align myself with the position of Enda Duffy in *The Subaltern "Ulysses,"* which, despite a surprising number of factual errors, makes a compelling antidote to complacency in the field of Joyce studies on the issue of Joyce's politics. Though Duffy mutes Joyce's critique of nationalist ideology and presupposes a theory of the postcolonial that is more in harmony with nationalism than I believe it to be, still he is absolutely justified in reclaiming *Ulysses* "for Irish readers as *the* text of Ireland's independence." He calls it "a covert, cautious 'guerilla text' in which the violence erupting in Ireland while the novel was being written is in a complex manner homologized by the modernist textual strategies of estrangement that characterize the work."[8] His study centers on what I have already referred to as the subaltern subject, a concept that he derives from Gramsci via Fredric Jameson. The latter defines "subalternity" as "the feelings of mental inferiority and habits of subservience and obedience which necessarily and structurally develop in situations of domination—most dramatically in the experience of colonized peoples." Nevertheless, Jameson insists that subalternity is neither purely psychological, "although it governs psychologies," nor purely economic. Rather, it is cultural, since neither "psychological therapies" nor "purely objective transformations of the economic and political situation itself" can transform subaltern subjectivity.[9] The concept of "subalternity" brings into focus less the individual than the group—in Gramsci's own words, a social group "deprived of historical initiative, in continuous but disorganic expansion, unable to go beyond a certain qualitative level, which still remains below the level of the possession of the state and of the real exercise of hegemony over the whole of society."[10] For Jameson, cultural revolution dialectically sublates the condition of subalternity.

So I would qualify Duffy's thesis about the homology between the violence of the Irish revolution and Joyce's textual strategies in *Ulysses.* Duffy privileges a concept of nationalism that in the history of colonized peoples, according to Edward Said, produced "the mobilizing force that coalesced into resistance against an alien and occupying empire." This movement is "a deeply problematic enterprise," however, since, as Said argues after Frantz Fanon, it tends "to replace the colonial force with a new class-based and ultimately exploitative one." Such a nationalism is only the first of "two distinct political moments" within the nationalist revival, "each with its own imaginative culture, the second unthinkable without the first." While these two moments can coexist both before and after the actual war of independence, the second moment does have a critical relation to the first:

> Whether in the Indian constitution, or in statements of Pan-Arabism and Pan-Africanism, or in its particularist forms such as Pearse's Gaelic or Senghor's *negritude,* conventional nationalism was revealed to be both insufficient and crucial, but

> only a first step. Out of this paradox comes the idea of liberation, a strong new post-nationalist theme that had been implicit in the works of Connolly, Garvey, Martí, Mariategi, Cabral, and DuBois, for instance, but required the propulsive infusion of theory and even of armed, insurrectionary militancy to bring it forward clearly.[11]

I would add the name Joyce to Said's list of postnationalist liberation theorists. In my view, Joyce's understanding of and relation to Irish history during the period of the Easter Rising, the War of Independence, and the Irish Civil War is doubly complex because as he developed his effectively postcolonial critique of British imperialism and Irish nationalism, he also witnessed the fact of an independence struggle without which no concept of liberation for Ireland could ever be realized in practice. At the same time, his writing concretely suggests that there can be no true human liberation within the framework of a revolution that does not go beyond national independence, that does not take, as Fanon stressed, "a rapid step . . . from national consciousness to political and social consciousness."[12] This step is the call to cultural revolution; and it is Joyce's attempt to produce this call, if not the revolution itself, that justifies Duffy's insistence on "the historiographic matrix of decolonization as an appropriate one within which to envisage the political trajectory of *Ulysses*."[13]

"Aeolus" dramatizes the material production of subalternity in the culture of colonialism and postulates several necessary conditions for its transformation. Central to this drama is the machine both as a real thing and as a figure for cultural production. Still, this episode reveals that such a distinction between the figure and the thing itself, while required by logic, is not altogether determinate *in the real* because it is precisely the cultural framework as a rhetorical process that produces the concept of the machine that would seem to be a figuration of that framework. In "Aeolus," Joyce demonstrates that our concept of the machine shapes and limits our understanding of the potential of the thing itself for human liberation. This concept from the earliest beginnings of the industrial revolution to the present cannot be detached from the history of imperialism and colonial domination. The project of this episode, therefore, is twofold. First, it dissects the concept of the machine that fosters the mechanical reproduction of imperialist culture. Second, it draws a sketch of and perhaps actually produces a revolutionary machine of cultural transformation.

From the opening of this episode, "IN THE HEART OF THE HIBERNIAN METROPOLIS," machines disruptively appear in direct connection with the symbols of empire: "Before Nelson's pillar trams slowed, shunted, changed trolley, started," and so forth (7.01–3). A few pages later, as he listens to the presses cranking out newsprint, Bloom thinks, "Machines. Smash a man to atoms if they got him caught. Rule the world today" (7.80–81). As Bloom watches the typesetters performing like machines, he imagines the machine itself as "almost human. . . . Doing its level best to speak" (7.175–76). Still, the foreman looks around at "his loud unanswering machines" (7.183). Passing Monks the dayfather, Bloom pictures the old man's "daughter working the machine in the parlour. Plain Jane, no damn nonsense" (7.201–2). In effect, the hegemonic machine of the imperialist culture has smashed human beings to atoms, or rather has atomized them in the sense of reducing them to discrete units that work silently within the system. The system encourages this silence not only as the absence of speech but as the absence of any political voice that would suggest the potential of the subaltern group to transform itself into a conscious class subject that could seize not only the machines of production but also the cultural machinery of hegemony. In the "Circe" episode, as the Lord Mayor of Dublin, Bloom dreams of such a machine as "the music of the future." Though his "tramline . . . from the cattlemarket to the river" may be an inadequate representation of that future, he at least asks the right question: *"Cui bono?"* (15.1367–69). Who benefits? Whose interests are served? He positions the interest of the subaltern group against the "bucaneering Vanderdeckens in their phantom ship of finance" (15.1369–70): "These flying Dutchmen or lying Dutchmen as they recline in their upholstered poop, casting dice, what reck they? Machines is their cry, their chimera, their panacea. Laboursaving apparatuses, supplanters, bugbears, manufactured monsters for mutual murder, hideous hobgoblins, produced by a horde of capitalistic lusts upon our prostituted labour" (15.1390–94). "Circe" here could be read as a subaltern fantasia, the political dream of the subaltern subject (understood here not as the individual but as the collective subject of the group or groups marginalized by imperialist culture), expressing both resentment and utopian desire. It is no accident that both Bloom and Stephen are feminized in "Circe"—Bloom by becoming a symbolic mother and Stephen by trying to rejoin his dead mother through submission to the death drive. "Aeolus," by contrast, maps out the social processes that produce and maintain subaltern subjectivity. Machines are not only the means by which labor is prostituted, supplanted, and always exploited. The subject itself operates within the framework of a machinal system, is itself engineered, hailed, or interpellated by the social machine as a determinate function within its overall operation. This particularly masculine episode also reminds us that the feminization of the subaltern subject does not necessarily point to a liberatory bond between oppressed men and women since the process of feminization presupposes and produces through performance the very gender hierarchy that a liberatory feminism would seek to overthrow.

As M. J. C. Hodgart has noted, "Aeolus" is the chapter in which "Bloom does some work."[14] But he is not the only one. The second section of the episode notes that "his Majesty's vermilion mailcars . . . received loudly flung sacks of letters, postcards, lettercards, parcels" (7.16–18) without explicit mention of the human agents who actually perform these tasks. The first section describes the movement of the tramcars as if there were no human beings attached to them, as if the machines simply responded to the commands of the "hoarse Dublin United Tramway Company's timekeeper" (7.07). Human operators have become functions of the machines they operate. By contrast, Bloom's job seems active and even creative; but we can also apply to him the phrase he applies to the machines that rule the world: "Working away, tearing away" (7.83). His first statement in the episode is the request to Red Murray about the Keyes advertisement in the *Telegraph:* "Just cut it out, will you?" (7.26). He carries the cutout to the foreman and explains that he wants it changed: he wants to paste on it a design from another ad from the *Kilkenny People.* Bloom's job, in other words, is indirectly one of cutting and pasting, which Joyce chose to emphasize when he inserted the words "scissors and paste" on the first placard in 1921 (7.32; *U*-G 240.14). These words appear immediately after Red Murray cuts out the ad, and they were inserted at the same time that Joyce began inserting the headlines or captions in the text. (Later I will return to the significance of these headlines and why, as John Kidd and others have argued, they probably should be in boldface.) The inserted phrase emphasizes that Bloom's job has its mechanical dimension, while the episode as a whole, which employs more obviously than the others the technique of montage, illustrates the creative possibilities of cutting and pasting.

Bloom's work on the Keyes ad produces a message about the national situation in Ireland. The icon of two crossed keys that he wants pasted onto the top of the earlier ad for "Alexander Keyes, tea, wine and spirit merchant" (7.143) alludes to the House of Keys, the parliament of the Isle of Man, which exercized some degree of home rule. Into this context Joyce inserted the phrase "Innuendo of home rule" (7.150) onto the second set of placards in late August or early September of 1921 (*U*-G 248.19) *after* the War of Independence had led to a truce in July.[15] Though the treaty was not yet negotiated, Joyce could not have missed the irony of a reference to home rule at a time when the revolutionary leaders of Ireland were seeking much more than home rule for Ireland. As it turned out, the republic would not be completely realized in the treaty of 1921; but Bloom's attempt to exploit Irish nationalism for commercial reasons suggests another dimension of subalternity as the ideological block to the desire for social liberation. Pacifist or not, Joyce could not have ignored the fact that Ireland was in a stronger position for negotiating with Britain after the War of Independence than she had ever been during the parliamentary movement for home rule. Critics like David Pierce who believe that Joyce's view never deviated from Parnellism, which "sought home rule for Ireland but not complete separation,"[16] imply that Joyce isolated himself from the dynamic realities of Irish history between 1904 and 1922. On the contrary, "Aeolus" examines the limitations of Irish nationalism in 1904 from the perspective of events unfolding between Easter 1916 and the treaty negotiations of 1921.

The concept of home rule, which had been effective as a counterhegemonic response to British imperialism in the 1880s under Parnell's leadership, had by 1904 begun to lose its threatening content. As Duffy stresses, between 1904 and 1921, "the structures were set in place so that Ireland would become . . . a culture and economy of consumers. It was perhaps the first modern colony in which the local culture could be successfully penetrated in precisely this manner." Bloom is the unconscious instrument of this hegemony, although, as Duffy elaborates, he has plenty of opportunity for resisting the lure of commodity culture in a community where only a few have the money to buy commodities. This culture "constructed only from advertisements . . . hails its subjects rather than reaching them directly through desire."[17] As Duffy suggests, such an interpellation without the concrete realization of the subject interpellated, that is, without the transformation of the colonial subject into a genuine consumer, creates a gap where resistance and critique become possible. Joyce exploits this gap in 1918 when he writes most of "Aeolus" and drives the wedge even further into the gap with the additions he makes to the episode in 1921; but he does not create the impression that either Bloom or the other colonized subjects in this episode can totally resist the call of commodity culture. Though it may not reach them as the satisfaction of their desires, it certainly awakens those desires and produces several phantasms as the objects of desire's realization.

These phantasms take shape in the three examples of nationalist rhetoric that harbor a secret identification of the colonized or subaltern subject with the culture of imperialism. The first example is Dan Dawson's panegyric, which paints such an idealized view of Ireland that it receives this appropriate caption: "ERIN, GREEN GEM OF THE SILVER SEA" (7.236). To the phrase, "*Our lovely land,*" Bloom responds, "Whose land?"; Professor MacHugh finds the question "pertinent. . . . With an accent on the whose" (7.271–75). While the men in the *Evening Telegraph*'s offices make fun of Dawson's *"peerless panorama of Ireland's portfolio"* (7.320), Bloom remarks to himself, "All very fine to jeer at it now in cold print but it goes down like hot cake that stuff" (7.338–39). This kind of writing conforms to the British stereotype of Ireland as a scenic paradise full of ineffectual natives, so that for the Irish to identify with it is to identify with the agency of their own domination. Yet while the men in "Aeolus" are not taken in by this empty rhetoric, they are impressed by the various alibis imperialism uses to promote its own cultural authority. The professor may hate the "material domination" (7.557) of the British, but he inadvertently accepts their cultural domination with something like Mulligan's call for the hellenization of Ireland: "The Greek! . . . *Kyrios*! Shining word! The vowels the Semite and the Saxon know not. *Kyrie*! The radiance of the intellect. I ought to profess Greek, the language of the mind" (7.562–64). Mulligan's experience at Oxford would suggest that Greek culture is no more unfamiliar to the British than anti-Semitism; and the language of the mind, or the "empire of the spirit" (7.567), as the professor refers to it a few lines later, may be precisely the means by which the empire interpellates the subaltern subject (witness Matthew Arnold). In "Telemachus," if Stephen is the Caliban figure, as Mulligan suggests (1.143–44), then Buck himself is Ariel, who does service for the British Prospero. If Caliban manifests the hypermasculinization of the subaltern subject, Ariel embodies gender ambivalence; and such a feminized spirit, in this case, is the instrument of material domination. Ironically, in "Aeolus," the outcome of this process of feminization-spiritualization is the production of masculine excess, a disavowal of gender ambivalence through an excessive and self-defeating performance of the masculine.

The second example of nationalist rhetoric is the forensic address of Seymour Bushe, the Irish barrister, who left Ireland to become king's counsel in 1904. Strictly speaking, this speech is not nationalist in content, but J. J. O'Molloy uses it as an example of Irish eloquence in the legal profession. In distinguishing Irish rules of evidence from British rules, Bushe contrasted Roman justice with the Mosaic code and, according to O'Molloy, "cited the Moses of Michelangelo in the Vatican" (7.756–57).[18] The word "cited," which Joyce substituted for "spoke of" in 1921 (290.21), emphasizes the arbitrariness of the process that Joyce foregrounds in "Aeolus." I refer to the citationality, or—after Derrida—the iterability not only of writing in the restricted sense but of culture itself as general writing, as performance. Because the words from Bushe's speech are noticeably decontextualized by comparison with the other citations in this episode, they dramatize the violence of quoting and the instability of context that such violence necessarily foregrounds. This does not mean that the original context is irrecoverable but that it is always possible to displace a context by grafting any part of the text onto another context. Joyce exploits this possibility in the very process of composing "Aeolus." For example, in 1921, he added the phrases *"in frozen music"* and *"of the human form divine"* (*U*-G 292.03–5) to the following segment of Bushe's description of the Moses: *"that stony effigy in frozen music, horned and terrible, of the human form divine, that eternal symbol of wisdom and prophecy"* (7.768–69). The second phrase comes directly out of Blake, while the first, in consonance with the rest of the passage, has a distinctly Paterian note (although, as Gifford comments, the phrase actually comes from Schelling's *Philosophy of Art*).[19] This hint of aesthetic idealism or decadence in the Bushe speech seems completely out of context in the courtroom (especially for the Childs murder case). Given Stephen's addiction to literary decadence in the last chapter of *A Portrait of the Artist as a Young Man,* it comes as no surprise that he should blush at these words, "his blood wooed by grace of language and gesture" (7.776). The phantasm that captures and derails subaltern desire in this case is the seduction of art itself, or at least the aesthetic effect of language. Stephen's blushing aligns him with the greatest Irish decadent of all, Oscar Wilde, who could be said to have fused Caliban and Ariel in the construction of an Irish subject-position that attempted to transcend subalternity through art. Wilde failed because in privileging homosocial desire across national and class boundaries he failed to take into account the material relations that actually shape and enforce social hierarchy. The social order he desired, wooed, critiqued, and transfigured through art could only read his desire as the ground of criminal action.

The third example of Irish rhetoric transcends the first two. John F. Taylor's defense of the Irish language movement and Irish cultural nationalism in general idealizes the goal of Irish independence by comparing it to the promised land of the Hebrews, Israel. It equates liberation with nationhood. It produces this meaning in a relatively austere and disciplined language, which does not call attention to itself as artistic. Joyce made very few changes in this speech after 1918, although the two most significant ones underscore the subaltern status of the Irish. The first change, made on the typescript before it went to the printer, contrasts the abject situation of the captive Hebrews with the power of their Egyptian captors: *"Yours serfdom, awe and humbleness: ours thunder and the seas."* Later, on the third set of placards, he added this sentence immediately after the preceding one: *"Israel is weak and few are her children: Egypt is an host and terrible are her arms"* (7.856–58; *U-G* 296.31–32). These additions were made shortly after the Irish republicans had forced the imperial British state, through a guerrilla war, to accept a truce and go to the negotiating table. The irony is unmistakable. Still, Joyce's irony cuts in more than one direction. In Taylor's speech, the Egyptian high priest poses this question to the Hebrews: *"Why will you jews not accept our culture, our religion and our language?"* (7.845). John F. Taylor responds to the British version of the Egyptian high priest in the English language, the primary language of *Ulysses* and *Finnegans Wake.* Furthermore, though the triumph of Irish Catholicism precedes the domination of Ireland by the British, there is no way of completely severing the cultural links between Britain and Ireland, these overlapping territories with intertwined histories, to use Said's phrase. According to Taylor, Moses came down from the mountaintop *"bearing in his arms the tables of the law, graven in the language of the outlaw"* (7.868–69). But Moses is not only a revolutionary but a patriarch—perhaps, after God himself, the supreme patriarch.

Joyce understood that the language of the outlaw becomes the language of the law.[20] As O'Molloy says "not without regret," Moses "died without having entered the land of promise" (7.872–73). In a sense, the real Moses never left the space of wandering in which the language of the outlaw was written. Ira B. Nadel has listed and analyzed the references to Moses that constitute a virtual typology in Joyce's work.[21] One of Joyce's heroes, Charles Stewart Parnell, was a type of Moses, as were all the great Irish leaders, including Daniel O'Connell. Immediately after the recitation of Taylor's speech, we encounter these references to O'Connell in Stephen's interior monologue: "Hosts at Mullaghmast and Tara of the kings. Miles of ears of porches. The tribune's words, howled and scattered to the four winds. *A people sheltered within his voice. . . . Love and laud him: me no more*" (7.880–83, emphasis added). The italicized passages were probably inserted into the manuscript after the declaration of the truce (*U-G* 298.23–25).[22] In these words, Stephen expresses his distrust of political rhetoric and the way it can seduce a people into the uncritical worship of authority, even though revolutionary. He refuses to give his support to the memorialization of O'Connell and other Irish nationalist heroes. These additions to the text suggest that at the conclusion of the War of Independence, Joyce, while he may have appreciated the tactical victory of Irish nationalism, continued to distrust visions of the promised land that appeal to hero worship and patriarchal authority.

In this context, it is worth noting that less than a year before Joyce wrote the first draft of "Aeolus" in 1918 the Balfour Declaration was made public; according to Nadel, this "event overtook the English and, no doubt, European papers: the *Daily Press* announced 'A State for the Jews,' *The Times* declared 'Palestine for the Jews.'" Although Nadel concedes that Joyce's view of Zionism was skeptical, he believes that Joyce would have found in the proposals of Theodor Herzl "a political spirit similar to the Irish—one that sought to transform a religion and a culture into a nation."[23] Nevertheless, Joyce surely would have seen some irony in the fact that Arthur J. Balfour, who gave his name to the British government's declaration, was known as "Bloody Balfour" for his coercion policy as chief secretary of Ireland from 1886 to 1892, though he later designed and implemented the "constructive Unionist policy" that culminated in the Wyndham Land Act of 1903.[24] Joyce also would not have been surprised to know Balfour's views on the native inhabitants of Palestine:

> *we do not propose even to go through the forms of consulting the wishes of the present inhabitants of the country*. . . . The four great powers are committed to Zionism and Zionism, be it right or wrong, good or bad, is rooted in age-long tradition, in present needs, in future hopes, *of far profounder import than the desire and prejudices of the 700,000 Arabs who now inhabit that ancient land*.[25]

Joyce probably surmised the imperialist and Zionist view of Palestine as "an empty territory paradoxically 'filled' with ignoble or perhaps even dispensable natives."[26] Bloom more or less endorses this view when he imagines Palestine as a "barren land, bare waste. . . . Dead: an old woman's: the grey sunken cunt of the world" (4.219–28), a politically problematic feminization not only of the subaltern subject but of the very space in which the subaltern can be said to exist. Joyce would have known Herzl's view in *Der Judenstaat* (one of the books in his Trieste library) that a Jewish Palestine would "form a part of a wall of defense for Europe in Asia, an outpost of civilization against barbarism."[27] In other words, Joyce could not have been naive about the imperialist implications of the Balfour Declaration.

The Zionist view of the Palestinians repeats the Egyptian high priest's view of the Hebrews. The "Aeolus" episode implies that nationalism could be a phantasm that merely reproduces the content of imperialist culture in a different form if it does not overcome itself by promoting a broader concept and practice of human liberation. This does not mean that Joyce saw no value in the nationalist struggle in Ireland, or, for that matter, in the Jewish quest for a homeland. But he also saw a problem that Seamus Deane formulates rather bluntly: "The point about Irish nationalism, the features within it that have prevented it from being a movement toward liberation, is that it is, *mutatis mutandis,* a copy of that by which it felt itself to be oppressed."[28] The question at the end of "Aeolus" is this one: how does one formulate a counterhegemonic vision within the framework of a hegemonic culture? Or, how does one construct an anti-imperialist rhetoric within the language and rhetorical traditions of empire? For Joyce, there should be no illusions. The language in which the citizens of Dublin speak is the English language, and that language can never be completely divorced from the culture and history of British imperialism. So how do the colonized, to use the terms of postcolonial theory, abrogate and appropriate the language of the colonizer?[29] Stephen Dedalus starts to give us an answer when he says, "I have a vision too" (7.917).

Stephen's vision is the story of the two Dublin women who "have lived fifty and fiftythree years in Fumbally's lane" (7.923–24). As Gifford notes, Fumbally's lane is in the Liberties, a Dublin slum in 1904.[30] Though they are called vestal virgins, their connection to hearth and home (after the Roman goddess Vesta) does not seem to have earned them the respect of the community. Professor MacHugh calls them "wise virgins" (7.937) with some irony; but it may be that, like the wise virgins in Matthew 25:1–13, these women are prepared in more than one sense for "the hour wherein the Son of Man [that is, Redemption] cometh." Joyce wrote the minimalist story that Stephen narrates during the summer after the passage of the Representation of the People Act in January 1918, which "granted the parliamentary vote to women of thirty years of age and over." The same act also enfranchised all men of twenty-one years. According to Rosemary Cullen Owens, this "partial attainment of suffrage objectives," for which Irish women had struggled since the latter half of the nineteenth century, produced "a changing approach to women who could now not only be party workers, but candidates and, above all, voters." It gave them the power to achieve complete suffrage for all women over twenty-one in the Irish Free State Constitution of 1922, so that Irish women beat their English counterparts to the vote by six years. Still, would these events have significantly changed the lives of Stephen's Dublin vestals? Probably not. From the beginnings of the Suffrage Movement in Ireland up to at least the time in which *Ulysses* is set, the women who formed the movement "were mainly middle and upper class and protestant in character." In the last decade of the movement, while there were more women involved, their interests were divided between separatism and commitment to the goals of nationalism. The movement may have achieved its primary goal in 1922, but it did not achieve "the related objective of complete equality for women in all spheres of life."[31] As Eric Hobsbawm grimly points out, "most working-class women laboured under disabilities which were more urgent than political disenfranchisement, which were not likely to be automatically removed by the right to vote, and which were not in the forefront of the minds of most middle-class suffragists."[32]

Stephen's wise virgins are probably virgins only in the political sense. As they buy their humble provisions and climb Nelson's pillar "to see the views of Dublin from the top" (7.931), it seems unlikely that they know to what extent their social and economic interests have been excluded by the various agents of political change who would claim to speak for them. Perhaps, as Gayatri Spivak says, "The subaltern cannot speak."[33] But then, as Enda Duffy insists, "the abject woman as subaltern can speak."[34] In this case, she speaks not with words but in what she does. I argued somewhat cryptically in *Paperspace* that the two women take a perverse pleasure, a *jouissance,* from eating forbidden fruit in the face of the patriarch, or the "onehandled adulterer" (7.1018).[35] As they peer up at Nelson's statue, they get "a crick in their necks" and "are too tired to look up or down to speak." Speechless, therefore, they eat their plums and spit "the plumstones slowly out between the railings" (7.1023–27). There is something that Stephen does not say about this moment, something that is implicit in the titles he gives the story, *"A Pisgah Sight of Palestine* or *The Parable of the Plums"* (7.1057–58). Joyce inserted the second title on the placards in 1921 (*U-G* 312.08–9), as if he meant to drive home the connection between the sight from Nelson's pillar and the plums. The point is simple but significant. These women, like Stephen, have *a vision of their own* as they look out between the railings. Of course, we don't know what it is; but in recognizing that it exists we recognize the fact of subaltern desire as the possibility of speech and social representation. It is the desire that counts and not the object of desire, which, since it is always only one of a series, has the structure of a phantasm. Therefore, Stephen employs a kind of rhetoric that enables him to articulate the ground or structure of desire without subordinating it to the object as phantasm. The truly revolutionary vision is always *A Pisgah Sight of Palestine,* just as the truly revolutionary Moses is the one who never reached the promised land, who never saw the language of the outlaw become the language of the law. Perhaps even more important, we recognize that this desire speaks for the subaltern group, which includes not only the two middle-aged women and all the other women of *Ulysses* but also the men in the offices of the *Evening Telegraph*. Both *despite* and *because of* their flaws and limitations, these men and women have their own visions; and, however phantasmic these visions may be, they channel and keep alive the material desires that are the necessary condition of any counterhegemonic strategy. To use a Lacanian distinction, they keep alive the *aim* of desire as the possibility of hope, even though the immediate *goal* of desire may be problematic. Though Stephen imagines the subaltern subject as feminine, he does not necessarily identify with the feminine or seek a bond with women on terms of social equality. He merely articulates the aim of desire as the reproduction of desire itself, or hope, through the representation of the desiring subject *as* feminine. He turns the machinery of imperialist representations, including the feminization of the subaltern subject, against itself by using it to foreground the process of social desire rather than its phantasmic goals. If you will, the machines of imperialist culture may feed the illusions of the colonized, but they also create the condition of those *decolonizing* desires that fuel cultural revolution.

Such a revolution is itself a machine—a machine for the destruction of another machine. In a sense, this machine is precisely what the Watch in "Circe" imagine Bloom to be hiding: "Infernal machine with a time fuse" (15.1199); but this time fuse represents an indefinite postponement of the explosion, or rather the explosion is itself a process that takes place over an indefinite period of time—the time of what Raymond Williams calls the long revolution. Surely, when Joyce made the final revisions on "Aeolus" in 1921, he had come to realize that the only effective way to dismantle one machine was with another. *Ulysses* is a machine that should have the effect, however limited that effect may be, of dismantling the hegemonic mechanisms of imperialist culture. It produces this effect by foregrounding its own mechanical form, by dramatizing the mechanics of cultural production. Furthermore, in response to the socioeconomic process through which imperialism binds the colony to the metropolitan center, *Ulysses* presents itself as what Adorno would call the absolute commodity, the commodity that calls attention to its own formation within the framework of commodity culture and thus discloses the determinations of that culture in the production of the aesthetic. Insofar as *Ulysses* is a work of art that calls into question the autonomy of art, not by dismissing it as politically vicious, but by showing that aesthetic autonomy is precisely the commodity form of art itself, it concretely materializes the liberationist potential of art. Art liberates when it dispels the phantasms to which culture (and art as the product of culture) necessarily give birth. It makes visible the operation of culture as general writing, as iterable performance, the product of a technology that is always subject to adjustment and that can always be short-circuited. In positioning culture as general writing, Joyce rejects the view that culture is natural or can be reduced to an evolutionary model. As Easter 1916 and the War of Independence demonstrated, cultural transformations can be abrupt and extremely violent; but at the same time such violence usually results from the enforcement of concepts or laws that try to put a stop to the processes of cultural change. For this reason, cultural revolution is necessarily permanent.

Joyce made two other dramatic additions to the "Aeolus" episode in 1921 that support the argument I am making. First of all, he added passages on the early placards that illustrate the operation of the empire as a machine. I refer to the opening segment that describes the movement of the trams before Nelson's pillar, and to a section near the end in which the tramcars are suddenly "becalmed in short circuit" (7.1047; see *U-G* 238.03–14, 310.17–24). It is surely no accident that this breakdown in 1904 takes place across the street from the General Post Office, where the British empire would begin to short-circuit in 1916. More emphatically, Joyce inserts these passages into *Ulysses* after the British empire has been forced to the negotiating table by the rebel leadership of one of its colonies for the first time. The second significant addition that Joyce made in 1921 are the headlines. They are significant because they demonstrate, perhaps better than anything else in *Ulysses,* the form of culture peculiar to the age of mechanical reproduction and the kinds of resistance such form permits. From this perspective, John Kidd is absolutely right to insist on the evidence that Joyce intended for the headlines to be in boldface.[36] They should disrupt the text since they create the effect of a counterhegemonic position that subverts the hegemony from within, using the instruments of hegemony itself.

As the subtext of "Aeolus" demonstrates, the events from the Easter Rising to the conclusion of the War of Independence in Ireland created a historical possibility for Irish liberation that cannot be strictly reduced to the form of the nation-state. Irish independence represents the short-circuiting of the empire. This event is the violent but absolutely necessary condition of a truly liberated Ireland. Still, achieving that liberation requires another step. The nation-state can either channel human desire into the process of cultural revolution or control human desire by limiting the forms of its representation. For Joyce, the nation-state could only work if it became the kind of machine that *Ulysses* is, "the most competent and reliable production and reproduction machine" that "simultaneously ruins its model. Or at least," as Derrida goes on to say, "it threatens to ruin its model."[37] Historically, the model of the nation-state has included within itself naturalized conceptions of gender, race, and class. One of the political meanings of *Ulysses* could be described in this way: any state that would seek social justice and freedom as the desire of the other (and, to some extent, every desiring subject is *an other* in relation to the machinery of hegemony) must disrupt the binary categories I refer to. "Aeolus," with its disruptive headlines and conflicting rhetorical visions, gives us an idea of what such a de-con-structive machine looks like from the inside. It is not Utopia, but it does promise another vision of things.

8

Legal Fiction or Pulp Fiction in "Lestrygonians"

KAREN LAWRENCE

"Real men eat beef." Something like this flesh-eating virility is suggested in the first sentences in which we are introduced to Leopold Bloom: "Mr Leopold Bloom ate with relish the inner organs of beasts and fowls. He liked thick giblet soup, nutty gizzards, a stuffed roast heart, liverslices fried with crustcrumbs, fried hencods' roes" (4.01–3). We meet "Mr Leopold Bloom" at home in his kitchen. If the first sentence begins with a distanced and polite form of address to Bloom, it quickly plunges deep into his interior, where we see him, in turn, receiving the "inner organs" of animals.

Or do we? For one of the many miscues we encounter in *Ulysses* (like the conclusion of the "Lotus-Eaters" chapter, which we might erroneously read as a scene in which Bloom regards his own body in the bath) is this supposed scene of eating, which turns out instead to be a description of Bloom's habitual likes and dislikes, his "taste" ("Most of all he liked . . ." [4.03]). We discover that this chunky, almost onomatopoetic description, is indeed a description of Bloom's *thoughts:* "Kidneys were in his mind as he moved about the kitchen softly" (4.06). This "real" man *imagines* himself eating flesh in his "real" kitchen—kidneys are *in* his mind as he putters around. This initial description gives substance to Bloom's interiority. It mimes for us the fullness of his inner life, a fullness and richness which the novel will increase in its pages. Although he subsequently *does* leave home to purchase a pork kidney at Dlugacz's, and is seen "chewing with discernment the toothsome pliant meat" (4.391), the initial culinary description pertains to his thoughts only.

The simulated dive inward—from third-person narration reminiscent of, say, "Emma Woodhouse, handsome, clever, and rich," to what feels like the *inside* of Bloom's gullet as he devours the inner organs of other creatures—extends the modernist project of the inward turn of narrative, extends it comically and corporeally, as if "fleshing out" the character from the inside out, an incarnation or embodiment of consciousness upon which fiction relies. Our surprise at finding ourselves in Bloom's *thoughts* reminds us that this graphic corporeality is, indeed, graphic—a representation in writing. The world made flesh is the flesh made word. Grammatically, the iterative narrative ("He ate with relish") emphasizes the fact that writing is made possible only through iterability, through the repeatability of the sign. Bloom first appears to us not in a particular scene of eating (an event) but under the sign of repeated and almost ritual feasting.

This first representation of Bloom in "Calypso" distinguishes his subjectivity from that of Stephen Dedalus, whose interaction with the world is ocularcentric ("thought through my eyes" [3.01–2]). Stephen takes in the world through what Kant calls the "objective" or mechanical sense of sight (not to be confused with "objectivity," but rather, signaling a distancing, a removal from the thing perceived).[1] His modality is the "ineluctable modality of the visible" (3.01). In contrast, despite the voyeurism in "Nausicaa," Bloom's prime modalities seem to be taste and smell, in Kantian terms the more "subjective" or chemical senses. With taste, unlike sight, the external object is transformed as well as taken in, through a process of liquefaction. "Lestrygonians" is the chapter in which Bloom is most clearly represented as taking in the world through his mouth and nose. The many puns and plays on food in the chapter construct a basic analogy between the processes of incorporating and digesting food in the stomach and the formation of the "self" through internalizing the environment. This analogy is structured as a kind of law of the chapter—"You are [or become] what you eat"—a law to which Bloom himself seems to subscribe. He looks at two Dublin theosophists and contrasts them with the beefy Irish policemen: "Dreamy, cloudy, symbolistic. Esthetes they are. I wouldn't be surprised if it was that kind of food you see produces the like waves of the brain the poetical. For example one of those policemen sweating Irish stew into their shirts you couldn't squeeze a line of poetry out of him" (8.543–47). Intake determines output. In "Lestrygonians," the chapter that derives its Homeric title from the cannibalistic tribe Odysseus and his men narrowly escape, Bloom recognizes the risks, even more than the pleasures, of incorporation. "Risky putting anything into your mouth" (8.859), he thinks, and, at the nadir of his experience in the Burton restaurant, his gorge rises in disgust at the sight of the beefy Irishmen who shovel food into their mouths like animals.

Orality in *Ulysses* culminates in "Lestrygonians," but it resonates throughout the novel, particularly in relation to the psychoanalytic concept of identification (a further twist on the idea that you are what you eat). For the figuring of mental processes as the bodily processes of ingestion or assimilation is crucial to the psychoanalytic discourse on the construction of the subject. The subject incorporates or ingests the "other" and is transformed, wholly or partially, after the model the other provides. The general name for this process is identification. "In Freud's works," Laplanche says, "the concept of identification comes little by little to have the central importance which makes it, not simply one psychical mechanism among others, but the operation itself whereby the human subject is constituted."[2] Originally, Freud seems to have thought of identification in terms of the oral or cannibalistic phase of libidinal development, and in *Totem and Taboo* (1912–13), he relates it to the relationship between the father and sons in the primal horde, according to which the sons devour the body of the father in an act of possession and identification.[3] Derrida's term for the speculative idealism according to which the law of the father is interiorized through a process of ingestion is *"carno-phallogocentrism."* He speaks of an "idealizing interiorization of the phallus and the necessity of its passage through the mouth, whether it's a matter of words or of things, of sentences, of daily bread or wine, of the tongue, the lips, or the breast of the other."[4] In Joycean terms, this carno-phallogocentrism establishes paternity as *the* legal fiction. It is central as well to the rite of the Eucharist, the offering of Christ's body in the form of the wafer and his blood in the form of the wine. "Take, this is my body," Christ says in the Gospel of St. John; the Christian is he who eats and identifies with the ideal father.

In an immensely suggestive plenary speech at the Frankfurt Symposium (which later appeared in print), Julia Kristeva takes on Joyce's special relationship to the central symbol of the Eucharist and its implications for his fictional exploration of the process of identification. She writes:

> In his intense experience of Trinitarian religion, resulting in his subsequent derision of it, Joyce was confronted by its central ritual, the Eucharist, exemplary rite of identification with God's body, pivot of all the other identifications, including the artistic and imaginary profusion favored by Catholicism. It is probable that this Catholic cultural context, profoundly assimilated by Joyce, met with a mechanism that was, in other respects, the motor of his fictional experience and which allowed him to concentrate his efforts of representation and elucidation upon the identificatory substratum of psychic function, so masterfully placed at the center of the ultimate of religions.[5]

From the first scene of the novel, in which the "wellfed voice" (1.107) of a "plump Buck Mulligan" (1.01) taunts Stephen Dedalus with the mock chalice containing the "body and soul and blood and ouns" of the "genuine christine" (1.21–22), both the general concept of hunger/nourishment and the specific oral ritual of the Catholic Mass, the Eucharist, are introduced as barometers of the way the characters partake of the world around them. "Personally I couldn't stomach that idea of a personal God" (1.623), Haines, the Englishman, says to Stephen. Haines's Protestant fastidiousness toward the rite of the Eucharist, his visceral disgust at the thought of Irish Catholics "stomaching" the body of Christ, demonstrates his refusal to risk any but the most intellectualized participation in the Irish culture around him. (Buck earlier refers to these "bloody English! Bursting with money and *indigestion*" [1.52–53, emphasis added]). On the other hand, the mocker, Mulligan, taunts Stephen with the thought of Christ's body and blood because his irony and thoroughgoing materialism neutralize the mystery of transubstantiation so that he sees only a wafer and a glass of wine, not the body and blood of Christ. In "Lestrygonians"

Bloom thinks "that last pagan king of Ireland Cormac in the schoolpoem choked himself at Sletty southward of the Boyne. Wonder what he was eating. Something galoptious. Saint Patrick converted him to Christianity. Couldn't swallow it all however" (8.663–67). Bloom's "Jewish" view is one of empathy toward the pagan king force-fed the body of Christianity; transubstantiation fails in Bloom's rendition of conversion because the pagan king, unlike the Platonizing Christians, who idealize the process, cannot "swallow" Christ's body. It is immediately after this thought that the beefy smells of men make his gorge rise, suggesting a link in Bloom's mind between the cannibalism he associates with the Eucharist and the manly eating he witnesses in the Burton. Earlier, as Bloom watches the ritual of communion in All Hallows Church, he thinks, "*Corpus*: body. Corpse. Good idea the Latin. Stupifies them first. Hospice for the dying. They don't seem to chew it: only swallow it down. Rum idea: eating bits of a corpse. Why the cannibals cotton to it" (5.350–52). It is useful to remember that Catholic children are warned *not* to chew the host but to swallow it whole, a practice which avoids the implication of cannibalism and emphasizes Christ's spiritual incorporation in the communicant. Throughout *Ulysses* images of and attitudes toward the Eucharist put in high relief the question of identification; that is, of what one can assimilate or swallow and make part of one's being. Bloom, the twice-baptized Jew, is alternately fascinated and repelled by the ritual of the Eucharist. Bloom rejects both the triumph of idealization—the swallowing without chewing—and its materialist "manly" opposite, the chewing of dead meat.[6]

I want to trace the displacements and realizations of the topos of orality in the "Lestrygonians" chapter, where Bloom's food for thought is most dramatically represented. Here Bloom refuses a particular kind of virile communion and remembers, and mourns, a different kind of assimilation, a more vegetarian one, his reception of the half-chewed seedcake from Molly's mouth on Howth Hill. This erotic identification tells a "pulp fiction," different from the eat and be eaten story in the Burton (all body and no spirit), different as well from the idealizing narrative of sacred communion through the host (all spirit and no body). The body of food Molly feeds Bloom is neither masticated brutally nor swallowed whole like medicine. This cherished memory of communion, savored in consciousness like Molly's photo in Bloom's pocket, is his weapon (a moly?) against the feeding frenzy that disgusts him in the Burton restaurant.[7]

In "Lestrygonians," it is lunchtime in Dublin. The Linati schema indicates that the technique of the chapter is peristalsis, the organ, the esophagus.[8] Lured by the smell of various foods, Bloom stops before several eating houses, debating about what he does or does not crave. He is hungry for lunch, and this hunger is intoned as general all over Ireland: he thinks of "the harp that once did starve us all" (8.606–7). Like the "famished ghosts" in *The Odyssey,* who can come to life (and speech) only by drinking "hot fresh blood" (8.729–30), the Dubliners, including (non-Kosher) Bloom, crave something to fill them up. "A barefoot arab stood over the grating," sniffing fumes from the nearby restaurant.

"Deaden the gnaw of hunger that way. Pleasure or pain is it?" (8.235–37), Bloom thinks, speculating on strategies for dealing with unsatisfied desire. These are the musings of Bloom, the husband who has not had full intercourse with his wife for ten years and is about to be cuckolded, as he deliberately stays close enough to home and far enough away to experience the pain/pleasure of Molly's adultery.

What distinguishes the representation of orality in "Lestrygonians" from its appearance at Bloom's introduction in "Calypso" is Bloom's sense of victimization and loss of control. In "Calypso" eating is part of a domestic routine over which Bloom presides: he thinks about eating, feeds the cat and then Molly, and breakfasts on a tasty, slightly charred pork kidney—all are comforting components of a ritual ordering of domestic life. His morning collation, replete with "burnt offering" (17.2044), is a comic, domestic sacrifice. In "Lestrygonians" Bloom fails to exert the same control over how and what to eat and increasingly his senses are assaulted by the sights and smells of flesh that surround him. Early in the episode he remembers the unpleasant sensation of going down to the pantry to get Molly something at nighttime and suddenly encountering the odor of leftover codfish: "Don't like all the smells in it waiting to rush out" (8.23). He associates the phosphorus of the decomposing fish with the body of Christ on a luminous crucifix ("Our Saviour. Wake up in the dead of night and see him on the wall, hanging. Pepper's ghost idea. Iron Nails Ran In" [8.19–20]). In his kitchen he can more or less control the unpleasant smells; in "Lestrygonians," however, his thoughts about food keep triggering a recognition of his own mortality, as corpus and corpse continually collapse. If in "Hades" he takes comfort in the idea of the ecological efficiency of the food chain ("It's the blood sinking in the earth gives new life. . . . Well preserved fat corpse, gentleman, epicure, invaluable for fruit garden" [6.771–73]), in "Lestrygonians" the vision becomes more personal—with horror he sees his own sacrificial place in the food chain. Bloom himself becomes the abjected, expelled body of food: "This is the very worst hour of the day. Vitality. Dull, gloomy: hate this hour. Feel as if I had been eaten and spewed" (8.494–95).[9] As he views the "men, men, men" chomping food in the Burton (8.653), Bloom is nauseated by his sense of their murderous cannibalism:

> Smells of men. Spaton sawdust, sweetish warmish cigarettesmoke, reek of plug, spilt beer, men's beery piss, the stale of ferment.
>
> His gorge rose.
>
> Couldn't eat a morsel here. . . .
>
> Every fellow for his own, tooth and nail. Gulp. Grub. Gulp. Gobstuff.
>
> He came out into clearer air and turned back towards Grafton street. Eat or be eaten. Kill! Kill! (8.670–73, 8.701–3)

Why is his reaction so violent? Why does the lover of inner organs of beasts and fowls, the man who likes the urinous tang of kidney, have such a strongly emetic response? In a provocative revisionary reading of Bloom's supposed nonviolence, Emer Nolan points out that earlier Bloom had accepted the joining of life and death in the food chain as an affirming part of life's process: "In the midst of death we are in life. Both ends meet. Tantalising for the poor dead. Smell of grilled beefsteaks to the starving" (6.759–61). Nolan says of Bloom's virulent reaction in the Burton: "However, in the face of actually existing human community and warm human bodies, this robust common man proves unable to imagine, for example, communal eating outside an economy of greed and selfishness." She sees the kill or be killed rhetoric of Bloom's interior monologue as evidence that "his own appetite . . . inspires this appalling vision of endless gluttony and savagery."[10]

Nolan is right to question the complacency of humanistic accounts of Bloom as the heroic common man who rejects the violence and masculinism of the Dubliners around him. She is accurate about Bloom's hesitancy to participate in a masculine community (although I think it is more appropriate to speak of his ambivalence than fear), and she offers a corrective to the view that his outsider status is solely due to the anti-Semitism that surrounds him (in her view, as in Fredric Jameson's reading of the father-son relationship in *Ulysses* in "Ulysses in History," the oedipal plot so often stressed is itself a symptom of a lack of full social participation). Indeed, Bloom's repulsion is even more puzzling in light of his earlier attraction to the social community that he recognizes is forged through the celebration of the Eucharist: "There's a big idea behind it, kind of kingdom of God is within you feel. First communicants. Hokypoky penny a lump. Then feel all like one family party, same in the theatre, all in the same swim. They do. I'm sure of that. Not so lonely. In our confraternity" (5.360–64). Given the strength of Bloom's nausea, however, the register of Nolan's analysis seems off the mark. Bloom doesn't merely reject "community" here, like a petulant child, as Nolan seems to suggest; rather, like Cormac, the pagan king, he "can't stomach" the idea of flesh as mere corpse. Despite Bloom's comic demystifications of the *idealization* operating in the rite of the Eucharist, he has as much trouble facing the nonsublimated version of incorporation, the atavistic image of the body wholly devoid of spirit. The food chain, a once comforting image of death providing nourishment for new life, is now "frozen" in Bloom's horrific vision of male meeting and meat-eating. At all costs Bloom attempts to avoid the taste of death.

It is possible to relate Bloom's repulsion here to the traditions that cling to this fallen-away Jew. In her essay on abjection, Kristeva reminds us that for Jews, the corpse is "a body without soul . . . it must not be displayed but immediately buried so as not to pollute the divine earth." In the Burton, Bloom confronts the unredeemed and unredeemable corpse, a vision exacerbated by his recent experience in the cemetery. As Kristeva puts it,

> The corpse (or cadaver: *cadere,* to fall), that which has irremediably come a cropper, is cesspool, and death; it upsets even more violently the one who con-

> fronts it as fragile and fallacious chance. A wound with blood and pus, or the sickly, acrid smell of sweat, of decay, does not *signify* death. In the presence of signified death—a flat encephalograph, for instance—I would understand, react, or accept. No, as in true theater, without makeup or masks, refuse and corpses *show me* what I permanently thrust aside in order to live. These body fluids, this defilement, this shit are what life withstands, hardly and with difficulty, on the part of death. There, I am at the border of my condition as a living being. My body extricates itself, as being alive, from that border. Such wastes drop so that I might live, until, from loss to loss, nothing remains in me and my entire body falls beyond the limit—*cadere,* cadaver. [Think of Bloom's pleasure in defecation.] If dung signifies the other side of the border, the place where I am not and which permits me to be, the corpse, the most sickening of wastes, is a border that has encroached upon everything. It is no longer I who expel, "I" is expelled. . . . The corpse, seen without God and outside science, is the utmost of abjection. It is death infecting life. Abject . . . it is thus not lack of cleanliness or health that causes abjection but what disturbs identity, system, order.[11]

The corpse—seen without God (or love/agape) and outside of science—this is the vision Bloom has in the Burton.

As James McMichael points out in *"Ulysses" and Justice,* thoughts of food and sex overlap in Bloom's mind in "Lestrygonians." In a very suggestive discussion of Bloom's hunger in the episode, he notes that Bloom puts off satisfaction of his hunger, rejecting the frenzied activity of "bolting to get it over" (8.661) that he sees: "As his continuing to say both 'yes' and 'no' to sex is, his thinking of food to say 'no' to it is Bloom's resistance to the time it takes for bad things to happen." McMichael sees deferral—deferral of sleeping with Molly and deferral of the satisfaction of his hunger—as Bloom's strategy of delay, a way of resisting time (McMichael links this to his idea that it is Bloom rather than Molly who resists "full carnal intercourse," out of fear of conceiving another child like Rudy). "Because his thoughts about food and sex collapse into one another, Bloom thinks of the progeny that come from lovemaking not as persons the body engenders so that they might live, but rather as what the body passes and disposes of as vile. The stillborn, for Bloom, are 'trouble for nothing' (8.389–90), waste, as Rudy is waste."[12] This remark is particularly suggestive in light of Kristeva's description of the corpse as "the most sickening of wastes."

This vision of Rudy as dead matter, like the vision of the host as dead meat, prevents the idealization of mourning. The "cannibalism" in the Burton is an image of corpse-eating without both the idealization of mourning and the space of deferral. Like Blazes "Boylan with impatience" (11.426), these men satisfy their urges immediately. Constantly thinking about Blazes and Molly's impending assignation, Bloom is himself stalling so as not to go home. As McMichael points out, this stretching out of time is Bloom's strategy; it is his means of feeling in control. He checks his watch throughout the chapter: "Time going on. Hands moving. Two. Not yet. / His midriff yearned then upward, sank within him, yearned more longly, longingly. / Wine" (8.791–94). The image of the men eating in the Burton is an image of blood-lust immediately gratified. The opposite of love, as Bloom states it in "Cyclops," is not only hatred, but force. Plot is a suspension of consummation, a refusal to force the moment to a crisis. The moment in the Burton seems to end the suspension of time in a vision of animalistic gratification.

In contrast, Bloom is an incorrigible savorer and planner, a man who lives between past and projected satisfactions, perpetually in mourning and anticipation. As reciprocal and prolonged hungers, food and sex are played off one another in the chapter, beginning with Bloom's entrance into the Burton to escape sexual temptation. The smell of food replaces that other smell that rushes out at him in the chapter, the perfume of female bodies. It is as if the body of the world presses in on Bloom's interiority, massaging his own cravings; yet he resists succumbing wholeheartedly to this lure: "A warm human plumpness settled down on his brain. His brain yielded. Perfume of embraces all him assailed. With hungered flesh obscurely, he mutely craved to adore" (8.637–39). This "warm human plumpness" is, of course, associated throughout the novel with Molly's body; the plumpness on Bloom's brain displaces his desire for Molly onto a general eroticization, as if diffusing her particular perfume ("what kind of perfume does your wife use" [5.258]) into the atmosphere. It is this threat of satisfaction that propels him into the Burton, as if he is choosing the lesser of hungers to satisfy. "He turned Combridge's corner, still pursued. Jingling, hoofthuds. Perfumed bodies, warm, full. All kissed, yielded. . . . His heart astir he pushed in the door of the Burton restaurant. Stink gripped his trembling breath: pungent meatjuice, slush of greens" (8.641–51). But in the Burton he finds that the smells of men are more dangerous than the scent of a woman.

As a temporary stay against hunger, Bloom does make a culinary choice—a cheese sandwich and wine. Tellingly, his meal is later dubbed "the unsubstantial lunch" (17.2047), a chosen alternative to meat as both substance and symbol (transubstantiated matter). Indeed, before choosing cheese, he mentally catalogs the various ways in which he can protect himself from unholy meat, through prescriptions both Kosher and vegetarian. "Kosher. No meat and milk together" (8.751), he thinks, again relying on Jewish traditions. Momentarily, he mulls over Jewish dietary exclusions and taboos which function as a purification—less violent than abjection, they are alternative forms of protecting oneself from the taste of death ("I hate dirty eaters" [8.696], he thinks as he witnesses the carnivorous orgy of men). Bloom's uncharacteristic fastidiousness further leads him to thoughts of the ritual fast of atonement at Yom Kippur, a "spring cleaning of inside" (8.752) as he puts it, that replaces the murderous sacrifice with rules of atonement. Vegetarian traditions also cross his mind: "After all there's a lot in that vegetarian fine flavour of things from the earth garlic of course it stinks after Italian organgrinders crisp of onions mushrooms truffles" (8.720–22). Of course, we know that Bloom is no vegetarian; indeed, he ridicules the dreamy theosophist vegetarians like a "real man" regarding a flower child eating tofu.

And even the pacific cheese sandwich cannot wholly free him from thoughts of death. In "Hades," only hours earlier, he thinks, "A corpse is meat gone bad. Well and what's cheese? Corpse of milk" (6.981–82). Cheese, too, reminds him of the food chain: "Cheese digests all but itself" (8.755), Bloom thinks before he eats his sandwich, projecting cheese, surprisingly enough, as the victor in the food chain, like paper winning over rock in the children's game. But the cheese and wine he chooses to eat suggest a different kind of ritual than either Catholic communion or cannibalistic frenzy. In "Ithaca," the "unsubstantial lunch" is linked, parenthetically, to the "rite of Melchisedek" (17.2047). Melchisedek is the archetypal priest of the Old Testament.[13] Ransacking various possible identificatory roles for himself, Bloom casts himself as a Jewish priest, engaging in a rite different from both the transubstantiation of the host in the Eucharist and the nontransubstantiation of the food in the Burton.

The cheese and wine he eats represent a kinder, gentler form of organic breakdown, the chemical process of fermentation:

> Wine soaked and softened rolled pith of bread mustard a moment mawkish cheese. Nice wine it is. Taste it better because I'm not thirsty. Bath of course does that. Just a bite or two. Then about six o'clock I can. Six. Six. Time will be gone then. She.
>
> Mild fire of wine kindled in his veins. I wanted that badly. (8.850–54)

The wine Bloom drinks is distinctly *not* the symbol of the blood of Christ, not, that is, the idealization of the divine body. It is a fermented drink that liquefies the bodies of food so that they achieve a consubstantiality. Furthermore, this is food that mixes rather than separates according to strict dietary code. Parts of speech liquefy in imitation of the process of transcorporeality occurring in Bloom's mouth, as he tongues the soft pulpy mixture. No brutal mastication, this softening in the mouth replaces force with enzymatic transformation. This image of satisfaction, represented in a kind of indolence of the lotus-eaters sort, fills up Bloom *and* the time it takes for Boylan to make his way to Molly: this "glowing wine on his palate lingered swallowed" (8.897). This image of ingestion links fermentation with the very action of memory: "Glowing wine on his palate lingered swallowed. Crushing in the winepress grapes of Burgundy. Sun's heat it is. Seems to a secret touch telling me memory. Touched his sense moistened remembered" (8.897–99). The present pulpy mixture evokes the remains of an earlier day. A ripening ("Sun's heat it is"), a pressure ("Crushing in the winepress grapes"), a liquefaction, produce a pulp fiction in the brain, a sweet, moist memory, different from Molly's brand of pulp fiction, her "sweets of sin." Bloom's senses are lubricated; a softening and yielding in his brain produces Molly herself and her seedcake, the metonymy for Molly as mollification.

> Softly she gave me in my mouth the seedcake warm and chewed. Mawkish pulp her mouth had mumbled sweetsour of her spittle. Joy: I ate it: joy. Young life,

> her lips that gave me pouting. Soft warm sticky gumjelly lips. . . . Kissed, she kissed me. (8.907–16)[14]

It is the woman who begins the process of transformation and sexual exchange. As Frank Budgen records it, Joyce told him:

> "Fermented drink must have had a sexual origin . . . In a woman's mouth, probably. I have made Bloom eat Molly's chewed seed cake."
>
> I told [Joyce] I had just read a German book in which was described a tribal orgy on a South Sea island. The drink was prepared by the women of the tribe. They chewed a certain herb and spat the pulp into a huge crock out of which the men then drank.[15]

This is Molly's Eucharist; in the gift of the seedcake she offers her transubstantiated body ("Take, this is my body") in a sacred rite. This identification through orality does not sublimate the body in pursuit of idealism, the kind of sublimation that is troped in Bloom's thoughts of the coldness of the Greek statues in the library, who have no anuses, no holes for food to enter or exit the body, or the coldness of the nymph in the picture, *The Bath of the Nymph,* above the Blooms's conjugal bed. This Eucharist is *warm,* tasted, an already chewed body that offers an exchange of sexual eros. But it is not the gross, material body eaten in the Burton, the profaned body of matter without spirit. It is, instead, a counterpart to the Eucharist, a symbolic satiation that makes of Molly a nourishing, yet not devouring, mother. This erotic identification through the transfer of pulp from Molly's mouth to Bloom's, between her "sticky gumjelly lips," contrasts with the terrifyingly vampiric "mouth to her mouth" kiss in Stephen's poem.[16]

Yet immediately Bloom thinks, "Me. And me now," then watches two copulating flies "stuck" on the windowpane, the antithesis of the erotic moment he has just remembered. It is shortly after this that we lose Bloom's interior monologue for a while as he goes to the urinal ("Dribbling a quiet message from his bladder came to go do not to do there to do. A man and ready he drained his glass to the lees and walked" [8.933–34]). The narrative pulls back to a dialogue between Nosey Flynn and Davy Byrne about Bloom, and it is as if he were robbed of his full, richly nourished interior, metaphorically to be replaced by his own full bladder. Nosey and Davy discuss Bloom, "—I noticed he was in mourning" (8.944), Davy says; this suddenly externalized view reminds us of the fact that the moment of oral exchange is a memory only, made more vivid and painful because of the ten years that have elapsed since full carnal intercourse has occurred between the Blooms—it is, indeed, a kind of mourning for a love already lost. The constant pressure of Molly's impending adultery and the reminder of the Blooms's less than full carnal relationship reveal the "incertitude and evasion of the love object," as Kristeva puts it in another context.[17] The tone of the chapter is indeed elegiac—"I was happier then. Or was that I?" (8.608).

Despite the numerous feedings and eatings in which Bloom participates in the chapter, his yearnings go unsatisfied, a sense of the mourning of his lost self and love pervades. This memory of amorous communion, so vividly *re-presented* (and also remembered in Molly's monologue), captures the elegaic quality of the sacrament of the Eucharist—a ritual that, through iteration, attempts to conserve an essence (the love of Christ), that simultaneously preserves the full sense of the loss of that love object. If Christ's sacrament is one way of getting at the problem of identification through incorporation, Molly's pulp fiction provides an alternative image of communion not constructed in the carno-phallogocentric mode, a communion culminating in the substance of Molly's words incorporated, as it were, on the final pages of *Ulysses*.

The mollification of the seedcake stands as the symbol of the fluidity and liquidity of identifications that mark Joyce's text. By thematizing and enacting moments of oral assimilation, present and remembered, the "Lestrygonians" chapter focuses our attention on the way in which texts are transubstantiations, marriages of body and meaning. Dominated by the "subjective" senses of taste and smell, "Lestrygonians" is, at the same time, one of the most metatextual of chapters, for it reminds us of the process of identification through assimilation that underwrites all fiction and the superfluidity of such identifications that marks Joyce's protean *Ulysses*.

9

The Perils of Masculinity in "Scylla and Charybdis"

JOSEPH VALENTE

James Joyce once pronounced the Scylla and Charybdis episode of *The Odyssey* a "splendid parable."[1] Taking him at his word, one might begin by noting that the generic essence of a parable lies in the exceptionally elastic simplicity of its symbolic valences, its surprising receptivity to conceptual translation. A newly en-gendered perspective on Joyce's own "Scylla and Charybdis," accordingly, might well proceed first by detailing how the Homeric original allegorizes a certain double bind in the masculine subject-position of its hero and then by examining Joyce's conceptual translation of this double bind, in light of the revised social condition of its operation.

Under patriarchy in its classical form, a man's place in the world takes its shape and so its limits in accordance with a regime of familial status and relations, alliance and filiation, beginning of course with the sexual division itself. This regime, in turn, functions to articulate social ties in such a way as to reserve the earmarks of subjectivity proper—autonomy, agency, authority—almost exclusively to men and, conversely, to make the exercise or proof of these endowments the very test of manliness: it defines masculinity as a position of relative transcendence and takes such transcendence as the insignia of masculinity. But inasmuch as any gender position remains strictly circumscribed by the social order, and is indeed the mark of this social inscription, a man can only journey toward transcendence by a negative road, through an experience of and an accession to his own gendered limitation or lack. This is also to say that such transcendence, the ostensible destiny of manhood, can be simulated or claimed but never actually achieved. Herein, then, lies the classical impasse in the assumption of the masculine subject-position: one's limiting inscription in the social must be accepted, but with an eye to its ultimate refusal; one's transcendence of the social must be attained through failure. Having been thus summoned to authenticate and vindicate his place in the world by a path which appears to question or undermine it, a classical hero typically undergoes a crisis of identification, a sense of disjunction between who he is and who he is called to be, which is precisely the effect of the contradictory mandates enjoined upon him. This double bind, in which a man attains to superordinate potency of various kinds by submitting to the symbolic order that underwrites such potency, is otherwise known as the law of castration.

At the outset of this essay, we will see the Scylla and Charybdis episode of Homer's *Odyssey*—the passage Odysseus navigates, the decisions he makes, the losses he accepts—as an allegory of this law of castration. It is in this incident that Odysseus must acknowledge and assent to his lack as an adventuring hero in order to become the hero of the *nostos* or homecoming, a man of all dimensions. The sanguinary nature of that homecoming, however, speaks to the insolubility of the classical impasse of manhood, the need for some sort of phallic overcompensation—ultimately embodied in the son—to cover up or re-dress the permanent deficit that castration entails.

The psychoanalytic conjunction of the law of castration with the law of oedipal desire testifies to an important shift in the nineteenth-century construction of gender—and specifically masculine—positionality.[2] As Michel Foucault has famously argued, the categories of sexuality, having previously been attached to actions or practices, were now seen as constitutive ingredients, and often the innermost, essential ingredients of one's social being.[3] In the process, the classical impasse of male gender identity was subsumed within the more complex modern impasse of male *sexual* identity. The delimitation of a masculine gender position, in which the will to transcendence waits upon the assent to castration, could no longer be disentangled from the dynamics of male sexual desire, its solicitation, expression, and regulation. That is to say, as an essential component of male identity, sexual desire becomes a direct stake in the dialectical interchange of castration and transcendence. On the one hand, a masculine gender identity can only be assumed by recognizing and accepting certain interdictions upon sexual desire, by renouncing certain aims and objects, modes and pleasures in favor of others. On the other hand, given the defining mandate of masculinity—to achieve transcendence—such sexual prohibitions necessarily operate as provocations as well, incitements to take control over the aims, objects, and pleasures forfeited in castration. The masculine sense of agency, autonomy, and authority thus finds itself simultaneously enhanced and compromised: perverse attachments—attachments formed at variance with one's place in the sex/gender system—are at once subliminally, even structurally, induced, and outwardly often violently sanctioned. Instead of a straightforward crisis of identification, then, the modern impasse of masculinity implies an ongoing crisis of ambivalence, in which the subject is impelled to transgressive desires even as he dreads, repudiates, and abjects them as a violation of his own sense of self.

During the same period in which individual identity was fundamentally sexualized, homosexuality became, in Foucault's words, "a species" of being, constituted discursively as "a certain way of inverting the masculine and feminine in oneself . . . a kind of interior androgyny, a hermaphrodism of the soul"—what was generally called sexual/gender inversion.[4] This historical coincidence was no mere accident. The modern impasse of masculinity, in which sexual desire itself becomes the focus of the law of castration, was enlisted from the start as a policing mechanism of compulsory heterosexuality, with homosexuality being defined as *the* affectional mode that must be forfeited if one is to avoid effeminacy and secure one's manhood. At the same time, this structure of heterosexist enforcement entails a fetishism of manhood as *the* transcendent state or property, and so demands a deep investment in masculinity that is itself implicitly homoerotic. Under such a dispensation, the crisis of ambivalence characteristic of the modern impasse of masculinity centers on the relationship between identification and desire, the will to be and the will to have. On the face of things, a man is called upon to want to have only that which he is not, his sexual "other," to oppose strictly his erotic desire and his identification. That is, in effect, the heterosexual imperative. But this imperative also entails wanting to have, eroticizing if you will, the *sexual* identity that one is called upon to be, and wanting to be at one with the sexual other that one is called upon to have: it entails conflating identification and desire from either end. That is the very condition of the heterosexual imperative, and is also the condition of its impossibility. The result of this (re)double(d) bind, a bind of gender and sexuality, is an irresoluble masculine anxiety, which often takes the form of what Eve Sedgwick calls "homosexual panic."[5] The anatomy of this anxiety and this panic is very much the subject of Joyce's rendition of "Scylla and Charybdis."

Joyce inscribes the conceptual border that joins and separates Homer's classical parable of besieged masculinity and his own modern translation across the fissure joining and separating Stephen's theory of Shakespeare and the extensive narrative context of its production. This splitting of the theoretical statement and its enunciative context is a direct function of Stephen's own psychical resistances, the changing deployment of which give the chapter as a whole its structure. In the theory itself, Stephen represents Shakespeare, his idealized aesthetic father, as undergoing a crisis of masculinity which, despite its sexual origins, appears to retain the basic contour of the classical Odyssean impasse: emasculation, overcompensation, (father/son) identification, (failed) transcendence. In drawing this portrait, however, Stephen omits the rumors and historical evidence of Shakespeare's homosexual affections, a complicating issue that slips to the surface, tellingly enough, in Stephen's account of the bard's identification with his son. At this point, as the entr'acte approaches, the sexual ambivalence that Stephen has been repressing and displacing in his theoretical discourse suddenly confronts him in the person of Buck Mulligan, whose very presence has two correlative effects: his presence brings the question of homosexuality to the fore, in a predominantly phobic light, and it broaches the larger narrative context in which Stephen's aesthetic interest in Shakespeare is shown to involve

Stephen's own decidedly modern impasse of masculinity, a double bind of (male) gender identification and (homo)erotic desire. To defend against this traumatic intrusion of his own unacknowledged anxiety, Stephen compulsively repeats his theoretical performance in another, more "panicky," key, elaborating new strategies for refusing what he can no longer repress.

A SPLENDID PARABLE

In order to return to his homeland and resume that dense cluster of distinctly masculine attachments which caused Joyce to nominate him "the complete man of literature,"[6] Odysseus must negotiate the monumental double bind of Scylla and Charybdis, the gendered outlines of which anticipate the topographical symbolism of *Finnegans Wake.* Although the monsters are both nominally female, their respective aspects differ along sexual lines. The more purely feminized construction, Charybdis constitutes a "whirling maelstrom," hidden by a "shaggy mass of leaves." Scylla features a set of similarly engorging maws, but also a set of patently phallic tentacles. She occupies a gynemorphic "cavern," but it is lodged within a "sharp" phallomorphic rock.[7]

The relevance of this asymmetry becomes salient when one considers Circe's admonition that Odysseus decline the temptation to pilot his ship by way of the seemingly passable Charybdis, who in fact threatens total destruction, and instead "hug the cliff of Scylla," who will surely remove a portion of his crew as a toll.[8] Now, since the objective of his voyage is to regain not just his homeland but also the prerogatives to his paternal and royal status, the figuration of Circe's challenge resonates of a rite of passage, a symbolic recapitulation of the assumption of a male subject position. On this reading, Charybdis allegorizes an extension of the presymbolic mother, offering apparent security that is the stillbirth of subjectivity proper. Scylla is an emblem of *achieved* oedipal separation—of child from mother and male from female—a mytheme of the passage to sexual difference. The lethal price of this passage, the loss of a part of the ship's crew, tropes on a collective scale the normative resolution of the male separation crisis in the acceptance of castration, the effect of lack attendant to a subject position delimited by exclusion. The disappearance of a body (part), particularly its ingestion by a terrible mother, is a paradigmatic castration fantasy, and Scylla actually heralds her incorporative practice by simulating the anguished shrieks of the mutilated men as the wailing of a child ("a newborn whelp's cry"). The effect upon Odysseus himself is, aptly enough, one of self-division: his subjectivity appears to split between the masculinized imperative to "invoke Blind Force" and an explicitly feminized attitude of helpless sympathy for those sacrificed—"deathly pity ran me through."[9]

It is important to observe why Odysseus initially resists Circe's advice and begs her to reveal some means of preserving intact the expedition, itself a phantasmatic extension of his own idealized identity as a great adventurer. Circe's response evinces the psychic stakes involved in Odysseus's symbolic castration:

"will you not yield to immortal gods? / . . . there is no fighting [the nightmare] . . . / All that avails is flight."[10] The need to accept, in flight, the divinely ordained loss of his men, a part of his crew, evidently correlates with a loss of his martially informed sense of manhood, a key aspect of his self-image as warrior-king. Put another way, Odysseus regards surrender to the symbolic law that enshrines the masculine values of conquest and mastery (the will of the "immortal gods") as paradoxically entailing a betrayal of the values so enshrined. This law, of course, is nothing other than what we are calling the law of castration, in which a submission to lack or limitation is the irrevocable toll to be paid for the promise of transcendence.

The paradox that Odysseus confronts in crossing Scylla and Charybdis can be seen to shape the whole arc of Odysseus's journey, where its relevance to the phallocentric construction of gender at large becomes clear. Odysseus can return to recover his estate as the complete private and public man only insofar as he assumes his irrevocable *in*completeness, acquiesces in the necessity of a course that he deems unheroic and, strangely enough, only insofar as he agrees to default on his particular symbolic mandate—as leader, captain, king—in deference to the patriarchal law itself. He thus comes to embody the perfection of classical male subjectivity as constituted in and by lack or deficit. And in a reflexive paradox, this lack or deficit must, as a condition of his distressed perfection, be persistently disavowed—displayed as his own and denied as other, excluded, "feminine."

Odysseus's arrival in Ithaca dramatizes the latter paradox quite precisely. Because lack defines Odysseus's (gendered) place in the symbolic, the restoration of which is his ruling passion, that lack must be displayed in some manner to identify him as the rightful (re)possessor of his kingdom. That is why he is first recognized by a positively overdetermined signifier of symbolic castration: the scar on his thigh from a wound that a white boar's tusk inflicted upon him during a visit to his mother's father, *who had given him the name Odysseus.* Yet because lack defines Odysseus's place in the symbolic, his desire for complete restoration cannot but be frustrated in its very fulfillment. Far from returning him to a fully consolidated masculine identity, his success can only intimate the impossibility of such a consummation. As a result, Odysseus must also contrive to deny this constitutive lack or deficit in the (futile) attempt to re-dress it. That explains the extreme brutality and bloodlust of his triumph over the suitors, which seems wildly discordant with the tone of both the poem and its hero. His triumph represents a barbarous moment of phallic overcompensation, an excess of manliness answering to and glossing over the lack *in* manliness. Indeed, Odysseus finally stays his hand only at the behest of Telemachus, whose timely plea for Medon's life serves to signal a general end to the carnage and a renewal of Odysseus's long interrupted familial and political authority. Thus, in a narrative turn that exemplifies Stephen's Shakespeare thesis *avant le lettre,* the figure of the son here functions as the privileged agent of reparation for the father's "lost" or vitiated manhood.

MR. WILLIAM HIMSELF, W. H.

Until the entr'acte, Stephen's bio-historical view of Shakespeare plays itself out as a fairly recognizable conceptual translation of Homer's masculine double bind. The initial resistance offered by his interlocutors establishes the Charybdian pole in this reconstruction of Shakespeare. A. E. objects first, in the name of an implicitly masculinist aesthetics of transcendence.

> All these questions are purely academic. . . . Art has to reveal to us ideas, formless spiritual essences. The supreme question about a work of art is out of how deep a life does it spring. The painting of Gustave Moreau is the painting of ideas. The deepest poetry of Shelley, the words of Hamlet bring our minds into contact with the eternal wisdom, Plato's world of ideas. (9.46–53)

In dismissing the significance of historical inscription, A. E. not only aligns art with the dominant values of the patriarchal code—separation, stratification, mastery—he treats the person of the artist, the presumptively male artist, as their virtual incarnation, a "deep" yet uncircumstanced "life" bearing the "wisdom" of "Plato's world of ideas." Like Odysseus importuning Circe, A. E. seeks to forestall the necessity of castration, to preserve the creative man complete and unimpaired by contingency. His masculinist aesthetics of transcendence is at the same time an aesthetics of transcendent masculinity.

A subsequent demurral evidences as much. When Stephen broaches the importance of "Ann Shakespeare, born Hathaway" (9.180) to Shakespeare's literary production, Russell responds,

> —But this prying into the family life of a great man. . . . Interesting only to the parish clerk. I mean, we have the plays. . . . what is it to us how the poet lived? As for living, our servants can do that for us. . . . Peeping and prying into greenroom gossip of the day. . . . We have *King Lear:* and it is immortal. (9.181–88)

In an elaboration on the hoary male/mind, female/body dichotomy, A. E. identifies properly aesthetic endeavor, aristocratic and "immortal," with the masculinized public sphere of the impersonal "we," and he identifies the material conditions and engagements he would dismiss with the female-identified private sphere of transitory gossip and domestic service. It is in the defense of this gender hierarchy that Russell rejects Stephen's critical approach. Unconsciously, he is less bothered that Stephen historicizes Shakespeare, reducing him from aesthetic transcendence to personal travail, than that he thereby feminizes Shakespeare as well, upsetting Russell's sexual division of labor and authority. Indeed, Russell's ally in the debate, John Eglinton, seems to sense what is at stake in the above diatribe, for he immediately intercedes to ratify this gender division from the other side, by categorically excluding the bard's wife from the empyrean of art: "Her ghost at least has been laid for ever. She died, for literature at least, before she was born" (9.215–16). With this assertion, Eglinton comes close to baring the masculinist device. For while he and Russell seem set on idealizing Shakespeare the dramatist at the expense of Shakespeare the man, they are covertly idealizing Shakespeare's art as a distinctively male triumph over the feminized cycle of mortality, the ultimate castration, here telescoped in the posthumous birth of (a) woman.

Stephen sees the pair's ultra-Platonic aesthetics (not just essential spiritual forms but "formless spiritual essences") as bound up with their theosophical mysticism. Each involves the regressive pursuit of an imaginary oneness, a state of plenitude before or beyond the bodily inscription of sex, and thus each ultimately tends toward a collapse of the symbolic order and, with it, the very possibility of verbal articulation. Stephen not only images this incoherence as an engorging vortex spun out of control, he strikes a close conceptual analogy between the path of Charybdis, as I have been reading it, and the intellectual and imaginative course chosen by his adversaries: "Filled with his god, he thrones, Buddh under plantain. Gulfer of souls, engulfer. Hesouls, shesouls, shoals of souls. Engulfed with wailing creecries, whirled, whirling, they bewail" (9.284–86). As in Homer, Charybdis tempts to security and escape, in this case the security of disembodied self-possession, an escape from gender division, but only to inflict outright destruction, in this case the disintegration of selfhood per se. The context of Stephen's meditation suggests that the same Charybdian (il)logic applies to Russell and Eglinton's vision of Shakespeare. Their attempt to enshrine the playwright in the hypermasculine sublime can only reduce him to a construct of gender indifference, placing him beyond the very lack or deficit which, as Homer's parable shows, is constitutive of masculine identity.

Stephen's less gynephobic (but no less phallocentric) interpretation of Shakespeare likewise interconnects the latter's assumption of masculine subjectivity with his achievement of literary greatness. But Stephen expressly posits Shakespeare's experience of symbolic castration as their *tertium quid,* their joint condition of possibility and the site of their mediation. He "gained the world of men" (9.254) and the laurels of dramatic fame by "hug[ging] the cliff of Scylla." Indeed, Stephen seems to have designed Shakespeare's personal Scylla, Anne Hathaway, as a miniaturized version of the archetype. Where Scylla's rock is phallomorphic, Anne is phallic in the sense of sexually aggressive ("stooping to conquer . . . a boldfaced Stratford wench" [9.259–60]); where Scylla is "monstrous," Anne is unattractive ("the ugliest doxy in all Warwickshire" [9.253]); where Scylla is "eternal evil itself," Anne is a nasty older woman; where Scylla is cannibalistic, Anne is castrating ("By cock, she was to blame" [9.257]). With an anachronistic flourish, Stephen even manages to identify Anne with Scylla's terrible mother role: "She saw him into and out of the world" (9.217–18). His purpose in crafting these negative parallelisms is to underscore an originally Homeric insight. A man's development or accomplishment is animated by a desire to re-cover the lack or deficit left by the exclusions determining his place in the patriarchal symbolic, so that some traumatic experience of dispossession provides a necessary spur to that recovery and development. For Shakespeare, as for Odysseus, "loss is his gain" (9.476).

But insofar as these primordial exclusions operate through maternal separation and gender division, and insofar as the resulting lack is figured as feminine, women constitute a privileged vehicle of this traumatic yet productive recognition. Thus Anne Hathaway performs the same androcentric function in Stephen's theory that Scylla allegorizes in Homer's epic. She affords the site of negation required for male self-overcoming. Stephen all but says so. When Eglinton smugly opines that "A shrew . . . is not the most useful portal of discovery, one should imagine," Stephen counters with the informing principle of his whole theory, "Dialectic" (9.232–36), thereby suggesting a colonizing dynamic in which women provide the lived resistance necessary to ground the circuit of overweening male enterprise and thus the energetic tension necessary to drive it.[11] In Stephen's model, women obstruct male genius, but only to enable it, and so they always turn out to be "errors . . . volitional" in the end (9.229). In other words, Stephen's theory, like Russell's, presupposes an ontology of gender wherein men bear the potential for cognitive transcendence, what Stephen later calls "the intellectual imagination" (15.4226), and women embody the countervailing force of material immanence. The difference is that by Stephen's lights a man compasses the *summum bonum* of transcendence only by undergoing the abjected state of feminization, for only a traumatic encounter with the instability of his fundamental social determination can impel him to realize his gendered potential, to re-cover his identity at all costs. For Stephen, the risk of suffering, if not yet engaging, gender difference has become indispensable to intellectual endeavor. The separatist alternative, he suggests, results in mental masturbation: "Unwed, unfancied, ware of wiles, they fingerponder nightly each of his variorum edition of *The Taming of the Shrew*" (9.1062–63). His own urgency to be seduced as Shakespeare was, even at the price of emasculation ("And my turn? When? / Come!" [9.261–62]), thus comprises an artistic as well as a sexual component, a hope that such an event might leave galvanizing scars on his imagination.

But the Scyllan course that Stephen charts in Shakespeare's life, and plots for his own, neither points toward nor terminates in the male artist's creative recuperation of his "feminine side," as Froula's recent quasi-Jungian readings have proposed.[12] On the contrary, the very idea of inner gender selves, as opposed to interactive gender positions, is ridiculed outright in Stephen's parody of theosophism ("Hesouls, shesouls, shoal of souls"). Moreover, Stephen never portrays Shakespeare as owning the feminine "in himself" or as experiencing the feminine as anything other than internalized trauma. That is why, as Stephen says, Shakespeare's feminization at the hands of Anne Hathaway did not assist him in fashioning credible female characters, but rather led him to leave a recognizably masculine impress upon them, a simultaneously defensive and appropriative signature: "Good: he left her and gained the world of men. But his boywomen are the women of a boy. Their life, thought, speech are lent them by males. He chose badly? He was chosen, it seems to me. If others have their will Ann hath a way" (9.254–57). Far from putting Will in contact with his feminine side, Anne's initial dispossession of his phallic sense of manhood only drives him to extend and intensify its expression. Anne plays the role of Scylla in Stephen's theory precisely in sending Will "home," to take up his entitled place in the sex/gender system.

A series of *positive* parallels between Shakespeare and Odysseus work to underscore *this* Homeric intertext. Indeed, Shakespeare emerges from Stephen's account as a kind of intellectual correlative to Odysseus's active heroism—a "myriadminded man," polytropic in his self-projections, replacing martial with aesthetic prowess. For Shakespeare, as for Odysseus, symbolic castration poses an impossible task of self-reclamation, in which success itself merely testifies to the lack compelling it: "he will never be a victor in his own eyes after nor play victoriously the game of laugh and lie down. Assumed dongiovannism will not save him. No later undoing will undo the first undoing" (9.457–59). This double bind provokes in Shakespeare, as it does in Odysseus, a correspondingly ambivalent response, a disavowal—display/denial—of castration.

On the one hand, aesthetic self-expression for Shakespeare entails the compulsive, coded display of his own mark of symbolic castration; his sense of identity, like that of Odysseus, is bound up with a particular form of social limitation or lack. To illustrate as much, Stephen adduces Shakespeare's famous romance, *Venus and Adonis,* in which his mythic alterego, Adonis, receives a mark of castration that closely matches that of Odysseus: "The tusk of the boar has wounded him there where love lies ableeding" (9.459–60). Only this time the responsible party is Venus herself, the mythic alterego of Anne Hathaway. On the other hand, the act of aesthetic self-expression becomes Shakespeare's method of denying his castration, of achieving a phantasmatic transcendence that devotees like Russell and Eglinton take as real. That is to say, Shakespeare's art, like Odysseus's warfare, manifests the sort of phallic overcompensation that the world calls greatness.[13] Instead of a (martial) show of mastery, Shakespeare dissimulates his lack in a mastery of the (dramatic) show. Moreover, like Odysseus, he does so in a doomed effort at fully re-covering his phallic self-image, an effort which Stephen, following Homer, narrativizes as a nostos: "He goes back, weary of the creation he has piled up to hide him from himself, an old dog licking an old sore. But, because loss is his gain, he passes on towards eternity in undiminished personality, untaught by the wisdom he has written or by the laws he has revealed" (9.474–78). Stephen punctuates this peroration, and the first act of the episode, with the crowning Shakespeare-Odysseus parallel, locating the final "haunt" of the playwright's masculine anxiety in "the heart of him who is the substance of his shadow, the son consubstantial with the father" (9.480–81). Having left home owing to Anne's emasculating forwardness, Shakespeare becomes a ghost through "absence," the absence left by symbolic castration. He then immortalizes his deceased son in *Hamlet* so that he may be to Shakespeare what Telemachus is to Odysseus: the ultimate compensatory agent of the father's damaged phallic authority and a vindicating witness against his enemies (the faithless wife/brothers, the treacherous subjects/suitors). Through the symbolic power of the son, Shakespeare's denial of castration passes into something like "resolution," as it does for Odysseus. Moreover, as the very image of masculine self-renewal achieved via passage through the feminine, this "consubstantial" son represents the culmination of Stephen's colonizing theory of (male) literary eminence.

To this point, however, there is in Stephen's account a duality, not to say duplicity, which encodes the powerfully defensive relation that binds Stephen's conscious discourse and his unconscious desire. The "primal [Shake]scene" of his narrative, in which Shakespeare's "belief in himself [was] untimely killed" (9.455–56), clearly engages what I have been calling the modern impasse of masculinity. The formative crisis in Shakespeare's gender identity is profoundly embedded in the problematics of erotic desire and ambivalence; and it is on these terms that Shakespeare *displays* his castration in a poem like *Venus and Adonis.* Yet Stephen nonetheless struggles to conceptualize Shakespeare's negotiation and resolution of this crisis primarily in the classical terms outlined above—castration pointing to transcendence by way of phallic overcompensation and paternal identification; and it is on these terms that Shakespeare *denies* his castration in a play like *Hamlet.* Through this economy of disavowal, Stephen's first walk through Shakespeare's career manages to sidestep its more perverse psychosexual aspects in favor of a normative patriarchal scenario in which the father finally secures his place in the symbolic order through the transmission of his name and authority—his "Will" in sum—to his son and heir. But in order to safeguard his investment in this patrilineal narrative, however, Stephen must elide or suppress both historical evidence and logical inference that would demand a more variably or complexly sexual analysis.

As the entr'acte approaches, however, the repressed begins to surface in a moment of symptomatic incoherence, setting the stage for its more dramatic return in act 2, with the appearance of Buck Mulligan. Eglinton has adduced the "spirit of reconciliation" (9.396) in Shakespeare's later plays to counter the genealogy of personal bitterness and marital treachery that Stephen has been tracing in *Hamlet.* Stephen turns the tables by citing the recurrent *vehicle* of this reconciliation, the figure of the daughter, as evidence of a previous rupture between husband and wife: "Will any man love the daughter if he has not loved the mother? . . . Will he not see reborn in her, with the memory of his own youth added, another image?" (9.423–28). This is probably Stephen's most effective pass in the verbal duel. But then he appends the sort of tangential and rhetorically vexed comment in which the unconscious typically encodes its messages: "—His own image to a man with that queer thing genius is the standard of all experience, material and moral. Such an appeal will touch him. The images of other males of his blood will repel him. He will see in them grotesque attempts of nature to foretell or to repeat himself" (9.432–35). Not only does this proposition do nothing to bolster Stephen's immediate argument, it controverts the general run of his thesis so far, which centers on the identification of embattled fathers with their deputized sons. Having proposed the son as the direct and therefore surpassing object of paternal alliance, Stephen suddenly withdraws the son as an overly direct and therefore troublesome object of paternal self-projection.

What is at stake in this about-face is precisely an unacknowledged shift from the classical to the modern impasse of masculinity, in which the task of assuring and aggrandizing one's place in the world becomes profoundly eroticized. The key conceptual index of this shift is the modern, psychoanalytic construct of auto-affection, what Freud terms "primary narcissism," which names the earliest phase of human psychic development, wherein the erotic investment of the infant in his own body lays the groundwork for both the assumption of a self-identity and the extension of desire outward to another.[14] Thus construed as the fundamental psychic estate—the common origin that galvanizes and binds together ego development and object-love—primary narcissism imports that *all varieties of personal identity are at bottom elaborations of sexual identity.* But not just any sexual identity. As Colleen Lamos has compellingly argued, the "mingling" of identification with erotic desire, "what a man wants to be and what he wants to have," is precisely "what is forbidden under the rule of normative heterosexuality."[15] In making the image of the self, a same-sexed image obviously, the primary object of erotic investment, narcissism has always already broken with the heterosexual regime to which it remains nonetheless fundamental. With this in mind, the clichéd and invidious ascription of narcissistic tendencies to avowed homosexuals can be seen as the "reverse discourse" of compulsory heterosexuality,[16] designed to disavow the homoerotic component of the primary narcissism which grounds *all* sexual expression. The bourgeois discursive register outlaws homoeroticism as the chief menace to its narrowly procreative sexual norms only to install homoeroticism as a necessary condition of that norm.[17] Thus, the modern psychodrama of masculine gender identification cannot but draw upon homoerotic energies that are officially abjected as unmanly.

If we return to the paternal genius of Stephen's fancy, we can see this logic in action. A confirmed narcissist, Stephen's man of genius not only posits his own self-image as "the standard of all experience" (9.432–33), but finds that universal image to be threatened by the proximateness (likeness/nearness) of his own male issue. And he experiences this filial encroachment, this identificatory menace, in powerfully if aversively sexual terms: not as pique or anxiety, but as a repulsion of the "blood," an eroticized phobia. The nature of his aversion, in turn, lends Stephen's citation of the phrase "that queer thing genius" (9.433) an unlooked-for resonance, activating the sexual ambiguity that had come to hover about the word "queer" during the preceding decade.[18] Understood as a narcissistic effect, the "queerness" of genius bears an implicitly sexual dimension.

Thomas Lyster seizes immediately upon these homoerotic undertones of Stephen's anatomy of genius. Dedalus no sooner concludes than the librarian introduces, seemingly from nowhere, the running debate over the nature of Shakespeare's relationship with William Herbert—whether it took the form of affectionate quasi-paternal identification or sexual passion. Lyster himself splits the difference and situates the connection safely within the zone of fraternal/homosocial affinity and heterosexual rivalry: "if the poet must be rejected such a rejection would seem to be more in harmony with—what shall I say?—our notion of what ought not to have been" (9.443–45). Nevertheless, the timing and substance of Lyster's remarks suggest that Stephen's shift of register has suddenly made accessible the very aspect of the Shakespeare legend that his theory had quietly occluded.[19] Seizing no less directly upon the implication of Lyster's comment, Stephen smartly returns to his earlier narrative focus. He embraces Harris's fraternalistic model—"that may be too" (9.450)—and traces the "unhappy relation" in the sonnets to the bard's unmanning at the hands of Anne Hathaway: "Why does he send . . . a lordling to woo for him? . . . Why? Belief in himself has been untimely killed. He was overborne in a cornfield. . . . No later undoing will undo the first undoing" (9.452–59). This irreversible castration, in turn, sets the stage for a real fraternal rivalry and betrayal, the cuckolding of Shakespeare by his brothers; and it is as recompense for this dual aspect of the family romance that Stephen envisages a positive interfusion of father and son through the medium of the word: "But, because loss is his gain, he passes on towards eternity in undiminished personality. . . . He is a ghost . . . a voice heard only in the heart of him who is the substance of his shadow, the son consubstantial with the father" (9.476–81). By this ventriloquism of the soul, the artist's masculine authority is reasserted in his patrilineal descent.

With the triumphal father-son resolution, however, Stephen's theory not only reaches its preordained climax (a newly arrived Buck Mulligan intones "Amen" [9.482]), but also discloses its central knot of contradictions. On the one hand, the girl child emerges as the figure of "reconciliation" for the paternal genius—"the lost [object] . . . given back to him" (9.422)—largely because the images of his male kin seem "grotesque attempts on the part of nature to foretell or to repeat himself" (9.435). On the other hand, just such a "repetition," the son consubstantial with the father, will serve as a vehicle for assuring that "loss is his gain," that the formative castration of the paternal genius will be redeemed in the end. On the one hand, the prospect of this profoundly intimate at-onement must "repel" the paternal genius, exacerbating his eroticized dread at the proximity of the filial image. On the other hand, the emblematic instance of such genius, Shakespeare, enshrines this "grotesque" intimacy for all time in the dramatic action of *Hamlet*. The son functions as a *pure* object of paternal identification, renovating the artist's masculinized self-definition; but the son also functions as an *eroticized* object of identification, disturbing that self-definition and the terms on which it is predicated. As a pure object of identification, the father-son tie poses as an antidote to the fraternal rivalry that proceeds from the homosocial exchange of women; as an eroticized gender identification, it threatens to reveal the homosexual stirrings in such rivalry and exchange.

These overlapping contradictions describe an insurmountable double bind at the heart of Stephen's dialectic of aesthetic mastery: the bonding of the paternal artist with his "son and heir" (6.43) indemnifies him in his necessary passage through heterosexual emasculation and thus restores his claim to a virility that is at once personal and cultural, sexual and aesthetic; but it can only do so at the risk of implicating him in a powerful homoerotic attachment to his "son and heir" and thus vitiating this claim to virility along other lines. This risk is an irreducible aspect of Stephen's theory. It can be embraced and celebrated or phobically occulted and deferred, as it is here, but it cannot be blinked away.[20]

But plenary father-son identification is but one side of the oedipal dynamic with the power to arouse homosexual panic in Stephen. As I have demonstrated elsewhere, the dominant and more urgent source of Stephen's panic corresponds with the dominant cultural and scientific model of homosexuality at the time. I am speaking, of course, of sexual/gender inversion. Stephen's own inversion anxiety stems from his deeply ambivalent identification with his *mother,* which her death has intensified.[21] Indeed, Stephen's failure to recognize, under the camouflage of negation, the homoerotic resonances of the father-son bond answers to the pressure exerted on his discourse by this other, maternally identified sexual anxiety. By turning now to the effects of this pressure upon Stephen's theory, we will be able to establish the contours of Stephen's ideological predicament, to which this *same form of negation* proves his ultimate, and ultimately self-defeating, solution.

ENTR'ACTE; OR S. D.: *SUA DONNA*

If incoherence is the price Stephen pays for shying away from the homoerotic dimension of Shakespeare's life and emblematic paternity, then what are the underlying stakes of this evasion? Why does Stephen sidestep an issue so obviously pertinent to his effort to locate Shakespeare's personal gender insecurities in his celebrated aesthetic achievements? Why in his negotiation of this Renaissance life does the classical impasse of masculinity overshadow the modern? A brief examination of these questions not only reveals how Stephen's own sexual insecurities haunt his critical performance, but also how these insecurities ultimately flow from the impossibility of an unalloyed heterosexuality.

Stephen is primarily interested in plotting a genealogy of Shakespeare's creative prowess that can serve as a paradigm for his prospective development as an artist. To this end, the masculine trauma he assigns Shakespeare not only objectifies and displaces his own profound sexual anxieties, it augurs their eventual transubstantiation on the altar of poetic invention: "loss is [Shakespeare's] gain" so that Stephen's present anomie might count as his future potential. Indeed, the explicit burden of Stephen's argument goes directly to his motive in making it.

He holds Shakespeare's public literary production to have been irritated into existence, like so many pearls, by the author's private agonies over the nature and status of his psychosocial identity, manifest in everything from a concern with his "fair name" (9.921) to an obsessive sense of property over "what he calls his debts" and "whom he calls his wife" (9.788–90). In this respect, anyway, Stephen's evaluation of the bard is almost entirely self-reflexive. He volubly confesses his own self-doubts in Shakespeare's name.

But by the same logic, his conspicuous omission, to this point, of the question of Shakespeare's feelings for W. H., his resistance to factoring the importance of homosexual love into the self-reflexive confines of his theory, would seem to bespeak still deeper doubts and anxieties about his own erotic economy and, by ideological extension, his masculinity. Moreover, insofar as what gets disclosed takes its specific gravity from what must be left undisclosed, and even unconscious—the dishonored, the taboo, that which "dare not speak its name"—it should come as no surprise that Stephen's narrative projection of one of his sexual insecurities, heterosexual emasculation, is a device for holding at bay a related and evidently more alarming one, homosexual panic, the experience of one's repressed homoerotic desires as dread at the prospect that one might harbor, signal, or attract homoerotic desire. What connects these two insecurities in Stephen's mind is a *fear of feminization*—feminization as castration on one side and as sex/gender inversion on the other.

Here again, Stephen's aesthetic analysis mimics the object it constructs. In the process of framing Shakespeare's art as a kind of socially redemptive symptom, Stephen fashions a similarly symptomatic discourse, using his loosely biographical Shakespearean narrative as a wishful restaging of his own family romance. Stephen's lecture must be understood as constituting a psychoanalytic mise en scène: a transferential drama about Shakespeare's *Hamlet* as transferential drama. In *Hamlet,* the paternal ghost enlists his son and namesake to expose the *mesalliance* of the wife/mother, thus personifying the power of fatherhood to parry the castrating effects of female sexual agency, which the play figures as death itself. In the *Hamlet* theory, correspondingly, the "eternal son" enlists a patrilineal model of aesthetic creation to parry a maternal ghost whose castrating power has been enhanced by death. Stephen's Shakespeare returns to his creation as a ghost in order to settle accounts with "the girl he left behind him"; Stephen creates this account of Shakespeare in order to exorcize the ghost of the girl who has and yet has not left him behind.

The surface of Stephen's narrative bears the mark of its transferential impetus in the muted connections that obtain between his imaginary projection of Anne Hathaway and his dream image of the ghost of May Dedalus. There is, for example, that catechresis whereby he seems to position Anne as Shakespeare's mother: "she saw him into . . . the world" (9.217–18), Stephen avers, thinking perhaps of his own mother's self-martyring pronouncements, as exemplified in "Circe." There is, moreover, a distinct trace of May's *spectral* bearing toward Stephen in Anne's *sexual* bearing toward Will: in either case, an aggressive older woman looms over the passive figure of her unmanned victim. To parrot Stephen's analytic method, "the greyeyed goddess who bends over the boy Adonis" is not only a "boldfaced Stratford wench who tumbles . . . a lover younger than herself" (9.258–60); she is also the wraith who "had come to [Stephen and] . . . bent over him with mute secret words" (1.270–72) the night before. In light of such couplings, it is easy to trace the emotional springs of Stephen's anxious paternal "dialectic" of creative mastery to his profound maternal abjection, the former being a kind of fantasy solution to the latter. Like any fantasy solution to the family romance, however, Stephen's theory about Shakespeare must not only repeat its basic terms, it must reconfigure them as well, subjecting them to significant omission and distortion.

Throughout *Portrait* and *Ulysses,* the nature of Stephen's filial bond to his mother exemplifies Julia Kristeva's specialized notion of abjection: an ambivalent eroticism, compact of desire and disgust, dependency and dread, at once emasculating and narcissistic in its refusal of any stable or solid boundaries between the psychic space of the child and its mother.[22] Stephen's self-referential aphorism, "*Amor matris,* subjective and objective genitive" (9.842–43), speaks precisely to this dyadic condition in which mother and child engage in a mutual, implicitly cross-gender identification so profound that it conflates the affections of each with the other. Abjection is sustained, in turn, owing to a crisis or failure of primal separation, where the infant assumes an emergent subject position by simultaneously excluding and eroticizing that portion of the "self" identified with the dissolving maternal dyad. As a repetition/reconfiguration of Stephen's own ongoing *"Amor matris,"* the Shakespeare narrative mystifies this infantile scenario, which the death of May Dedalus has unconsciously reactivated, by refashioning the gradually interrupted union of mother and child as the abruptly foreshortened distance between a sexual predator and her prey. With this alteration, Stephen's narrative not only disguises its personal incestuous origins, but labors to dissolve the symbiosis of eros and identification which, as we have seen, precludes full accession to compulsory heterosexuality. The surrogate mother figure, Anne Hathaway, is shown to descend upon Will as an irresistible alien force imposing her desire on him. By the lights of late Victorian/Edwardian culture, masculinity and femininity were virtually defined by their alignment with sexual activity and passivity respectively,[23] so this transaction, with Anne on top, so to speak, would count as a wholesale *gender reversal:* Shakespeare's "undoing" is tantamount to his feminization. However, it is important to note that because this feminization does not irrupt from within, as an eroticized impulse to cross-gender identification, but rather supervenes from the outside, it is not implicated in sex/gender inversion. Not being an expression of *his* innermost desire, Shakespeare's feminization is not properly a part of his (sexual) identity, and thus may be overcome, dialectically, in his art.

To be sure, cross-gender identification is an essential facet of the masculine oedipal scenario, as Freud himself finally acknowledges in his revisionist masterpiece *The Ego and the Id.*[24] But this dynamic closely approximates the condition of *sexual/gender inversion,* the reigning construction of homosexuality during the period that *Ulysses* represents. Originally defined by Ulrichs as describing "a feminine soul enclosed in a male body,"[25] the inversion paradigm was advanced not only by prominent sexologists like Symonds, Ellis, Carpenter, and Krafft-Ebing, all of whom Joyce read, but also that Viennese doctor whom Eglinton invokes on the question of Shakespeare's rumored pederasty.[26] In order to finesse the erotic confusion implicit in the oedipal scenario, Freud came to posit a universal bisexuality, which substitutes a *coexistence* of distinct sexual tendencies within the subject for the more threatening *coimplication* of these tendencies logically required by his overall theory.[27] In this manner, Freud was able to peg the resolution of the male oedipal complex to the normative intensification and election of one erotic current (desire for the mother) and one form of identification (emulation of the father) at the expense of all other alternatives or combinations. He thus salvages the oedipal complex as an explanatory clause of the heterosexual contract through a reduction, hence a denial, of its very complex-ity. Just such a denial, I would submit, informs Stephen's transferential Shakespeare narrative, the quite oedipal "resolution" of which treats Shakespeare's "castration," his unmanning, as a dialectical moment of feminine *dis*identification.

We are confronted here with the other, more powerful reservoir of Stephen's homosexual panic, the maternal counterpart to his patriarchal model of "that queer thing genius." The double bind attaching to the identificatory father-son tie redoubles itself for Stephen with respect to the erotic mother-son umbilicus. Joyce thereby points up an impasse in the circular cultural strategy of naturalizing heterosexual attraction. Just as the narcissistic basis of the father-son identification necessarily (homo)eroticizes the bond thus formed, so the narcissistic basis of Stephen's *amor matris,* with its conflation of "subjective and objective genitive" (9.843), induces a degree of cross-gender identification, which must be repudiated but cannot be eradicated. The oedipalized son cannot separate from the mother without internalizing her lost imago. Here again, a popular cliché about male homosexuals turns out to be part of the "reverse discourse" of a compulsory but deeply compromised heterosexuality, a projection of its hidden inconsistency onto its designated other. Emerging concurrently with the rise of psychoanalysis, the stereotype of the homosexual as effeminate momma's boy countersigns the law of gender disjunction by disavowing as pathological a strain of feminine identification intrinsic to the oedipal formation of masculine subjectivity. By the same token, the "scientific" concept of male gender inversion, which was selectively applied to sustain the myth of an integral heterosexual norm, would have been better understood as "gender involution," a universally applicable identity form whose correlative sexuality is never directly homo, hetero, or bi, but always hybridized, irreducibly "queer."

Whereas Stephen remains in denial about the homoerotics of paternal identification, he has always lived in dread of its maternal counterpart. This is one reason why Stephen owns his paternal likenesses ("his eyes," "his voice") while disregarding the stronger maternal resemblance detected by Bloom ("Face reminds me of his poor mother" [15.4949]).[28] Stephen's oft-remarked gynephobia, in fact, is deeply complicitous, even coextensive with his homophobia, each being interchangeably a determinant and an effect of the other.[29] As the ideological principle in which these phobias coincide, gender inversion is the key to the sexual anxieties besetting Stephen throughout *Portrait* and *Ulysses.*

In "Nestor," for example, Stephen remembers his Clongowes self as a "mother's darling . . . slightly crawsick" (2.315–16), a feminized self-image that harkens back to the scene in *Portrait* where Stephen undergoes questioning as to whether he kisses his mother before bed. His initial answer, yes, provokes immediate ridicule, presumably because it suggests his excessive, hence unmanly proximity to his mother, a sense that his inquisitor, Wells, underscores by repeating his answer with the phrase "every night" superadded (*P* 14). Stephen's revised answer, no, provokes like ridicule, presumably because it suggests his excessive, hence unnatural, distance from his mother, a sense Wells underscores by deleting the temporal marker. At one level, the interrogation and Stephen's febrile response to it ("He felt his whole body hot and confused in a moment" [*P* 14]) foreshadow his profound ambivalence toward his mother in later years. At another level, the interrogation illuminates an affective double bind attaching to the norm of heterosexual virility: since the oedipal desires in which virility supposedly originates are at once prescribed and proscribed, their indulgence and their refusal alike can be taken to evidence a lapse of manliness.

Significantly, this double bind "returns" in Stephen's theory of Shakespeare at precisely the moment that he projects himself into the primal seduction scene. Having bolstered his theory with the claim that Shakespeare had read his name in the stars after his trysts with Anne, Stephen imagines his own name written in the firmament, and what he discerns there is a distinctly feminized sexual identity: "Wait to be wooed and won. Ay, meacock. Who will woo you? / Read the skies. . . . Where's your configuration? . . . *S. D.: sua donna* (9.938–40). He takes his passive enjoyment of the primal scene ("Wait to be wooed and won") and his effeminate removal from it ("Ay, meacock. Who will woo you?") as complementary possibilities tending toward the same end, a sense of sex/gender inversion *("sua donna")* fraught with homoerotic connotations: "*Gia: di lui, Gelindo risolve di non amare S. D.*" (9.941).[30]

This last connection has likewise been prepared earlier in *Ulysses.* In "Proteus," Stephen rewrites Hyde's "My Grief upon the Sea." He interpolates a vampire into this revivalist song, unfolding a popular cultural trope that not only locates his propensity for cross-gender identification in a context of flagrantly oedipal eroticism, but also incorporates his homosexual panic as well.[31]

> He comes, pale vampire, through storm his eyes, his bat sails bloodying the sea, mouth to her mouth's kiss.

> Here. Put a pin in that chap, will you? My tablets. Mouth to her kiss. No. Must be two of em. Glue em well. Mouth to her mouth's kiss.
>
> His lips lipped and mouthed fleshless lips of air: mouth to her moomb. (3.397–402)

In crossing the blood feast of the fetus with the oral fixation of the neonate (scarcely displaced from breast to neck), the myth of the vampire conflates the various phases of the oedipal fantasy from immersion in, to recontact with, to penetration of the maternal body, a spectrum neatly encapsulated in Stephen's portmanteau phrase, "mouth to her moomb." But insofar as Stephen already thinks of his mother as a "Ghoul" (1.278) and succubus "ghostwoman" (3.46), his erotic, vampiristic fantasies about her are also a means of identifying with her. In the move from poetic revery to poetic inscription, Stephen enacts this confusion of wanting to have and wanting to be. Shifting fantasy positions from vampire to quarry—*"He comes pale vampire, / Mouth to my mouth"* (7.524–25)—he suddenly finds himself in the alternating roles of the penetrator and the penetrated, the active and the passive party, the filial and the maternal presence, the agent and the object of his oedipal desires. The escalating climax of his poem, and the "Proteus" episode, "pin" or "glue" together the two sides of the culturally entrenched sexual divide through the prospect of a masculine maternal identification. Stephen himself finally seems to sense the undecidably queer implications of this climax upon rereading the poem in "Aeolus": "Would anyone wish that mouth for her kiss? How do you know? Why did you write it then?" (7.711–12).

Unconsciously, Stephen may take up "My Grief Upon the Sea" in particular because the title speaks to his own mourning/morning activities in the Martello Tower and, more specifically, Buck Mulligan's part in them. Mulligan, of course, approvingly cites Swinburne's personification of the sea as "a great sweet mother" (1.77–78), and then proceeds to taunt Stephen for refusing to comply with his mother's last wishes. But Mulligan proves no less important to the subtext of Stephen's revision, specifically his introduction of the vampire, for Mulligan represents the dominant figure around which Stephen's homoerotic and homophobic energies circulate in *Ulysses.* If these two narrative functions seem wildly disparate, a couple of related points need to be considered: first, the only friend who seriously engages Stephen's homosexual panic in *Portrait,* Cranly, is also the only person to remonstrate with Stephen for refusing to obey his mother's demands; second, Stephen draws an incipiently libidinal connection between Mulligan and Cranly not once but twice ("Cranly's arm. His arm" [1.159] and "His arm. Cranly's arm" [3.451]). These repeated and layered textual "coincidences" mark a durable unconscious intersection of Stephen's embattled oedipal and homoerotic desires.

The nature of that intersection, Joyce subtly suggests, involves a cross-gender identification originating in the oedipal scenario. On the one occasion when Stephen's libidinal cathexis of Mulligan decisively intrudes into consciousness, the motif of sex/gender inversion comes to the fore, implicitly organizing his sense of their relationship:

> His gaze brooded on his broadtoed boots, a buck's castoffs, *nebeneinander.* He counted the creases of rucked leather wherein another's foot had nested warm. . . . foot I dislove. But you were delighted when Esther Osvalt's shoe went on you: girl I knew in Paris. *Tiens, quel petit pied!* Staunch friend, a brother soul: Wilde's love that dare not speak its name. His arm: Cranly's arm. He now will leave me. (3.446–52)

Joyce here mixes indirect free style and interior monologue for the purpose of illustrating Stephen's profound ambivalence in a classic act of denegation: Stephen explicitly denies ("foot I dislove") his own unconscious perception that the wearing of Mulligan's boots represents something like displaced sexual contact ("wherein another's foot had nested warm"). But Stephen's "delighted" memory of having fit into a girl's shoe momentarily breaches his defenses. Establishing a typically Joycean correspondence between the present incident and the legend of Cinderella, Stephen's memory marks his feet as the focus of a powerful feminine identification. He cherishes and enjoys publicly demonstrating their dainty size, a property so generally prized in women that it is the stuff of fairy tales. The allusive field of Cinderella also suffuses this moment of gender inversion with overtones of genital activity, since any shoe-fitting that clinches a marriage proposal bears an unmistakably coital significance. The immediate effect upon Stephen is to extort a recognition, however provisional and ironic, of a romantic/erotic valence in his dealings with Mulligan, and he clarifies this affect, significantly, by reference to Wilde, whose name was synonymous not just with homosexuality but with the homosexual as effeminate, as invert, as "queer."

Only in "Scylla and Charybdis," however, does this interlude finally accrue its full meaning. Stephen no sooner finishes piecing together the feminine "constellation" of his identity—"*Stephanoumenos.* . . . S. D.: *sua donna*" (9.939–40)—than his mind reverts to his borrowed footwear: "*Stephanos,* my crown. My sword. His boots are spoiling the shape of my feet" (9.947–48). Not only does Stephen hereby rewrite his part in the Cinderella legend, denying the connubial fit of his foot and Mulligan's boot, his words also glance at the founding pun of another, darker tale of orphanage, resentment, and consummation, the story of Oedipus, a name which translates as swollen foot. In both of these legends, the foot stands forth as both a phallic substitute and the key to the protagonist's secret identity. Accordingly, the convergence of these male and female counterparts in Stephen's struggle for self-definition overdetermines his feet as just this sort of signature fetish, a part object that incorporates desire and identification indirectly. As a site of feminine identification (small-footed Stephen as

Cinderella) and incestuous desire/castration (spoiled-footed Stephen as Oedipus), Stephen's feet reveal both his gender involution and his homosexual anxiety to be unconsciously grounded in his maternal attachment and abjection.

Just as Mulligan's boots become the receptacle for Stephen's feet, Mulligan himself becomes the receptacle of the dread desire encoded in those feet. That is to say, the eroticized menace that Mulligan seems to pose is in large part a projection of Stephen's psychomachia. The logic at work in this psychic process is not unfamiliar. In Stephen's theory of Shakespeare, the emasculation of the seduced artist is the occasion of fraternal treachery and cuckoldry. In Stephen's oedipal drama, which his theory transposes and mystifies, the "inversion" of the seduced son, the "momma's boy," is the occasion of fraternal coupling and penetration. In combining the roles of "brother soul" (3.450) and maternal spokesman, Mulligan comes to objectify Stephen's repudiated and ambivalent oedipal longings as a fear of inversion.

THE COMPANY OF MEN

More than a casual outpouring of antagonism, then, Stephen's response to Mulligan's grand entrance—"Hast thou found me, O mine enemy" (9.483)—identifies the latter as a threat to the psychic barricades raised in the Shakespeare narrative. The nature of this threat manifests itself in Mulligan's dress and demeanor, which almost seem to be cued by Stephen's anxieties and the perceptual filter they create. The "enemy" appears to Stephen as a dandy of the Oscar Wilde sort, the prevailing image of the invert: "Primrosevested he greeted gaily with his doffed Panama as with a bauble" (9.489–90).[32] As if to confirm Stephen's impression, the presence of Mulligan has the immediate effect of steering the Shakespeare debate quite decisively onto the track of the bard's homosexual affinities, alliances, and associations, beginning with the possibility of gender bending in *Hamlet*. It is as if Mulligan's return into Stephen's experiential space embodies and mobilizes a return of the repressed. Indeed, the remainder of the chapter, which is to say the entire reprise of Stephen's Shakespeare theory, unfolds by way of an insistent recurrence to questions of homoeroticism, which Stephen can no longer overlook but must instead find a means of disavowing.

When Lyster directly inquires about Mulligan's theory of Shakespeare, John Eglinton interrupts with a lament on the late eccentricities of Irish bardology, and his chief example brings us to the very center of the episode's gender concerns: "—The bard's fellowcountrymen . . . are rather tired perhaps of our briliancies of theorizing. I hear that an actress played Hamlet for the fourhundredandeighth time last night in Dublin. Vining held that the prince was a woman. Has no-one made him out to be an Irishman?" (9.516–20). Considered in the light of Stephen's recently completed elaboration of "that queer thing genius," Eglinton's words broach a situation in which Hamlet, "the son consubstantial with the father" (9.481), a privileged object of empowering male identification, may already be "a girl," the daughter, privileged vehicle of sexual reconciliation (9.406). With this gender doubling, the erotic possibilities lodged in Stephen's theory of paternal identification begin to emerge into full view.

Mr. Best's response to Eglinton indicates as much. It links the notion of a cross-gendered Irish Hamlet to the uncertain relationship of Shakespeare and William Herbert by way of Oscar Wilde's erotically suggestive account of Shakespeare's poetic muse: "—The most brilliant of all is that story of Wilde's, Mr Best said. . . . That *Portrait of Mr W. H.* where he proves that the sonnets were written by a Willie Hughes, a man of all hues. / —For Willie Hughes, is it not? the quaker librarian asked" (9.522–25). Not only did the public image of Oscar Wilde play a large part in conflating male homosexuality and effeminacy in the public mind, as I noted earlier, but *The Portrait of Mr. W. H.* itself assumes a gender inversion model of same-sex desire. The painting of "Willie Hughes" that passes from Cyril to Erskine to the narrator shows "A young man . . . of extraordinary beauty, though evidently effeminate. Indeed . . . the face, with its dreamy wistful eyes, and its dark scarlet lips, was the face of a girl." This "physical beauty was such," Cyril claims, "that it became the very cornerstone of Shakespeare's art, the very source of Shakespeare's inspiration; the very incarnation of Shakespeare's dreams." What is more, Cyril finds in Hughes's extraordinary features a looking-glass maternal resemblance of a kind shared by Stephen Dedalus. Shakespeare is even made to testify to Hughes's profound at-onement with his mother ("thou art thy mother's glass, and she in thee / Calls back the lovely April of her prime"), much as Bloom does to Stephen's ("the image of his mother" [16.1803–4]). Finally, Cyril Graham, Willie Hughes's author and doppelgänger, likewise displays both a pronounced effeminacy and a rare physical beauty and he, like Hughes, spent a portion of his life playing Shakespeare's "boywomen" (9.254).[33]

At the same time, however, the relationship that Wilde and Cyril "discover" in the sonnets involves a father-son identification between an older playwright and a boy actor, whom Shakespeare grooms and counsels even as he passionately adores.[34] So while Best does err in suggesting the sonnets were written *by* rather than *for* Willie Hughes, this error too turns out to be one of those "portals of discovery" (9.228), for in confounding the object of the love poems with their author, he inadvertently penetrates to the profound symbiosis of eros and identification essential to Wilde's *The Portrait of Mr. W. H.*[35] Such confusion reigns throughout *The Portrait,* wherein the sexual, emotional, and intellectual passion—of Shakespeare for Hughes, Graham for Hughes, Eveline for Graham, and so on—repeatedly passes into a fantastic and fatal emulation. What makes Best's *lapsus* especially threatening to Stephen, however, and important to us, is that the desire to have in this instance, the object relation, is constructed along the lines of a sex/gender inversion, so that the desire to be, the narcissistic relation, carries a transsexual charge. On the terms given in *The Portrait of Mr. W. H.,* Shakespeare's desire to possess or incorporate Hughes on account of his specifically feminine charms—his enactment of what Chauncey calls "the heterosexual paradigm" of homosexuality[36]—implies some sort of degree of an identification with Hughes, from which those same charms cannot be excluded. Taking up the same aesthetic icon, Wilde's text has in effect preempted the patrilineal model of genius at the heart of Stephen's theory, showing how it is put to rout by the coexistence of its maternal counterpart, so that the identity of the players themselves, sexual and otherwise, grows confused. As Stephen thinks, responding to Best's confusion, "Or Hughie Wills? Mr William Himself. W. H.: who am I?" (9.526). Thus what Stephen sees as the castrating touch of female sexuality, exemplified by Anne's "undoing" of Shakespeare, is not finally recuperated nor dialectically overcome in the father-son bond that it mediates, but is repeated there, in the feminine-maternal identification it leaves behind. If, as Craft rightly argues, Freud's "redaction of the inversion metaphor," with its "heterosexual paradigm" of homosexuality, ultimately tends to reduce "male homosexual desire to a mere simulacrum" of "the boy's heterosexual desire for the mother," Joyce's redaction of the inversion metaphor here takes the same premises in the opposite direction and challenges the Freudian assumption that an unambiguous (hetero)sexual desire could ever be distilled from the oedipal complex.[37]

Stephen's immediate reaction is to redirect the "charge of pederasty brought against the bard" (9.732), in this case by Wilde, and to project it onto Richard Best, who is profiled as an effete and effeminate version of Oscar Himself: "he smiled, a blond ephebe. Tame essence of Wilde" (9.531–32). A prolonged bout of ridicule directed at Best culminates in yet another snide sketch combining effeminacy and ephebic initiation: "the douce youngling, minion of pleasure, Phedo's toyable fair hair" (9.1138–39). The particulars of Stephen's ridicule leave no doubt as to his motive. He indulges in the essence of homophobia, the stigmatizing of another to displace self-doubts, in which questions of gender performance and sexual preference overlap.

Indeed, Best's by/for confusion touches a nerve precisely because *The Portrait of Mr. W. H.* so closely approximates the transferential impetus and structure of Stephen's performance. In either case, the truth value of the theory is specifically discounted by the person retailing it. Cyril Graham concocts his tale of a grand passion between Shakespeare and Hughes out of his own homoerotic identification with the latter, a figment of his own imagination; and in a restaging of this transferential dynamic, Erskine "believes" in Willie Hughes strictly owing to his homoerotic identification with Cyril. As we have seen, Stephen's theory reduplicates this pattern *via negativa.* He has framed Shakespeare's life in answer to his need for an ego ideal and, to this point, he has sought to downplay Shakespeare's homosexual notoriety in order to dissociate himself, *in his own mind,* from same-sex desires and adherences. With its reliance on father-son gender inversion, Wilde's *Portrait* indicates that the *act* of identification on Stephen's part harbors the homoerotic valence that the *form* of his identification would repudiate. Stephen cannot seek to perform the masculine ideal of aesthetic creator, cannot aspire to be William Himself without, in the same motion, investing that ideal with libidinal or erotic energy, implicating himself in the "invert" role of a W. H.[38] Nor, by the same token, can he articulate a homophobic notion of masculine identification that is not immediately reversible into a homophilic notion like Wilde's: "You ought to make it a dialogue, don't you know," Best declares, with complex and unwitting irony, "like the Platonic dialogues Wilde wrote" (9.1068–69).[39]

It is therefore appropriate that having trained Mulliganesque mockery upon Best, Stephen should find himself "Bested," in turn, positioned as a W. H. figure by Mulligan himself. The virulently homophobic comment in question, moreover, goes directly to Stephen's prized father-son connection as it is projected into the larger narrative of *Ulysses.* Having espied Bloom's "dark figure," Mulligan "suddenly turned to Stephen," proclaiming, "—He knows you. He knows your old fellow. O, I fear me, he is Greeker than the Greeks. His pale Galilean eyes were upon her mesial groove. Venus Kallipyge . . . *The god pursuing the maiden hid*" (9.613–17). Mulligan here invokes twin racial stereotypes, the "Greeks[']" long-standing reputation for pederasty and the "Galilean['s]" modern racial classification as feminine; and he thereby places Stephen at the nexus of the ephebe and the invert, where Stephen had placed Best.[40] At the same time, he makes Stephen both a surrogate son to Bloom ("He knows your old fellow") and a quasi-daughter or "maiden," much the same convoluted symbolic affinity that Mrs. Palmer's Hamlet bears toward her/his "author." Taken in tandem, these sallies lend a different spin to the climactic Circean formula, "Jewgreek is greekjew" (15.2097–98).

MAN DELIGHTS HIM NOT NOR WOMAN NEITHER

Stephen's final strategic reaction to the challenge posed by the sudden and repeated convergence of same-sex identification and gender inversion represents a quite sophisticated form of disavowal. He concedes, in effect, what he has so far resisted—the fundamental imbrication of hetero- and homosexual desire. Then he proceeds to associate both affective categories with the fraternal/maternal axis of his family romance, while disjoining the father-son axis from sexuality altogether.

The first step takes place in delayed response to Best's preferred solution of the W. H. mystery. Returning to Shakespeare's relations with William Herbert, Stephen admits a homosexual motive in their heterosexual fellowship and rivalry. That is, he deems Shakespeare complicitous in his own competitive overthrow.

> Love that dare not speak its name.
>
> —As an Englishman, you mean . . . he loved a lord. . . .
>
> —It seems so, Stephen said, when he wants to do for him, and for all other and singular uneared wombs, the holy office an ostler does for the stallion. (9.659–64)

In the next breath he links the "French triangle" (9.1065) of the sonnets with the Shakespeare family triangle which is to round out his narrative: "But she, the giglot wanton, did not break a bedvow. Two deeds are rank in the ghost's mind: a broken vow and the dullbrained yokel on whom her favour has declined, deceased husband's brother. Sweet Ann, I take it, was hot in the blood. Once a wooer, twice a wooer" (9.666–69). But Stephen's earliest reference to "all other and singular uneared wombs" suggests that Shakespeare is complicitous in his overthrow here as well, that he abandoned Anne so that he might return, by fraternal proxy, to the site of his original, artistically energizing sexual trauma, just as Stephen gnaws on his mother's memory through fraternal rivalries with Cranly and with Mulligan.

Standing against this scenario is Stephen's last attempt to install the father-son relationship as a lever for dialectically recovering masculine integrity and creative authority in the face of castration. The set piece upon "A father" (9.828–71) is triggered in part by his memory of a phrase, "He knows your old fellow" (9.824), previously used by Mulligan to announce Bloom's supposedly sexual designs upon Stephen. With this in mind, Stephen takes up his earlier negation of father-son at-onement, the idea of a narcissistic blood repulsion, and transposes it into the register of object relations under the sign of "bodily shame" (9.850). Such is the intensity of this sexual phobia, Stephen insists, that the estate of fatherhood passes *beyond* sexuality, becoming a "mystical estate, an apostolic succession" (9.838). As the spiritual and religious vocabulary suggests, Stephen has elected to reclaim his patrilineal model of aesthetic legitimacy from its homoerotic embarrassments by casting it on the plane of the immaterial, and his core tenet of incertitude, which has prompted so many ethical and aesthetic interpretations, serves him first and foremost as a *principle of disembodiment*. Robbed by the preceding discussion of any other way to shield father-son identification from the erotic energies that fuel them, Stephen resorts to a kind of negative transcendence, a grounding in "the void" (9.842).

That homosexual panic unconsciously animates Stephen's soliloquy is evident first in the fact that paternity is a "legal fiction" (9.844) for Stephen only when it comes to male children. Daughters have disappeared entirely from his discourse on paternity proper. Only sons create fathers so driven by "shame" as to identify without desire: "Who is the father of any son that any son should love him or he any son?" (9.844–45). And only sons can produce and extend the true sense of fatherhood, which is precisely about nonlibidinal connection: "he was not the father of his own son merely but, being no more a son, he was and felt himself the father of all his race, the father of his own grandfather, the father of his unborn grandson" (9.867–69). Homosexual panic is evident secondly in the texture of Stephen's language, which undoes the repressions of his conscious argument. When he proposes that "[father and son] are sundered by a bodily shame so steadfast that the criminal annals of the world . . . hardly record its breach" (9.850–52), the double pun on "an(n)als" and "breach" not only signals but enacts the fundamental dependency of male "bodily shame" on the homoerotic desire it would deny. Stephen's very enunciation of his argument draws us back from "the void" toward which the argument itself tends, so that Joyce may allow us to glimpse the libidinal forces to be contained and concealed there.

At the same time, however, the disappearance of the daughter at this stage of Stephen's exposition illustrates how far the heterosexist design of his theory of genius subserves the end originally pursued by Russell and Eglinton: the exclusion of women from the domain of intellectual and aesthetic production. Given the role of sex/gender inversion in Stephen's thinking, this tendency should come as no surprise. Indeed, in some sense, Stephen's homosexual panic is always already about being "castrated" by "feminine" involvement. That is to say, it is not just that Stephen reacts to the homoerotic as A. E. and Eglinton react to the feminine, that is, as a dangerously uncontrollable otherness; rather, understanding homosexuality in terms of sex/gender inversion, Stephen sees it as the persistence of the feminine and all that it represents for him (material immanence, embodiment, heteronomy, death) within a male space and so beyond the reach of dialectical recuperation. For Stephen, homosexuality is the feminine deconstruction of the masculine, the subversion of its logic of (gender) identity/identification. His homophobia *is* their gynephobia once removed; his acceptance of oedipal castration is but a provisional form of their refusal.

This meta-French triangle of Stephen's discourse, the secret complicity of his position with those it rivals, is borne out in his concluding agreement with Eglinton on the ontological status of Shakespeare. Stephen begins by combating A. E. and Eglinton's aesthetics of transcendent masculinity, the vision of the artist as occupying an imaginary zone of narcissistic plenitude, preserved from castration and its attendant desire, detached from social circumstance, sexual inscription, and material corruption. But he winds up projecting Shakespeare into a similarly resplendent state of self-sufficiency, the dialectical enrichment of which is purely formal. To be sure, Stephen's Shakespeare is seen to absorb particulars, being "all in all" (9.1018–19), instead of negating them like the "formless spiritual essences" of A. E.'s "deep" life (9.49–50). But he remains unaffected and unimpaired by them just the same. He too stands beyond desire ("Man delights him not nor woman neither" [9.1030]), beyond castration and its attendant sexual difference ("an androgynous angel, being a wife unto himself" [9.1052]), and beyond contingency ("He found in the world without as actual what was in his world within as possible" [9.1041–42]). The aesthetics of A. E.'s Charybdian "world of ideas" (9.52–53), with its masculinist values of separation, autonomy, and mastery, are resurrected in Stephen's "economy of heaven" (9.1051).[41] The unconditioned and the omni-conditioned, the indifferent and the totalized body, finally join in an ostensibly compensatory but ultimately self-defeating fantasy of a hypermasculine sublime.[42]

10

Diversions from Mastery in "Wandering Rocks"

BONNIE KIME SCOTT

O, rocks! (4.343)

Molly Bloom

I should never be able to fulfil [*sic*] what is, I understand, the first duty of a lecturer—to hand you after an hour's discourse a nugget of pure truth to wrap up between the pages of your notebooks and keep on the mantelpiece for ever.

Virginia Woolf, *A Room of One's Own*

"Wandering Rocks" has rarely been seen by the critics in a positive light.[1] Molly's protest against male pedantry, cited above, is one possible response. To Michael Seidel "Wandering Rocks" is the "black hole" at the center of *Ulysses*.[2] For Hugh Kenner, this episode marks the point after which all of *Ulysses* becomes fissured.[3] Though regarded as unpleasant or treacherous terrain, "Wandering Rocks" offers both a last outpost for controlled readings of *Ulysses* and a point of departure for postmodern feminist ones. Despite its (almost) central placement, "Wandering Rocks" contains numerous moments of being that enact the marginal experiences of minor characters who seem to have little control over their lives. Its narrator is disliked by critics partially because his methods exert a devious form of control. The episode offers ideal material for studying issues of mastery, both in the author's writing and the critics' interpreting. Postmoderns must develop new attitudes and terms to comprehend the differences deployed in this elusive episode.

The Joyce industry has densely packed the "author's horizon" for *Ulysses*,[4] preserving Joyce's masterful schemas and descriptive letters to early readers, cataloging his books, recovering his Jesuit school curriculum, and collecting accounts of his personal exchanges and his creative processes. The authorized statements Joyce left on "Wandering Rocks" have daunted successive generations of critical readers, though for different reasons. An important issue is textual control. Quite early in Joyce's writing of the episode (October 24, 1920), he told Frank Budgen that he planned an *"Entr'acte"* to follow episode nine, "Scylla and Charybdis." It would be "short with absolutely no relation to what precedes or follows like a pause in the action of a play" (*SL* 273). While this contemplated break in the text may not be "Wandering Rocks," the published episode does pose various problems of "relation," problems which can be explored as an aspect of control.[5] By this point in *Ulysses,* readers know that they may be required to switch from Stephen's plot to Bloom's, but they probably still seek narrative relation to a major textual player. "Wandering Rocks" denies this, granting them only two brief glimpses of Stephen and one of Bloom. In terms of symmetry, Bloom has an important location in the chapter's central, tenth section. But he is crowded out by the texts he contemplates in the bookshop; crowded out as well by minor characters, Bloom will concern us little in this study.[6]

On October 21, 1920, Joyce sent Carlo Linati a masterful schema to help a reader who was confused with the complexity of his "damned monster-novel" (*SL* 271).[7] Joyce's description of his own composition suggests that even he was laboring under difficulties of control. The categories and lists of what became known as the Linati schema pose new challenges. "Persons" to be followed in the episode include an incongruous collection of "objects, places, forces, Ulysses," complicating what readers must relate to and raising issues of agency and selfhood. We might well ask, *what* wanders and *who* are the rocks? Though Joyce lists "Ulysses" among the "persons" of "Wandering Rocks," he loosens his classical parallel; the episode takes us where even Homer's hero never sailed, jumping ship to cruise the course of Jason and his Argonauts. Joyce also seems to play confusing games with the reader. From visits made to the Joyce family while "Wandering Rocks" was being composed, Budgen posits the influence of "Labyrinth," a board game that Joyce played with his daughter Lucia. The term "labyrinth" reappears on various schema under the category of "technique." Budgen notes that Joyce found six errors of judgment that a player of "Labyrinth" might be susceptible to.[8] Joyce offers a shorter list of "Errors" as one category of "symbols" in the Linati schema.[9] It is reasonable to expect, as Clive Hart has, that he plotted mistakes for his critics and readers, using as his agent the aforementioned narrator, whose "difficult personality" has been remarked on as the "most salient thing about the chapter."[10]

The Linati schema raises other issues to a postmodern community of readers who are not so troubled as their predecessors by narrative gaps, and who consider game play—pitfalls and all—an integral part of reading texts. The schema identifies "the hostile environment" as the "Sense (meaning)" of the episode. That Joyce would list "meaning" at all is an issue in itself, as it implies a will to control interpretation—a move alien to a postmodern theoretical generation set on pondering indeterminacies. "Sense (meaning)" was dropped from the second schema Joyce sent to Valery Larbaud late in 1921, and all along he wanted to limit the Linati schema to "home use only" (*SL* 271). That he was more than willing to grant critics their indeterminacies has proven a good long-range marketing strategy, even if it hints at disrespect for the critical industry.[11]

Joyce's theme of "hostile environment" may pose problems to critics invested in finding increased stylistic complexity as *Ulysses* progresses. However acceptable to *Dubliners,* this naturalistic category is ill-suited to a modernist, let alone a postmodern project. A return to *Dubliners* is affirmed by the reappearance of a great number of its characters in "Wandering Rocks." Joyce depended upon *Thom's Directory* for numerous members of his cast and for place-names used in the episode. He worked with a map spread before him, marking paths and calculating distances. These writing practices have allowed Hart to assign the episode to another category not normally thought of as modernist—documentary realism.[12]

For postmodern critics, Joyce may return to *Dubliners* territory with a difference that shifts notions of authority and offers previously neglected, marginal, "minoritarian" matter for cultural analysis. Florence Walzl was one of the first critics to reread cultural history for its positioning of women, as recorded in *Dubliners* by Joyce.[13] Margot Norris has offered important rereadings of such stories as "Clay" and "The Dead," using narrative and psychoanalytic tools and turning a new eye to history. Norris has gendered as masculine the narrator of "The Dead," detecting his evasions of the crises in women's lives and their countertext of "back answers."[14] Something analogous exists, I feel, in the respective roles of the narrator and women characters of "Wandering Rocks."

Giles Deleuze has theorized about "the minoritarian as a potential, creative and created becoming." His first example of the minoritarian subset is "Woman," and "becoming-woman" affects "all of humankind" but is achieved not by "ownership" of a process, but by entering into it.[15] Carol Gilligan offers an alternate developmental scenario for female "becoming" that helps us read relationships among characters of "Wandering Rocks." Her theory suggests that while "for boys and men separation and individuation are critically tied to gender identity," girls and women are defined more by "intimacy" and their relationships to other individuals.[16] She notes that in the theories of Freud, Piaget, Ericson, and others, women fail to progress from one stage to another. As we look to other priorities, even "progress" becomes a suspect motion and notion.

Twenty years ago, in the landmark collection *James Joyce's "Ulysses,"* Hart explored "Wandering Rocks" as a tour de force. Hart's own love of mapping places and measuring time sustains Budgen's firsthand view, which imagines Joyce as "an engineer at work with compass and slide-rule."[17] Hart offers his own masterstroke, a chart titled "'Wandering Rocks'—Times and Places." It is a model of formalist organization and control. The Hart chart negotiates the labyrinth of Joycean Dublin minute by minute, setting straight twenty-nine wandering paths. Read horizontally, it captures Joyce's accomplishment of a multiple narrative by recording simultaneous occurrences for any of the sixty minutes between 3:00 and 4:00 P.M. Linear readings emerge as we read the chart vertically, following the course taken by Dublin characters, some of them so minor as to be nameless. The chart is impressive, folding outward on an oversized sheet, comprehensive of wanderers and landmarks of all sorts. It is of lasting value to readers of the episode.

While Hart justifies his approach with reference to Joyce's supposed pursuit of documentary reality, he also identifies a Joycean will to possession that I want to take a step further. I would tend to attribute Hart's work—and indeed much of the formalist study of Joyce—to a comparable will toward possession, not so much of the material city Joyce had scrupulously retained in exile (though knowing Joyce's Dublin does convey pedagogical authority), but rather of the design of *Ulysses*. In one early manifestation we have the quest for a mythically ordered, well-scaffolded *Ulysses* conducted by T. S. Eliot. Hart's chart has affinity to the schemas Joyce provided to Linati and Larbaud, the latter leading to the master chart first published in Stuart Gilbert's *Joyce's "Ulysses,"* and to the commentary on *Finnegans Wake* encouraged by Joyce and eventually published together as *Our Exagmination Round His Factification for Incamination of Work in Progress*. As forms of textual possession, we can include not only the stylistic analyses of *Ulysses* but also directories of Joyce's characters, listings of his allusions, and studies of intertextuality.[18] This last category becomes particularly important in and beyond "Wandering Rocks," which contains new characters for subsequent episodes (Mina Kennedy, Lydia Douce, and Gerty MacDowell, for instance), and which flings its own "persons" over interpolated gaps and from one of its sections to another.

The will toward textual mastery is something that I think all Joyceans experience and participate in, though such command of the text has been increasingly open to critique in the en-gendered readings of our postmodern era. Kathleen McCormick's ideas about the sources of pleasure in the text identify "mystery" as an alternate position to "mastery" and allow for the possibility of oscillating between these two options. She also gives the less than reassuring diagnosis that readers may satisfy their "repetition compulsion" with the episode.[19] Authority, a concept closely related to mastery, is seen less as an achievement and more as a site for cultural analysis by Vicki Mahaffey.[20] Positions devoid of ownership, another related term, interest Deleuze, as noted previously. Postmodern readers consider it unlikely that there is a stable order to discover in *Ulysses*. Classical foundations and geographical locations no longer suffice in an era when the complex of gender, race, and colonial status command attention, and when we pose questions about the power of institutions and categories to privilege or exclude segments of the public. For example, Reverend Conmee's judgments, which could appear benevolent to Frank Budgen, are as open to question now as the direct path he treads.[21]

Hart's work with a stopwatch and map became the basis of one of the most memorable events of the 1982 Centennial Joyce Symposium, where between 3:00 and 4:00 P.M., "Wandering Rocks" was reenacted. This exercise in exactitude was also a massive performance. Probably unintentionally, it ushered in the postmodern appreciation of the performative nature of Joyce. Joyce's script not only called for precision but also allowed for costumes and the complex language of gesture. The strolling street scenes played the best, while typically women characters were left hanging out of windows, if they were to appear at all. Was anyone able to play the role of Maggy Dedalus? Does this lack in its 1982 staging reflect upon the episode itself?

Hart's chart sets up narrative units and vocabulary that remain invaluable for working with the "Wandering Rocks" episode. First we have the nineteen numbered "sections." These were separated by Joyce with three asterisks in a triangular array; the asterisks have wandered in various editions, though the divisions remain.[22] Hart offers the term "interpolations" for intrusive material within the sections—thirty-one brief passages that often take us simultaneously to another site in and around Dublin. One distinction lost in Hart's chart is between characters met in the regular sections as opposed to those who appear in the interpolations, though he lists and comments upon each interpolation in an appendix. Hart's leading explanation for these intrusions is irony, a privileged principle in 1950s formalism.[23] In correcting the impression made by bogus interpolations, Hart asserts his own control over the narrator.

More complex explanations of the placement and rationale for interpolations have become an enterprise and even a source of delight for readers of intertextuality. McCormick offers five classifications for the interpolations based on their different appeals to the reader—a decided move away from authorial control. Schooled on Roland Barthes, McCormick tries to account for the pleasure and bliss readers may encounter in "cruising the interpolations" with minoritarian, urban wandering practices in the "queer sites" of modernism, to borrow a phrase from Joseph Boone (though the contemporary activity of cruising television channels comes more immediately to mind, taking *Ulysses* into another genre).[24] The interpolations are certainly the product of elaborate aesthetic patterning, forming verbal relationships and registering simultaneity. But we should also heed politically suggestive asymmetries in these patterns. The interpolations are unevenly distributed within the nineteen sections, suggesting that the narrator finds some sections' characters less important, and hence more interruptible, than others. Seen another way, the interpolations are a minor subset of the chapter, with their own minoritarian way of insinuating the struggles of very minor characters for personal and textual survival.

In their *Topographical Guide to Joyce's "Ulysses,"* Hart and Leo Knuth had to be at their most expansive to cover the ground for "Wandering Rocks," and particularly to track two of its most powerful characters/forces. One of the most extensive routes was Reverend Conmee's as he moved from Upper Gardiner Street on a northeastward vector to the O'Brien Institute near Artane, where he sought a place for the Dignams's oldest son. The second long and continuous vector was for the viceroy's cavalcade, progressing from the Viceregal Lodge in Phoenix Park along the north side of the Liffey River, and then south and east to Ballsbridge, site of the Mirus Bazaar, which the viceroy had the duty of opening on June 16. The direct progress and the relative lack of interruption in these two ventures by men on professional business are worth remarking.

Conmee and the viceroy are the primary representatives of what I shall term "professional progress" in the episode. Though Martin Cunningham does not go as far, he belongs to this category too. He has a clear sense of his route from the Castle to the environs of city hall, seeking signed pledges on behalf of the Dignam family. He is linked professionally with Conmee by his letter, which sent the priest on his mission toward Artane. Conmee is confident, in turn, that he can count on favors from Cunningham at mission time.

I want to draw attention to the less directed characters of "Wandering Rocks." Hart and Knuth notice that a number of characters turn back upon their own paths. This group includes Lady Maxwell, who has visited Conmee in the morning; Cashel Boyle O'Connor Fitzmaurice, whose eccentric path leads to one collision; the blind piano tuner, who has to retrieve his forgotten tuning fork; and an elderly female dressed in black, who wanders back and forth among courts and offices.[25] A "minoritarian" set of women, children, the mad, and the blind steer what I shall term "zigzag courses" through Dublin, seeking objects that cannot readily be located or owned.

In their *"Ulysses" Annotated,* Gifford and Seidman make a related distinction. They register sections where characters "progress" and ones in which there are "fixed locations."[26] Reverend Conmee and the viceroy, obviously, are in sections of "progress." Movement is also shown by the one-legged sailor (section 1), Lenehan and M'Coy (section 9), Kernan (section 12), Stephen (section 13), Cunningham (section 15), Artifoni (section 17), Cashel (section 17),[27] and Master Dignam (section 18). Predictably, if we are aware of Gilligan's work, no women make it into sections of "progress." But there are additional sources of omission. Lady Maxwell, the elderly lady in black, and the women who share a tram ride with Reverend Conmee are too minor to register on map or list. The focus on movement within sections misses the paths of characters who take up different positions from one section to another; we could call them the "skipping stones" of the narrative. Dilly Dedalus is a prime example, jumping from 11 to 13 to 19, with parts of her perambulations omitted. Dennis Maginni is the lightest of skipping stones, marginal to other men's trajectories. "Wandering Rocks" also acquaints us with people who may have returned from earlier wandering, as is the case for Maggy Dedalus. She is my prime example of a "scavenger," whose survival tactics are harder to map than linear, progressive motions. Her type has been missing from traditional history and neglected in the criticism of this episode, although ALP assumes mythic proportions as a scavenger in *Finnegans Wake*.

In developing an en-gendered course through "Wandering Rocks," I have diverted considerably from the orderly ranks and columns of Hart's chart, restive with time and space as vertices to register adequately vast differences in movement, connections, and narrative—particularly in relation to the women characters, who largely disappeared into the system. I have read against the critical grain of setting down for all time a complex master design crafted by the author/genius, allied to a "difficult" narrator, as seen and served by the formalist reader. My second epigraph, taken from Virginia Woolf's *A Room of One's Own,* critiques a pedagogy that produces inert nuggets (or rocks, for current purposes) for collection and permanent, static display. I offer instead zigzag and skipping courses traced by characters well down the hierarchy of textual prominence or previous academic interest. Many of them are women, though the category of gender merges with other social determinants, including colonial economies shared across gender. Thus I shall attend to a set of less directed male figures: Lenehan and M'Coy (section 9), Simon Dedalus (sections 11 and 14), and Master Dignam (section 18). Gilligan has noted that the ideal used in the male developmental studies is the successful professional man—a group not inclusive of many of the male characters in "Wandering Rocks" (and not even inclusive of Stephen Dedalus, unable at this later phase of his life to conceive of a vocation as the artist/priest of his race). The course of Lenehan and M'Coy is indirect and frequently interrupted by interpolations. Indirection is expected in Lenehan, perhaps, given his record as a voyeur of Corley's questionable commerce in "Two Gallants." Lenehan and M'Coy's section is also valuable for its interpolations of one of the most fugitive characters of *Ulysses,* the elderly woman in a black silk skirt.

Before studying these characters, and as access to still more minor characters, I want to suggest that even the most directed wanderers of this episode are subject to disruption. Despite his painstaking charting of their paths in red on a Dublin map as he wrote this episode, and despite the length and directedness of their course, Joyce also undermines Reverend Conmee and the viceroy. They were demoted in his schema over time. In the early Linati schema, we have noted "Christ and Caesar" as the symbols of the episode; it is "Citizens" who have this designation in later schemas—a designation that still falls short of attending to the disenfranchised women of the episode. The viceroy rarely emerges as a character in the episode; he qualifies more under the category of "force" listed for the "persons" who become Joyce's various rocks, and is elided with ceremonial wandering. His most (and perhaps only) individual action is to distract his lady's attention from the flirtatious performance of Blazes Boylan. Though his passage is not interrupted by interpolations, the viceroy is robbed of the readers' attention in section 19 by the return of almost all the minor characters, as well as "a tongue of liquid sewage" (10.1197), the back of Artifoni's trousers, and other distracting sights. That Conmee, Stephen, and Bloom miss the cavalcade also robs it of importance. The performance of gestures—many of them deceitful or absentminded, many of them erroneous or subject to misreading—is a hallmark of the section.

On the other hand, though Conmee is a force of the church and has a great deal of individuality in his personality, he exudes a host of quirks and prejudices in both dialogue and internal monologue. These traits set him out to self-destruct in the minds of readers sensitive to his religious and social prejudices.

Although we can trace Father Conmee through a relatively coherent, linear journey, at the end of which he is to accomplish a goal, his one interruption is significant. Maginni is launched as a skipping stone in the first interpolation of "Wandering Rocks" in section 1. However fleetingly, the narrator thus insinuates the gay community upon the rock of the church and the course of empire. Maginni is unnoticed by Conmee and the viceroy, though he is seen by many lesser citizens in midchapter. His description gets the maximum value from clothing reminiscent of Oscar Wilde: "Mr Denis J Maginni, professor of dancing &c, in silk hat, slate frockcoat with silk facings, white kerchief tie, tight lavender trousers, canary gloves and pointed patent boots, walking with grave deportment" (10.56–58). Maginni's full path and purposes are undeveloped. Yet his selection of costume, his deliberate style of movement, and projection of an emotional tone encourage us to read here self-styling performance (a shared trait of an array of characters in "Wandering Rocks"). Maginni's living equivalent was listed in Thom's Directory as a resident of 32 Great George's Street North (*JJ* 365),[28] and he can still provide a lead into a lost gay community of the turn of the century.

Conmee's first actual meeting on his walk is with the one-legged sailor, whom he gives a blessing, but not a coin. In section 3, this veteran beggar introduces the marginal course of reading "Wandering Rocks." Female charity is represented by a stout woman who drops a coin into his cap. Soon afterward, he encounters a "generous arm" (10.251)—the only part of Molly Bloom included in the episode; her donation becomes a community effort, as street urchins retrieve the tossed coin for the sailor. The sailor also crosses paths with Katey and Boody Dedalus, little more than urchins themselves, as they return home from school. Given the conditions of the home we will soon encounter, it is little wonder they cannot respond to his appeal to *"home and beauty"* (10.235).

Conmee begins his walk with a fairly strong professional orientation, sustaining an important political contact through Mrs. Sheehy, "wife of Mr David Sheehy, M.P." (10.17 and 10.26–27), getting off his letter to the father provincial (while shaping the behavior of the three schoolboys who will mail it for him), reflecting that "aged and virtuous females who take the blessed sacrament may be "badtempered" (10.80–82), and acting condescendingly toward the free church and the souls to be saved in Africa. This final thought is stimulated by the blackface minstrel poster of Eugene Stratton, and allows him to think of his sermons and his readings of Jesuit positions on the doctrine of salvation. Once he leaves the tram, however, Conmee is lost in fantasies built on secular reading and idealized memories, such as the regal one of Clongowes, where "his reign was mild" (10.188). When a young couple emerging from a gap in the hedge escape with a blessing, gravely given, he remains absorbed in his breviary.

As representatives of official power, both Conmee and the cavalcade collect salutes, with the former usually stopping only briefly in exchange of greetings, and the latter not at all. Conmee's relatively long exchange with Mrs.

Sheehy shows familiarity with a family that sends its sons to Conmee's school, Belvedere. His repetition of the phrase "the wife of Mr David Sheehy, M.P." (10.17 and 10.26–27) shows a political motivation for lavishing attention here. We never learn where Mrs. Sheehy is headed, only that she has remained in Dublin while her husband is in London, since "the house was still sitting" (10.22). She expresses a slightly surprising interest in the zealous Father Bernard Vaughan, whose success with her is unaffected by the Cockney accent mentally mocked by Conmee. If we want a full fictional narrative of Mrs. Sheehy's British equivalent, we could turn to another wife of an M.P. in Woolf's *Mrs. Dalloway*. Clarissa's traversal of London in search of flowers for her party takes the place of Conmee's perambulations. She worries much more than Conmee does about old relationships, and instead of maintaining a confident air, feels "schoolgirlish" when encountering Hugh Walsh.[29] Assessment goes two ways, as the people Clarissa meets contribute to her characterization. Despite a stiff aloofness engendered by class, she merges into an understanding of Septimus Smith, whose death as a postwar victim is as wasteful as the alcoholic death of Paddy Dignam.

While in Conmee's case there is usually a salute on both sides of an encounter, the sharing of attentions is less reciprocal with the cavalcade, which is positioned above the people, with outriders' hoofs fending them off. Tom Kernan cannot get to a position where he can even see its passage. Kernan's inclusion in section 19 is an excuse for a narrative pun. His pride in his newly acquired coat doubles with the denied view: "Mr Thomas Kernan beyond the river greeted him vainly from afar" (10.1183–84). But there are other vain gestures. From the second carriage, "the honourable Gerald Ward" singles out for hasty reply the salute of the demented Dennis Breen, whose wandering has nearly got him hit by the outriders (10.1231–36). Some salutes are not that at all, as in the case of "a charming soubrette, great Marie Kendall" (10.1220), whose dauby smile (like that of Eugene Stratton) has been flashed from mechanically reproduced posters all over the cityscape of "Wandering Rocks." Blazes Boylan jauntily flashes the rose he holds between his teeth to the ladies, doubly defying decorum. Bernard Benstock sees Simon Dedalus's lowered hat as a gesture to hide his fly, not yet closed after leaving a urinal.[30] Through a chain of events, this nongesture emerges from Simon's consumption of alcohol, the mark of a debilitated, but all too typical, man about Dublin.

Within the privileged textual and political bindings of the characters who make professional progress in the chapter we find persons of seemingly lower orders, wandering and encountering one another with varying levels of personal and textual relationship. This second tier of characters assumes the focus of the sections interior to 1 and 19. They are often tracked again in an interpolation or two, and all but Stephen and Bloom have some contact with the viceregal cavalcade.

Although his path is relatively short compared to those of Conmee and the cavalcade, Martin Cunningham also displays the characteristics of professional progress. Having already fired off a letter suggesting how Conmee should proceed on behalf of Master Dignam, he undertakes his own mission of collecting the signatures of donors to the Dignam family. Cunningham's stature is shown by the fact that he can signal for an empty jarvey to shadow his progress. His movement is so determined that John Wyse Nolan, "lagging behind," must hurry to catch up with him (10.968–69). Nolan and Power follow in formation as he seeks support from the assistant town clerk, Jimmy Henry, and the sub-sheriff, Long John Fanning, though nothing is settled as the section ends. Readers may recall from the "Hades" episode that Cunningham's home life seems less orderly: reports of his "awful drunken wife . . . pawning the furniture on him every Saturday almost" come to Bloom through the source of Simon Dedalus (6.349–57), hardly a model himself of family values. Simon's own property is pawned by desperate women.

Far less successful than Cunningham as professionals are the cluster of men who inhabit section 9. Lenehan attempts to play a professional role in promoting Tom Rochford's invention to Blazes Boylan,[31] but Lenehan's professional route is far from direct or complete. He reveres Rochford more as a hero than an inventor, diverting his narrative to this subject. Completion of his mission depends upon a meeting at the Ormond bar, which he has arranged through Miss Dunn, Boylan's secretary, in section 7. Miss Dunn remembers to mention this appointment at the Ormond bar only at the very last moment of a phone conversation with her boss. We hear only one side of this conversation, revealing some communication from Belfast and Liverpool. But on this day, the road to Belfast clearly leads through Eccles Street and an unprofessional contact with Molly Bloom. Lenehan is diverted from his path to the Ormond by a call at Lynam's to check on the betting odds for Sceptre—a mission more tied to a personal addiction than to his ill-defined employment at *Sport*. Lenehan and Boylan, like Bloom, are haphazard professionals at best.

Joyce achieves a sense of distractions from business in brief internal monologues of decidedly minor characters. In section 18, Master Patrick Dignam dawdles along wayward paths on his errand for pork steaks, his meandering thoughts taking form in coarse colloquial language. He is relieved to be away from the "blooming dull" (10.1125), primarily female company in the family parlor. He is distracted by posters—both Marie Kendall and a pair of boxers (or "puckers" in his lexicon)—and he is willing to deceive his mother to get to their match. It may presage the future of mass culture that he relates to the hoardings more than to any living creature, and that he has cultivated his critical sensibility on sport. Like his cohort in "The Sisters," Master Dignam is studying his reaction to the death of a father figure; his memory of his last experience with his father is naturalistic, recording Dignam's grey face, his boozed behavior, and his last-minute effort to remind his son to be good to his mother, struggling to get the message past his tongue and teeth. The youngster is intrigued by the prospect of having his name in the paper beside his father's, for all his schoolfellows to read. There are premonitions that his own progress will be halting: the boxing match is already over. It took his father's death to bring about a relationship to him, and it is compounded of paternal guilt and printer's ink. Master Dignam is already showing symptoms of self-indulgence and is apt to join the ranks of a haphazard working class.

But let us turn now to the Dedalus girls—in some ways the female counterparts to Master Dignam. The girls demonstrate considerable variety in character, including their attitudes toward specific relationships and personal progress. The one-legged sailor of sections 1 and 3 leads us to Katey and Boody on their way back from school; we move in section 4 to a bare, subsistence household run by Maggy, who has spent much of her day scavenging. There has been clear direction in her day, though in the selection of text offered by the narrator, this is seen only briefly and in retrospect. Maggy has been both to Mrs. M'Guinness's pawnshop, seeking in vain to turn books into sustenance, and to Sister Mary Patrick, who has supplied the family with pea soup. Maggy gets double use out of the kitchen. The kettle has been converted to the warming of soup. The largest pot, where Katey expects to find food, is used for boiling shirts. As Kimberly J. Devlin suggests in her essay in this volume, while these might be family linens, it is possible that Maggy is taking in laundry so that characters such as Lenehan can attend "boiled shirt" affairs (10.537). Hot-water cleaning would be reserved for whites; Katey's "stained skirt" (10.275) suggests that the family's tattered clothing rarely sees soap and water. If Maggy, like Nora Joyce, is a part-time laundress, the collection, processing, and delivery of her product goes almost unnoticed by the narrator. It serves mainly to produce another error of judgment in his narrative, as Katey squints hopefully at the pot. Boody is the most forceful and ironic of the sisters; like Lily in "The Dead," she is quick with back answers, challenging male assessments. For example, while Reverend Conmee is impressed by the queenly walk he assigns to Mrs. M'Guinness, Boody curses her face for her refusal to broker the Dedalus's books: "Boody stamped her foot and threw her satchel on the table. / —Bad cess to her big face! she cried" (10.268–69). She also plays an ironic literary turn on their absent, irresponsible father in "Our father who art not in heaven" (10.291). Upholding religious sanctity, Maggy censors this outburst. This eldest sister, however, seems to have antipatriarchal strategies afoot. She reports that Dilly has "gone to meet father" (10.289), which everyone knows means that she hopes to seize on family funds before they go down Simon's throat.

In recent work, the ill-clothed, ill-postured, and presumably ill-nourished Dilly Dedalus has emerged as a hero from her brief appearances in "Lestrygonians" and "Wandering Rocks." Bloom makes prognostications about her health when he sees her outside Dillon's auction rooms in "Lestrygonians." She confronts male members of her family in her two appearances in "Wandering Rocks." In section 11, she loiters with a purpose, securing funds from her father before he can spend them in the Scotch House. After the Dignam funeral, drink and chance encounters with male cronies seem to be his business for the day. Nor is his part particularly positive. He perpetuates anti-Semitism and makes sartorial jokes at the expense of Ben Dollard, who does manage to use some legal knowledge for the benefit of Father Cowley (section 14). Dilly's ambiguous arresting words, "It's time for you" (10.656), suggest possibly that she has Simon's movements well timed. As she calls upon his responsibility to the family she is not deterred by Simon's diversionary gestures—his unflattering mimicry of her posture, which she arrests by pointing out that "All the people are looking at you" (10.666), or his comic plan to do a systematic search for funds in gutters, though this elicits a spontaneous grin. Dilly's persistence gets her two pence beyond the original shilling, but even as he walks off, she vents her suspicion that Simon is holding back at least another shilling. He expresses his own suspicions of the "little nuns" as providers of Dilly's "saucy" resistance (10.676–77). Simon's parting allusion to "little sister Monica" (10.716) evokes a Catholic charity for women, St. Monica's Almshouse.

In section 13, Dilly interrupts the flow of Stephen's perambulatory musings, which have brought him to quayside bookcarts where he does offhand research on "how to win a woman's love" in the secret book of Moses (10.847). Dilly issues a pert, "What are you doing here, Stephen?" (10.853). Ducking the question of his reading, he asks about hers. She shows her purchase, the French primer, and admits "reddening and closing tight her lips" that she plans to learn French (10.869–70). It is an appetite that he may well have created; Stephen recalls, "I told her of Paris" (10.859–60). He has mentally recorded her shabby dress, broken boots, and her token from Dan Kelly, who may have won her love without the advice of the secret book of Moses. Stephen relates to his sister only in the sense that he sees in her his own reflection, or perhaps others' views of him: "My eyes they say she has. Do others see me so? Quick, far and daring. Shadow of my mind" (10.865–66). Theirs is the story of Shakespeare's sister, told more centrally and directly by Virginia Woolf in *A Room of One's Own,* where the son progresses into a public world that refuses and in effect kills his sister. Stephen's perception of Dilly is that she is drowning, but his only help is to warn her to protect her newly purchased French primer from Maggy's pawning efforts.[32] He is remote from the family. Dilly answers his supposition, "I suppose all my books are gone," with "Some . . . We had to" (10.872–74). It registers upon him that she thinks in terms of "we" (10.878). He can feel guilt, but not such community. It is also appropriate at this point to note Gilligan's reference to Stephen Dedalus in an anecdote presented near the end of *In a Different Voice.* Students compare the attitudes expressed by Mary McCarthy's persona in *Memories of a Catholic Girlhood* with those of Stephen in *A Portrait of the Artist as a Young Man.* Each character is weighing responsibility against individual rights in setting a life course: "comparing the clarity of Stephen's *non serviam* with Mary McCarthy's 'zigzag course' of compromise," women students studying the two texts "were unanimous in their decision that Stephen's was the better choice."[33] Dilly Dedalus, like Mary McCarthy, is performing a zigzag between individual intellectual development and family responsibility. Her path is forked and divided, zigzagging between public and domestic spaces, consorting with both sides, and compromising. She will presumably carry a shilling and one pence home to her sisters, having spent a penny on her own development.

More minor still are characters who emerge only in the interpolations, along Reverend Conmee's path, or in the final section featuring the viceregal cavalcade. Many are late scribal additions made to the final manuscript or the proofs. In this class, too, is the crumpled "throwaway," an announcement of an evangelist's coming, which threads its way down the Liffey with more direction than most of the "persons" of the episode.

Although much of Reverend Conmee's thinking as he encounters people on his travels is judgmental and flattering to his own responsibilities and system of values, he calls additional minor characters to our attention. His tram ride offers a reading of ordinary people akin to that of the exemplary train ride in Virginia Woolf's "Mr. Bennett and Mrs. Brown." He identifies a woman traveler as "wife" because the gentleman with the glasses in the next seat had been explaining something to her. When an old woman with a market net and basket exits hurriedly, he assumes that she must stay within the penny tram fare. Here is another trace of a woman scavenging out her existence with a very careful use of resources, and another zigzag course not followed.

Gerty MacDowell has a significant miniature amid the passage of the viceregal cavalcade in the final section. Her brief internal monologue of "Wandering Rocks" has different diction from the half of "Nausicaa" that inscribes her thoughts in the language of popular romance. Here Gerty has a directed task in place of her indisposed (and presumably drunkard) patriarch. Thus like Dilly and Maggy, she takes responsibility for the family, while her father lets it down. Gerty's fascination with fashion persists, frustrated by a blocked view of "Her Excellency" (10.1209). Critics have chided Gerty for getting her titles wrong, though she should be credited with knowing the discourse of fashion that interests her more. Like Dilly, she takes some time out for herself.

One of the second-order minor characters who intrigues me most is the elderly female in a "black silk skirt of great amplitude" (10.474–75): she zigzags among the four courts in sections 9, 10, and 19, remaining a mystery. She seems to be following three legal cases. The description of divisions of the court and stages of an appeal wanders incomprehensibly through six lines of text (10.626–31). The elderly woman in black may well be a widow, though unlike Mrs. Dignam, she is apparently unassisted in making legal claims (if that is her interest in the proceedings of the courts of chancery). We last see her smiling "credulously" on "the representatives of His Majesty"—acquiescing to both the viceroy and the labyrinthine proceedings of the legal system (10.1193–95). This enigmatic figure wears the voluminous black garb of the aged Queen Victoria, who had moved through Dublin in her own cavalcade in 1900, denied the salutes of many Dubliners thanks to the efforts of Maud Gonne and other nationalists to keep the audience away. Her zigzags through the courts suggest the legal convolutions of the Victorian novel *Bleak House*.

Her seemingly mindless smile joins many others as one of the most persistent gestures in the chapter. The smile wanders around from face to face—from Conmee's smile with teeth well polished with areca-nut paste, to Dilly's grin, to the mechanical smiles plastered on the poster people, Marie Kendall and Eugene Stratton (the latter, as a white performer in blackface, preserves the illusion of gaiety among the oppressed). In her darting about, the elderly woman in black may be at least trying to read the system for her survival, perhaps for the sake of her own set of dependents.

Gender is a factor in the narrative array of characters in "Wandering Rocks"—in the decisions of whom to follow, when to interrupt, and what minds to enter. On the whole, women as a group are underrepresented: through their "minoritarian" presence in "Wandering Rocks," the episode leaves a suggestion of a significant gap in Joyce's work, or in his Dublin.

Where people go in "Wandering Rocks" has a lot to do with the sorts of relationships and responsibilities they assume. Given Gilligan's theory that women are socialized to attach more importance to relationships, it is not surprising that one of the first feminist Joyceans, Marilyn French, attempted to read the "moral relationships" between characters from "Wandering Rocks," and that she was disappointed when she could not find "genuine encounters" in the episode.[34] What male networking exists may or may not challenge Gilligan's findings. Paddy Dignam's circle of friends is working on his behalf throughout the day. Ironically, their relationship to him becomes most productive after some of them have helped him drink himself to death, as Molly Bloom notes in "Penelope." Dignam and friends do not touch the root cause of alcoholism, just as the male power figures of *Mrs. Dalloway* never question the merits of war. A more basic social critique never emerges from the minds and zigzagging paths of women characters of "Wandering Rocks"; it originates there when readings are repositioned for sensitivity to gender and marginalization.

11

Political Sirens

JULES LAW

Minuet of *Don Giovanni* he's playing now. Court dresses of all descriptions in castle chambers dancing. Misery. Peasants outside. Green starving faces eating dockleaves. Nice that is. Look: look, look, look, look, look: you look at us. (11.965–68)

Music. Gets on your nerves. (11.1182)

THE "OUTSIDE" OF MUSIC

I begin not so much out of an active impatience with music in "Sirens" as with a conviction that some of the most intriguing developments in the chapter occur "outside" its psycho-philosophical meditations on music, and, indeed, outside the Ormond bar, saloon, and restaurant altogether.[1] In Leopold Bloom's meditative daydream these excluded themes are figured as "green starving faces" exiled from the bastions of high culture. But what "green faces" hover "outside" this particular chapter, demanding that we pay attention to them? And to what social forms does the alleged nervous exhaustion of music point? I begin, then, with two observations: first, that the entire chapter is framed by a political context (signaled most immediately by the passing of the viceregal cavalcade) which it is Bloom's project to repress or avoid; and second, that the Ormond barmaids function as ambivalent mediating figures who register—but refuse to return—the dysfunctional male gaze. This latter ambivalence points us, in turn, back to the frame, which we may understand both as the chapter's political context and as the formal device (the "overture" to the *fuga per canonem*) which marks the boundary between "Sirens" and "Wandering Rocks" while containing the movements of the "Sirens" chapter proper. The overture separates the interior of the chapter—a narrative about music and desire—from its political exterior, and in this sense is like the window at which the barmaids are sitting at chapter's opening, surveying the passing cavalcade. But the overture also offers itself as a spectacle in its own right, a tour de force of linguistic materiality. Like the barmaids themselves, the overture is *on display*—for stakes, and in ways, which we have to determine.

"Sirens" is not unique among the chapters of the novel in staging the deconstruction of the male gaze. "Nausicaa" and "Circe," too, counter Bloom's gaze with the perspectives of Gerty MacDowell and Bella/Bello, respectively.[2] But the chapter is unique in aligning the male gaze, and its various consequences and evasions, with the spectacularization of nationalist politics which the novel elsewhere so adroitly inspects (as in "Cyclops," for instance). For the drama outside the Ormond bar which captures the interest of the Sirens-barmaids is precisely the spectacle of the viceregal cavalcade; and to Bloom, at least, what is most alluring about the Sirens is the question of what they are looking at. The chapter thus structurally aligns the classic anxious subtext of the male gaze ("what do women want?") with questions about the modern consumer of politics. With this twist, of course: that as *icons* of *the act of consumption,* the Sirens are both objects and subjects. In the end the chapter does not say anything (new) to us about female sexuality, but the Sirens's double role makes them a kind of hinge or relay in the chapter's argument, helping to make visible the articulating function of female sexuality in (straight) male public life. Thus, Bloom's flight from politics at the chapter's end is arrested by his encounter with a hystericized version of the Sirens's sexuality, an encounter which ironically returns him to politics as refuge.

THE OVERTURE

Let us assume for a moment that the overture unfolds synchronously with the passage of the viceregal cavalcade and with Bloom's tour of the Liffeyside shop windows ("Moulang's pipes," "Wine's antiques," and "Carroll's dusky battered plate" [11.86–88])—the two parallel events with which the chapter's narrative proper begins. A three-ringed circus, then: the barmaids watch the cavalcade roll by; Bloom surveys the flow of commodities; the reader beholds as several dozen phrases and strands from the chapter parade by in all their material splendor.

The overture is an extravaganza of material signifiers cut loose from their once and future narrative context. It is at once a tableau of visual signs ("bronze," "gold," "blue") and a catalog of aural ones ("hoofirons, steelyringing" [11.01], "husky fifenote blew" [11.05]), but beyond that still it is a display of pure signifiers. Indeed, the strands of the overture mingle and merge at the level of the signifier, whether through puns, contractions, synecdoches, metonymies, or more unorthodox orthographic distortions ("Goodgod henev erheard inall" [11.29]).[3] This foregrounding of the signifier fits quite neatly with Bloom's tour through the half-lives of commodities (as Hugh Kenner points out, most of the shops Bloom passes are secondhand or antique stores)[4] and the barmaids' treatment of the viceregal party as a fashion show ("—Is that her? asked miss Kennedy. / Miss Douce said yes, sitting with his ex, pearl grey and *eau de Nil.* / —Exquisite contrast, miss Kennedy said" [11.66–68]). Language here is just one more commodity on display, like antique plate or the viceregal wardrobe.

Why should we regard the overture as a display specifically of *commodities* rather than simply a celebration of the *materiality* of language? In purely formal terms, the overture reduces linguistic signs to the musicality of pure sound; or, conversely, subjects musicality to the vicissitudes and materiality of the orthographic sign.[5] Let us tease out for a moment the various implications of a formalist reading. According to such a reading, the function of the overture would be to defamiliarize linguistic signs while at the same time reorienting us to a specifically Joycean way of reading. This double movement is achieved in several different ways.

The first characteristic we notice about the stylistic ethos cultivated by the overture is that it is essentially Bloomian. Though it might be argued that many of the stylistic devices developed here—free association and the plasticity of the signifier in particular—are the signatures of stream of consciousness more generally, the overture still places us firmly within the hypotactic, ever-condensing bricolage of Bloom's mind:

> Blew. Blue Bloom is on the. (11.6)

> Appropriate. Kidney pie. Sweets to the. Not making much hand of it. Best value in. Characteristic of him. Power. (11.617–18)

> Coincidence. Just going to write. Lionel's song. Lovely name you have. Can't write. Accept my little pres. (11.713–14)

If the overture does evoke Bloom's consciousness, then a strongly paradigmatic subject/object structure is established at the very beginning of the chapter. The chapter must then be concentrically organized, like a kind of parodic Platonic cave: Bloom's mind at the center, outside of which we find the bar and its shadowy denizens, outside of which is the jostle and glare of the "real" world, the world of imperial cavalcades and sexual betrayal. This organization fits nicely into the Homeric schema, for it presents Bloom as an Odyssean hero and the barmaids quite unambiguously as the seductive objects of desire, sheltering and distracting the hero from the *telos* of plot. In other words, such an organization suspends narrative syntax and places Bloom implicitly inside the Ormond hotel from the very beginning of the chapter, thus allowing him to be the presiding consciousness of a chapter which begins by *watching* the barmaids *watching* the viceregal cavalcade.

Pursuing a formalist reading further, we find in the overture an assertion of the relationship between the self-manipulability of the body's sensory faculties and those stylized distortions that may subsequently be incorporated as "art." Take, for example, a line from later in the chapter ("Good God he never heard in all his life" [11.780–81]), which the overture renders as "Goodgod henev erheard inall" (11.29). While the overture version retains the belatedly "original" syntagmatic sequence of phonemes, it gathers and spaces them in new and defamiliarizing ways. Thus we have two simultaneous processes: on the one hand, the extraction and isolation of short sequences of signs from their context; on the other hand, defamiliarizing shifts of rhythm and emphasis within the extracted chains. The combined effect corresponds to a kind of sensory self-manipulation that Stephen/Joyce had experimented with in *Portrait*: "It was like a train going in and out of tunnels and that was like the noise of the boys eating in the refectory when you opened and closed the flaps of the ears. Term, vacation; tunnel, out; noise, stop" (*P* 17). Stephen Dedalus's experiment splits the difference between Odysseus and his crew, between the stopped-up and unstopped ear. "Sirens" suggests that regulating the flow of phonic material in this way produces a particular kind of acoustic attention. The overture thus performs a certain kind of work on, and produces certain kinds of effect from, the materiality of language. In doing so, it attempts to naturalize a particular style: at once lyrically associative and comically abbreviated. The overture attempts to demonstrate that as we move closer to the register of the material signifier and actually *listen* to language, we can begin to hear its distinctive music. This music is, not surprisingly, consubstantial with Joyce's own default- or house-style in *Ulysses,* the style of Leopold Bloom's interior monologue.

The overture, then, attempts to set free the musicality of language by foregrounding the linguistic signifier; not surprisingly, the newly liberated material side of language turns out to sound a lot like the Joyce we already knew. This strategy of defamiliarizing so as to refamiliarize remains in force even when we turn to consider the narrative aspect of the overture. For while at one level the overture appears to materialize and thus denarrativize Joyce's discourse (extending and intensifying the decomposition of the unit of narrative in "Wandering Rocks"), it must be admitted that the overture's narrative syntagmas unfold more or less in the same order that they do in the chapter proper. Thus the overture does not so much suspend narrative as reduce it to the purer temporality of sequence. Rather than disappearing, narrative is simply redacted to a synecdochical code. The point of the overture, then, is to reassure us that the apparent randomness and contingency of the purely material side of language inevitably resolves itself into familiar patterns and meanings.

We have dwelled here on the formal implications of the overture at the expense of its status as a display of commodities. As a formal set piece it orients us toward specifically "Joycean" reading even as it indulges in the fiction of a pure materiality (that is, musicality) of the sign. But as we have noted, this parade of signifiers is situated alongside two other displays: the shopwindows of the Liffeyside merchants, and the viceregal cavalcade.[6] What do these various spectacles have to do with one another? To begin to answer this question we must look at the structural positioning of the overture, poised as it is between two narrative rehearsals of the same event: the passage of the viceregal cavalcade outside the Ormond hotel. The final segment of "Wandering Rocks" recounts this event from a narrative position outside the bar and hotel, while the opening movement of "Sirens" recounts it from the perspective of the barmaids looking out the window of the bar. The overture thus becomes a hinge articulating the two accounts and the two perspectives. Regarding the overture as part and parcel of the spectacle which articulates the two chapters rather than as some metalinguistic code instructing us how to read "Sirens" invites us to think of the chapter as centrifugally, rather than centripetally, oriented: as pointing outside itself (to some concrete, public event) rather than as cultivating some psycho-philosophico-musical interiority. The overture, then, *points us* toward the chapter's political context, but it is not a *transparent* window. It is precisely this recognition that is at stake in regarding the overture as a display of commodities rather than simply as an extravaganza of signifiers. For if the chapter is framed by a signifier of supreme British imperial authority, the "political" meaning of that signifier is nonetheless complicated by the relationship of the "authentic" Irish gaze toward that signifier, and by the ironic ways in which the relationship between barmaids and patrons mimics that between the barmaids and the cavalcade. In short, the overture points us toward the highly gendered and commodified nature of icons which mediate "Englishness" and "Irishness."

THE SIRENS

For fifty years the Sirens have plagued political philosophers. I refer not simply to Joyce's rendering of the Homeric episode—which has itself attracted significant political commentary—but to the Homeric myth itself. For Adorno and Horkheimer, Homer's Odysseus represented the spirit of proto-enlightenment rationality, the victory of regulative reason over an unruly natural and social world, represented principally by the snares of undomesticated female sexuality: the Sirens, Calypso, Circe.[7] According to the classic Frankfurt School interpretation, Homer thus has one foot in myth and one foot in enlightenment. Extending this line of interpretation, critics such as Franco Moretti, Terry Eagleton, and David Lloyd have regarded Joyce as having one foot in the enlightenment and one foot beyond, in some decentered, post-Kantian conception of the subject.[8]

Specifically, Adorno and Horkheimer argue that in the Sirens myth, Homer narrates the divorce of art from labor. Odysseus's enlightenment solution to the problem of the Sirens is simple: those that labor must not listen; those that listen must be bound impotently to the mast. Adorno and Horkheimer are careful to emphasize that the split does not precede Odysseus's solution: it would be a mistake to regard the Sirens' song as symbolizing the seductions of art or sexuality abstracted from knowledge or labor. The Sirens' song is enthralling precisely because of its cognitive content: they "know all that has happened" and offer a totalized understanding of the individual life.[9] But their mythic knowledge distracts Odysseus from the teleology of hearth and home, which it is the duty of regulative reason to enforce.

How does Joyce's *Ulysses* play havoc with this myth of enlightenment? Who are the Sirens in *Ulysses*? And how does Joyce's handling of the myth subvert or reinforce the gendering of "authentic" identity—particularly national identity—which the myth seems so conveniently to support? We can begin with a simple observation: like many of the episodes in *Ulysses,* the "Sirens" episode seems to begin at the end of the previous episode, where, as form begins to disintegrate, random phrases, clues, and allusions begin to anticipate the coming chapter. In this case, it is the figure of the Sirens and the bound Odysseus who appear in ironic, inverted fashion. As the viceregal cavalcade flashes by at the end of "Wandering Rocks," Blazes Boylan, his hands occupied, is able to offer no more than a rakish glance of appreciation to the three women in the carriages: "His hands in his jacket pockets forgot to salute but he offered to the three ladies the bold admiration of his eyes and the red flower between his lips" (10.1245–46). The passage raises the question, Who are the Sirens? The English countess and her entourage, or, as the next episode would have it, the Irish barmaids? From the point of view of an analysis of gender and nationality—of the gendering of nationality—the difference may not amount to much. For Joyce seems to have been acutely aware of the ways in which the iconic component of late-nineteenth-century nationalism recapitulated traditional sexual politics. Viceregal processions were in fact a case in point.

THE CAVALCADE

In February 1886 Lord Aberdeen, the new viceroy of Ireland, and his wife, Ishbel Marjoribanks, prepared to make their state entry into Ireland.[10] The event promised to be an auspicious one, for only a month earlier Gladstone had swept into office, pledging to resolve the Irish question, and the new viceroy was widely regarded as ambassador and broker for a transition to home rule. Lady Aberdeen herself was regarded as something of a social missionary, whose plan of adopting Irish culture and Irish causes caused considerable chagrin to members of the Ascendancy, who felt such sympathies to betray bad taste as well as bad politics. The marchioness had planned to deck out her children and herself in green velvet coats for the occasion, but this spectacle was vetoed by officials in Dublin Castle, who determined the signifier of Irish green to be too subversive under the circumstances. (The popular song of the day, "The Wearing of the Green," contained the line, "they're hangin' men and women for the wearin' of the green.") On the opposing side, Irish patriots were equally resentful of what they saw as a cynical ploy to appease, or even to co-opt, nationalist sentiment. In his memoir, Lord Aberdeen recalls:

> we always attributed much of the subsequent kindly feeling shown to us by the Dublin public to the impression created on that first day by the little folks' spontaneous delight in the gay show, which they evidently thought was organized for their special benefit. They were dressed in white Irish poplin, and amused the crowd by the zest with which they responded to any signs of salutation by waving their hands and blowing kisses. We learned afterwards that some people indeed imagined that this feature of the show had been carefully devised beforehand, and

> remarks were heard to the effect that it would not do for Lady Aberdeen to suppose that she would "get round" the people by the blandishments of her children.[11]

If Lord Aberdeen came belatedly to recognize the complex ways in which the viceregal wardrobe—as a spectacle of domesticity—might be interpreted, he seems to have remained strangely obtuse as to the military-political implications of other aspects of viceregal "ceremony":

> From Kingstown we proceeded by train to Westland Row Station, where the customary State entry into Dublin was made, in accordance with usage, the Lord-Lieutenant riding, accompanied by the Commander-in-Chief of the Forces in Ireland, and a brilliant *military staff*, and escorted by a *detachment of cavalry*. This was for *purely ceremonial purposes*; and in the same manner *the streets were lined by troops*.[12]

Lord Aberdeen was hardly obtuse as to the military nature of the British presence in Ireland. His and Lady Aberdeen's memoirs record their frequent frustration with Dublin Castle's constant level of military surveillance and security precautions, and Lord Aberdeen frequently presents himself as deliberately opting for smaller "ceremonial" contingents of military guards. (We should regard this, then, as a textbook example of the kind of blindness and insight that allows imperialism to pursue its course in "good faith.") Nonetheless, Aberdeen's inability to see British military displays in the Irish context as anything other than "ceremonial" is at least ironic, given his (and his wife's) sensitivity to the meaning and advantages of symbol and spectacle (Lord Aberdeen, for instance, had insisted on being publicly introduced to T. D. Sullivan, the author of "The Wearing of the Green," and to Michael Davitt).[13]

What the controversy over the wardrobe of the viceregal processional points to is that the "meaning" of any nationalist or imperialist spectacle in this period was actively contested rather than taken for granted. And further, it points to the central role of domestic ideology in the fashioning of such spectacle. It is the domestic face of imperialism that draws fire from unionist and patriot alike. There is no record of what Lord Aberdeen wore for the occasion, or of the public reaction to it; it is left to the "family"—wife/mother and children—to sentimentalize imperial rule. And the "family" distills, ultimately, into the figure of the woman, for whom the children are mere extensions. The ruse of sentimentality, after all, is attributed to Lady Aberdeen ("it would not do for Lady Aberdeen to suppose that she would 'get round' the people by the blandishments of her children"). Lady Aberdeen becomes the mobile signifier at the intersection of the English and Irish gazes. We might say that it is upon her body that the political contest is waged and inscribed, providing we note that she is herself (owing to her position of privilege) an active participant in the fashioning of the national-female body.[14]

The Aberdeens' first stay in Ireland turned out to be a short one (they returned for a second vice-regency in 1906 through 1915), for in June 1886 Gladstone's home rule bill was defeated in parliament, and by August the Liberals had been turned out of office in a general election. In the interim, however, Lady Aberdeen had established the Irish Industries Association to promote domestic industry, introduced Irish-made-clothing-only garden parties at Dublin Castle, and arranged for a display of "pretty Irish girls spinning and lace-making" in a special Irish industries stall at the 1886 Edinburgh Exhibition.[15] And on August 3, as the family prepared to decamp from their Dublin Castle residence amidst great fanfare, Lord Aberdeen happened to glance out of the carriage, across the street, and to glean some symbolic affirmation of the changes he believed they had wrought: "We could not help thinking as we sat there, of the window opposite, which once had been hired with a design to shoot a former Lord-Lieutenant, Lord Cowper, instead of which now there was a photographer's camera."[16] Viceregal spectacle as the object of the journalistic lens rather than the rebel gunsight—Aberdeen must have thought that his family's "blandishments" had indeed worked well! Where once had been the gaze of hatred and suspicion there was now the gaze of desire and fetishization.

As these various events and anecdotes suggest, the Aberdeens were at once immensely sensitive and immensely obtuse as to the political significance of public spectacle.[17] During their administration, every kind of spectacle or effect that could be viewed as expressing aspirations of the "Irish" was celebrated and put on display (Irish commodities, Irish "girls," Irish clothing): every kind of spectacle that announced British imperial authority was either regretted or, more likely, deliberately misread. What were the subsequent effects of this? By 1904, Lord and Lady Aberdeen were safely ensconced in new philanthropic and ambassadorial projects abroad, and viceregal spectacles in Dublin were looked to for less "political" statements of fashion. "Wandering Rocks" and "Sirens" provide us with exemplary instances, as Lord and Lady Dudley's viceregal cavalcade flashes through the streets of Dublin:

> Gerty MacDowell, carrying the Catesby's cork lino letters for her father who was laid up, knew by the style it was the lord and lady lieutenant but she couldn't *see what her Excellency had on*. . . . (10.1206–9, emphasis added)

> —Is that her? asked miss Kennedy.
> Miss Douce said yes, sitting with his ex, pearl grey and *eau de Nil*.
> —Exquisite contrast, miss Kennedy said. (11.66–68)

Old-fashioned narrative (and political) questions such as "Where are they going?" or "What are they doing?" are relegated to an afterthought here. One of the bar denizens will later ask Miss Kennedy if she knows where the cavalcade is headed this afternoon—on what ceremonial state mission—and Miss Kennedy will turn to the newspaper for the viceregal itinerary. But such narrative tropes of nationalism as the bureaucratic journey and the newspaper—

identified by Benedict Anderson as crucial to the formation of colonial-nationalist identity—are here subordinated to the purer spectacle of fashion.[18]

Popular-cultural, mass-cultural, and state-cultural images converge here in historically resonant ways.[19] The second half of the nineteenth century saw an increasing commodification of ostensibly popular-cultural Irish material, a commodification mediated (as we have seen in Lady Aberdeen's case) precisely by aristocratic English patronage. Toward the end of the century, the Tara brooches and other reproductions of antique Irish jewelry popularized by the patronage of British aristocrats in the 1850s, were filtering down to the mass-cultural worlds of fashion and cosmetics.[20] Now imperial culture reflected back to Irish nationalism not a simulacra of its own aspirations, but a commodification of it.

In both the viceregal procession of February 1886 and the viceregal cavalcade of June 1904, the main spectacle—and cause for speculation—is the viceroy's wife, who becomes a symbol of the threat to "authentic" Irish identity. In both cases the differences between Irish and English identity is elided: in one case, submerged in a spectacle of Irishness; in the other, submerged under the general sign of fashion. The two cases outline a spectrum of possible threats to the nationalist project, spanning not so much from Anglicization to commodity-fetishization, as from the illusion of authenticity to the illusion of inauthenticity. On the one hand, as D. G. Boyce remarks, there was the danger that Irish cultural nationalism might succeed too well; that its greatest success might lie in a commodification that erased any difference between the respective cultures of the occupied and the occupier.[21] Though it was officials from Dublin Castle who vetoed Lady Aberdeen's plans to parade in Irish costume, we have also seen that it might just as easily have been officials from the Irish Parliamentary Party or the Gaelic Athletic Association. Irish nationalism could not afford to have its own distinctiveness appropriated. In fact, Boyce argues that the vacillation in the Irish Parliamentary Party's position during the 1880s and 1890s, between the more moderate demand for home rule and the more radical demand for repeal of the Union, reflects in part a concern about the degree to which English *cultural*, and not just *political*, hegemony threatened Irish self-determination.

On the other hand, there was the danger of postulating—in response to an ostensibly insidious and inauthentic consumer culture—an authentic and monolithic Irish culture which erased those internal differences crucial to nationalism as a mass political program (chief among these was class, though religion and gender figured prominently as well). This latter danger, emphasized by recent theorists of nationalism such as Hobsbawm and echoed by Seamus Deane, among others, is in some senses not symmetrical with the first.[22] It would seem to derive from late-twentieth-century critiques of totalizing political programs, and not to be a part of the late nineteenth century's own understanding of national aspirations. But as Hobsbawm has emphasized, nationalism rarely succeeded after the turn of the century unless harnessed to some genuine and independent social movement.[23] Attacks on the inauthenticity of commodity culture were useful when they helped highlight the critical links between imperialist and capitalist oppression; but they easily tilted over into a politically naive Puritanism.

Thus the temptation of 1886 and the temptation of 1904 turn out to be the same: whether the threat to Irish nationalism lies in the simulation of Irish identity or in the simulation of cosmopolitan identity, the real danger lies in the very hypostatization of identity. And here is where the figure of gender enters the scene. For what happens when the threat to the authentic body politic comes to be symbolized in terms of a woman's body? And what is the difference between figuring the threatened and the threatening body as a woman's?

THE NATIONAL BODY

The barmaid's appreciation for viceregal fashion is disruptive on a number of accounts. It suggests a preference for fashion over either "high" or "folk" culture; it values cultural assimilation over patriotism; and it hints at currents of erotic identification that exceed the bounds of domestic heterosexuality. The result is to prevent any simple reduction of nationalist fronts to the fault lines of sexual politics. The male gaze and the imperialist gaze do not align neatly here. Of course this does not prevent the attempted realignment of such gazes in the chapter's interior.

As we have seen, one of the crucial effects of the overture is to suspend the chapter's narrative syntax, placing Bloom effectively in the bar at the same moment the cavalcade passes by (and, conversely, making the cavalcade pass by repeatedly as the chapter proceeds). Thus we have the following situation: Bloom watching the barmaids watching the cavalcade. The mirroring is more than casual. Later in the chapter Bloom will scrutinize the barmaids with the same critical eye for cosmetic appearance as they displayed in watching the cavalcade: "Her ear too is a shell, the peeping lobe there. Been to the seaside. Lovely seaside girls. Skin tanned raw. Should have put on coldcream first make it brown" (11.938–40). Here the professional ad-canvasser turns the barmaids into advertising props, much as they had done to Lady Dudley. There has been a considerable amount of critical commentary in recent years on the spectacle of advertising in *Ulysses*. Following the pioneering lead of Franco Moretti, both Garry Leonard and Jennifer Wicke have explored the ways in which *Ulysses* speaks ironically from within the false consciousness of a consumer culture, reflecting the arbitrary equivalence of commodities with an equally and implacably arbitrary array of styles. And Thomas Richards has demonstrated that the "Seaside Girl" is the quintessential advertising trope in this system: an aura-less sexual icon circulating freely among the advertising pages and commercial logos of late-nineteenth-century consumer culture; an all-purpose signifier of desirability in an economy that has moved more and more toward pure conspicuous consumption, pure exchange value.

According to this thesis, the advertising, fashion, and cosmetic industries supply modern culture with a particular kind of false consciousness, whose contours are shaped by a highly gendered circulation of commodities. But as I have suggested, there is another system of exchange at work here, and one which is also mediated by conspicuous images of cultural femininity. In short, *national* identities and allegiances too are being mediated by the performances, constructions, and negotiations of gender. As David Lloyd, Eve Sedgwick, Peter Stallybrass, and Ann Rosalind Jones have demonstrated, the figure of the nation is defined by policing the borders of the sexual body—nowhere more so than in the case of Irish nationalism, where the sexual scandals of Parnell, Wilde, and Casement in particular played into a centuries-old English strategy of gendering the Irish.[24] In Lloyd's words,

> If the spectre of adultery must be exorcized by nationalism, it is in turn because adulteration undermines the stable formation of legitimate and authentic identities. It is not difficult to trace here the basis for nationalism's consistent policing of female sexuality by the ideological and legal confinement of women to the domestic sphere.[25]

By this measure, the sexually unruly barmaids are but poor guardians of Irish nationality; but of course such policing is not Joyce's intent—nor is it particularly the desire of Bloom, whose consciousness presides over this episode.

The spatial staging of "Sirens" emphasizes the ways in which figures of gender hover at the borders of the national body, but the episode emphasizes at the same time the complexity of gender mingling that takes place at the border. The barmaids are border figures, first standing at the window and mediating the passing of the viceregal cavalcade for the inhabitants of the bar (including, implicitly, Bloom), then standing at the bar itself and providing mediating images for Bloom, who cannot actually see the patrons singing patriotic ballads in the adjoining saloon, and who contents himself instead with that dangerous supplement, erotic spectacle.

National identity is constructed in this scenario as a series of concentric exteriorities, rendered ironically equivalent to the interiorized subject, Bloom, precisely through the images of commodified cultural femininity which link them. For Bloom there is little or no difference between the English and the Irish Sirens. Nor is there, from his point of view, anything particularly radical about the appreciative gaze or regard of Siren for Siren, which for him simply betokens the ironic democratizing effects of consumer culture. I have argued elsewhere that the autoerotic and homoerotic component of such scenes provides them with a certain amount of critical leverage. If the sexual dynamic of the scene does not provide a coherent alternative to nationalist politics, it nonetheless cuts across the grain of those politics. Neither Irish nationalism nor English imperialism can become pure spectacle in these scenes—there will be no convenient juxtaposition or tableau of national difference, because there is too active a process of mimicking and desiring going on between the two groups of Sirens.

THE MATERIALITY OF THE GAZE

The figure of the viceroy's wife genders—or perhaps we should say literalizes the implicit sexualization of—the spectacle of the imperial cavalcade. But in "Sirens" this spectacle is not produced—at least immediately or directly—for the classically constructed male gaze.[26] For as we have seen, it is the Irish barmaids—themselves objects of the gaze—who scrutinize Lady Dudley and cast an approving critical glance at her dress. The barmaid-Sirens are thus doubly mirrored from the beginning: not only mirrored in advance *by* Lady Dudley and her entourage (Boylan, as we have seen, plays the bound Odysseus to the viceregal Sirens in the preceding chapter [10.1242–46]), but engaged as well in an active attempt to mimic the "exquisiteness" of Lady Dudley's fashion and bearing. It is not surprising, then, that the barmaids are visually framed for most of the episode by a gigantic bar mirror, in which most of the bar denizens glimpse them reflected and doubled: "[Boylan's] spellbound eyes went after, after her gliding head as it went down the bar by mirrors . . . where it concerted, mirrored, bronze with sunnier bronze" (11.420–23). The various mirrorings and overdeterminations of the Sirens (not to mention the displacement of their appeal from the aural to the visual register) significantly complicates the play of desire in this chapter. Though Bloom cannot "hear" the barmaids hearing Simon Dedalus, he can watch the barmaids watching the men who watch them. But are the barmaids really watching the men?

The one point at which the barmaids are not framed by the mirror is at the opening of the chapter, when they sit at the window gazing across the expanse of the overture at the cavalcade outside. Significantly, this produces a moment of anxiety for the male gaze, which *cannot tell what the Sirens are looking at:* "—What is it? loud boots unmannerly asked. / —Find out, miss Douce retorted, leaving her spyingpoint. / —Your beau, is it?" (11.94–96). The scene hidden from the boots' gaze is a complicated one. It comprises political spectacle (which hereafter enters the bar only through the medium of song), "fashion" (which mediates and in a sense displaces the "political"), homosocial desire (the barmaids' appreciation is reserved for Lady Dudley, while the ogling men receive only their contempt), and the reconfiguration of epic perspective (in which the Sirens of "Wandering Rocks"—that is, the members of the cavalcade—become the Odyssean crew of "Sirens," "killed looking back" [11.77] at the barmaids).[27]

What makes the scene at the window proleptic for the rest of the chapter is, first, that it relegates the "political" to some offstage event, and, second, that it displays the Sirens's literal disregard for male spectatorship. With the exception of Lydia Douce's brief pursuit of Boylan (which takes her momentarily back to the window), the barmaids are ostentatiously contemptuous of the male gaze. In fact they seem intrigued only by dysfunctions of sight: "—O! shrieking, miss Kennedy cried. Will you ever forget his goggle eye?" (11.146); "O greasy eyes! Imagine being married to man like that! she cried" (11.169); "—So sad to look at [the blind piano-tuner's] face, miss Douce condoled" (11.284). When not commenting on dysfunctional male gazes, the Sirens simply disregard their admirers:

> Miss gaze of Kennedy, heard, not seen, read on. Lenehan round the sandwichbell wound his body round.
>
> —Peep! Who's in the corner?
>
> No glance of Kennedy rewarding him he yet made overtures. . . .
>
> Girlgold she read and did not glance. (11.240–46)

For the barmaids, the play of gazes is a gambit within the field of sexual politics. One of Bloom's functions in the chapter will be to adopt this gambit ("See, not be seen" [11.357–58]) and then to philosophize randomly about its various psychological and physiological implications, resituating sexual politics within the supposedly naturalizing discourse of empiricist aesthetics.[28]

Both imperial and sexual politics frame the chapter, then, and both must be neutralized. On the one hand, as we have seen, there is the nationalist-imperialist frame: the chapter begins with the sound of the viceregal cavalcade passing by (the line describing its hoofbeats is repeated like an echo or leitmotiv throughout the chapter) and concludes with Robert Emmet's scaffold speech, announcing the deferral of his epitaph until Ireland *"takes her place among. . . . [the] Nations of the earth"* (11.1284–89). On the other hand, we have the broadly sexual frame: the episode begins with a classic *blazon,* disarticulating the barmaids into synecdochical body parts ("Goldpinnacled hair" [11.07], "satiny breast" [11.08], "Thigh smack" [11.18]), and concludes with Bloom's discharging of a bodily function, with all these elements delicately linked by the chapter's nostalgic atmosphere of sexual tragedy.[29] Though it is the very linkage of the two frames that provides the key to their neutralization (that is, to their replacement by the more familiar philosophico-musical thematic), the linkage is also, as we shall see, the clue to the inevitable reemergence of politics. How, then, are the two frames linked?

Most immediately, by a pun. "Imperthnthn" (11.02). The second line of the chapter begins with what begs to be read as a distorted form of the word "imperial," given the immediate context of the viceregal cavalcade, with which the previous chapter concludes and this one begins. "Imperthnthn." Is the word sticking in someone's throat, or simply merging with the hoofbeats of the chapter's first line ("Bronze by gold heard the hoofirons, steelyringing" [11.01])? But of course "Imperthnthn" turns out, a few pages later, to be only the snuffling, suppressed signifier, "impertinent"—the impertinence of the "boots," who quizzes the two barmaid-Sirens on their love lives. Thus, the imperial context is dissolved into petty sexual and workplace rivalries, which are in turn dissolved into the plasticity of the signifier.

The reduction to the signifier is hardly a neutral operation here. The chapter as a whole contains two reciprocal movements: one in which politics is decomposed into the materiality of the sign; the other in which materiality is recontextualized within a political frame. And just as the discomfiting political sign "imperial" is reduced to "imperthnthn," so the potentially subversive relationship between the Irish and English Sirens—so threatening to nationalist and imperial politics alike—is also reduced to linguistic play. Initially, the barmaids' expression of admiration for Lady Dudley ("—Exquisite contrast, miss Kennedy said" [11.68]) is loosed from its context in order to provide the terms for the barmaids' own self-image: "Most aggravating that young brat is. If he doesn't conduct himself I'll wring his ear for him a yard long. / Ladylike in exquisite contrast. / Take no notice, miss Kennedy rejoined" (11.104–7). However, the relentlessly materializing current of the narrative eventually submits this empowering sign to the play of the signifier: "She drew down pensive (why did he go so quick when I?) about her bronze, over the bar where bald stood by sister gold, inexquisite contrast, contrast inexquisite nonexquisite" (11.462–65). Here the phrase "exquisite contrast" has lost its function as a trope from the discourse of fashion, in which capacity it had forged a link (albeit an unstable one) between the Irish barmaids and the English marchioness. Now the signifiers are mere combinatory terms in a play of sounds.

The materializing *telos* of the chapter fits in quite nicely with Bloom's own (slightly confused) empiricist aesthetics, the most amusing manifestation of which is, of course, his account of "musemathematics":

> Numbers it is. All music when you come to think. Two multiplied by two divided by half is twice one. Vibrations: chords those are. . . . Musemathematics. And you think you're listening to the etherial. But suppose you said it like: Martha, seven times nine minus x is thirtyfive thousand. Fall quite flat. (11.830–36)

Throughout the latter part of the chapter, Bloom is continually translating questions of mediated sexual desire, voyeurism, and sexual jealousy into conundrums of aesthetic physiology. He ponders how Richie Goulding can produce the whistling "answer" to Simon Dedalus's "All is lost now" (11.635), and vacillates between materialist and formalist explanations in meditating on the relation of music to language, visual perception, and "mood": "Wish I could see his face, though. Explain better. . . . Still hear it better here than in the bar though further" (11.721–23); "Might be what you like, till you hear the words" (11.838–39); "Question of mood you're in. Still always nice to hear" (11.841–42). In these passages Bloom performs one of the quintessential functions of the chapter, neutralizing potentially disquieting sexual material by reducing it first to an intellectual speculation about the psychology and logic of sense perception, and then even further to a kind of jocular play with the materiality of the sign. But even Bloom recognizes that this is an evasion. Maneuvering around the Scylla of sexuality brings him face to face with the Charybdis of politics:

> Sea, wind, leaves, thunder, waters, cows lowing, the cattlemarket, cocks, hens don't crow, snakes hissss. There's music everywhere. Ruttledge's door: ee creaking. No, that's noise. Minuet of *Don Giovanni* he's playing now. Court dresses of all descriptions in castle chambers dancing. Misery. Peasants outside. Green starving faces eating dockleaves. Nice that is. Look: look, look, look, look, look: you look at us. (11.963–68)

In this evocation of poignant, imperative voices from the "outside," Bloom pauses to resituate his musings in a social context. Aesthetic theory and aesthetic play are recognized momentarily as an elite privilege, the guilty pleasures of high culture. Though Bloom's spontaneous next step is to put the best face on things ("That's joyful I can feel" [11.969]!), the spell is nonetheless broken. As if in response to Bloom's invocation of repressed political considerations, the denizens of the bar suddenly turn from love songs to patriotic songs ("—No Ben, Tom Kernan interfered. *The Croppy Boy*" [11.991]). Bloom's immediate response is to leave: "I'll go" (11.994).

From Bloom's point of view, politics exercises a threatening, almost sexual influence over the passions of the men at the bar: "Low sank the music, air and words. Then hastened. The false priest rustling the soldier from his cassock. A yeoman captain. *They* know it all by heart. The thrill *they* itch for. Yeoman cap" (11.1081–83, emphasis added). In order to see just how completely the threat of politics has merged with the threat of unruly sexuality here, we have to keep in mind that in Bloom's discourse the pronoun "they"—especially when there is no clear antecedent—is always a code word for "women," and more generally for the alleged mysteries of female sexuality: "*They* can't manage men's intervals. Gap in their voices too. Fill me. I'm warm, dark, open" (11.973–74, emphasis added); "Is that best side of her face? *They* always know" (11.1046–47); "What do *they* think when they hear music?" (11.1049). Thus "the thrill they itch for" conflates the alleged mysteries of political and sexual passions. But the men's political passions are not directly visible to Bloom, who can actually see only the barmaids. The barmaids must thus mediate the men's passions, and this allows Bloom to filter out the political content of the desires being expressed, since in his view the object of the barmaids' rapt attention is the singer, not the song ("Ha. Lidwell. For him then not for. Infatuated" [11.1110]). Bloom's last attempt to keep nationalist politics from intruding requires him to hypostatize the barmaids as figures for a generic sexual gaze, onto which one can graft any sexual fantasy.[30] Watching Lydia Douce listening in rapt attention to Ben Dollard's song, Bloom observes:

> Thrilled she listened, bending in sympathy to hear.
>
> Blank face. Virgin should say: or fingered only. Write something on it: page. If not what becomes of them? Decline, despair. Keeps them young. Even admire themselves. See. Play on her. Lip blow. Body of white woman, a flute alive. (11.1085–89)

In Bloom's fantasy, women gaze "blankly"; thus the female gaze, which to this point has variously threatened, withheld, and refused, is refigured as a page awaiting inscription. The potentially disruptive question of who and what the barmaids are really gazing at is contained. This is a double move on Bloom's part. For by insisting on the nonpolitical and conventionally heterosexual nature of the barmaids' desires, he not only domesticates the barmaids but neutralizes as well the political sentiments of the men in the bar: the "thrill they itch for" is mediated by—and transformed into—a "blank face."

The apparition of Lydia Douce's "blank face" provides only temporary respite for Bloom, whose resolve is nonetheless still to leave. But Bloom fares no better out of the bar than in, for outside as well he must navigate between the Scylla and Charybdis of unruly sexuality and nationalist politics. As a "frowsy whore" careens down the quay toward him, Bloom, embarrassed, seeks refuge in the window display of Lionel Marks's antique shop: "Sees me, does she? Looks a fright in the day. Face like dip. Damn her. O, well, she has to live like the rest. Look in here. . . . Let her pass" (11.1259–64). But the averted gaze brings Bloom face to face precisely with (a variation on) the patriotic sentiment he had fled from at the bar. Concentrating on the shopwindow, his eyes alight on a portrait of martyred patriot Robert Emmet, whose defiant gallows speech *("When my country takes her place. . .")* concludes the chapter, albeit interspersed with Bloom's fart.

In *Ulysses*, it appears, there is no "inside" or "outside" to politics; no interior retreat from, or exterior reference to, the political that is not already implicated in its opposite. The medium for Bloom's negotiations with his world, thus, is not the cozy bar or the shopwindow display but the more complicated figure of the woman. It is the absence or failure of "properly" domestic femininity in the bar that exposes Bloom to the vicissitudes of nationalist passions, and thus the figure of "woman" that sends him shuttling back and forth between politics and sexuality, a "between" whose complex mirrorings and doublings cannot be schematized precisely in terms of interior and exterior. Yet in thus opposing political aspirations to the putative anarchy of feminine sexuality, Joyce ends up with a fairly conventional containment of sexual politics and a fairly traditional opposition of femininity and domesticity to the public sphere. Where does that leave us? We could wish that *Ulysses* was not in the end just as much a critique of Irish cultural nationalism as of English imperialism. We could wish that its sexual anarchy did not proceed along such predictable and ultimately recontainable lines. But we can say, nonetheless, that the episode demonstrates the inextricability—and tactical intertranslatability—

of two of the most vexing identities in modern identity-politics: gender and nationality.

By way of emphasizing this, let me in closing recapitulate the structure of the episode. In the viceregal cavalcade we have an event laden with political meanings, whose terms of analysis are well known. These meanings, however, are complicated by the insistent gendering of the imperial-bureaucratic procession, and this process is in turn complicated by the fact that it is staged most immediately for the barmaids and not for the male gaze. A fourth level of complexity is added when Bloom gazes at the barmaids (while both imperial hoofbeats and Irish patriotic songs echo about him), and finally the whole schema begins to collapse when we realize that neither Bloom (who is the ultimate interiorized subject of this drama) nor the cavalcade (which is at the drama's furthermost horizon) are really *present*—not consistently present throughout the chapter, anyway, and certainly not present to each other. One can see here what Eagleton, Lloyd, and others have analyzed as *Ulysses*'s destruction or decentering of the Kantian subject—that paragon of autonomous, self-consistent, self-present consciousness. Doubtless this is a deconstruction of consciousness that goes on all the time in *Ulysses*. But here it is a question of national identity that precipitates it, and a question of sexual identity that mediates it. Bloom, as we have seen, flees from each of these crises of consciousness into the arms of the other. Joyce's alignment of the two is, I think, proleptic of the convergence of gender and nationality in identity politics, a tension that still haunts contemporary Irish nationalism, according to Seamus Deane.[31] Thus if the Sirens are the figures policing, and being policed at, the borders of contemporary nationalist politics, perhaps we can appreciate Joyce's situation of them at the interface between imperial English spectacle and patriotic Irish song. And perhaps we can appreciate—even as we remain dissatisfied with—the fact that the Sirens show so little regard for Bloom's and Joyce's gaze.

12

When the Saints Come Marching In

Re-Deeming "Cyclops"

MARILYN REIZBAUM

In the "News" section of a July 5, 1992, edition of the *Irish Sunday Tribune,* under the bold headline of "Martyrs move closer to sainthood," we read that of the seventeen Irish martyrs to be beatified, one, "a widow," is a woman, the rest men. Here is her story: "Margaret Bermingham was born in Corballis, near Skyrne, Co Meath in 1515 and moved to Dublin as a teenager. In 1580, her son Walter, who had converted to Protestantism, was elected mayor of Dublin and decided to do something to finally defeat Catholicism. He had his mother arrested and thrown into jail for the rest of her life. She died there in 1584."

This seems a remarkable story for a number of reasons. After reading the whole article, one is struck by the contrast between Mrs. Bermingham's "sacrifice" and that of her martyr compatriots, who—as priests, bishops, brothers, or even sailors—died for their faith through rebellious acts, being punished for them by a "glorious" death of some sort: they were hanged, perhaps thereafter drawn and quartered, or beheaded. Mrs. Bermingham's death seems all the more horrible for having, as it were, no agency or heroism attached to it. Yet it seems better martyr material precisely because her life itself becomes the sacrificial act. What seems absurd here—that the mother's incarceration and death constitute a "defeat" of Catholicism—is at once historically resonant (in religious terms, of Mariology; in other, contemporary terms, of Freudianism). From a certain, perhaps modern, perhaps secular vantage point, women's sacrifice to achieve sainthood seems always to approach the absurd; that is, it crosses some threshold of appropriateness for the occasion. It must be more, somehow greater, and it must always involve the expunging of the self, almost always in sexual terms, where proving the self is disproving it. Women saints register what is simultaneously the highest and lowest kind of sacrifice. How important is this mother that she should become a stand-in for Catholicism? And what is Catholicism's role in exacting such a price and such a victim? For it is not only that Catholicism rewards such "acts," or, commensurately, that such cruel punishment should be measured in terms of martyrdom; surely it is also that future martyrs are primed by hagiography, by the catechisms of piety and devotion.

I begin here because "Cyclops" is to a great degree about the subjects of sacrifice and heroism, as well as the parody thereof. There is, in fact, an economy of sacrifice at work, where everything and everybody gives too much or too little.[1] And it is, I will argue, also about the way in which these subjects, in tandem with the politics of race and national identity, are illuminated by the however recessed categories of gender and sexuality. The appearance of a list of women saints that comes at the end of a longer list of male saints seems—more than many of the other interpolations—obscure. In the context of a chapter that was identified by Joyce and taken up by its critics as employing narrative excess, this list registers as both too much and too little too late. Yet, as I will argue here, it is an opening into the chapter, characterized by its recessiveness and obscurity, as well as by its sense of elaboration and allure.

Many critics have worried the question of the political vision of the chapter. Inasmuch as the chapter, according to the schema, employs the "art" of politics, they have asked to what degree it promises redemption, as it were, in either an artistic or political sense. In his study of the notesheets, Phillip Herring wonders about or laments what he sees as the impossibility "of taking anything in this episode seriously," and attributes this to his sense that all statements and events "become mythopoeic," are "magnified to such absurd dimensions."[2] He refers specifically to the national(ist) issues posed by the chapter, as do most critics who have treated this chapter and also wondered about its excesses, despite the schema's pronouncement of the "technique" as gigantism.[3] Whatever else has gone on, the dramatic climax of the chapter—Bloom and the citizen's "grand" altercation at the end—has been read as the dynamic focus. And most critics have made the interpolations fit this narrative moment. It sets up, at the very least and however parodically or "mythopoeically," the classic territorial duel between men/titans (as national types), and seems to promise a victor and a victory.

More recent critics, such as Enda Duffy, have "redeemed" the text from its (undermining, or overwhelming) comedy by seeing the dramatic altercation between the citizen and Bloom as a "comic interlude" in the enormity of the violence taking place around Barney Kiernan's, in a space outside of the novel, not long before this chapter was written.[4] But in wishing to deflect from this focus to the "real" politics that inform it, Duffy nevertheless returns to it to make his point, a point which seems unconvincing in its facileness about Irish history as a context for the chapter. Mark Osteen is more convincing in his restatement of the "art" of the chapter as "politicoeconomy," a term he borrows from the *Wake*:

> We laugh at the sheer excess in the Cyclopean lists, but our laughter is tempered by the suffering we experience when reading through them and attempting to fit them into our interpretive economies. Joyce's comic economy of excess

finally disarms the monologic discourses of Nameless and the Citizen, and the very excessiveness of the second narrative zone produces a dialogic effect through the comedy that undermines even its own claims to authority. Through this extravagance, the political economy of "Cyclops" is transformed into a "politicoeconomy." (*FW* 540.26)[5]

Osteen, in his analysis, integrates elements of excess (for example, politics and parody) with(in) an economy of sacrifice that is destructive (he calls it "a cult of martyrdom"), so that what emerges victorious is Joyce's labor of art, an expenditure that demonstrates the virtue of excess. "Through his cramming of excess into the novel, Joyce himself becomes a kind of gambler, risking both loss of meaning and loss of readers by his verbal largesse. Yet, ultimately his writing is also *politically* productive labor: the 'superabundance' of description in the insertions does reconstitute the lost wealth of Ireland, not in money but rather in words."[6] In Osteen's terms, the victor is the loss; that is, the loss of one kind of political identity or autonomy becomes "literary capital," "its verbal gifts turning losses into gains." Such a reading not only recasts the cliché of the Irish "gift of the gab," it reformulates the classic duel.

Another way to address this re-formation is in the consideration of how these positions are gendered. One might ask where the woman as eroticized object of the classic duel resides in this text, since there always seems to be one around such showdowns, however marginalized she may be. Unlikely as such a connection might at first seem, the women saints of "Cyclops" provide one path of illumination: they are the recessed damsels in distress literally dying to be acknowledged/saved, and it is through them that the chapter is re-deemed, if you will (just as, for example, the Grace Kelly figure in the 1950s classic American western *High Noon* is the medium and prize of victory and salvation, and just as dubiously).[7] The women saints bring together what is excessive (the political verbiage, sacrificial acts, the parodies and fables of heroism) with what is recessive or repressed (sex and sexuality). At the same time, the fact of their sainthood suggests a religious register (from a feminist angle of vision, a kind of reverse register) of Osteen's characterization of the positively compensatory nature of the narrative excess. For as the hagiography reveals, these women had to betray their own sexuality, their womanliness, before it and its excesses betrayed them. Such a betrayal is a revelation (Grace Kelly's "disguise"—her buttoned-up long-sleeved full-skirt dress—is at once the revelation of that body, just as the fact of her existence as an object of desire and salvation is simultaneously acknowledgment of her potential for betrayal). Now their excess of love is suitably aimed at God. They were potentially like, as I will show, the other women of the chapter—Kitty O'Shea, Sarah Curran, Helen of Troy, Molly—Eves one and all, lost or loose women, who threaten or bring about the downfall of men and civilizations (of course, synonymous), just as the "excesses" of the Cyclopean narratives have been seen by many readers to undermine the "serious matters" of the chapter. In fact, it is these peculiar combinations of excess and recess that complement the very narrative mode of the chapter which counterbalances exaggeration with lack, comedy with history, assertion with retraction and/or equivocation.[8]

The appearance of the saints is signaled in the plot by Martin Cunningham's prayer for the assembled in Barney Kiernan's; Bloom has conveniently left the pub at the very moment when such prayer is meant to deliver and achieve inclusiveness, but has the ironic (and perhaps desired) effect of demonstrating its partiality.

> —Well, says Martin, rapping for his glass. God bless all here is my prayer.
> —Amen, says the citizen.
> —And I'm sure He will, says Joe. (12.1673–75)

Then the sacring (sanctus) bell is sounded and the procession commences, beginning with the crucifer followed by the maintenance squad (thurifers, boatbearers, etc. . . .), the clergy of all manner and kind, and finally "came all saints and martyrs" (12.1689). The caboose, as it were, is Father O'Flynn, who according to the song, "would make hares of them all," and he is attended by Malachi and Patrick, sage and saint of Ireland.[9] There are some eighty-four ostensible saints listed, thirteen of which are women—not including Theresa of Avila, mentioned earlier in the list as leading "the children of Elijah prophet" (12.1683), or one Marion of Calpensis, alias Molly Bloom, whose status as saint in these terms I shall address later. The final two attendants remind us of one crucial context for the chapter, one which Joyce seemed to have had in mind from its inception (in June 1919): "Religion—Saints (Isle of)" appears in the early notes for the chapter as number one in the list of order of events.[10] Despite this, the fair copy had only twenty-one saints to begin with, eight of which are women. It is unclear why Joyce added so many saints and why he selected these in particular (although I will speculate about this second question). It is in any case clear from the notes that this dimension of the chapter was an integral part—not these saints per se, but the dramatic interaction of national and religious issues—whereas he created the parodies, the narrative voice, and what has become the critical focus, "the barroom scene," last.[11]

After the procession, the plot breaks in with the return of Bloom, whose arrival is announced by the Nameless One in rhetoric exactly antithetical to a blessing: "I was just looking around to see who the happy thought would strike when be damned but in he comes again letting on to be in a hell of a hurry" (12.1754–55). While it may appear that it is Bloom's departure in a literal sense that brought on the saints, it is his presence altogether in literal and figurative terms (in the pub, in Ireland) that has stirred things up. "That's the new Messiah for Ireland! says the citizen. Island of saints and sages!" (12.1642–43). This new messiah, "the perverted jew" (12.1635), as Martin Cunningham calls Bloom shortly before, is being savaged here by the men as Jew, or more accurately, as Jewish stereotype, for his excesses and his withholding or lack. He is a marked man, marked by the presumption of what is lacking—a literal tip (prepuce); he has too much money and gives neither drink nor tip ("a prudent member"); he talks too much, but won't divulge; he has many national and religious affiliations, and he lacks the capacity for Irishness; the double entendre inherent in his (supposedly) withheld tip generates a sign both of an abundance of money (the winnings on *Throwaway*) and impotence (the circumcised penis). As Molly later observes, "Poldy not Irish enough" (18.378–79), which is tantamount to not being man enough. The "tip" epitomizes the ironic and contradictory heart of Bloom's character. He is a hybrid/half-breed, in sexual and racial terms, and his Jewishness is the key to that hybridity. "Saint Patrick would want to land again at Ballykinlar and convert us, says the citizen, after allowing things like that to contaminate our shores" (12.1671–72).[12]

It is perhaps historically simple to say that Bloom's Jewishness, however dubious, renders him suspect, dangerous, so capable of harm and pollution. Such views about Jews are presented early in the novel, before we even get to Bloom—by Haines in "Telemachus" and Deasy in "Nestor." The "Cyclops" episode serves to spell out the dimensions of the danger in a way that aligns Bloom with our Mrs. Bermingham, who in her very being represents the Catholic threat to an ascendancy Ireland, in need of humiliation and elimination, a necessary sacrifice. The passage that is framed by these remarks of the citizen—about Bloom as the false messiah (*Throwaway*/Dowie) and as contamination—has the men catalog and construct the elements of Bloom's danger, for them, for Ireland, and for the novel:

> —That's the new Messiah for Ireland! says the citizen. Island of saints and sages!
>
> —Well, they're still waiting for their redeemer, says Martin. For that matter so are we.
>
> —Yes, says J. J., and every male that's born they think it may be their Messiah. And every jew is in a tall state of excitement, I believe, till he knows if he's a father or a mother.
>
> —Expecting every moment will be his next, says Lenehan.
>
> —O, by God, says Ned, you should have seen Bloom before that son of his that died was born. I met him one day in the south city markets buying a tin of Neave's food six weeks before the wife was delivered.
>
> —*En ventre sa mère*, says J. J.
>
> —Do you call that a man? says the citizen.
>
> —I wonder did he ever put it out of sight, says Joe.
>
> —Well, there were two children born anyhow, says Jack Power.
>
> —And who does he suspect? says the citizen.
>
> Gob, there's many a true word spoken in jest. One of those mixed middlings he is. Lying up in the hotel Pisser was telling me once a month with a headache like a totty with her courses. Do you know what I'm telling you? It'd be an act of God to take a hold of a fellow the like of that and throw him in the bloody

> sea. Justifiable homicide, so it would. Then sloping off with his five quid without putting up a pint of stuff like a man. Give us your blessing. Not as much as would blind your eye.
>
> —Charity to the neighbour, says Martin. But where is he? We can't wait.
>
> —A wolf in sheep's clothing, says the citizen. That's what he is. Virag from Hungary! Ahasuerus I call him. Cursed by God. (12.1642–67)

In this exchange, Bloom's virility is put on the block, beginning and ending with his ethnic (or racial) identification as Jew. At the start of the passage, the difference between Christians and Jews is delineated through a reference to the division in messianic traditions. But by invoking Christ here, the men unwittingly point to the "mixed middling" in ethnic or cultural terms that is the figure of Christ, Jew and non-Jew, like Bloom (as he will soon point out, unwittingly too), despite—or perhaps explaining—the men's need to fix him in the position of the threatening other.[13] The reference to Bloom as "mixed middling" refers specifically to questions here surrounding his male prowess (we shall come later to the issue of Christ's maleness). The curious reference in J. J.'s remark to the ambiguous pronoun "he" begs the question of gender; what it can mean to say that the sex of the child will determine the sex or gender of the father—the implication of J. J.'s statement—has not been satisfactorily explained. It recalls the persistent myths about virility (though they are not peculiarly Jewish), wherein a man who could not bear sons would be deemed impotent, unmanly, even womanly.[14] And the myth entails a displacement of blame onto the woman/mother, despite the biological reality. We then read this statement to suggest both that the sex of the child determines the gender of the father and that the woman's involvement is really only acknowledged in cases of failure to produce a son. One easily extends from this to the apprehension that the woman is vilified as an active agent of birth and production but sanctified as a passive vessel of the same ("Paternity may be a legal fiction" [9.844]). In this regard, the French phrase meaning "in the belly of the mother" is taken to be yet another invocation of Christ, referring here to the fetus of Rudy, whose sex, by this theory (by all accounts) should validate Bloom's virility, and whose birth is—in Bloom's terms—nothing short of miraculous. But both Bloom's behavior as described by Ned, implied as womanly (buying baby food), and the fact of Rudy's death, delivered here along with the evidence of Bloom's domesticity ("before that son of his that died was born"), along with the assumption of diminished sexual capacity ("A bit off the top" [12.20]), reconfirm for the men what they are bound to prove—that Bloom is no-man and Molly is no-saint ("and who does he suspect").[15]

The danger of Bloom's "unmanliness" becomes equated in this passage with the taboo of blood, especially that of menstruation, when it is suggested that he can be as incapacitated as a "totty with her courses." The taboo of blood can be cited from a number of sources, both modern and ancient, and has a number of incarnations and manifestations, but most relevant for our purposes here is the way in which the taboo from its Judaic source is inverted to instantiate the disease of Jews and all of the associated myths of smell and contamination, even to suggest that Jewish males menstruated ("I'm told those jewies does have a sort of queer odour coming off them for dogs" [12.452–53]).[16]

The Jewish ritual practices of purification connected to the menses, birth, and dietary practices were not only changed/eliminated within Christianity, but the changes led both to the association of impurity with Jews, and to a metaphorical extension of such practices in relation to the sexuality of Christian women. The icon of Christian womanhood in this respect is, of course, Mary: though she does obey the injunction of purification ("mikveh"—ritual bath) after the birth of Christ, she has not engaged in sexual activity.[17] She is literally emptied of her sexuality. As Marina Warner points out in her compelling study, the ideal of chastity embodied, as it were, by Mary, has had the historical effect of encouraging the physical onset of amenorrhea in women, symbolically the elimination/denial of blood.[18] History seems to have elided the way in which the Jewish taboo against menstruation and blood—kashrut law—has been inverted to become a taboo against Jews who become themselves the pollutants (Jewish men rather than Christian women menstruate). The "disease" of Jews is often associated with blood (the "social diseases" of ritual murder and syphilis. Despite the counterhistorical evidence that Jews have a much lower incidence of the latter than their non-Jewish counterparts, it has been established as prevalent among them and thereby mythically connected to the ritual of circumcision).[19] Disease/circumcision becomes the mark of the Jew which cannot be hidden; in the racial discourse of the period, Jewish bodily features—nose and penis—were the symbolic extensions of Jewish sexuality. "The Jew's sexuality, the sexuality of the polluter, is written on his face in the skin disease which announces the difference of the Jew."[20] Given this historical weight of evidence against Jews and the danger they represent, it becomes "justifiable homicide"—laughable as it is in its tellingly ironic expression here—to throw Bloom, the Jew, into the "bloody sea." The citizen's final remarks in this passage then reinforce all that has been tacitly understood about the threat of the Jew. He is "a wolf in sheep's clothing" (how can you hide that nose?), in many respects pretending to be what he is not: an Irishman, an insider, a man of his word *("Mauscheln")*, a man. Instead he is "Virag from Hungary! Ahasuerus, I call him. Cursed by God": the pretender, false messiah, outsider, the betrayer of Christ doomed to wander the earth without a home. A bloody Jerusalem cuckoo (12.1571–72).[21]

The idea that Bloom is pretending to be something he is not takes on a number of twists and turns here since one might just as likely characterize him as a sheep who has been given wolf's clothing. He is famous among critics for playing his part in the duel, for finally taking on the mantle of Jewish identity—an identity that is only partially his; he is pretending in at least two ways (with his Protestant and Catholic mantles), to be what he is not. Bloom's pretense/bravado receives the blessing of the saints, who intervene between these sections of the text to inspire Bloom, as it were, to the "heights" of the role of the sacrificial lamb, a role that is forced upon him and that he produces in the guise of muscular defense (a sheep in wolf's clothing).[22] For as we shall see, his claim to Jewishness is not only ambiguous and/or equivocal, but highly provocative in its rhetoric of identification with Jesus. It gives a whole new meaning to the idea of "cross"-dressing.

And so the wolf that is Bloom is at once the sacrificial lamb in this section, imaged as the ravenous wild animal (this reference to Matthew 7:15 brings together all the associations of false prophecy, disguise, and the etiology of danger), suggestively both the scapegoat that is historically the Jewish figure, and the martyr, the rehabilitated lamb of God that is the metaphor of Christ.[23] We see in negative relief the way in which the challenge to Bloom is gendered. His sexuality is a metonymy for his religious affiliation, his alien status, and just as ambiguous in the very terms that are used to mark it. He has been unmanned by circumcision, that very lack leading to an excess of blood (or a lack of the Y chromosome), by the blood libel—here of menstruation—and by disease. Whatever the truth—since, of course, Bloom is not circumcised—he can do nothing to change or dislodge the associations. He is the necessary outsider, against which the national and sexual authenticity of the men in the pub can be measured and verified.

But what of the women saints? Theirs is a resonant placement, as I suggested before, both in holding up the rear of the procession of saints and in their interpolative role at this point in the chapter. Like Bloom, they perform a necessary function. They are first scourged (as humans) and then lauded (as saints) for their lacks and their excesses. They are the idealized other to Bloom's evil other. And yet, the woman saints are themselves conceptually Bloom's complementary others. They too are sacrificial lambs, mirrored in Christ's martyrdom, whose sexuality had to be disguised/expunged because proven and therefore dangerous, just as the "proof" of Bloom's otherness/Jewishness is mediated through his sexuality. (We might think of "Little Red Riding Hood," where the wolf wears grandma's clothing, associatively aligning in yet another powerfully mythic way the danger of the Jew with the danger of woman.)[24]

Rather than attempting to address all of the women saints mentioned here, I will discuss a few individuals at some length and several others in terms of characteristic groups, groups that have a particular import for this chapter and this moment in it. Almost all are celebrated and revered for what are tantamount to acts of self-mutilation and abnegation, and in almost all cases their sexuality—either literally through the genitalia or through symbolic terms—is the arena of that mutilation. The procession begins with St. Theresa of Avila, the saint born in the sixteenth century, whose worldly or heavenly agony is captured in the magnificent seventeenth-century statue by Bernini that stands in the Coronaro Chapel in Rome. What one sees in the statue is what one can read in Theresa's accounts of her "ecstasies," that they are palpably physical though their source is purportedly spiritual. While the poetic translation of physical sexuality into spiritual ecstasy is not new (for example, "Song of Songs"), this translation (much like, for example, the poetry of John Donne) has physical pain as its necessary medium; these sainted figures become "transsexuals" as E. M. Cioran suggests in his aphoristic *Tears and Saints,* by which he means they become sexual beings of a different order, and that sex is in fact the necessary ingredient of their ecstatic transformation:

> Ecstasy replaces sexuality. The mediocrity of the human race is the only plausible explanation for sexuality. As the only mode of coming out of ourselves, sexuality is a temporary salvation from animality. For every being, intercourse surpasses its biological function. It is a triumph over animality. Sexuality is the only gate to heaven. The saints are not a-sexual but trans-sexual. They no longer need the revelations of sexuality. To be a saint means to be always outside yourself. What else would sexuality *add* to this? Sexual orgasm pales besides the saints' ecstatic trance.[25]

Theresa of Avila was a controversial figure in her lifetime, where her excess of piety and suffering were interpreted as the excess of human vanity by the sisters of her first order. She is associated with the reinstitution of the discalced discipline for the Carmelite order, and practiced ascetic austerity, for example, by wearing a painful haircloth. Because she was so shrewd and so self-effacing, she was thought by some to be a man (therefore a transvestite as well as a transsexual). In other words, her piety and position were always questionable, and always through the attribute of her gender or sexuality (a woman pretending to be a saint, a man pretending to be a woman saint; or, indeed, a wolf in sheep's clothing). Her womanliness made her suspect; she had to be in disguise. Her body was mutilated after death as well, and often exhumed for the purposes of a kind of religious occupation or fetishization—relic making. Her brother cut off her hand, which was thought to have miraculous powers, and it is noted that a scent of violet and fragrant oil emitted from her tomb. Cioran says that "saintliness is the cosmic apogee of illness, the transcendental forescence of rot," resonantly suggesting what he believes to be the true matter of such sacrificial imperatives.[26] Theresa is the patroness of Spain and is invoked against headaches and heart disease, while, according to one source, her heart is on display at the convent of Avila, complete with crown and lance marks for the pain of God's love she has suffered.[27] She is emblematically the bride of Jesus, who "entered" her in many a vision.

The procession of women saints in the passage ends with a procession of its own, that of Ursula and the eleven thousand virgins, who, as the story goes, undertake a pilgrimage from Britain to the holy land, and meet a "glorious death in defense of their virginity from the army of the Huns," whom they encountered along their way in Cologne.[28] Like so many of the women saints, Ursula is driven to her martyrdom by an original wish to defend herself against human marriage and sexuality; their slaughter, then, becomes a grandiose (and gross) symbol of the very thing Ursula wishes to avoid, wherein the denials of worldly consummation become the devotions of spiritual wedlock. She is emblematized by her cloak, which is imaged to be sheltering her companions (all eleven thousand of them), a mere synecdoche in another kind of disguise.

In between we have many examples of women who sought to eschew worldly love and to avoid marriage at great expense to their physical well-being; some, like Barbara, had this visited upon them in the form of possessed and possessive fathers. In the cases of Lucy and Brigid, such resistance takes the form of mutilation of the eyes and face: Lucy is emblematized by her gouged-out eyes, which she holds in a dish; Brigid, patroness of Ireland, prayed for deformity. Both Lucy and Brigid were purported to have regained their sight and visage through grace. For Brigid, this happens oxymoronically when she receives her veil.[29] The reference to missing eyes, of course, is resonant in this chapter about blinds of all kinds, but works particularly to connect the myths about sexuality and vision, where, as we gather from these saints' lives, the threat of the first may mean the destruction of the other. In every case, blinding sight is the aim, a rewriting of self-destruction, just as sexuality is displaced and rewritten, repressed and reformulated into ecstatic devotions and postures. These women are wedded to Christ, who is ironically eroticized by their reformulation, their physical deformities or lack (just as Bloom's lack makes the men men).[30]

Finally, there are a number of saints here who are associated with roses, by name and/or by flower. We know that the Virgin Mary is symbolically associated with roses: hers is a crown of roses in counterpoint to Jesus' crown of thorns. Theresa of Avila is often depicted with roses, as is Therese de Jesus/Teresa de Lisieux (1873–1897), or The Little Flower, as she is called, whose life of domestic sacrifice and endurance was recorded in her memoir, *Story of a Soul.* She is always depicted with flowers. There are Rose of Lima (1586–1617) and Rose of Viterbo (1235–1253). The first, named Isabela at birth, is noted for her deprivations and self-inflicted disfiguration; she would often emerge from her house dragging a cross and had a vision that Christ called her soul his spouse. She always wore a crown of roses. At the age of eight, Rose of Viterbo had a vision in which the Virgin commanded her to wear the habit of St. Francis of Assisi, to be, as it were, a transvestite. She was refused entry to St. Mary of the Roses convent because of her lack of dowry and was buried there after appearing in a vision to the Pope Alexander IV. She is the patron saint of florists.[31]

The emblem of roses here seems then to rephrase the connection between the denial of the material and the acquisition of the heavenly. As Bloom puts it in his ruminations about perfume and flowers (and Martha and Molly), "no roses without thorns" (5.277–78). As far as these saints are concerned, the only good body is a dead body or "bitchbody," as Mulligan says of Stephen's mother in "Circe" (15.4179); in Stephen's dream her sainted body emits an odor of rosewood (1.271). The references to roses are appropriate for Molly—though rose is not technically her scent—reminding us that "roses" is slang terminology for menstruation, a reference that Bloom makes in relation to Martha in "Lotus-Eaters" (5.285). The no-saint of the above passage from "Cyclops," Molly is a misfit precisely because of her physicality and sexuality, which she does not rewrite or forfeit, and which she displays rather than displaces. In fact, she "gets her roses" in "Penelope" (18.1105–48) while her memories merge the flowers of Calpe and the blooms of Howth. Molly's materiality is the source of her displacement in the cultural and narrative landscapes of the text. As those within and without the narrative demonstrate, she is worshiped but without heavenly reward. What makes her an object of admiration and desire—she is somebody—makes her simultaneously subject to vilification and innuendo. Her sexuality is always represented as excessive, but it is also a sign of her lack. It will undo her for what she will not (un)do to it. Molly's roses in saints' terms is the sign of her womenly detritus, the symbolic dis-ease. But for Bloom and like Bloom (Mr. Flower himself), her smell is associative, tropic: her redolent underwear is fragrant to Bloom, containing the traces of her body and his desire; Jews smell bad because of the tropes/bodies they are.[32]

The indirect or covert reference to menstruation among the women saints ("the flower as an indecent and glaring sacrilege"[33]) returns us to the passage in "Cyclops" where such reference is made quite directly in relation to Bloom. The reference rehearses the emblematic relation between what is Jewish and what is womanly and traces it to what might be considered the originary moment, in the garden, from which the physical bloodiness of women's menses will emerge as the literalization of Eve's "betrayal" (where woman's punishment is extended to the pain of childbirth); the relation is the source and symbolic tag of their danger and pollution, for which Jesus will die. His bloody wounds are the metamorphic cure.

These women saints then remind us of the links among motherhood, sacrifice (of sexuality), and betrayal, and are thereby linked in turn to the politics of the chapter, of Irish nationhood, freighted with such associations. While no physical women appear in the plot of "Cyclops," many figments of women—"saints" or no-saints / heroes or villains (depending on your angle of vision)—appear by reference and innuendo:

> —The strangers, says the citizen. Our own fault. We let them come in. We brought them in. The adulteress and her paramour brought the Saxon robbers here.
>
> —Decree *nisi,* says J. J.
>
> And Bloom letting on to be awfully deeply interested in nothing, a spider's web in the corner behind the barrel, and the citizen scowling after him and the old dog at his feet looking up to know who to bite and when.
>
> —A dishonoured wife, says the citizen, that's what's the cause of all our misfortunes. (12.1156–64)

In these few lines the citizen intones a historiography of female betrayal and sacrifice, alluding to the reproduction (within contemporary Irish myth and history) of the religious or canonical sources of such betrayal and sacrifice. These lines come in the midst of, and really as part of, the citizen's xenophobic pronouncements on Irish national integrity, a transparent guise for racial hatred and intolerance directed at Bloom the Jew, but troped, here as elsewhere, through the dis-ease of female sexuality. The first "adulteress" he refers to, Devorgilla, became the wife of Dermot, who joined forces with Henry II after being deposed as king of Leinster, and with whom he invaded Ireland (in 1169); but first she was the wife of O'Ruarc, prince of Briefny and East Meath.[34] The second "adulteress" seems to be Kitty O'Shea, though the chapter provides us with a number of possible stand-in candidates for the dishonored wife, all of the ancient and modern myths of female treachery possessing the almost identical narrative structure. One might think that the citizen has recently consulted with Mr. Deasy, who in "Nestor" produces almost this same litany of female acts of betrayal, adding to it the "woman [who] brought sin into the world" and commenting also on Helen ("a woman no better than she should be"), because of whom "ten years the Greeks made war on Troy" (2.390–92). He uses almost the exact same phrase as the citizen when he talks about bringing the "strangers" in, an implication by historical necessity of the English; and in both places, the "Saxon robbers" are projected through and on the figure of the Jew.[35] Deasy's remarks follow his by-now infamous proclamation that the Jews are the "signs of a nation's decay" (2.347–48), just as the citizen's remarks are directed at Bloom. In both cases, there is a shifting subject and object, and the resting place for blame is a matter of historical interpretation, a fact or distortion, depending on the point of view. For in the case of the blameworthy woman, Devorgilla, she seems insufficiently accountable as the cause for Dermot's act (her guilt so primary, her actual part so insignificant); and the second historical elision or alignment between the English and the Jews is the "elevation" of Jews and, by association, women, to the level of danger represented by the English.[36] And both cases speak to the displacement of the object of derision—in other words, do unto others what has been done unto you. The difference in these rehearsals resides in the speaker's identification as subject; unlike Deasy, whose shiftiness reflects his equivocal identification with the Irish, the citizen sees himself momentarily in analogue with betraying woman, responsible for letting the stranger in, in this case Bloom ("our own fault"), suggesting the notion of Irish self-destruction, the other side of the idealization of the nation figured in the sacrificing woman—Kathleen ni Houlihan, soon to be invoked by the citizen (12.1375).[37] The citizen glimpses for just a moment, or allows us to see, the personification of the nation gone wrong, the sow who eats her farrow, the old woman of "Telemachus," bereft of pride and place. Emblematically then, like these mythic women, he becomes Ireland (like Padraic Pearse—"Mise Eire" [or Misery, as some have suggested]).[38] He must recover both from the analogue and the demoralization, and "stand up to it then with force like men" (12.1475). The injustice of xenophobia and/or nationalism to which Bloom refers and which prompts John Wyse's ironic pronouncement about the duty of men to show force will be turned on Bloom. "Our own fault" becomes "ourselves alone"; "—*Sinn Fein*! says the citizen. *Sinn fein amhain*! The friends we love are by our side and the foes we hate before us" (12.523–24).

Of course, Deasy and the citizen would not have to consult one another to produce the same *his*tory of female betrayal, nor do they have to stray outside of the Irish realm of myth, when, as the chapter informs us, Ireland has done well to produce its own honor rolls. Bloom and the citizen's famous exchange on the question of national integrity—"—What is your nation if I may ask? / —Ireland, says Bloom. I was born here. Ireland" (12.1430–31)—is a seeming parody of the fight scene from *Henry V*: in it, the external threat is momentarily deflected by the potential strife among the Irishman, Scotsman, and Welshman, soldiers in England's army, whose national affiliation is highlighted or questioned and itself becomes a threat and thereby deflected under or by England's banner (act 3, scene 3). While Bloom produces the legal definition of nationality, the succeeding interpolation presents *The Book of Ballymote* (fourteenth century), which contains Gaelic historical, legendary and genealogical material, law texts, a section on grammar and metrics, and translations of classical works, including *The Destruction of Troy, The Wandering of Ulysses, The Aeneid,* and the *History of Alexander,* adapted for a "Gaelic Audience."[39] "Take that in your right hand and repeat after me the following words" (12.1436–37) introduces the book into the chapter and into the debate. It becomes a kind of bible of national identity—the Irish cultural landscape—and the point would seem to be that Bloom will not find himself there. However, he is mirrored there, the final lines of the interpolation anticipating Bloom's next remarks.

> *all these moving scenes are still there for us today rendered more beautiful still by the water of sorrow which have passed over them and by the rich incrustations of time.*
>
> —Show us over the drink, says I. Which is which?
>
> —That's mine, says Joe, as the devil said to the dead policeman.
>
> —And I belong to a race too, says Bloom, that is hated and persecuted. Also now. This very moment. This very instant.
>
> Gob, he near burnt his fingers with the butt of his old cigar.
>
> —Robbed, says he. Plundered. Insulted. Persecuted. Taking what belongs to us by right. At this very moment, says he, putting up his fist, sold by auction in Morocco like slaves or cattle.
>
> —Are you talking about the new Jerusalem? says the citizen.
>
> —I'm talking about injustice, says Bloom.
>
> —Right, says John Wyse. Stand up to it then with force like men. (12.1461–75, emphasis added)

Many links between the Irish and the Jews emerge here, despite the fact that the citizen's remarks and even Bloom's are intended to draw the differences. By establishing the distinction between nationality and "race," Bloom at once debunks the racialist currency of the period that would connect the two and points to the way in which that connection has served to subjugate the Irish as well as the Jews, producing the sorrow mentioned at the end of the passage on *The Book of Ballymote,* and the persecution to which Bloom refers in his impassioned outburst.[40] David Hayman's classic reading of this section suggests that Bloom is signaling his "persecution" at the hands of Boylan, who is at that very instant indeed, to put it crassly, robbing, plundering Molly in Bloom's fantasy/nightmare and thereby insulting him.[41] Such a reading makes the double entendre of historical fact and literary metaphor work to reinforce the view of race, or racial hatred, through the lens of gender, in this case, sexual exploitation or impropriety. But in doing so, it seems to belittle both, literally to disavow the one (the lacking Bloom) and diminish the other (the excessive woman). This makes Hayman's other claim for Bloom here—that he is victorious despite his lacks—unconvincing. In fact, the chapter seems to deprive Bloom of a classical kind of heroism by parodying and preventing him from becoming the classical kind of victim in and, perhaps, of this chapter.

Which brings us to the fine line between victimhood and martyrdom that both this section and the subject of women saints reveal (sheep or wolf / scapegoat or lamb of God). For in referring to their respective histories of persecution, as before, the citizen and Bloom are linked, and in their stands they inscribe themselves into the book of martyrs. Each act of martyrdom is spurred by the notion that sorrow enhances and that persecution makes for self-righteousness; there is a supreme value placed on suffering then and a kind of willful participation in the same. We have heard it before, but Mark Osteen puts it well when he writes, "in sacrifice destruction acquires value."[42] These are the sources and aims of national(ist) and religious fervor. Like that of Robert Emmet, the "darling of Erin," as the song goes (and as the songs go), one's death for the cause is the ultimate act of heroism for a man, emblematized through the sacrifice of the woman (Kathleen ni Houlihan)—or by her danger and act of betrayal (Dark Rosaleen); after all, as the chapter reminds us, legend gives Sara Curran, Emmet's fiancée, partial blame for his undoing, making him vulnerable to capture as he is vulnerable to her charms (he is captured when he returns to bid her good-bye). She becomes the object rather than the subject of the romanticization process at work here.[43] Furthermore, Curran was later reviled for marrying, for in that act she would offend and betray the martyr who, it has been intimated by history, died for her just as he died for Ireland (she and Ireland becoming emblematically entwined). So, in other words, Sara should have prayed for deformity, like her saintly sister, Brigid, and become a saint for the cause rather than succumb to worldly desire and womanly excess. We come to understand that canonization is its own form of colonization, with analogous if not identical sources and aims as that of nationalism. Women betray and sacrifice; men fight and die. Woman's sacrifice makes the man. And such losses become gains, the "value of destruction in sacrifice." "Saintliness draws blood," remarks Cioran, reminding us of the paradigm of blood at work here, in all its racial/sexual, sacrificial/vampiric splendor.[44] He continues in what can be read as a characterization of sainthood as a distinctly human enterprise, a kind of heavenly imperialism, the ultimate colony:

> Could saints have a will to power? Is their world imperialistic? The answer is yes, but one must take into account the change of direction. While we waste our energy in the struggle for temporary gains, their great pride makes them aspire to absolute possession. For them, the space to conquer is the sky, and their weapon is suffering. If God were not the limit of their ambition, they would compete in ultimates, and each would speak in the name of yet another infinity. Man is forever a proprietor. Not even the saints could escape this mediocrity. Their madness has divided up heaven in unequal portions, each according to the pride they take in their sufferings. The saints have redirected imperialism vertically, and raised the earth to its supreme appearance, the heavens.[45]

Despite Bloom's bravado, he signals his own difference and departure from such acts of heroism through the offer of love rather than force as remedy for persecution and injustice; by proclaiming it, he at once pronounces himself, yet again, unmanly, as the immediate display of Gertyesque prose suggests (12.1493–1501). He is like a lamb to the slaughter, or perhaps more accurately, the sacrificial scapegoat/martyr for love. I continue to quote here from the text where the above passage from "Cyclops" ended:

> That's an almanac picture for you. Mark for a softnosed bullet. Old lardyface standing up to the business end of a gun. Gob, he'd adorn a sweepingbrush, so he would, if he only had a nurse's apron on him. And then he collapses all of a sudden, twisting around all the opposite, as limp as a wet rag.
>
> —But it's no use, says he. Force, hatred, history, all that. That's not life for men and women, insult and hatred. And everybody knows that it's the very opposite of that that is really life.
>
> —What? says Alf.
>
> —Love, says Bloom. I mean the opposite of hatred. I must go now, says he to John Wyse. Just round to the court a moment to see if Martin is there. If he comes just say I'll be back in a second. Just a moment.
>
> Who's hindering you? And off he pops like greased lightning.
>
> —A new apostle to the gentiles, says the citizen. Universal love.
>
> —Well, says John Wyse. Isn't that what we're told. Love your neighbour.
>
> —That chap? says the citizen. Beggar my neighbour is his motto. Love, moya! He's a nice pattern of a Romeo and Juliet.
>
> Love loves to love love. Nurse loves the new chemist. Constable 14A loves Mary Kelly. Gerty MacDowell loves the boy that has the bicycle. M. B. loves a fair gentleman. Li Chi Han lovey up kissy Cha Pu Chow. Jumbo, the elephant, loves Alice, the elephant. Old Mr Verschoyle with the ear trumpet loves old Mrs Verschoyle with the turnedin eye. The man in the brown macintosh loves a lady who

> is dead. His Majesty the King loves Her Majesty the Queen. Mrs Norman W. Tupper loves officer Taylor. You love a certain person. And this person loves that other person because everybody loves somebody but God loves everybody. (12.1476–1501)

It is ironic here, as Mark Osteen has pointed out, that "the Jewish Bloom voices the Christian idea of charity," especially in light of the citizen's stereotyping of Bloom as a kind of shyster or Shylock—"beggar my neighbour is his motto."[46] But it is doubly ironic when we consider Portia's role in Shylock's fate. The seeming injustice or cruelty of Shylock's demand for justice from the merchant of Venice (Antonio) is diffused or deconstructed by Portia's mirroring uncharitable acts, for it is the Christian Portia, that would-be exemplar of Christian charity, who speaks but does not perform it. In fact, the play seems to prove by her guises that as woman, she has as little value as the Jew she belittles and dispossesses by legal definition. (The price of "a pound of flesh" seems a thinly disguised reference to the accusation of blood libel, Antonio being the martyred victim of Shylock's bloodlust.)[47]

And so I now come to the very place—the duel—that I have protested has too much governed readings of this chapter, to the final rather than the central movement in the showdown between Bloom and the citizen. In the course of their exchange, Bloom has become the marker against which the forces of colonization (canonization) and nationalism must be measured, the stranger who permits the men in the pub to be men as he assumes the position, however parodically, of the crucified. The Jew is not only voicing the ideal of Christian charity, but is approaching the state of canonization (a "martyr moving toward sainthood"), imaging Jesus himself, who proves that the road to heaven is just as badly paved as the one to hell; the exemplar of sacrifice itself. Or is he? Does Jesus not become more sacrificed than sacrificing, and has that not been a vexed aspect of his image, how to make the victim heroic, the ultimate in love and charity, manly? Bloom seems to address this question. In a gesture that is both comic and threatening—he is mockingly accused by a "slut of the nation" of having his fly open, as though to reveal the mark of the Jew—Bloom delivers his famous exhortation:

> And says he:
>
> —Mendelssohn was a jew and Karl Marx and Mercadante and Spinoza. And the Saviour was a jew and his father was a jew. Your God.
>
> —He had no father, says Martin. That'll do now. Drive ahead.
>
> —Whose God? says the citizen.
>
> —Well, his uncle was a jew, says he. Your God was a jew. Christ was a jew like me.
>
> Gob, the citizen made a plunge back into the shop.
>
> —By Jesus, says he, I'll brain that bloody jewman for using the holy name. By Jesus, I'll crucify him so I will. Give us that biscuitbox here.
>
> —Stop! Stop! says Joe. (12.1803–13)

When Bloom compares himself to Jesus, he is doing at least two things: first, he points to the irony of his own crucifixion, as it were, at the hands of the barbaric unbeliever (a duel between infidels); second, by making the analogy, he points to the question of Jesus' origins, a threatening gesture in itself. Jesus is like Bloom a Jew and a non-Jew, by practice, perception, and history. And he is like Bloom's other exemplars of Jewishness here, Bloom's "icons" of representation—Mendelssohn, Marx, Mercadante, and Spinoza—who respectively suggest conversion, apostasy (really conversion), mistaken identity (a Freudian slip perhaps, since this Catholic was the composer of "The Seven Last Words of Christ"), and heresy or excommunication.[48] But it is not, I would suggest, because of these analogues that the citizen is provoked. It is, instead, the specter of sameness, of relation, or perhaps even more disturbingly, the suggestion of ambiguity which presents the problem and for which it has become a historical necessity to rehabilitate Jesus, from Jew to non-Jew; and in order to do so, it would become just as necessary to stabilize (Bloom's) Jewish identity. Further, given the historical representation of Jews as discussed here, it becomes indeed an ironic blasphemy and at once a revelation to make the connection. As one scholar of religion puts it, "as a Jew and the first Christian, yet neither a Jew nor a Christian, Jesus is the ultimate theological transvestite."[49] The idea of the transvestite suits so well when we think about all the ways in which Bloom is either accused or suspected of being something other than he seems or *is,* for that matter (a wolf in sheep's clothing); again, it is the ambiguity that represents the danger, the threat of invasion and pollution. And, therefore, this ambiguity produces the need not only to maintain his difference, but in the case scenario of which we are all too familiar in this century, to eradicate the dis-ease.[50]

Worse yet, if we take the metaphor of transvestism to consider the "facts" of Jesus' life, the threat may be from within. He has no father, to paraphrase Martin Cunningham, and he is no father, after all. He may not even be a man. (Could he be circumcised?) "The gender indeterminacy with which Jesus is represented in the gospel literature further enhances his potential for transvestite performance: his teachings laud gentleness, the meek and the cheek; he is himself pierced, wounded, bleeds, suffers and dies. At the same time, however, he is a man whose closest associates are men, not women; who proclaims himself one with the Father; whose death is overcome by the erection of resurrection."[51] (Of course, Jesus' women associates created the paradigms of sexual sacrifice for the likes of Sara Curran, for example, to follow). One might wonder whether Jews were demonized and emasculated in response to the need to culturally differentiate them and rewrite Jesus' origins or whether Jesus' initial characterization as (feminine) distinct from the warmongering and merciless, unfeeling Jews (all too male) created the need to turn this difference back on the Jews themselves in order to transform the Christians from victims to martyrs for Christ, from sacrificed to sacrificing, and finally into agents of their own heroism.

As the chapter seems to argue, such categories of national and sexual and even literary identity may not be capable of being sharply distinguished. The ambiguity derives in part from the conceptual nature of vision—the beam in someone's eye may be the mote in your own. The ambiguity and excess of Joyce's text, threatening, dangerous as it may seem, like Bloom, is finally redeeming, if not redeemed. But what of the women saints, and poor Mrs. Bermingham (initials, M. B.), whom Joyce surely would have added to his list if she had only made the grade in time? The mock ascension of Bloom and the suggestion of Elijah's fiery chariot at the conclusion of this chapter mirror or parody the ascension of the *true* Messiah (or, the devil goes to heaven), and of all the saints, suggesting the way in which such movements take on a political trajectory when, as Cioran points out, they seek to "colonize upwards"; but it speaks to the women saints most poignantly of all, in that their ecstatic rise becomes a displacement, a veiled image of the heliotropic gesture of desire, a bloodstone sacrifice.[52] They are history's scapegoats, as much as Bloom, as much as even the citizen, whose mission to banish false gods (one of Elijah's tasks), is not only mocked but a mockery. In the "politicoeconomy," this creation by means of loss, the idols of nationalism/sainthood and the cult of martyrdom are replaced by the labor of art, where the verbal excesses and extravagances become a kind of productive rather than destructive indulgence. Joyce's labor of art in all its excess and economy is, like Bloom's labor of love, just less than a saving grace.

13

A Metaphysics of Coitus in "Nausicaa"

JOHN BISHOP

"Nausicaa" develops the "parallactic" technique put lengthily into play in "Cyclops" by presenting its reader with alternate perspectives on the same scene, though here only two of them rather than many: the first half of the episode, an indirect (and female) monologue, offers a mediated account of Gerty MacDowell's view of a flirtatious encounter with Bloom on Sandymount Strand; the second half, a direct (and male) monologue, offers Bloom's unmediated reflections backward over the same events. A few weird internal references to "Cyclops" within "Nausicaa"—Gerty's grandpapa Giltrap owns Garryowen, the dog with which the citizen "ars[es] around" Dublin (12.752–53, 13.232–33)—perhaps encourage us to see large contrasts and parallels being drawn between the two chapters. "Cyclops" parodically erodes idealized representations of "the best traditions of manly strength and prowess" (12.911), of heroism and ideal masculinity; "Nausicaa" analogously undercuts representations of the "womanly woman" and of idealized femininity and purity (13.435).[1] The first of three chapters to which Joyce respectively assigned the symbols of Virgin, Mother, and Whore, "Nausicaa" moreover initiates in *Ulysses* a sustained exploration of conventional representations of women—an exploration that comes to incomplete completion only when Molly, in "Penelope," gives voice to her own idiosyncratically unconventional womanhood and declares that she doesn't "like books with a Molly in them" (18.657–58).

Why Joyce chose to write "Nausicaa" in two distinct parts and styles, from two points of view—in a doubly gendered and genred form—is one of the larger critical questions posed by the chapter. Karen Lawrence, seeing Joyce amplifying the contrastive technique put into play in "Cyclops," finds the chapter's "parallactic" comparativism and parodic exposure of sentimental fiction superfluous—more of what had already been done well enough in the chapter before.[2] And other readers have accounted for the distinctly binary form of "Nausicaa" by playing up the obvious difference between its two sections and reading the chapter as a Joycean version of "he said, she said"—or, in Bloom's idiom, "says she and says he" (13.1146). Gerty's monologue, from this perspective—densely mediated by her immersion in the language of advertising and of sentimental and domestic fiction of the kind epitomized by Maria Cummins's *The Lamplighter* (13.633)—exemplifies something like the cultural constructedness of femininity ("the nature of woman [as] instituted" [13.457]), her interiority an effect of the external social forces and discursive systems that have come to shape her. Stimulated by advances in commodity aesthetics and in feminist theory and criticism over the past decade, recent critics of Joyce have in fact done so much brilliant work on Joyce's intricate differentiation of Gerty's femininity from Bloom's masculinity—on his analytical critique of its constructedness—that "Nausicaa" has come to seem in the criticism a chapter that centers on Gerty. The emphases necessitated by such studies, however, have the effect of minimizing attention to the second half of the chapter, seeing it in a deterministically gendered relation to the first part and so construing the relation between Gerty and Bloom as one of victim and victimizer, symptom and disease, effect and cause. As a female, an unreflexive pawn of commodity culture, and even a commodity herself, Gerty resolves, often enough, into a victim of a system of production in which Bloom, as male, predator, and advertising agent, is the complicitously participating counterpart.

Why and how these two parts (and partners) are coupled, however, may be questions central to a chapter that seems profoundly invested in an exploration of the singularity of pairing—of why and how couples come together, and mating comes about. Having "gone together" in Joyce's conception and writing of the chapter, certainly—or, to give the verb its Latin equivalent, *coitus* ("having gone together")—the two parts of "Nausicaa" arguably require analysis together, as surely do any two partners in any other two-body relation ("Always see a fellow's weak point in his wife" [13.972–73]). The chapter itself highlights its thematic interest in pairing and doubling by focusing on twins in its opening pages—indeed, in the narrator's insistently tautological phrasing, on "two twins" (13.41, 13.363, 13.492, 13.505). The redundancy calls attention to the cognate relations of the word "*tw*ins" to the number "*tw*o," and in turn to the chapter's setting at "*tw*ilight," "be*twee*n" two agents and states of illumination: all three of these words—"twins," "twilight," "between" (Derrida's *entre*)—derive from a common proto-Indian European root designating "two."[3] Their structural centrality to a chapter otherwise full of references to divided halves and twinned pairs in turn highlights the chapter's interest in the cipher for the couple, the number two: Gerty, we learn, "would be twentytwo in November" (13.221–22) and is situated not simply between "two twins," but between two girlfriends as well: Edy Boardman, "one of your twofaced things, too sweet to be wholesome" (13.279–80), "as cross as two sticks" (13.260); and Cissy Caffrey, who "in two twos . . . set that little matter to rights" (13.614–15). At once virtually identical and indistinguishable, and yet discernibly individualized, the "two twins," like the two girlfriends and the two priests conducting the benediction in the Star of the Sea Chapel, moreover exemplify forms of pairing and doubling that are central to the chapter and recur at almost every level of its design.[4] In part because of its imitation of the alliterative style of the sentimental romance, for instance, but also because of its intrinsic thematic interest in pairing, the first part of the chapter resorts to an almost incessant form of alliterative doubling: phrases like "away in the west," "sun was setting," "lingered lovingly," "sea and strand," and "proud promontory" (13.02–4) occur everywhere in Gerty's monologue—"she tickled tiny tot's two cheeks" (13.257, need they have been counted?). Equally prominent are curiously doubled terms and phrases: "boys will be boys" (13.41); "honour where honour is due" (13.96); "hoping against hope" (13.179–80); "a might that he might be out" (13.149); "and often and often she thought and thought" (13.459–60); "and yet—and yet!" (13.188); and so forth.[5] Proper names, comparably—both those that Joyce invented and those that he borrowed—are subject to a peculiar kind of consonantal doubling: apart from Cissy Caffrey and baby Boardman—"Cissy Caffrey told baby Boardman to look up, look up" (13.253)—the chapter introduces us to "grandpapa Giltrap" (13.232, 13.343), "the Widow Welch" (13.85), "Madame Vera Verity" (13.109–10), "Flora MacFlimsey" (13.35), "the litany of Our Lady of Loreto" (13. 287–88), and "W. E. Wylie who was racing in the . . . races" (13.135). Manifold doubling operations pervade Bloom's monologue, too, though they seem to take a more substantive than formal shape, simply perhaps because Bloom thinks more explicitly than Gerty about coupling ("Man and woman that is. Fork and steel. Molly, he" [13.992–93])—and also about pairs: "Pretty girls and ugly men. Beauty and the beast" (13.836–37); "Long and the short of it. Big he and little she" (13.982–83).[6] Cumulative attention to various copulative effects like these, at any rate—no matter whether we attribute them to Joyce's intention or the binary properties of language—makes the act of coupling itself, in countless forms and manifestations, a central feature of a chapter dramatically built around a couple and the fantasy of coupling. The need to read Gerty's monologue dynamically through and against Bloom's is signposted in the text not only by these pairing effects, but also by the chapter's attention to various focalizing objects which move back and forth between them: the Caffrey twins' ball, in the first section, which links Bloom and Gerty as a ball links Odysseus and Nausicaa in *The Odyssey;* the characters' erotically correlated game of throwing and catching glances and eyes; and the movement of a bat between Gerty's and Bloom's sections. "Nausicaa," finally, takes place *between* two parts and partners, each differentiated and both united, whose interdependence requires their analysis together. "Suppose there's some connection" (13.1014), as Bloom puts it; "must be connected" (13.1036). Rather than holding the two sections of "Nausicaa" in a fixed and simple relation of gender opposition, the chapter's sustained thematic attention to forms of twinning, coupling, and pairing invites us to see them connected in every possible way that pairs can connect: under operations not simply of opposition, but also of doubling, parallelism, likeness, differentiation, sequentiality, complementarity, asymmetrical reflection, inversion, and so forth. What otherwise might be a statically drawn episode becomes under this form of analysis a variety of "mutoscope pictures" (13.794) in which perspectives and understandings continually change if we "look at it other way round" (13.1219); "yes now, look at it that way" (13.1030).

Some of the chapter's doubling effects also arise, perhaps, from its preoccupation with mirroring and—in both specular and speculative senses of the word—"reflection." While both parts of the chapter provide us with the characters' mental "reflections" on events and circumstances, both also reflect on physical mirrors and reflections (13.162, 13.192, 13.919–20, 13.1261–62). This happens, in part, because mirrors, like other frames that contain images, represent representation—as do the various pictorial magazines in which Gerty sees the ideal images after which she models her "real" self ("*Art thou real, my ideal?*" [13.645–46]). "The lovely reflection which the mirror [gives] back to [Gerty]" (13.162)—a cipher for her own self-reflexivity—emerges also from the frames of "the Woman Beautiful page of the Princess Novelette" (13.110) and "the *Lady's Pictorial*" (13.151), either of which, as titles, could fittingly be assigned to the first half of "Nausicaa." Because the "action" of Gerty's monologue is so ocular and voyeuristic, but also because Gerty tends almost autonomically to translate her perceptions into idealizing representations, Joyce designated the eye as the organ governing the first half of "Nausicaa" and painting as the art governing the chapter as a whole. Frank Budgen, himself a painter, was the first to elaborate on these schematic clues by pointing out how pictorially Gerty frames and views "the evening scene" on Sandymount Strand (13.09–10), how reflexively she pictures herself to herself and throws her perceptions of "reality" into idealizing representations:[7] "she could see far away the lights of the lighthouses so picturesque she would have loved to do with a box of paints because it was easier than to make a man" (13.627–29). The stoppage of Bloom's watch—in turn suggesting the stoppage of time—intensifies these pictorializing effects by calling attention to the largely static "action" of the first half of "Nausicaa": since both characters (even Bloom, despite his manual activity) largely stay still while theatrically posing and modeling for each others' voyeuristic benefit, the first half of the chapter entails the staging of something like pictorial *tableaux* or charades (13.486, 13.815, 13.1106–16) and so takes on the representational status of a painting. The world here is spectralized in ways suggested by the chapter's continual evocations of portraiture and painting—"pictures and engravings and the photograph" (13.231–32), "edifying spectacle[s]" (13.285), "illuminated views of Dublin" (13.465). In details like these, as in his schema, Joyce calls such elaborate attention to "painting" and the eye, surely, because the eye is the organ of idealization: "ideas," along with their more perfect forms ("ideals," "idols," "eidolons," and "idealizations"), all derive from the Greek *eido* ("to see"), in part because the process of looking enables one to "know" an object or person in the absence of any real contact with it at all. This is Gerty's (like most adolescents') experience of the world in the first half of "Nausicaa": in the absence of any real contact with Bloom (or other potential mates), she draws her romantic and sexual speculations about men from literary and pictorial idealizations; the romanticizing style of her monologue, complementarily, presents her not as she is, but as she would like to see herself and as she would like Bloom to see her.[8] Bloom himself is framed and idealized in her vision, finally, as if he were her "beau ideal" (13.209), "a foreigner, the image of the photo she had of Martin Harvey, the matinée idol, only for the moustache which she preferred because she wasn't stagestruck like Winny Rippingham" (13.416–18). Insofar as the two halves of "Nausicaa" might be seen to stand in more than an oppositional relation to each other, however—as sequential complements or asymmetrical reflections—everything that might be said about Gerty during her specular coitus with Bloom might also be said of Bloom as well.

"LOOK AT IT OTHER WAY ROUND"

In the schema for *Ulysses* that he passed on to Gorman and Gilbert, Joyce labeled the "technic" of "Nausicaa" "tumescence"/"detumescence"—suggesting not only that the chapter follows out the rhythm of sexual excitation and deflation (with orgasm occurring at the moment in which Gerty's monologue slips over into Bloom's, in the paragraph in which fireworks go off [13.715–40]), but also that its two parts may be related more as sequential complements than as contrastive opposites: Gerty's monologue, to put it simply, is precoital, while Bloom's is postcoital. Narrative omissions and asymmetries in the episode's representation of events of the hour, moreover, reinforce this sense that the chapter's two narratives complement as much as they oppose each other. Readers of *Ulysses* have long noted that odd gaps of unrepresented time punctuate Joyce's otherwise detailed account of June 16, 1904, and that one such gap takes place between "Cyclops" and "Nausicaa": we only learn after the fact that between his visit to Barney Kiernan's pub and his appearance on Sandymount Strand, Bloom has traveled with Martin Cunningham to the Dignams's house to help arrange the affairs of the widow and orphans.[9] Two no less critical, yet unexamined gaps of unrepresented time transpire within "Nausicaa" itself, since we never learn exactly what moves through Bloom's mind during the first part of the episode, while he is undergoing tumescence and masturbating, or what occurs to Gerty during the second part of the episode, while she travels home and Bloom desultorily fights off his deflated thoughts of agedness, fatigue, and the manifold miseries of domestic life. Even so, details scattered through both parts of the episode enable us to draw inferences about what happens when, as Bloom recommends, we "look at it other way round" (13.1219).

As her monologue comes to its climax, we learn that Gerty

> knew too about the passion of men like that, hotblooded, because Bertha Supple told her once in dead secret and made her swear she'd never about the gentleman lodger that was staying with them out of the Congested Districts Board

> that had pictures cut out of papers of those skirtdancers and highkickers and she said he used to do something not very nice that you could imagine sometimes in the bed. (13.700–6)

Her recollection of a story heard about a man masturbating while viewing pinup girls or cheesecake photos resonates with Bloom's recollection, in the second part of the episode, of his experience in Dublin's "adult" bookstore: "A dream of wellfilled hose. Where was that? Ah, yes. Mutoscope pictures in Capel street: for men only. Peeping Tom. Willy's hat and what the girls did with it. Do they snapshot those girls or is it all a fake?" (13.793–96). If we want to know what the girls did with that hat, Gerty cannily provides us with the only possible answer: "something not very nice that you could imagine." The conflation of the two passages suggests that Bloom's (male) equivalent to the kind of pictorial idealizing that Gerty engages in while allowing Bloom to stare at her is pornographic scene staging ("for men only"); or, more bluntly, that the male equivalent to the kinds of sentimental and romantic fiction in which Gerty finds compensatory relief for her own real-world deficiencies is pornography. If Gerty frames Bloom in such a way as to staticize him and enhance his resemblance to a culturally produced image of the ideally desirable male (Martin Harvey, the matinee idol), it cannot be surprising that Bloom complementarily seems to have staticized and framed Gerty in such a way as to minimize her ordinariness and to enhance her resemblance to a pornographically yielding pinup girl ("I'm all clean come and dirty me" [13.797]). "Thought something was wrong by the cut of her jib," Bloom thinks when he discovers, in the aftermath of his orgasm, that Gerty is lame; "Jilted beauty. A defect is ten times worse in a woman. . . . Glad I didn't know it when she was on show" (13.773–76). Insofar as we are able to reconstruct Bloom's fantasies about Gerty retrospectively, in the absence of their direct representation, he seems to have indulged in a form of pictorializing indistinct from that practiced by the fellow "Wilkins," whom he recalls later in his monologue:

> Did she know what I? Course. Like a cat sitting beyond a dog's jump. Women never meet one like that Wilkins in the high school drawing a picture of Venus with all his belongings on show. Call that innocence? Poor idiot. His wife has her work cut out for her. Never see them sit on a bench marked *Wet Paint*. Eyes all over them. (13.908–12)

Bloom's judgmental condescension notwithstanding, he does not seem at all that different from Wilkins, since in the first part of "Nausicaa" he himself—though in his head and not with a pen—seems to have been "drawing a picture of Venus with all his belongings on show," complementing and spectrally accompanying Gerty's pictorially idealizing fantasies with painted—and wet—ones of his own.

That Bloom engages in a form of pornographic iconicizing while Gerty is romantically idealizing him is furthermore suggested by the ease with which, in the second half of the chapter, he elides her with Martha (who has provided him with a verbal, rather than pictorial, form of excitement). At one point in his monologue, in fact, recalling a phrase from Martha's letter ("Then I will tell you all"), he thinks that she and Gerty might be the same:

> Then I will tell you all. Still it was a kind of language between us. It couldn't be? No, Gerty they called her. Might be a false name however like my name and the address Dolphin's barn a blind.
>
> *Her maiden name was Jemina Brown*
> *And she lived with her mother in Irishtown.*
>
> Place made me think of that I suppose. All tarred with the same brush. (13.943–50)

Though Dolphin's Barn might well resemble Irishtown in being in a poorer section of Dublin, it may be Bloom's thoughts on sexually exciting agents more than on "place" which lead him into reflection, in a couplet, about the allures that lead to coupling.[10] "Tarred with the same brush"—painted in the same style—Martha and Gerty respectively represent in his mind the verbal and visual forms and media of pornographic allurement.[11] In turn, then, the continual pairing of Gerty and Martha in Bloom's monologue ("Martha, she" [13.782]) raises the interesting question of whether the masturbatory fantasy that Bloom entertained about Gerty can have been all that different from the fantasies we see him cultivating under the memory of inducements like Martha's letter elsewhere in *Ulysses.* "Like to be that rock she sat on. . . . Also the library today: those girl graduates. Happy chairs under them" (13.1084–88): indications like these raise the possibility that Bloom may have imagined masochistically submitting to Gerty in much the same ways that he imagines submitting to Martha or, for that matter, Bella ("little naughty boy. . . . I will punish you" [5.247–52]; "Exuberant female. Enormously I desiderate your domination" [15.2777]). If so, it is finally hard to see Bloom simply as the predatory male in "Nausicaa"; in some ways, he emerges from the chapter as the familiarly disempowered male known to us through other parts of the novel, a disabled twin to Gerty.

Joyce's decision to give the wishfully "perfect" Gerty a "defect," a "shortcoming"—a limp—becomes, from this perspective, more strategic than malicious, since the word "limp," after all, is applied more than once—and more than to Gerty—to Bloom throughout *Ulysses.* In "Lotus-Eaters," where Bloom initiates the line of thought that will come to its climactic realization only in "Nausicaa" ("Also I think I. Yes I. Do it in the bath. . . . Combine business with pleasure" [5.503–5]), his penis is figured as "the limp father of thousands" (5.571); and in "Circe," where he humiliates himself into thumb-twiddling inaction in what is traditionally the arena of male sexual prowess, the brothel, he imagines the massive brothel keeper sizing him up and finding him coming up short: "What else are you good for, an impotent thing like you? . . . It's as limp as a boy of six's doing his pooly behind a cart" (15.3127–31). In "Nausicaa," comparably, Bloom thinks of Gerty's limp in a way that reflects ambiguously on his own: as he rearranges his wetted clothing, he thinks, "O Lord, that little limping devil," in a context that makes it not entirely clear whether the phrase refers to Gerty or his own exhausted member:

> Funny my watch stopped at half past four. Dust. Shark liver oil they use to clean. Could do it myself. Save. Was that just when he, she?
>
> O, he did. Into her. She did. Done.
>
> Ah!
>
> Mr Bloom with careful hand recomposed his wet shirt. O Lord, that little limping devil. Begins to feel cold and clammy. Aftereffect not pleasant. Still you have to get rid of it someway. (13.846–53)

Bloom and Gerty are made to reflect on each other by way of the "limp" in "limping" here, which bears the weight of both their real-world deficiencies. "But for that one shortcoming," Gerty thinks, "she knew she need fear no competition" (13.649–50); and something comparable might be said of Bloom, whose marital unhappiness we know to be occasioned by one psychogenetic "shortcoming" which in his mind leaves Molly resentfully unfulfilled and willing to entertain Boylan. Indeed, the word "limp" appears again late in the chapter, while Bloom thinks of avoiding a return home in order not to have to face his wife ("Better not stick here all night like a limpet. . . . Go home. . . . No. Might still be up" [13.1211–13]). The distinct kinds of "limp" borne by Gerty and the profoundly emasculated Bloom, furthermore, tend to equalize them as victims. One of the many distinct effects served by Bloom's discovery of the stoppage of his watch at 4:30 in "Nausicaa," in fact, is to foil Boylan's and Molly's aggressively real and not uninjurious coupling against Bloom's and Gerty's fantasized liaison and to ask us, as readers, to weigh the difference between the pairings. Bloom and Gerty, we realize, both severely disempowered, have real-world shortcomings for which they seek compensation through fantasy—Gerty in a fantasy of sentimental love and domestic romance made available to her through romantic fiction, Bloom in a fantasy of unproblematized virility and sexual conquest made available to him through pornographic fiction. Pornography, from this perspective, serves much the same function for the disempowered male as romantic fiction does for the disempowered female, supplying him with the illusion of unproblematized masculinity ("Still, I feel. The strength it gives a man. That's the secret of it" [13.859–60])—and in turn forcing a reformulation of the well-known and astonishingly oversimplistic formula coined by Robin Morgan and enlisted by movements against pornography: "pornography is the theory, masturbation is the practice."[12] "Nausicaa," we might finally note, is a chapter panoramically full of vignettes of males in trouble and need—not simply Bloom, but Wilkins, Gerty's alcoholic father, the drunkards praying for their reformation at the retreat, and others to be noted below.

If the narrative asymmetries of "Nausicaa" enable us to infer that Bloom was doing a (male) version of what Gerty herself was doing during the first half of the chapter—pictorially idealizing her, although as a pornographically compliant pinup girl rather than as a romantic matinee idol—they also help us to resolve the vexed question of how much Gerty "knows" about the sexual character of her flirtation with Bloom by enabling us to see that she, too, is doing a version of what he is when he masturbates. Though Joyce called the technic of "Nausicaa" "tumescence"/"detumescence" in the schema that he passed on to Herbert Gorman and Stuart Gilbert, the character who most clearly experiences tumescence in "Nausicaa" is the masturbating Bloom, whom we only see in the second, detumescent half of the chapter. His reflections on the rhythm of sexual release that he experiences in the hour during which "Nausicaa" takes place, however—"My fireworks. Up like a rocket, down like a stick" (13.894–95)—enable us retrospectively to see that Gerty, too, though in displaced form, undergoes a kind of tumescent, sexual excitement during her monologue. Tumescence (literally the swelling up of parts of the body as a result of their engorgement with blood during sexual arousal) is something that Gerty seems to experience more in the upper than lower parts of her body—"the blood of the south" (13.969), as Bloom puts it, rushing north and, rather than engorging her loins, suffusing her face with displaced symptoms of sexual excitation in the form of a blushing that seems only to deepen and swell as her monologue progresses:

> And just now at Edy's words [intimating that Gerty has a "sweetheart"] . . . a telltale flush, delicate as the faintest rosebloom, crept into her cheeks. . . . (13.119–21)

> Gerty MacDowell bent down her head and crimsoned at the idea of Cissy saying an unladylike thing like that out loud she'd be ashamed of her life to say ["beeoteetom"], flushing a deep rosy red. . . . (13.264–66)

> A delicate pink crept into her pretty cheek. . . . She felt the warm flush, a danger signal always with Gerty MacDowell, surging and flaming into her cheeks. (13.360–67)

A "telltale" sign and "danger signal" because it reveals that "embarrassing" but unexpressed thoughts have begun drifting into her awareness—thoughts that "she'd be ashamed to say" out loud—Gerty's blush is something like a (clitoral) erection gone haywire: occasioned by sexual thinking (or, at times, a stifled rage), it shows that her blood has become tumescently animated but, in ways mapped out by Freud in his accounts of hysteria conversion, has rushed to the wrong part of the body—the head, rather than the genitalia. Worrisome enough to have caused Gerty to notice an ad for "blushing scientifically cured" (13.113) on "the Woman Beautiful page of the Princess Novelette" (13.110), her flushing is a form of confession that not coincidentally reveals itself in confession: "when she told him [the handsome Father Conroy] about that [menstruation] in confession, [she] crimson[ed] up to the roots of her hair for fear he could see" (13.453–54). As she succumbs more and more deeply to her erotic flirtation with Bloom over the first half of "Nausicaa," therefore, the increasingly tumescent ensanguination of her face amounts to an unconscious confession of a sexual arousal which—because of her youthful inexperience and Catholic inhibition—she seems unwilling and unable fully to acknowledge:

> the swift answering flash of admiration in his eyes . . . set her tingling in every nerve. . . . He was eying her as a snake eyes its prey. Her woman's instinct told her that she had raised the devil in him and at the thought a burning scarlet swept from throat to brow till the lovely colour of her face became a glorious rose. (13.513–20)

> she had to lean back more and more to look up after it [the Roman candle], high, high, almost out of sight, and her face was suffused with a divine, an entrancing blush from straining back and he could see her other things too, nainsook knickers, the fabric that caresses the skin . . . and she let him and she saw that he saw and then it went so high it went out of sight a moment and she was trembling in every limb. . . . (13.721–28)

A number of terms here furthermore suggest that just as Gerty's tumefying bloodstream is displaced upward from her loins to her head while she daydreams about Bloom, so too her sexual thoughts, which, because they are not consciously articulate, are displaced from "lower" to "higher" forms that help account for some of the peculiar investments of her monologue. "Suffused with a divine . . . blush," for instance, her face becomes "a glorious rose" as she flirts with Bloom—likening her, even more fully than her blue and white wardrobe, her statuesque pallor, and the conflation of her monologue with the Litany of Our Lady of Loreto already do, to the Blessed Virgin, the "mystical rose" of Catholic literature (13.374); and in imagining Bloom "eying her as a snake eyes its prey," she seems comparably to biblicize his penis. These adjustments clearly enable Gerty to think of herself as a good girl—again, like the Blessed Virgin, "a radiant little vision in sooth, almost maddening in its sweetness" (13.511–12)—while she is in fact half-consciously entertaining naughty thoughts and encouraging them in Bloom. The fact that she visualizes her underwear and even imagines its caressing feel while leaning back, ostensibly, to view a Roman candle that itself fades out of view—at least until it begins "gush[ing] out . . . a stream of rain gold hair threads" (13.738–39)—suggests that even while her attention is cast upward, her mind gravitates toward lower things which never quite achieve full representation in her awareness. Bloom's reflections on the displaced sexual energies of frustrated convent-school girls and "nuns with whitewashed faces" in the second half of "Nausicaa," however (13.809–13)—the manual agitation of "their rosaries going up and down" recalling the masturbatory activity which he comparably displaced by winding his watch—enable us to see the whole of Gerty's spiritually swollen and empurpled monologue as a form of "pantomimic" masturbation in which she unconsciously entertains all the thoughts that might normally accompany the process of sexual excitation and gratification (tumescence and detumescence) while allowing them to undergo a sublimating conversion that at times makes them almost unrecognizable.[13] From a passage quoted earlier—where Gerty fantasizes about "the gentleman lodger" (see 13.700–706)—we know that Gerty knows more about male sexuality than her monologue explicitly acknowledges. Her awareness of exactly what Bloom is doing when he masturbates is suggested not simply by passages like this, however—or by Bloom's canniness to her maturity ("Did she know what I? Course. Like a cat sitting beyond a dog's jump" [13.908–9])—but also by her monologue's recurrent preoccupations with what Joyce advertised in his well-known letter to Frank Budgen as the "namby-pamby jammy marmaladey" style of "Nausicaa": the many jams, puddings, and syrups that occur to Gerty while she daydreams about Bloom seem to be displaced indications that she knows full well what happens when he climaxes and produces his own "jam."[14]

"IN THE HIDING TWILIGHT"

In Gerty's empurpled monologue, a glorious sunset erotically "fold[s] the world in its mysterious embrace" (13.01–2)—coloring it, like Gerty and the Virgin herself, a "mystical rose" (13.374) and in turn leading Gerty to reflect on its romantic scenic splendor:

> She gazed out towards the distant sea. It was like the paintings that man used to do on the pavement with all the coloured chalks and such a pity too leaving them there to be all blotted out, the evening and the clouds coming out and the Bailey light on Howth. . . . (13.406–9)

Bloom, by contrast, whose detumescent monologue everywhere tends to flatten the illusions of hers, sees the same sunset with a distinctly unromantic scientific disinterest, as an effect of difractible electromagnetic radiation ("Colours depend on the light you see" [13.1132]):

> Some light still. Red rays are longest. Roygbiv Vance taught us: red, orange, yellow, green, blue, indigo, violet. A star I see. Venus? Can't tell yet. Two. When three it's night. Were those nightclouds there all the time? Looks like a phantom ship. No. Wait. Trees are they? An optical illusion. Mirage. (13.1075–79)

Insofar as "twilight"—once again etymologically meaning "between-light" or "two-light"—can be interpreted not simply as the blazened close of day but also as the beginning of the descent into night, Bloom also tends to see its darker and more sinister sides. For him, the twilit seascape on Sandymount Strand signifies not the rosy horizons of romantic possibility, as it does for Gerty, but the fading of day and—again, like the stoppage of his watch—the winding down and ending of time: "Useless. Washed away. . . . Hopeless thing sand. Nothing grows in it. All fades" (13.1259–67). These deflationary perspectives arise in Bloom's mind in part because of his disillusioned middle age ("Never again. My youth. Only once it comes. Or hers" [13.1102–3]), but also because his detumescent monologue takes place in the depressive postcoital letdown following the chapter's orgasmic turning point. As Bloom puts it in remarks that might apply not only to his reflections on sexual climax but also to the whole second half of "Nausicaa," "My fireworks. Up like a rocket, down like a stick" (13.894–95)—or, "aftereffect not pleasant" (13.852).

Bloom is aware that a certain amount of romantic illusion building and idealizing theatricality is essential to the act of lovemaking: "See her as she is spoil all. Must have the stage setting, the rouge, costume, position, music. The name too. *Amours* of actresses. Nell Gwynn, Mrs Bracegirdle, Maud Branscombe. Curtain up" (13.855–57). And in the first half of the chapter he not only embraces such illusions (by not "see[ing Gerty] as she is"), but encourages them also in Gerty by doing some acting and posing himself: "Saw something in me. Wonder what. Sooner have me as I am than some poet chap with bearsgrease plastery hair, lovelock over his dexter optic. To aid gentleman in literary. Ought to attend to my appearance my age. Didn't let her see me in profile" (13.833–36).[15] But details like these, by exposing the posturing and stagecraft of their flirtation, make Bloom and Gerty both begin to seem, in the deflationary second half of "Nausicaa," indistinct from the bee that Bloom recalls "last week [getting] into the room playing with his shadow on the ceiling" (13.1143–44): in the first part of the chapter, each has cultivated in himself and projected onto the other a wishfully idealizing "mirage," indulging a form of "optical illusion" by seeing in his partner and himself—as if with a semi-blinding "lovelock over his dexter optic"—the shadow of fertilizable attractiveness.[16]

One effect of Bloom's detumescent monologue then is to undo massively such illusions by reconsidering, from the perspective of a soberingly postnaturalistic scientism, the romantic and medievally spiritual understandings of love sustained in Gerty's section: to say this in another way, if Gerty's tumescent monologue resembles the kind of inflationarily aggrandizing fantasy that goes into foreplay prior to the act of lovemaking, Bloom's detumescent monologue reads like the set of depressing realizations about oneself and one's partner that follows.

Where Gerty daydreams of "love [as] a woman's birthright" (13.200), for instance, a fulfillment of personal destiny in the realization of a dream come true ("Here was that of which she had so often dreamed" [13.427–28]), Bloom tends to see their mutual attraction, in the deflationary aftermath of their spectral coitus, as the unremarkable consequence of sheer animal and physical forces. "Still you have to get rid of it some way" (13.853), he thinks, considering the pressures that have led him to discharge his pent-up sexual fluids over a girl who now begins to seem not the model "specimen" of Irish girlhood of Gerty's monologue ("Gerty MacDowell . . . was, in very truth, as fair a specimen of winsome Irish girlhood as one could wish to see" [13.79–81]), but as a "specimen" in the more rawly detached and scientific sense: "Curiosity like a nun or a negress or a girl with glasses" (13.776–77).[17] Far from being "perfect," Gerty becomes most distinguishable from her friends by her "defect" ("Jilted beauty. A defect is ten times worse in a woman. . . . Glad I didn't know it when she was on show" [13.774–76]). And where, like all young people smitten with an infatuation, she thinks of herself, Bloom, and their relations as unique and special—"she felt instinctively that he was like no-one else" (13.429–30), "he was her all in all, the only man in all the world for her" (13.671–72)—the middle-aged and maritally burned-out Bloom, who has earned his scars and come to "understand all the ways of the world" (13.897), tends to see himself and Gerty in the aftermath of their flirtation as just another random couple among millions doing the quotidian business that millions have done for millions of years: "All quiet on Howth now. . . . Where we [he and Molly]. . . . All that old hill has seen. Names change: that's all. Lovers: yum yum. . . . Nothing new under the sun" (13.1097–1105). At moments in his monologue, Bloom even tends to regard their meeting as a random collision indistinct from billions of others that ensue from globally vast and impersonal processes of animal mating. Women are figured in his thoughts as schools of fish or groups of other creatures, individually indistinguishable and driven to pair under animal impulsions:

> Because they want it themselves. Their natural craving. Shoals of them every evening poured out of offices. . . . Catch em alive, O. (13.790–92)

> Mat Dillon and his bevy of daughters. . . . (13.1106–7)

> Women buzz round it [the "mansmell" of sperm] like flies round treacle. (13.1037–38)

And men emerge no differently, as creatures subject both to physical forces of magnetic attraction and repulsion (13.984–96) and to fundamentally Darwinian motivations: "Dress they [women] look at. Always know a fellow courting: collars and cuffs. Well cocks and lions do the same and stags" (13.829–30).[18] Gerty, from this naturalizing perspective, comes to resemble not the singularly desirable "ideal" of her own monologue (13.211), but a creature as ordinary as "a cat sitting beyond a dog's jump" (13.908–9), fascinated but scared by the animal she has roused. Even the smiles that she and her girlfriends exchange while flirting with Bloom—"showing their teeth at one another" like Molly and Josie

Breen (13.814–19)—start to seem a matter of competitive fang baring among mammalian rivals over the meager available prey. Where Gerty's monologue apotheosizes and deifies the act of lovemaking, in short, Bloom's detumescent monologue deflates its significance to animal and physical levels—making the two sections of "Nausicaa," in part, something like the contradictory accounts of a "beauty and the beast" (13.837).

The antisentimental naturalism of Bloom's monologue heightens the poignancy of Gerty's situation, finally, by allowing us to see how utterly ordinary and unromantic her life likely is. Surmising that Gerty, like "shoals" of single women, is "out on spec probably" (13.808)—hoping to find someone—he infers her loneliness and her eagerness to escape the tedium of a servile home life ("Go home to nicey bread and milky and say night prayers with the kiddies" [13.854–55]), commiserating with her in turn for the dependent passivity with which she, like her companions "and the children, twins they must be, [are] waiting for something to happen. Want to be grownups. Dressing in mother's clothes. Time enough, understand all the ways of the world" (13.895–97). He also sees that the acquisition of that understanding will bring an end even to the ephemeral, constrained freedom which he has just seen her enjoy on Sandymount Strand:

> Sad however because it lasts only a few years till they settle down to potwalloping and papa's pants will soon fit Willy and fuller's earth for the baby when they hold him out to do ah ah. No soft job. Saves them. Keeps them out of harm's way. Nature. Washing child, washing corpse. Dignam. Children's hands always round them. Cocoanut skulls, monkeys, not even closed at first, sour milk in their swaddles and tainted curds. (13.952–58)

In the same way that Joyce enables us to infer what Bloom might have been imagining during the tumescent half of "Nausicaa," he allows us, through Bloom and the romance-puncturing revelations of Gerty's own monologue, to infer what likely happens to Gerty when, in the detumescent second half of the chapter, she returns home to her alcoholically abusive father and bedridden mother and the thrilling prospect of "gazing out of the window dreamily by the hour at the rain falling on the rusty bucket" (13.294–96).

"YOU HAVE A BEAUTIFUL FACE BUT YOUR NOSE?"

As the explosion of fireworks causes "Nausicaa" to pivot from Gerty's to Bloom's point of view, a host of broad metamorphoses sweep over the chapter: the evening star called "Mary, star of the sea" in Gerty's monologue (13.08) becomes the fleshier "Venus" in Bloom's ("A star I see. Venus? Can't tell yet. Two" [13.1076–77]). Veneration concordantly modulates into venery; and, as the dominant colors in the first half of the episode—mystical "rose" (13.121, 13.230, 13.520) and shrinking "violet" (13.230, 13.642)—evaporate into invisible fragrances (13.1002, 13.1009), Bloom's nose gains ascendancy over the idealizing eye.

In his schema for *Ulysses,* Joyce indicated that the organ governing the first half of "Nausicaa" was the eye, the second half the nose—for reasons, no doubt, demonstrated by the profoundly anti-idealizing function that Bloom's nose exercises throughout his monologue. Ideal forms of love and sex are visualized, spectralized, in daydreams and fantasies like those that both Bloom and Gerty entertain as they pose for and eye each other in the first part of the episode. Real love, by contrast, necessitates an actual gritty contact with another person in all of his or her unpredictable psychological and physical peculiarity.[19] A realization of this kind occurs gradually to Bloom as twilight deepens on Sandymount Strand, visibility diminishes, and he awakens to the gradually diffusing scent of Gerty's "rose" perfume and the darker aroma of "roses" which he imagines it to be masking ("Roses, I think. She'd like scent of that kind. Sweet and cheap: soon sour" [13.1009–10]).[20] She becomes to him an object of scent rather than of vision. Prompting him to reflect on the inverse relation of light and smell—the darker it is, he reflects, the more powerfully smells become evident (13.1012–15)—the perception awakens him to the aroma of the world around him, but also causes him to compare Gerty, with her unseasoned taste for the generic, unfavorably to Molly, the poignantly articulated memory of whose manifold scents and aromas ("the perfume of the time before" in her worn dresses, the scent of her stays and bathwater, and even her shoes) attest to a long and intimate personal history together (13.1010–13, 13.1022–25). What wakens in Bloom's monologue as darkness obscures the visible and his nostrils open to the world, in other words, are dimensions of coupling that may be more intimate, immediate, and primitive, less susceptible to idealization and cultural coding, than the kinds of idealization in which both Gerty and Bloom indulge in the first part of the chapter—dimensions of coupling, in fact, that Gerty's sentimental monologue, given its recurrent preoccupations with deodorization, perfumatory censing, and the "look" of the nose, does everything to obscure.[21] Bloom's monologue teems with the kind of olfactory reminiscence that could only ensue from the experience of intimate contact with actual and imperfect people ("Because you get it out of all holes and corners" [13.1026–27]). He recalls not simply Molly's alluringly familiar aromaticism ("Clings to everything she takes off" [13.1022]), but also, among other things, the smell of menstrual discharges (13.826–27, 13.1031–33); the odor of armpits (13.1026); the smell of baby's diapers (one real consequence of the act of lovemaking), "sour milk in their swaddles and tainted curds" (13.957–58); the smell of both good and bad breath (13.936, 13.1035–36);[22] the idiosyncratic weirdness of people's predilections for strange aromas ("All kinds of crazy longings. . . . Girl in Tranquilla convent that nun told me liked to smell rock oil" [13.779–81]); and the experience of waking up next to someone with a hangover ("Worst of all at night Mrs Duggan told me in the City Arms. Husband rolling in drunk, stink of pub off him like a polecat. Have that in your nose in the dark, whiff of stale boose. Then ask in the morning: was I drunk last night?" [13.963–66]). Whether they repulsively deromanticize or merely familiarize, the range of minuscule and humanizing smells that Bloom recalls here has the effect of eroding with particularity the conventional portraits of lovemaking drawn in the first part of "Nausicaa."

These aspects of adult amatory relations, enabled by intimacy and fleshy contact, fall well outside the idealizing conventions of Gerty's monologue, and in turn help to explain a number of weird preoccupations around which Bloom's thoughts gravitate in the second half of the chapter: his comic speculations on the erotic power of musk, for instance, and the pheronal attraction to each other of dogs, other mammals, and, by implication, humans ("Animals go by that. Yes now, look at it that way. We're the same" [13.1026–31]); his correlated interest in the movements and motivations of birds and, more prominently, the humanoid little bat that flits from Gerty's monologue into his own;[23] and, everywhere beneath these objects of curiosity, his obliquely conveyed absorption in the ideas of unconscious attraction and "animal magnetism." This is yet another function served by Bloom's discovery of the stoppage of his watch in "Nausicaa": his puzzlement about its malfunctioning leads him, immediately before his thoughts on olfaction, into a meditation on "magnetic influence" (13.984)—a term popularized by Mesmer—and, in particular, the "magnetic influence" of Boylan and Molly on each other and himself, the "hidden attraction" that mysteriously draws Gerty and himself together from different poles of Dublin (13.982–96). Whether "magnetic fluids" of the kind postulated by Mesmer, Puységur, and their successors shared the physical characteristics of a fluid irradiated like the musky grains of scent that Bloom's nose detects emanating from Gerty (13.1015–21) or those of radiation transmitted through an invisible ether was a matter of debate while belief in animal magnetism flourished; even so, some reflection on its hidden "intercessory" power—a correctively sexualized and physical counter to the spiritualistically "pure radiance" (13.08) attributed to the Blessed Virgin in the "radiant little vision" of Gerty's monologue (13.511)—seems to underlie Bloom's thoughts on olfaction and its permeating role in coupling. Particularly because historians of science have come to see eighteenth- and nineteenth-century theories of animal magnetism as precursors to a modern theory of the Unconscious—but also because Bloom characterizes smell as a "mysterious thing" (13.1015) capable of impinging on consciousness "without [one's] knowing it" (13.1021)—what seems at stake in his reflections on the subliminally attractive and repulsive powers of smell in lovemaking are large questions of the unconscious determinants of human coupling, the role of "personal magnetism" and even that of what Bloom calls "instinct" (13.1129).[24] When coupled with and read against Gerty's monologue, accordingly, Bloom's in turn raises even larger and more irresoluble speculations about the delicate ways in which culture and nature—"the conventions of Society with a big ess" (13.666) and "crazy longings" (13.779)—must mutually intervene to enable the act of human pairing. As happens everywhere else in the double narrative of "Nausicaa," "twice nought makes one" (13.977).

Something of this conflationary sort occurs, perhaps, in many of the memories Bloom sustains in "Nausicaa" of Molly—in passages where eye and nose, romantic scene painting and familiarizing olfactory intimacy come synaesthetically together rather than standing opposed:

> And when the painters were in Lombard street west. Fine voice that fellow had. How Giuglini began. Smell that I did. Like flowers. It was too. Violets. Came from the turpentine probably in the paint. Make their own use of everything. Same time doing it scraped her slipper on the floor so they wouldn't hear. (13.1000–1004)

> Nightstock in Mat Dillon's garden where I kissed her shoulder. Wish I had a full length oilpainting of her then. June that was too I wooed. The year returns. (13.1090–92).

Passages like these, in which Bloom dwells paradoxically on the smell of painting (or of a visually memorable scene), complement those in which Gerty dwells on the look of the nose. Bloom's (mnemonic) romantic scene painting in passages like these is altogether different from the kind of visual idealizing in which he and Gerty indulge in the first half of the chapter.

"WHEN YOU GO OUT NEVER KNOW WHAT DANGERS"

The coordination of Gerty's romantic and domestic fantasies in the first part of "Nausicaa" with the Litany of Our Lady of Loreto—given their mutual glorification of the figure of an idealized mother who, capable of "powerful protection" (13.380), serves as a "comfortress" (13.442) and "haven of refuge for the afflicted" (13.444–45)—leads to a view of domestic love as a source of protection, shelter, and security. For the adulterously wounded Bloom, by contrast, marital love is anything but secure, since it leads to the immense pain of betrayal and, potentially, abandonment. If one effect of Gerty's monologue is to play up fantasies of the kinds of bliss and protective comfort that love can afford, one countereffect of Bloom's monologue is to dramatize the kinds of pain and anguish to which it makes one vulnerable. These range, in his characteristically encyclopedic thinking, from forms of mere physical or venereal pain—thoughts on friction burns, "white fluxions," rashes and skin irritations punctuate his monologue (13.979–81, 13.1081–84, 13.1194)—to forms of psychological pain like those ensuing from but not exclusive to adultery. His meditations on the bereavement of widows and widowers, for instance (13.1225–39), and on the separation of sailors (like Odysseus) from their wives (13.1152–62)—both reflecting the anguish of the loss of attachment—are an overdetermined effect of both his visit to the Dignam household and his fears of losing Molly. Revealing the matured experience of someone who has long ago passed through the excitement of romance and courtship rituals into the anguish of a long-soured marriage, his thoughts open up yet another contrastive way of reading the two sections of "Nausicaa": Gerty's monologue is not simply postcoital, but also premarital, while Bloom's is not simply postcoital, but postmarital as well. Bloom's susceptibility to these darker kinds of thought on the consequences of loving is deepened, moreover, not simply by his recent experience of betrayal, but by the gathering darkness into which the second half of "Nausicaa" moves.

The beginning of the fireworks display, at the exact moment when Gerty's monologue gives way to Bloom's, indicates precisely the time when "twilight" becomes more dark than light, dark enough for man-made illumination to become visible and outshine sunlight. In the darkness that gathers as the fireworks display continues and Bloom's monologue progresses, accordingly, a world once pervasively visible and aglow with illumination starts to produce from within itself, in isolated and scattered spots, specks of light that ward off a deepening night: stars, glowworms, and streetlights start to appear, along with homes and lighthouses illumined from within (13.1068–80, 13.1124, 13.1137–38, 13.1166–84, 13.1212). At the same time, the vision which made possible the erotic posing and flirtation of the first part of the chapter becomes occluded and fallibly deceptive (13.1076–79). Under these conditions, it becomes harder for Bloom to see, easier for others out there on the prowl in the dusk to see him:

> A last lonely candle wandered up the sky from Mirus bazaar . . . and broke, drooping, and shed a cluster of violet but one white stars. They floated, fell: they faded. The shepherd's hour: the hour of folding: hour of tryst. From house to house, giving his everwelcome double knock, went the nine o'clock postman, the glowworm's lamp at his belt gleaming here and there through the laurel hedges. And among the five young trees a hoisted lintstock lit the lamp at Leahy's terrace. By screens of lighted windows, by equal gardens a shrill voice went crying, wailing. . . . Twittering the bat flew here, flew there. Far out over the sands the coming surf crept, grey. Howth settled for slumber, tired of long days, of yumyum rhododendrons (he was old) and felt gladly the night breeze lift, ruffle his fell of ferns. He lay but opened a red eye unsleeping, deep and slowly breathing, slumberous but awake. And far on Kish bank the anchored lightship twinkled, winked at Mr Bloom. (13.1168–81)

If Bloom, like Gerty, was the aggressive voyeur in the first part of the chapter, here, by contrast, he imagines himself spotted and watched. Not unreasonably, he becomes vulnerable in this position and is put in mind not of the excitement, but of the danger of chance encounters, particularly for women, and even of the possibility of being mugged and hurt:

> Howth. Bailey light. Two, four, six, eight, nine. See. Has to change or they might think it a house. Wreckers. Grace Darling. People afraid of the dark. Also glowworms, cyclists: lighting up time. Jewels diamonds flash better. Women. Light

> is a kind of reassuring. Not going to hurt you. Better now of course than long ago. Country roads. Run you through the small guts for nothing. Still two types there are you bob against. Scowl or smile. Pardon! Not at all. (13.1068–74)

In the same way that the twilight, romantically scenic to Gerty, begins to seem ominously gloomy and even dangerous to Bloom, so too do the lighthouses, lightships, beacons, and ocean-going vessels that recur to him here and throughout his monologue (13.1068–70, 13.1164–65, 13.1180–87). For Gerty, these were picturesque components of a romantic seascape illumined by the sun (13.02–8, 13.627–28); for Bloom they become emblems of frail, huddled, human families—like Grace Darling's—seeking mutual protection by illumining from within a universe dark with always encroaching disaster. Much the same is true of Gerty's and Bloom's reflections on "vessels": in Gerty's monologue, underscored as it is by the Litany of Our Lady of Loreto ("spiritual vessel, pray for us, honourable vessel, pray for us, vessel of singular devotion, pray for us, mystical rose" [13.373–74]), "vessels" are conceived as repositories of spiritual power capable of benevolent intercession in worldly affairs; in Bloom's monologue, by contrast, they become frail containers of human cargo barely strong enough to ward off the catastrophe of imminent engulfment:

> Dreadful life sailors have too. Big brutes of oceangoing steamers floundering along in the dark, lowing out like seacows. . . . Others in vessels, bit of a handkerchief sail, pitched about like snuff at a wake. . . . Hanging on to a plank or astride of a beam for grim life, lifebelt round him, gulping salt water. . . . (13.1148–61).

Retrospectively, of course, Bloom's thoughts on the dangers of the chance outing or encounter—"Something in all those superstitions because when you go out you never know what dangers" (13.1159–60)—reveal an awareness of the possibility that Gerty might well have encountered in the strange man with whom she has flirted more the ill-intentioned "scowler" than the benignly smiling admirer ("two types there are you bob against. Scowl or smile"); indeed, this awareness leads him in a later section of his monologue to worry more particularly about the safety and security of his daughter, who resembles Gerty in being too young to have learned the need for cautiously prudent fear ("Milly, no sign of funk. . . . Don't know what death is at that age" [13.1187–89]).

"MUTOSCOPE PICTURES"

In the schema he prepared for Carlo Linati, Joyce called the style of "Nausicaa" a "retrogressive progression" rather than a tumescent/detumescent sequence—in part perhaps because Bloom's matured and postcoitally disillusioned realizations cast retrospective insight back over Gerty's; in part because Bloom's dalliance with Gerty within view of Howth causes him, like Rip Van Winkle, to return in memory to the time of his courtship with Molly

(13.1109–16); but also perhaps because "Nausicaa" "quotes" and critically reworks earlier scenes from Joyce's writing. A chapter whose two parts are already crisscrossed by proliferating doublings and contrasts, in other words, becomes even more elaborately paired with yet other scenes in Joyce's works. "Nausicaa" takes place in the same locale as "Proteus," for instance—on Sandymount Strand—and countless parallels, as critics have shown, accordingly weave the two chapters into each other.[25] Stephen's interest in the Aristotelian "diaphane" returns in Gerty's and Bloom's fascination with her "transparents" (13.426, 13.502, 13.716, 13.929, 13.1262); Stephen's morbid study of a dog sniffing another dog's corpse gets comically reprised in Bloom's thoughts about the sniffing of dogs in love (13.1028–30); and the bat that appears in Stephen's disturbing quatrain about the life-draining powers of love sails out of literature and into the twilight in which Bloom and Gerty woo. Bloom also gives concrete life to Stephen's more abstract thoughts on menstruation (3.393–98, 13.777–84, 13.822–27, 13.1031–33); and he recalls, like Stephen, the shards of a dream from the night before (3.365–69, 13.878, 13.1240–41).

But in another form of "retrogressive progression," as critics have extensively shown, "Nausicaa" also heavily evokes the fourth chapter of *A Portrait of the Artist* and, in particular, the scene in which Stephen, like Gerty and Bloom, stares with erotic fascination at the bird-girl on the beach.[26] The twinning of these two scenes—one in which an adolescent girl and the other in which an adolescent boy gazes in beatifying rapture at a member of the opposite sex—makes it difficult to see the division of "Nausicaa" into two parts as one of gender opposition. Since, in many ways, Gerty might be regarded as a female version of Stephen, the two parts of the chapter seem divided more along generational than gender lines: Gerty and Stephen are young, while Bloom is middle-aged, hurt, and beyond the kind of idealizations to which Gerty and Stephen are given. Gerty, who "would be twentytwo in November" (13.221–22), is a few months younger than the Stephen of *Ulysses,* and, like him, though she reflects a different level of culture and educational experience, might be said to have been contaminated by literature:[27] Stephen reads the philosophers and fathers of the church, while Gerty reads magazines and romances, but both have let literature and the imagination overpower their experience of the world. Gerty's imaginary relations to Reggy Wylie, moreover, are not that different from Stephen's equally spectral relations to "E. C.": her desire to discover her "beau ideal" (13.209) somewhere in reality—in Reggy Wylie, in Bloom *("Art thou real, my ideal?"* [13.645–46])—recalls pretty directly Stephen's desire to "meet in the real world the unsubstantial image which his soul so constantly beheld" of a female who would "transfigure" him (*P* 65). Both Gerty's monologue and *A Portrait,* furthermore, offer extended accounts of adolescent pretension: the Byronic posturing of Stephen's "Madame, I never eat muscatel grapes" (*P* 63), for instance, reappears in Gerty's "wonder[ing] why you couldn't eat something poetical like violets or roses" (13.230). Even the pervasive theological undercast of Stephen's character and consciousness in *A*

Portrait and *Ulysses* reappears in "Nausicaa," though in a distinctly feminized and Mariolatrous form. The effect that Joyce gets by enabling us to see Gerty as a female version of Stephen is also, finally, Homeric.[28]

Given their mutual preoccupations with painting and portraiture, it might even be said that Gerty's half of "Nausicaa" evokes the whole of *A Portrait of the Artist as a Young Man*—for which, incidentally, "the *Lady's Pictorial*" is nothing much more than a re-gendered synonym. Like that novel, though in capsule form, the chapter offers a telescopic account of male and female acculturation and development from infancy to adolescence. Striking details from early parts of *A Portrait* reappear in mutated form in the first part of "Nausicaa": the infantile language, a bedwetting incident (13.393–403), "little mariner[s]" (13.64)—Stephen sings a hornpipe while the twins, like Joyce in the earliest photographs ever taken of him, wear "sailor suits" (13.14)—a child being pushed and falling in the dirt (13.47–62), and, of course, the exploration of adolescent pretension. In the chapter's first line of dialogue, baby Boardman is ominously being taught how to say, as any full-grown Irishman must if he is to survive, "I want a drink" (13.26). And in the "altercation" of the twins over a sandcastle modeled on the Martello tower—one of them as "headstrong" as the other is "selfwilled" (13.42–48)—we see the primordia of the rivalry between Stephen and Mulligan: rather than fighting over the key ("It is mine. I paid the rent" [1.631]), they fight with their sister for possession of a ball (13.247–50). The twins' names, it has been suggested, "represent warring soldiers and sailors (Tommy Atkins and Jack Tar respectively),"[29] and so map out two possible futures for these boys, as do parallel traits attributed to the three girlfriends: Cissy Caffrey, the athlete and tomboy (13.275–77, 13.478–84, 13.754); "squinty Edy" Boardman (13.128), the girl with glasses and all that they might imply; and Gerty, "the womanly woman" (13.435). All three girls are also obviously in training to become mothers: Gerty, already "just like a second mother in the house" (13.325–26), has taken on her mother's and father's responsibilities (10.1205–11, 13.320–34); Cissy, gifted with a "quick motherwit," is helping to raise her twin brothers (13.75); and Edy, too, is "pretending to nurse the baby" (13.522–23). Gerty and her companions, Bloom notes—all of them like Milly Bloom in undergoing "growing pains" (13.1202)—"want to be grownups. Dressing in mother's clothes. Time enough, understand all the ways of the world" (13.896–97). Their posturings and pretensions, like Stephen's, are an essential part of their growing up, since only by pretending can they grow into the roles they aspire to fill.

Like all young people, as Richard Ellmann has pointed out—and not least like Stephen of *A Portrait*—Gerty thinks of herself as unique and exceptional ("she was something aloof, apart, in another sphere, . . . she was not of them and never would be" [13.602–3]), though her sense of singularity is paradoxically conveyed in a style that is imitative, conventional, and heavy with implications of mass reproduction.[30] One effect of this tension is to highlight the youthful naïveté of Gerty's thinking, the vast discrepancy between her own belief in her exceptionality and our perception, corroborated by Bloom, of the sheer iterative ordinariness of her circumstances and desires ("Names change: that's all. Lovers: yum yum"). Bloom's monologue, by contrast, not only puts Gerty's into perspective but also works in just the opposite way: though Bloom thinks of himself as barely passing muster in the ranks of the ordinary (even his wife finds him dull on June 16), he does so in the signal stream-of-consciousness style for which *Ulysses* in part earned its reputation as a work of avant-garde literary innovation. As a counterfoil to Gerty's monologue, one of the effects of his, paradoxically, is to recuperate a sense of how exceptional and singular the ordinary can be. In reading Bloom's monologue, the reader may also feel—in another form of "retrogressive progression"—the pleasure of a return to the familiar, particularly after the virtuosic stylistic experimentation of *Ulysses* from "Wandering Rocks" through the first part of "Nausicaa," and even something of a nostalgia for the "normative" stream-of-consciousness chapters that placed us "inside" of Bloom early in the novel. This nostalgia for a past experience doubles with Bloom's nostalgia for Molly and the early years of his marriage (and with Odysseus's for home), and arguably solidifies our attachment to Bloom as a character here. For the style of his monologue in "Nausicaa" is not quite the same as that of the interior monologues of the chapters extending from "Calypso" through "Lestrygonians": it is much more elliptic and fragmentary. "Suppose I when I was? No. Gently does it" (13.831–32 [undid my trousers]); "Besides I can't be so if Molly" (13.837 [ugly]); "It's so hard to find one who" (13.869). One has to be familiar with Bloom, canny to his tics and habits of association, to fill in the blanks and read fragments like these.[31] The experience of reading his monologue therefore complements and contrasts with the experience of reading Gerty's: rather than experiencing the delight and thrill of novelty, as Bloom and Gerty do in their tumescent states, we experience the pleasure of returning to the familiar. Somewhere between two such poles as these, too, our experience of pairing happens—whether we look, like Gerty, for the foreign and exotic and unique in our partners, or like Bloom, for the comfort and security of the familiar.

"STILL THERE'S DESTINY IN IT"

"Nausicaa" is also thematically preoccupied with the question of whether the mysteriously intimate business of pairing is determined by what the chapter variously calls "fate," "kismet," or "destiny" (13.99, 13.973, 13.1062, 13.1239); or occasioned by the opposing operations of luck, accident, contingency, and mere chance (13.179–85, 13.226, 13.349, 13.651, 13.808, 13.1157, 13.1249–51, 13.1271). At the end of the chapter, on the one hand, when Bloom tosses away the stick with which he wrote his incomplete message to Gerty in the sand, he thinks of their meeting as fortuitously random:

> He flung his wooden pen away. The stick fell in silted sand, stuck. Now if you were trying to do that for a week on end you couldn't. Chance. We'll never meet

> again. But it was lovely. Goodbye, dear. Thanks. Made me feel so young. (13.1270–73)

From this perspective, couples match up, rub together, and blaze up into frictive heat for the same indeterminably fluky reasons that fires burst out in grass:

> Howth a while ago amethyst. Glass flashing. That's how that wise man what's his name with the burning glass. Then the heather goes on fire. It can't be tourists' matches. What? Perhaps the sticks dry rub together in the wind and light. Or broken bottles in the furze act as a burning glass in the sun. (13.1137–41)

But "Nausicaa"—its tumescent first half in itself a kind of hypermagnifying and "burning glass"—makes it clear that there is more to the stirring up of heat and fire than sheer indeterminacy. Bloom, after all, has been seeking some form of sexual attention and gratification since he picked up Martha's letter and the idea of masturbating at nine in the morning (hence the pressing density of phrases from her letter throughout "Nausicaa"). And Gerty, "wearing blue for luck, hoping against hope . . . because she thought perhaps [Reggy Wylie] might be out" (13.179–83), is also obviously culturally primed and "waiting for something to happen" (13.896). "Out on spec," as Bloom puts it while meditating on Gerty and her friends—out, that is, on the chance of finding someone—"they believe in chance because like themselves," presumably, they do not know exactly what they are looking for except that they are certainly looking (13.808–9). And those who look tend to find, though not perhaps what or where they thought ("never know what you find" [13.1249]): "they say if the flower withers she wears she's a flirt. All are. Daresay she felt I [was flirting]. When you feel like that [flirtatious] you often meet what you feel" (13.827–29). Bloom's and Gerty's spectral liaison, in short, seems to come about "accidentally on purpose" (13.485), as a result of forces somewhere halfway between aleatory happenstance and purposive determination. Isn't this the way it always happens? For, as Bloom notes while thinking about the odd circumstance that brought the Caffrey twins' ball—and Gerty's attention—rolling his way, "every bullet has its billet" (13.951): nothing, that is, happens by chance. In Bloom's case, moreover, dalliance with Gerty within view of Howth serves the therapeutically wishful and hardly random purpose of somewhat undoing the injury he has incurred on June 16, by rejuvenating a sustained memory of his youth and courtship of Molly ("Made me feel so young"): "June that was too I wooed. The year returns. History repeats itself. . . . All quiet on Howth now. . . . Where we. . . . So it returns. Think you're escaping and run into yourself. Longest way round is the shortest way home" (13.1092–1111). Who knows but that Bloom under different circumstances—were he ten years younger and, by chance, unacquainted with Molly—might not have pushed his meeting with Gerty one stage further: "Suppose I spoke to her. What about? Bad plan however if you don't know how to end the conversation [that is, to stop the escalating involvement]" (13.862–63); "French letter still in my pocketbook. Cause of half the trouble. But might happen sometime, I don't think" (13.877–78). For Gerty has, in another of the chapter's innumerable doublings—and notwithstanding the condescension with which readers have often understood her—enough of Molly in her to enable us to see back through her naïveté into the naïveté of Molly's youth, too: the breathless strings of conjunctions (particularly "becauses") that link her thoughts at times anticipate the peculiarities of Molly's "style" (13.179–87, 13.695–708); she is also like the young Molly in Gilbraltar in being superstitious, and in "waiting, always waiting to be asked" (13.208); and she is, after all—however great the "mistake in the valuation" (13.1125)—attracted to the "foreign gentleman that was sitting on the rocks" (13.1302; compare with 13.415–17, 13.656–59) for all the same reasons that Molly was:

> Looking out over the sea she told me. Evening like this, but clear, no clouds. I always thought I'd marry a lord or a rich gentleman coming with a private yacht. *Buenas noches, señorita. El hombre ama la muchacha hermosa.* Why me? Because you were so foreign from the others. (13.1206–10)

The only difference between then and now is the clarity and conviction with which Bloom wooed Molly ("Evening like this, but clear, no clouds"), as opposed to the moral and emotional ambiguity with which he relates to Gerty. Even so, "Molly and Milly" (13.785), "Molly and Josie Powell" (13.814), "Martha, she" (13.782): Gerty spectrally evokes and doubles for so many of the significant women in Bloom's life that she comes to resemble "that half tabby-white tortoiseshell in the City Arms with the letter em on her forehead" of Bloom's recollection (13.1136–37)—an amalgamation of remotely recognizable prototypes amid which stands out the primary sign of Molly.

"Still there's destiny in it, falling in love" (13.973), Bloom therefore thinks, in considering how strange it is that from the limited pool of eligible candidates who form a person's inevitably small and circumscribed social world—think of Smalltown, USA—and especially given the infinite idiosyncrasies of desire ("it's so hard to find one who" [13.869]), people nonetheless manage regularly to find each other, pair up, and mate: "as God made them he matched them" (13.976). Do they do so for romantically fated and impelling reasons or simply because of a circumstantial luck of the draw? Part of the wonder of Bloom's monologue is its spectacular meditation on the ubiquity and weirdness of coupling, the mysteriousness with which individuals of all shapes and proclivities somehow manage—like the exotic orchid which the Duchesse de Guermantes keeps on her balcony in Proust's novel—to find an appropriately receptive other:[32]

> Just compare for instance those others. Wife locked up at home, skeleton in the cupboard. Allow me to introduce my. Then they trot you out some kind of a nondescript, wouldn't know what to call her. Always see a fellow's weak point in his wife. Still there's destiny in it, falling in love. . . . Chaps that would go to the

> dogs if some woman didn't take them in hand. Then little chits of girls, height of a shilling in coppers, with little hubbies. As God made them he matched them. . . . Or old rich chap of seventy and blushing bride. Marry in May and repent in December. . . .
>
> Other hand a sixfooter with a wifey up to his watchpocket. Long and the short of it. Big he and little she. . . . Woman and man that is. Fork and steel. Molly, he. (13.970–79, 13.992–93)

And the characteristically encyclopedic list goes on: "pretty girls and ugly men marrying. Beauty and the beast" (13.836–37); "a married man with a single girl" (13.873); Milly and a "young student" (13.928); "nurse Callan" and "young doctor O'Hare" (13.960–61); "poor man O'Connor" and "some good matronly woman in a porkpie hat to mother him" (13.1232–34); "and Mrs Breen and Mrs Dignam once like that too, marriageable" (13.1232–34). Even the citizen has a wife—and a sister-in-law with "three fangs in her mouth" who is on the marriage market ("Imagine that early in the morning at close range. Everyone to his taste as Morris said when he kissed the cow" [13.1221–25]). Like Bloom and Gerty—and the two stylistically disparate monologues through which they are mediated—even the weirdest of all things in "Nausicaa" pair. The chapter is infinitely preoccupied with the process through which this happens: with the circumstantiality of meetings; the dynamics of flirtation and ways of advertising availability (13.916–17, 13.922–23); the tricks and subterfuges of invitational allurement (13.796–805, 13.993–96, 13.1007–8); the awkwardness of first dates ("Worst is beginning" [13.879; compare with 13.862–66]); the fashions and forms of courtship rituals (13.829–33, 13.838–40); the monumental significance of the first kiss (13.886–91); the disillusionments and habituating routine following marriage ("aftereffect not pleasant"). In one way of reading it, "Nausicaa" amounts to a metaphysics of coitus. Its two parts (and partners) draw out an immense field of tensions and contrasts—between femininity and masculinity, youth and age, culture and nature, conventionality and idiosyncrasy, idealism and practicality, fate and chance; between tumescent idealization and detumescent letdown; between naive inexperience and world-weary maturity; between the wish to be and find someone singular and unique and the wish to be and find someone companionably familiar; between the wish for security and union with a mate and the fear of being hurt and afflicted with loss. Somewhere amid the play of all these proliferating tensions and differentiations, pairing up surely and sometimes love take place.

14

Interesting States

Birthing and the Nation in "Oxen of the Sun"

ENDA DUFFY

> *Voglio essere in un stato interessante* (I would like to be in an interesting state [country], *or* I want to be pregnant).
>
> Italian comic Roberto Benigni punning on the phrase "interesting state"

First, three vignettes from Irish life since "Oxen of the Sun" was written in 1919–20 that cast light on the issues raised in the episode:

In the village I come from in Ireland there stands, opposite the gates of the Catholic church, a statue of "Mother Eireann." In her shadow, speeches are made at election time. The white marble from which she was carved in the early 1920s and the Howth granite of her plinth are the same as those used inside the church. On the plinth are written, in Irish, the names of the men from the townland who were killed in the War of Independence of 1919–21, a war which had just begun as Joyce was reflecting ferociously on young men, motherhood, and some versions of nationhood in "Oxen of the Sun." Strikingly, "Mother Eireann" does not look "motherly"; rather, she seems extremely youthful, innocent, virginal. As such, she resembles the Virgin whose statue may be venerated within the church.

A turning point in the "domestic" politics of the Irish Republic was the failure of legislation on the "Mother and Child" scheme of 1951. In a relatively new nation where social assistance was rudimentary, the legislation proposed that the state offer free medical assistance to pregnant women and newborn infants. In a scenario reminiscent of the "Parnell split" of the 1890s, the scheme was defeated by the determined opposition of powerful Catholic bishops, the government was out voted, and the scheme's proposer, Noel Browne, generally regarded as one of the most promising reformers ever to enter politics in the Irish republic, found his career ruined.[1]

In the 1980s, apart from savage incidents in the Northern Irish "troubles," the news story that most vividly captured the imaginations of the Irish people was the murder investigation that became known as the "Kerry babies" case. A dead infant was found on the beach in Kerry. The police accused a local woman; she appeared to confess, but then led the police investigators to the body of another child. The police suggested that she had been the mother of both babies—by different men. The tribunal that followed transfixed the nation, chiefly because it set in high relief the contrast between state-sponsored ideologies and women's rights, in a period when the Irish government was beginning to consider legalizing the sale of contraceptives, divorce, and abortion in some cases, for the first time.[2]

These are scenes from the fraught relationship between the representations and realities of motherhood and the modern Irish state. Behind each of them stands Joyce's strange rumination on precisely the relationship between the mother's act of giving birth to a child and the national and communal significance of this event, in the "Oxen of the Sun" episode of *Ulysses*—an episode written, we know with hindsight, when the Irish state was, with great difficulty, itself being born. In each of the three scenes I've presented, the effort to hold sacred the figure of the mother as a starred site for the representation of statehood is combined with an apparent determination all the while to avoid the physical reality constituting that motherhood: there is in each case a recoil from the physical act of giving birth. In "Oxen of the Sun" Joyce attempts a potentially disruptive gesture by taking exactly the opposite tack: he attempts to replace discussions of the symbolic power of representations of motherhood with an account of one mother, Mina Purefoy, giving birth. Up to this point in the novel, motherhood has figured predominantly as an issue of the potential symbolic power of women over men. The text has worked almost invariably to contest the specter of the dead mother, as in Stephen's discussions with Buck Mulligan in "Telemachus" or in the moments of his "Proteus" soliloquy. In "Oxen of the Sun" all this, in a radical move, is replaced by an engagement with the event of birth itself. Such an engagement, given the nation's subsequent attempts to avoid it, might be expected to force a reconsideration of the symbolic deployment of the images of motherhood and of women generally in the iconography of nationhood, to be followed, perhaps, by a reexamination of the specific rights and roles of actual women and men as citizens of the state.

The enormous difficulties Joyce experienced in facing up to motherhood at its point of origin, however, is readily visible in "Oxen of the Sun." First, consider the famous panoply of English literary canonical styles, from mock Old English to mock Carlyle, that are orchestrated in the episode: it is as if the author had to try out every British, and many Anglo-Irish, literary styles as a suitable medium for the description of a birth, and still did not succeed in placing an account of that birth before us, except as a brief report of a nurse and doctor.[3] Second, although the episode is set in the Holles Street Maternity Hospital, it veers resolutely away from the nurses, mothers, and children to focus on a group of male interns, medical students, and hangers-on—Lenehan, Stephen, Bloom—who carouse in a common room while Mina Purefoy gives birth within earshot upstairs. (Bloom at one point poignantly "heard on the upfloor cry on high and he wondered what cry that it was" [14.170]). The birth, then, occurs offstage. Joyce, of course, throughout *Ulysses,* continually uses this strategy of sidestepping accounts of apparently crucial events in favor of the mundane and quotidian: in "Hades," the corresponding episode to "Oxen of the Sun," for example, we are given only briefly and at secondhand the actual death of Paddy Dignam and the reaction of his widow, while the rituals of his funeral are minutely detailed. Further, accounts of varied groups of men engaged in witty discussion are possibly the most characteristic scenes in all of Joyce's writing. In an episode constructed around a woman giving birth to a baby, however, the continuous focus on a crowd of carousing young males must strike any reader as at least incongruous; from the writer's viewpoint, a potentially moving account of a difficult birth is sacrificed for a description of the rambling, often inchoate chatter of drunken young men. In this sidestepping of the actual birth, it is as if the disrespect of Costello, Mulligan, Lynch, and the rest for that birth is repeated in the episode itself: the text is more attentive to the banter of drunkards than to the birth of a baby. What the critic must consider is the space for a critique opened by such an incongruity as this.

The episode purports to describe a birth, but instead, in a plethora of imitations of English literary styles, describes a revel among a group of male medical students. Through the setting, the trope of "embryonic development," the discussions of Mrs. Purefoy, her husband, and family, the correspondences and oppositions to "Hades" (the episode centered on death), *birth* is clearly and unremittingly suggested as the central concern throughout; what we are mostly given, nevertheless, is a highly incongruous chorus to comment on the grand theme. This incongruity, I suggest, is forced upon the reader, and its resolution will determine one's reaction to the episode. By focusing at the moment of birthing upon a chorus, the episode sets before us the *social* implications of a birth, while eliding its private significance either for child or mother. Further, by making this chorus male, the text asks us what the social significance of birth can be in a male-dominated culture—in a culture where virtually all narratives of the social are constructed by men. As such, also, the episode is particularly concerned with how masculine identity is constructed, specifically, how its continual process of (re)construction by the different male characters who share the common room in "Oxen of the Sun" is inflected by the birth of a baby to a woman upstairs. These characters may be said to stand in for the stereotypical figures of nervous fathers in the maternity hospital waiting room who have populated twentieth-century urban domestic fiction (Roddy Doyle's *The Snapper* provides a recent Irish example);[4] Burke's public house, to which the young medicals of "Oxen of the Sun" retreat at the end of the episode, was well used to the custom of such fathers, just as Mooney's of Parnell Street was used to the custom of fathers waiting at the Rotunda Hospital at the north end of O'Connell Street. In considering birth by focusing on a group of men's reactions to it,

"Oxen of the Sun," whether consciously or not, presents its readers with an unremittingly accurate, bleak account of the prospects for narrating the birth of a child, or for having such a representation alter either the male-dominated society's view of itself or even the roles of its male or female members. It does, however, show men who are forced—by their proximity to a woman in child-birth—to consider, however jocosely, the viability of their adopted gender personae in relation to their productivity in the larger community. Featuring near the close of the episode one of the most significant sightings of the novel's least known and uncategorized male characters, the man in the mackintosh, this episode attempts to re-envision the social significance of motherhood and its use as a symbol by focusing on a mother giving birth; but it turns out to be insightful in gender terms mostly to the extent that it charts, first, the resistance of male-dominated cultures to any potentially disruptive representation of birthing, and second, a tenuous questioning by these men of their gender roles and status in a society that nevertheless cannot entirely suppress the reality of women giving birth.

NARRATING A BIRTH

The first question to consider in understanding the scope of this episode, therefore, is this: what is the effect of including the birth of a baby in *Ulysses*? Initially it allows the novel to display Bloom's solicitousness: he had inquired about Mrs. Purefoy to Mrs. Breen when they met in "Lestrygonians," and now he goes to inquire about the progress of her three-day labor at the maternity hospital itself. Displaying this solicitousness, the novel establishes Mrs. Purefoy's birthing as a *social* fact: that is, one of concern to the entire community of Dublin. Such a presentation of the birth is continually enhanced in the episode itself, by the reiteration of the fact that the labor takes place in a publicly provided maternity hospital, by the manner in which the rowdy young men are in a sense in attendance at the birth, by their eagerness to be informed of the progress of the labor, and by the way in which it in turn informs the progress and subject matter of their conversation. Thus the initial question may be focused as follows: what is the effect of including in *Ulysses* a birth that is presented as an event of social and even communal significance? In the most general sense, the birth is a socially significant augur of new life, hope, and regeneration; Paddy Dignam has died, and "they took the liberty of burying him this morning" (12.323), while the baby that will be known as Mortimer Edward Purefoy, "after the influential third cousin of Mr Purefoy in the Treasury Remembrancer's Office, Dublin Castle" (14.1334), is born, and these tangible mementos of death and birth frame the quotidian perambulations of Bloom, Stephen, and all the living of the city. Beyond such base tones, however, the specific social effects of representing birth in early-twentieth-century Ireland are also crucial to "Oxen of the Sun," and the social significance of birthing in the West generally needs to be considered in the context of some associated early-twentieth-century discourses. Havelock Ellis, in his *Studies of the Psychology of Sex* (which Richard Brown in *Joyce and Sexuality* argues that Joyce had read and used in his fiction), likewise insists on the social significance of birthing and implies its symbolic implications: "The sexual act is of no more concern to the community than any other private physiological act . . . but the birth of a child is a social act. Not what goes into the womb but what comes out of it concerns society. The community is invited to receive a new citizen."[5] While Ellis's brutalist practicality ("not what goes into the womb but what comes out of it") has a eugenicist tinge, his focus on the social significance of birth reflects a common assumption of a series of discourses—nationalism, women's rights, the birth control movement, eugenics, and Christian doctrine—in the West in the first decades of the twentieth century, discourses that are both employed and undermined in "Oxen of the Sun." These were all, it should be noted, varieties of *political* discourses; by presenting birthing as a social fact, "Oxen of the Sun" politicizes it and questions its potential political significance. It considers too how birthing can be narrated from the viewpoints of these discourses in ways that might alter its specific political effects.

The first word of "Oxen of the Sun" is "Deshil," which, despite its Latin appearance, is said to be an Irish phrase meaning "to the right of," or "to the house of." With the two lengthy paragraphs that succeed the initial incantation citing as a priority "the prosperity of a nation" (14.13), national interests—and specifically Irish national interests—are introduced at once as the discursive priority of the episode. When we consider that "Oxen of the Sun" was begun in 1919, at the time of the commencement of the guerrilla War of Independence, which would end with the Anglo-Irish Treaty of 1921 and the founding of the Irish Free State, the particularly charged nature of any intervention in Irish nationalist discourse at such a moment becomes apparent. By casting its birth announcement initially in somewhat garbled but nevertheless vividly marked nationalist terms, at the least the episode intervenes in the discourse that for long and in an increasingly vehement manner had associated the notion of the Irish nation with the figure of woman and in particular with that of the mother. Patrick Pearse, the leader of the 1916 rebellion and possibly the chief mythologist and rhetorician of early-twentieth-century Ireland's version of the sanctified nationalism prominent in Europe in the years leading up to the First World War, perhaps best distilled this tendency in his short powerful poem in Irish, "Mise Eire" ("I am Ireland"), whose incantatory tone, spoken by a national mother, betters that of the jokey incantations that open "Oxen of the Sun." In "Mise Eire," it is the mother figure that speaks, albeit in the male poet's words; Joyce would use this same strategy, to different effect, when he put words in Molly's mind in "Penelope." Pearse's final and most dramatic poem, written in his cell on the night before he and his brother were executed for their roles in the 1916 Rising, is entitled "The Mother"; it puts into his own mother's mouth the moving words of a cry of anguish over her dead children:

I do not grudge them: Lord, I do not grudge
My two strong sons that I have seen go out
To break their strength and die, they and a few,
In bloody protest for a glorious thing[6]

Cast as a prayer and as renunciation of suffering, this dramatic poem reinscripts, in advance, his own mother's personal anguish as political, communal pride. His mother's presumed anguish is located in the Christian context of Christ's sacrifice and Mary's sorrow, so that the focus is kept firmly on the sons' martyrdom (itself endured, it is implied, on their mother's behalf). Her reaction is moving precisely to the degree that it too is a sacrifice involving her self-restraint: she must keep her personal sorrow in check for the common good. Hence, in a representational imperative of which this poem might be seen as paradigmatic, while it may be said that the use of maternal imagery in relation to the nation grew markedly more intense as the independence of Ireland grew imminent, spurred on by various highbrow variants on the theme such as Yeats's earlier *Kathleen Ni Houlihan* and by numerous popular songs and images, the increasing attention to an idealized woman as national icon was matched, or even was founded upon, an increased dematerialization in such images of the actual realities of women's feelings and lives. This was occurring at the moment when women's rights in the public sphere may in fact have been increasing, partly due to the involvement of many women both in the Rising and in the War of Independence. Constance Gore-Booth, the Countess Markiewicz, who had been commandant at the College of Surgeons in Stephen's Green during the Rising, was the first woman ever to be elected to the British House of Commons following the Sinn Féin victory in Ireland in the election of 1918, although, as promised, she never took her seat there. Nevertheless, regarding the use of images of women as symbols of the new nation, what is striking is that while demands placed on the abstraction "woman" as figure of the new nation grew more vehement, the realities of women's daily lives, as we have seen in the case of Pearse's poem, were called upon to be narrated only in specific, narrow, nationalist terms. It is in this context that "Oxen of the Sun"'s attention not merely to motherhood as a lived reality but rather to the very act that originates the role, giving birth itself, needs to be considered as a potentially radical gesture.

While this representational gesture is at the core of the episode, it is clear also that the birth turns out to be represented circumspectly, so that the disruptive potential of its immediacy is largely diffused. First, since the novel is set in 1904, it can disavow any awareness of contemporaneous advances in the status of women, and hence, of alterations in the significance of representations of motherhood in relation to that status. Nevertheless, the episode both participates in and overturns the representational imperative by which the greater symbolic importance granted to the female subject, the lesser the actual freedom allowed female subjects themselves. In the first place, it refers to, and ultimately undercuts, versions of Catholic Mariolatry that may be said to have underpinned the symbolic significance of largely Catholic nationalisms such as that of Ireland. The second of the three invocations that open the episode ends with the word "wombfruit," echoing the final words of the "Hail Mary": "Blessed is the fruit of thy womb." Later, however, a drunken speech by Stephen on whether or not Mary "knew" God substantially undercuts any respect for Mary as "our mighty mother" (14.296) that specific isolated references might seem to imply. Second, "Oxen of the Sun" broadens discussion of motherhood and the relation of its representation to nationalist ideology by introducing, particularly in the discussions of the young men, the issues of the broader debate, common throughout Europe in the aftermath of the Great War, on the relation between population growth and a "healthy" nation—issues such as whether, in countries with a falling birthrate, procreation is not a national duty and contraception almost a crime. Nationalist discourses of this period were preoccupied with this last particular question, and it had a particular resonance in Ireland, where the population question was deeply anomalous. By 1919, Ireland was one of the few countries in Europe where the birthrate was rising—that is, where large families were still common—while paradoxically, it was one of the only European countries where the population had fallen, and fallen drastically, from about eight million people before the famine of 1845–47 to about four million people early in the twentieth century. Given this anomalousness, it might well have been deemed very useful that Irish nationalist concerns with parenthood go beyond pathos-laden representations of powerful mothers who must be honored and served. By showing us the idolatry that underpinned the nationalist version of motherhood and then casually undermining it ("let the lewd with faith and fervor worship" insists the drunken Stephen, on the doctrine of the Immaculate Conception [14.311]), and by extending the discussion to issues of population control, "Oxen of the Sun" dissipates some of the power of the old versions of motherhood, but at the cost, as we shall see, of almost having the mother as subject disappear altogether from the text.

By moving our attention away from the central fact that Mrs. Purefoy is giving birth, and on to strands of a discussion of possible moral imperatives to conceive, become pregnant, and give birth, "Oxen of the Sun" certainly discovers a means to recast representations of motherhood outside of the issue of mother-son relations that had preoccupied Stephen, the novel itself, and much of nationalist rhetoric in early-twentieth-century Irish culture, up to now. Such a mother-son narrative, as epitomized in the Irish context by Pearse's "The Mother," may be considered the ur-narrative of mothers as nationalist icons; Stephen's relation to his dead mother, therefore, turns out to be his personal version of a story cast irredeemably in nationalist terms, so that despite the fact that he rejects his mother's conservative influence rather than fighting on its behalf, Stephen still lives out his relation to his mother in terms thoroughly recognizable within the patterns of the nationalist ur-narrative. "Oxen of the Sun"'s turn to "fecundity" rather than maternal influence as the trope of motherhood may appear as an escape from the nationalist discourse's hold on representations of maternity; however, it moves the discussion into another area also rife with nationalist polemics, that of population growth. By having the young medical students discuss the mechanics of fecundity, "Oxen of the Sun" moves the context of motherhood from one inflected by religious motifs, especially veneration of the Virgin Mary, to one dominated by quasi-scientific thinking. This move, however, can serve to further instrumentalize the role of the mother, who in the scientific context can come to be seen as merely a tool in the mechanics of population growth.

At a crucial moment in the episode, as the baby is about to be born, Joyce presents us with perspectives from each of these two contrasting tendencies, in the voices, as it turns out, of two thoroughly different eighteenth-century Irish writers, Burke and Goldsmith (whose statues, in a further ironic twist, now grace the forecourt of Trinity College in Dublin's College Green). The episode invites us to laugh at the drunken Costello's defense of his rowdy behavior, a defense cast in Goldsmithian language, that sentimentally resorts to the notion of faithfulness to the mother's memory, a notion central to the quasi-religious nationalist version of motherhood: "Them was always the sentiments of honest Frank Costello which I was bred up most particular to honour thy father and thy mother that had the best hand to a rolypoly or a hasty pudding as you ever see what I will always look back on with a loving heart" (14.841–44). While such mother love is devalued, it is nonetheless allowed to drown out any extended account of the birth that is almost accomplished, news of which has just been given in the chipped, sententious tones of Burke: "Merciful providence had been pleased to put a period to the sufferings of the lady who was *enceinte* which she had borne with a laudable fortitude and she had given birth to a bouncing boy" (14.820–23). Bloom's solicitude, which had been the reason for his visit to the hospital in the first place and hence, as it were, the occasion for this episode, is here transformed into a coldly moralist officialese quite in keeping with the rationalist social concern of much early-twentieth-century population literature, whether written in favor of birth control or population increase. Behind these two rhetorics, both of which invade the text as self-conscious parodies so that neither is valorized, the cry that Bloom had earlier heard upstairs, the cry of Mrs. Purefoy in childbirth—a *chora* which it would have been fascinating to see Joyce transcribe in *Ulysses*—is drowned out. Further, while the Mariolatry-based narrative of motherhood that underpinned nationalist dogma is dismissed as grossly sentimental, the new alternative doxa of scientific population control and its discourses—whether from the conservative, nationalist pro-growth or the progressive birth-control factions—is hardly offered as a serious alternative, either as narrative or as guide to action.

A considerable portion of the criticism of "Oxen of the Sun" has been concerned with the perspectives the episode may offer on birth control. Much of this criticism has set out to understand exactly what Joyce meant when in his famous letter to Frank Budgen on his progress with "Oxen of the Sun" he claimed that the "idea" behind the episode was "the crime committed against fecundity by sterilizing the act of coition" (*Letters I* 138–39). Joyce wished to continue to develop the Homeric parallels of *Ulysses:* the murder of the oxen of the sun, symbols of fertility, is matched in this episode by discussions among the carousing young men, and various discourses of more anonymous narrators throughout the episode, on such issues as whether the mother or child should die during childbirth in cases where such a choice needed to be made (14.202ff), virgin birth (14.214ff), Immaculate Conception (14.309), condoms (14.462, 14.784), causes of sterility (14.668), irreverence for mothers (14.832), monstrous births (14.995ff), "the bride, evervirgin" (14.1101), and infant mortality (14.1267ff). Amongst this deluge of snippets of opinion given, and controversies canvassed, various critics have discerned an emerging consensus of opinion. In *Ulysses on the Liffey,* for example, Richard Ellmann decides that both Stephen and Bloom "take sides against unnaturalness," so that by implication in the episode "the fecundity of the natural order" is upheld.[7] Mary Lowe-Evans, in her rigorous study that takes its title from the contentious phrase in Joyce's letter on "Oxen of the Sun" to Budgen, concludes more cautiously that the episode presents aspects of both the discourses of population-growth proponents and those who advocated birth control, showing both viewpoints to be guilty of foisting overly vehement arguments upon individual citizens whose own independence could not but be lessened as they tried to grapple with the "cultural mandates" from either side.[8] Both Richard Brown[9] and Mary Lowe-Evans have shown how Joyce both read and used arguments from both sides in a debate that was still raging as he wrote, between the advocates of larger families, generally Catholic theologians or nationalists worried about declining birthrates particularly in the aftermath of the mass slaughter of the Great War, and the proponents of birth control, often feminist or socialist-Fabian commentators and activists like Marie Stopes and the members of the Malthusian league, who recognized that the control of childbirth would be a revolutionary step for women and who worried that the world would soon be peopled beyond the level of resources needed to sustain the burgeoning population. Given the welter of perspectives and sources from the theology of St. John Chrystotomos to George Bernard Shaw's preface to *Getting Married,* which Joyce read and incorporated into "Oxen of the Sun,"[10] and given that references to these perspectives were then generally reencoded into the specific literary style being used at that moment to narrate the episode, it is extremely difficult to assert that a single viewpoint is being supported by the narrative-as-chameleon. However, it seems clear that to ascertain its effect we must not only look at the spirit of a given reference to birth or birth control, but simultaneously, at the tone of the passage in which it is set; as I will now demonstrate with three examples, once the tenor of a given setting is considered, what appears at first to be narrative support for what Ellmann termed "the fecundity of the natural order" can turn out to be a parodic mimicry of a rhetorical line that the overall narrative seems loath to accept.

From the perspective of the episode's representation not only of a birth, but of birth in general, particularly as it affected narratives of gender, it is surely significant that virtually all of the sources of birth control read and referred to by Joyce in the episode are by men, even though some of the most important advocates of the control of birth—such as Annie Besant (who is named in *Finnegans Wake* at 432.31–33) and Marie Stopes—were women. Likewise, one needs to remember that every one of the passages from English literature that the episode parodies are by male authors, even though, as prose and prose fiction is the genre that is being parodied, there were many examples by women (especially from the nineteenth century onward) available to Joyce. Having chosen to echo only the work of male commentators, and having chosen to imitate only models of canonical English style by men, Joyce goes on nevertheless to offer most of the pro-"fecundity" arguments in contexts that, at the least, cause the reader to feel deeply uneasy as to the sincerity of any of the claims. Thus the two famously obscure paragraphs that follow the opening invocation of the episode, for example, which Joyce in his letter to Budgen claimed were a "Sallustian-Tacitean prelude (the unfertilized ovum)" (*Letters I* 139), are centered on the thought that "as no nature's boon can contend against the bounty of increase so it behoves every most just citizen to become the exhortator and admonisher of his semblables and to tremble lest what had in the past been by the nation excellently commenced might be in the future not with similar excellence accomplished" (14.20–25). What we are being given here, I suggest, is a parody of the windy officialese of a testimonial presented by a subservient group to a privileged personage or institution, a form written in a degraded and flowery political jargon of its own that was particularly common in the late Victorian period in Ireland and elsewhere and that put into discourse a kind of clientist political relationship based on asking for and granting favors, and, consequently, an often hypocritical gratitude. If the episode's initial apparent support for the necessity for population growth is cast in such degraded political terms, then it would seem likely that "Oxen of the Sun" is setting out to undermine it even as it presents it.

The same point seems to me true of a second major diatribe against contraception in the episode, launched by none other than Stephen himself. He asks, "But, gramercy, what of those Godpossibled souls that we nightly impossibilise, which is the sin against the Holy Ghost, Very God, Lord and Giver of Life?" (14.225–27). This apparently unequivocal version of Catholic moral teaching on the evils of contraception is presented, however, by an extremely drunken Stephen who spends the evening offering parodies of priestly sentiments and points of theology, for, as the text notes, "he was of wild manner when he was drunken" (14.261–62). Later, we hear him turn the church's teachings to joking ends: when asked what should happen to a second Siamese twin if the first should die, "he delivered briefly and, as some thought, perfunctorily the ecclesiastical ordinance forbidding man to put asunder what God has joined" (14.1007–9). The more apparently obsequious his delivery of church doctrine, it would appear, the greater the sacrilege intended. One can read all of the incantations of ecclesiastical teaching by this apostate as bitter expositions of their implied hollowness.

Finally, in the last of the episode's passages that imitates English prose style, given in the style of Carlyle, there is a rousing paean to Mina Purefoy's husband and his role as father of a huge family:

> By heaven, Theodore Purefoy, though hast done a doughty deed and no botch! Thou art, I vow, the remarkablest progenitor barring none in this chaffering allincluding most farraginous chronicle. Astounding! In her lay a Godframed Godgiven preformed possibility which thou hast fructified with thy modicum of man's work. Cleave to her! Serve! Toil on, labour like a very bandog and let scholarment and all Malthusians go hang. Thou art all their daddies, Theodore. . . . Copulation without population! No, say I! Herod's slaughter of the innocents were the truer name. . . . With thee it was not as with many that will and would and wait and never — do. Thou sawest thou America, thy lifetask, and didst charge to cover like the transpontine bison. (14.1410–31)

The grandiosely exaggerated address here reverses the order of the testimonial offered in the long paragraphs of the opening of the episode; now it is the "common man" who is being patronized by the oratorical leader. The pomposity of the language, however, the piling up of adjectives, the alliterative exaggeration, and the quasi-religious judgmental tone, all combine—with the final zoological simile—to make this one of the most comic parodies in all of *Ulysses* and a sweeping indictment of the nationalist calls for population growth on which it is based. It is also a moment of high and rather desperate drama in the representation of masculine identity that, as I will discuss next, is a crucial concern of the episode; by attending to Theodore rather than Mina Purefoy for the second time in an extended passage, it also makes evident the tendency of male-authored discourse on "family planning" to conclude by attending to the role of men, so that the crucial role of the woman and the representation of motherhood are elided.

The episode, I suggest, betrays the masculinist bias of many of the discourses, whether pro or con, about birth control that Joyce had encountered; it also—in its extended treatment of, and even compulsive return to, this subject—allows discussion of population control or increase to elide the representation of the birth that is at the center of the episode. As such, it participates in the trajectory of many of the discourses presented in "Oxen of the Sun," to drown out, as it were, the birth that is the episode's crucial event. Not only does the birth take place offstage, but it is finally, officially, reported to us at third-hand, in an account in turn filtered through the driest Johnsonian tones: "The news was imparted with a circumspection recalling the ceremonial usage of the Sublime Porte by the second female infirmarian to the junior medical officer in residence, who in his turn announced to the delegation that an heir had been born" (14.942–45). Hence not only are the mother and the child silenced and rendered invisible, but so too are the two female nurses. Both of these women had continually called on the young men to be quiet; as such, silence is associated with the women in the episode, language with men (and especially the playful, even carnivalesque use of language to form ideas). Further, Joyce's overall plan—that the procession of literary styles should mirror the act of gestation—means that, in effect, another child (of language, perhaps) is symbolically born in the episode; even if this is represented merely by Stephen and the others leaving the hospital common room for Burke's pub ("Burke's! outflings my Lord Stephen, giving the cry" [14.1391]), it means that this other, symbolic birth is more integrally encoded in the stylistics of the episode than the actual birth of Mina Purefoy's baby, so that hers is further abstracted. Ellen Carol Jones captures the effect of this opposition of real and literary gestation and birthing when she states that "the language of the literary forefathers is played out on the body of the mother, its linguistic virtuosity sounded on her silence."[11] Finally, in this cacophony of styles, delineating increasingly scientific disputations on aspects of birth and birth control, the initial solicitude of Bloom ("Woman's woe with wonder pondering" [14.187]) is also forgotten. The scientization of discourses on and representations of birthing, in other words, is shown to dissipate the narrow nationalist fixation on mothers and motherhood as symbols, but it also makes any consideration of mothers as subjects virtually impossible altogether; all that gets to be discussed at the end, after the language of Victorian science is represented, is the status of men. What the episode has given us, then, is an account of an actual birth and a range of alternative discourses, beyond that of the Catholically inflected nationalist iconography of motherhood, to represent it; these alternative discourses, whether of population growth or of birth control, turn out, however, to be so thoroughly male directed that they contribute to the abstraction and almost total erasure of the mother as subject altogether. "Oxen of the Sun," despite its apparent intention, turns out (like the greater part of Joyce's oeuvre) to be comfortable only when representing men. However, as I will consider next, although the stylistic baroque of "Oxen of the Sun" serves the representation of masculinity, this is an agitated baroque because these are, after all, men in a maternity hospital, whose all-too-stereotypical gender identities are placed under threat by their proximity to a woman giving birth.

MEN'S STYLE

"Oxen of the Sun" is the noisiest episode in *Ulysses;* the young men gathered downstairs in Holles Street Hospital may appear to be celebrating a birth, but it is more likely that they are noisily covering up the threat to their own masculinity that the setting suggests. In its recounting of a set of apparently frivolous debates among these males not only about birth control but more commonly about such matters as their experiences with women and their own sexual prowess, "Oxen of the Sun" embarks on the ambitious task of redefining versions of masculinity and attempting to discern alternative narratives of male subjectivity at a historical moment when traditional paternalist narratives of male worth were coming under intense pressure. Maurizia Boscagli has shown how for the large, recently created class of metropolitan white-collar young men—which is precisely the class to which the denizens of the common room belong—the early twentieth century witnessed a profound crisis in traditional masculine identity.[12] For these urban and ambitious young men (Boscagli cites Forster's Leonard Bast in *Howards End* as a prime literary example), the patriarchal narratives of male power, featuring a strong paterfamilias as the ruler of his family, were no longer tenable. In "Oxen of the Sun" it is precisely the redundancy of such a paterfamilias model of masculinity in the early-twentieth-century metropolis that makes the Carlylian praise of Theodore Purefoy ring so hollow; likewise, an earlier address to Purefoy *père* as ardent family man, couched in the style of Dickens (with whom Joyce had little sympathy[13] [14.1319ff]) comes across as one of the most lachrymose passages in the episode. It is therefore appropriate too that Theodore Purefoy, "older now (you and I may whisper it) and a trifle stooped in the shoulders" (14.1322–23), that is, worn-out from the duties implied in an outmoded version of patriarchy, is not present at the hospital at the time of his own child's birth. Likewise, Bloom's own memories of his father here, "the head of the [family] firm, seated with Jacob's pipe after like labours in the paternal ingle" (14.1057–58), recounted in the style of Charles Lamb, are some of the most sentimental in the episode; as the oldest man present, and one whose own son has died, Bloom still has about him the wistfulness of not having lived up to the old paterfamilias model. For the other members of the group, however, it is the escape from sonhood rather than the duties of fatherhood that concerns them. From the Irish nationalist perspective, for example, the narrative of valorized motherhood, as in Pearse's poem "The Mother," also implies a reciprocal narrative of how to act as a son: it is this narrative, rather than that of motherhood, per se, that this episode ultimately shows most interest in overcoming. Presented by Mrs. Purefoy's birthing with the physical reality of motherhood rather than any mythology concerning it, the young men are granted an opportunity which they seize here to begin to fabricate alternative gendered identities for themselves.

When the revelers toss insults based on what they perceive as degraded births at Punch Costello early in the episode—"thou chuff, thou puny, thou got in peasestraw, thou losel, thou chitterling, thou spawn of a rebel, thou dykedropt, thou abortion thou" (14.327–29)—they show a characteristic willingness to consider birth and sexuality in the crudest terms, often with a carnivalesque vulgarity that is a counterpoint to the sacred quality of traditional family narratives, and to ensure that it comments ultimately on the status of one of themselves. Often this vulgarity takes the form of male sexual boasting: Costello had earlier told Dixon "that he would ever dishonest a woman whoso she were or wife or maid or leman if it so fortuned him to be delivered of his spleen of lustihead," at which Crothers, "pricked forward with their jibes wherewith they did malice him," claimed "that he was able to do any manner of thing that lay in man to do" (14.230–37). On occasion this boasting veers into true carnival, as for example when Buck Mulligan presents his newly printed visiting card designating himself *"Fertilizer and Incubator"* and announces his plan to set up in Lambay island off the coast of Dublin:

> a national fertilising farm to be named *Omphalos* with an obelisk hewn and erected after the fashion of Egypt and to offer his dutiful yeoman services for the fecundation of any female of what grade of life soever who should there direct to him with the desire of fulfilling the functions of her natural. (14.684–88)

Mulligan's tour de force is backed by numerous phallic puns and jokes ("all masts erect" [14.642], whore "Bird-in-the-hand" [14.457], "saint Foutinus his engines" [14.236], and so on) scattered throughout the episode[14] without much reference to either subject matter or style, so that the whole becomes a low, barely covert celebration of male sexual excess. Even when Bannon and Lynch speak of their encounters earlier in the day with young women—accounts narrated in a fetchingly "affecting" style in the manner of Sterne—what might have surfaced as love stories become instead narratives of male predation, with Lynch boasting of his own knowledge of the availability in Dublin of condoms and diaphragms and extolling their usefulness on such occasions. What we are left with from this whole series of young men's boasts and jeerings is a catalog of the strategies and topics of what used to be called "smoking-room humor" from a period when male sexuality, and sexuality in general, was only beginning to be put into public discourse, and when public discourse itself was only beginning to be opened up to both sexes. We are made aware too that these raucous vulgarities betray a misogyny born of a deep insecurity about male gender identity that has no polite public discourse available for its expression.

Some of the unease shielded by the jokes is unearthed by Stephen, whose slightly uncomfortable presence and more complex gender persona acts as an irritant to the more jovial tacit agreement of most of the rest to humor each other. The radical persona that Stephen adopts in this episode is that of the mock priest. This would certainly have been read as a controversial and ambiguous role in early-twentieth-century largely Catholic Ireland, especially when Stephen adopts it mostly to mock "*mother* Church that would cast him out of her bosom" (14.241, emphasis added). At the same time it allows him to strategically deploy a male identity that has strong implications for the pursuit of high social status, for reworking the God-given power of the priest as a version of his own artistic powers, and for the exploration of male sexuality, given that the church supported large families among the laity but demanded celibacy of its priests. Stephen's priestly parodies, we should remember, are merely an imitation of those of Buck Mulligan, one of which opens *Ulysses:* what he presents, then, is a parody of a parody. A double parody can, however, go some way to making a more accurate imitation: Stephen betters Mulligan's jocose mockery by offering his version of the priest with deadpan seriousness. In his first major intervention in the common-room discussions he speaks against contraception ("those Godpossibled souls that we nightly impossibilise" [14.225]), of how "in all our holy mother foldeth ever souls for God's greater glory" (14.248), and the like. Such talk jars against the general low tone, permits Stephen to sound oracular, and grants him access to a discipline (theology) with a vast tradition and to the use of a prophetic voice. The effect is to suggest that Stephen is trapped in a discourse that he mocks—and to imply that the carnivalesque mockery of the young men can include even the most rarefied discourse in the critical purview. As such, Stephen's repetition of the priestly language that he might have been using in earnest if his life had taken another direction is a means to exorcize its power. By persisting in using it, Stephen is implying that he is a kind of "spoiled priest," an often uncanny and deeply unsettling figure in more traditional Irish fictions, of the young man who might have made a priest but gave up in the attempt. (An outstanding Irish fictional treatment of this figure is Francis McManus's later novel, *The Greatest of These.*) Stephen as "spoiled priest" at once betters the company in its mockery of conventional mores that would confine their freedom to express their gender identities; at the same time he jars it by reminding his associates that this discourse and the power that supports it will haunt both him and them for a long time to come.

Through Stephen, Catholic patriarchal power—the predominant guardian in Irish culture of the moral code that rules the kinds of sexual and gender matters of which the young men speak—gets to haunt the episode; above all, however, it reminds the group of the church's interest in celibacy and hatred of all sexual excess. When Dixon laughingly asks Stephen "what was the reason why he had not cided to take friar's vows" (14.335), Lenehan goes on to report that Stephen has "besmirched the lily virtue of a confiding female" (14.339). By adopting the priest's persona, Stephen gets to adopt the church's paradoxical emphases: on the one hand, to avow celibacy, on the other, to oppose birth control and support "natural" fertility. For himself here he resolves this paradox by ensuring that all know that his role is indeed parodic: he may grandiloquently cry the reproaches of the Old Testament or of Christ on the cross to his people, but he rewrites the friar's vows of "Poverty, chastity and obedience" for himself as "obedience in the womb, chastity in the tomb but involuntary poverty all his days" (14.336–37). Hence the condemnation of his interest in brothels in the comic parody of Bunyan which follows (14.429ff) seems mostly a means to demonstrate that his role as a mock priest is in no real sense disruptive of the norms of heterosexual behavior being fostered by the group as a whole: he too has been beguiled by "Bird-in-the-hand," who, as we are soon told, "all that company that sat there . . . the most lusted after" (14.455–56). Stephen is happy to play the lecherous priest to show that patriarchal Catholic asceticism can cohabit comfortably with masculinist sexual boasting, and thus allay his peers' discomfiture.

The priest, however, is also father, and it is in its potential for an alternative kind of fatherhood—as progenitor of words and art rather than, as in the Lambay island plans of Mulligan, of children—that Stephen takes his priestly persona very seriously. In a crucial early passage, moving from biblical incantation to a lie about the origin of his money, he veers wildly through a series of sources that makes evident the desperation of his attempt to forge an identity:

> His words were then these that as followeth: Know all men, he said, time's ruins build eternity's mansions. What means this? Desire's wind blasts the thorntree but after it becomes from a bramblebush to be a rose upon the rood of time. Mark me now. In woman's womb word is made flesh but in the spirit of the maker all flesh that passes becomes the word that shall not pass away. This is the postcreation. (14.288–94)

Here he careens from biblical phrases to the visionary poetry of Blake and on to Yeats, attempting, in a wild grasp of associated images, to escape from religious into secular visions, from images of generation to those of desire, from narratives of human to artistic reproduction, and from a world of passing generations (in Yeats's phrase) to art that is "a rose upon the rood of time." Deploying images from the art of earlier visionary, secular priest-poets, he decides that he has defined "postcreation"—both a pun on procreation and the post-Nietzschean *Übermensch* artist's riposte to the biblical creation narrative. The "new man's" version of fatherhood will at its best be beyond narratives not only of procreation, but even beyond those of potentially dangerous sexual desire; it will escape patriarchal models altogether, perhaps, while enhancing images of male power. At moments such as this, and later when Stephen declares himself "lord and giver of life" because of his art, it can appear as if the male poet is envious of the procreative act of the woman who is giving birth and wishes to equal her power which impresses him so much.[15] The fact that he has not yet composed more than "a capful of light odes" (14.1119) and that he has lied by claiming that his money has come from his poems shows up the fragility of his project and the tenuousness of his claims. Stephen deploys a mock version of Catholic priesthood as a means to forge a new version of nonalienated male subjectivity based on the practice of a visionary poetics; this project, these lies and dreams imply, is nevertheless the most concerted effort on display here to escape the paterfamilias model of male worth, a model which, despite their moments of would-be carnival, relentlessly interpellates these young men, as it has already interpellated the hapless bank employee Theodore Purefoy himself.

What is striking is that Stephen's forward-looking project to imagine a "postcreation" post-fatherhood encounters in this episode Bloom's nostalgic backward-looking attempt to cover the lack left by what he sees as his own failed fatherhood, in that his son and heir died soon after being born. This is, famously, the episode where Stephen and Bloom finally meet and even come to odds, appropriately over motherhood. Stephen and Bloom are the only two men present who offer more complex versions of masculine subjectivity than the raucous carnival carnality proposed by the rest: Stephen, because he is struggling to formulate a post-Yeatsian version of male artistic power that would be deepened by a reworking of the role of the priest derived from religion; Bloom, because he has not yet surrendered his faith in the old paterfamilias model of ideal masculinity as fatherhood, in which the fathering of a male heir is paramount. Yet Stephen's masculinist ambition and Bloom's fatherly nostalgia, although both find themselves estranged from the brutal comedy of the dayroom, have in fact little in common, so that the stage is set here for Stephen's refusal of Bloom's offer of a night's lodging that the reader witnesses in "Ithaca." Rather, both are interested in what each imagines that the other represents: for Stephen, Bloom, as a Jew, represents the alienation from both national and family narratives he himself cultivates, and the "chosen people" to whom Stephen's priestly reproaches are specifically addressed; for Bloom, Stephen is his lost son returned, with whom he can re-create, with a difference perhaps, a new patriarchal family narrative. That these visions are at odds is proven in the chaotic conclusion to the episode, when even the drunken revelers at closing time in Burke's pub are still seeking the identity of two people, first Bloom ("Bloo? Cadges ads. Photo's papli, by all that's gorgeous" [14.1535–36]) and then the man in the mackintosh ("Golly, whatten tunket's yon guy in mackintosh" [14.1546]), and finally, Bloom again ("Whisper, who the sooty hell's that johnny in the black duds?" [14.1575]). As the drunken young men run hither and thither, to the red-light district, after a fire brigade to Mount Street (appropriately), or home to the tower, their crude masculinist carnivalesque discourse dispersed in a spatter of dialects, their sense of community still turns out to be relentlessly normative, while those who—like Bloom and the stranger in the mackintosh—appear at all strange are clearly monitored and, if possible, excluded. Besides Stephen's art shades and Bloom's nostalgia for Purefoyesque fatherhood, what this episode leaves us with is the certainty that these insecure young males are unable to fabricate any alternative discourse of modern masculinity, but are determined nevertheless to police the shreds of an identity which they continue to celebrate.

Underlying this double task of delineating the torn fabric of masculine identity and still policing deviation from the old patriarchal norms is the episode's enormously complex armature of the historical sequence of literary styles. Critics have often seemed confused by the way in which each new style embodies a new tone: some have looked for the holy grail of sincerity and seriousness that they imply must be buried in one of the styles of the episode and that, once found, could be a base against which to measure the strength of the parody in each of the others. What seems in fact to be occurring, however, is a relentless examination not of the styles themselves, but of the parodic possibilities hidden in every historical style of the English language: that is, an exploration of how easy or how difficult it is to subvert the kind of official ideology that any particular style, when used officially and sincerely, is best at transmitting. It is evident from the episode that some styles are best at transmitting specific behaviors and the assumptions that underlie them: for example, the language of Sterne is excellent for the first recounting of Lynch's interlude with a young woman (14.777ff), and Carlyle's declamations are fitting for an attack on Malthusianism (14.1420ff). As such, the cavalcade of styles is also a cavalcade of ideologies: the styles make specific behaviors seem much more natural and inevitable. Because every style is a parody, however, the episode is in fact systematically investigating to what degree each dialect can be used against itself to put into question the specific ideology it supports. And in virtually every case, these are ideologies of the masculine conquest, degradation, or government of women. Yet as each parody shows up the ideology that underlies such misogyny, the effect is often simply to glory in the subversion rather than to express the significance of the exposure. The effect is oddly similar to that of some drunken would-be-witty sayings of Lenehan that are scattered throughout the episode. Lenehan is, apart from the man in the mackintosh, perhaps the most thoroughly lost character here: as a hanger-on at racecourses and a gambler, he is a prototypical modernist subject in Walter Benjamin's terms. Apart from stories of races and gambling exploits, his contributions here take the form of quizzical sayings: for example, when Lynch wonders if Stephen will prove himself a writer and an artist, Lenehan states that "He could not leave his mother an orphan." The witty meaninglessness of this phrase, based on a double reversal and an adaptation of a conventional phrase, is similar in effect to some of the parodies here. It echoes an "old saying," that is, conventional wisdom, reminding all (as did Stephen's priest pose) of its continuing residual power, but implying its current meaninglessness, the fact that it is now posed as an unsolvable riddle, merely good for a laugh.

And that is perhaps about as far as the parodies of English prose get us in "Oxen of the Sun." As in the extremely funny discussion of the "Irish bull in an English chinashop" (14.580ff), the parodies often allow the young men to speak covertly and in riddles about their situation and that of the community requiring them to conform. Such riddle language is, nevertheless, the code of the weak: the ventriloquism of the censored, and of those who know no other discourse than that of those who keep them as they are. The parodied styles, therefore, subvert a succession of styles of masculinist discourse, largely used in discussions of issues of gender, but they do not replace them with an alternative: rather, we witness at the end a lapsing into a cacophony of contemporary dialects, rather like the language of a radio dial turned idly. If there is a pattern in this final polyphony, it turns out to be about fixing identities by policing the strangers—Bloom and the man in the mackintosh—on the margins of the group.

In upturning so many varieties of masculinist style and their underlying ideologies, "Oxen of the Sun" also manages to abstract and even forget the initial central fact of the episode: the birth of a baby to the mother, Mrs. Purefoy. To the extent that this display of maternal power is once again veiled in this episode, it turns out to be less a project that searches for an alternative narrative of motherhood by publicizing the act of giving birth, than the episode of *Ulysses* that tries to confront the conventional male identities derived from narratives of patriarchy and sonhood and to show up the stylistic underpinnings of such tales. Once again, it keeps the woman offstage and implies that she is lying on a bed,[16] and if it celebrates birth, it notes from the start that this is the birth of a male heir. Even Mrs. Purefoy, giving birth, has worked "manfully" (14.1313). The young men, meanwhile, confused, boastful, and often lying, are granted extensive opportunities to recast the terms of the discourses in which their gender identities are formulated. Their confusion at the close implies the powerlessness of their carnival to imagine actively such alter-identities or the discourses that might be used to articulate them. This is why the episode is open to the voice of an American preacher announcing a new version of Nobadaddy, a modern strong businessman God as male role model, at its close.

15

Disenchanting Enchantment

The Theatrical Brothel of "Circe"

MARGOT NORRIS

Homer's account of Circe, even before Joyce transmogrifies it in *Ulysses,* links highly charged figurations of fluid ontology—shifting categories of human and animal, god and mortal, man and unmanned—to the relationship between sexuality and power, and to the investment of that relationship in perception and illusion. But *The Odyssey*'s poetry curiously implicates itself in the romantic seductions and enchantments it triple narrates—as it iterates Eurylochos's experience, reiterates his story of the experience, and iterates Odysseus's undoing of the prior experience with the antidote. In transposing the episode to *Ulysses,* Joyce refuses to reproduce the blandishments of a gorgeous poetry that itself enchants as it tells of enchantment. Instead, he transforms Circe's magical glen and polished stone hall with its "shining doors" into Bella Cohen's brothel, a space theatricalized by culture, by the art of pornography, and by the dramatic expressionism that replaces the Homeric narration.[1] Through this investment of the story of sexuality and domination in layers of theatricality, Joyce's "Circe" does what *The Odyssey*'s poetry refuses: it disenchants enchantment. By transforming Circe's tools of magical transformation (drugs, wands, music) into technologies of eroticism of the sort Bloom has earlier cataloged—"Must have the stage setting, the rouge, costume, position, music" (13.855–56)—the text dismantles not only the bordello's ethos into theatrical artifice, but the constructedness of sexuality and gender as well.

The mysterious magical processes that transmogrify men into grotesque and enslaved forms in Homeric myth serve as paradigms for the mysterious, hidden processes by which modern human beings become men (and women) only through a palpable vulnerability to threats of gender loss, sexual hybridity, and symbolic enslavement.[2] "Circe" helps demonstrate that sexuality—the ontological category we tend to equate with what is "natural" and that we take to stand for the "natural"—is culturally and historically constructed by the pressure of hidden laws and compulsions in the service of larger social controls, whose implementation takes form in discourses that, according to theorists such as Michel Foucault and Teresa de Lauretis, function as "social technologies."[3]

These technologies inevitably include cultural practices and art that serve social institutions charged with the organization and regulation of sexual behavior and its significance. In "Circe" Joyce uses several interrelated social systems—including theater, pornography, and prostitution—to demystify the relationship between sexuality, pleasure, and power. Their function in the chapter exceeds the thematic, as enchantment and delirium infect perceptual experience on all intra- and extra-textual levels. In "Circe," the theater of the mind, the theater of the brothel, and the theater of language all contribute to the theater of a text that enmeshes the reader, too, in the Circean web of sexual thrills and terrors, domination and control, and illusion and delusion.

The enchanted reader is gendered in relation to the social systems depicted and operative in "Circe," much as living subjects are gendered by being positioned in relation to institutions and symbolic systems. "The term gender is, actually, the representation of a relation, that of belonging to a class, a group, a category," writes Teresa de Lauretis.[4] For example, the way the brothel is coded in "Circe," as a bourgeois pleasure palace—a site of pornological activity patrolled by police to ensure male safety—is recapitulated when psychoanalytical criticism decodes "Circe" as a scene of transference in which male pathologies are relieved through transgressive eroticism, gender play, familial rememoration, and social experiment. The structural principle externalized in the Homeric myth, that finds the locus of narrative concern and interest in male vulnerability to the hidden powers of female sexuality, perdured extratextually when the U.S. court designated *Ulysses* as a pornographic text requiring judicial protection of *l'homme moyen sensuel,* the normative person of average sex instincts. The book was tried, in a sense, as advertisement and handbook for the brothel, and Judge Woolsey's decision to test *Ulysses* for obscenity against male literary assessors (in contrast to the standard of "the young girl" appealed to in the obscenity trial of Radclyffe Hall)[5] gendered readers into analogues of Odysseus's seducible sailors, bourgeois men as potential swine. This construction of the male as ingenue in and by "Circe" has had consequences for the psychoanalytic and political construction of the female,[6] and the equally seductive construction of the text. Joyce becomes the figure of Circe the enchantress in the typologies of the obscenity trial, capable—like the magical witch of "tending to stir the sex impulses or to lead to sexually impure and lustful thoughts"[7]—while the female becomes the hidden source of powerful control and morbid contamination palpable only as a dangerous effect[8] invested in reified metonymies and fetishistic figurations.

Reading "Circe" thus becomes an exercise in resistance to enchantment, requiring a critical moly. I would construe the most effective critical antidote to the text's enchantments as a *pharmokos*—a potion, drug, or agent with the power of a double effect, capable of acting as either poison or cure. I will designate theater as this *pharmokos* because it functions as a technology that creates illusions but simultaneously makes illusion apparent and visible, and that inherently constructs and deconstructs perception. Because the specific enchantment at issue in "Circe" is sexual and gendered—constructed as male enchantment by the female—a female critical perspective that can recognize the function of artifice, masquerade, and theatricalization in the production of woman as an "effect" is the catalyst applied to theater to activate its pharmaceutical function. But this gendered perspective must de-essentialize itself if it is to be usefully trained on prostitution and pornography as technologies of male enchantment. The assumption of a generic "female gaze" can easily equate the imago of woman as a single, monolithic entity, an essentialized subject, with the sort of bourgeois subjectivity that masks oppressive differences between women. Even though she is quite canny in recognizing her own theatricalized constructions,[9] Molly Bloom's thoughts about "those night women . . . bad enough to get the smell of those painted women off him" (18.36, 18.57) refuse to penetrate the extent to which those "painted women" are theatricalized products of a technology to create a specific female effect for male appreciation and consumption.

The female perspective most effectively employed as a moly might be one modeled on the political alliance between Victorian feminist activity on behalf of prostitutes and working-class women that galvanized the campaign to repeal the Contagious Diseases Acts of 1864, 1866, and 1869. The disenchantment of the brothel—best effected by the perspective of the prostitutes whose work is to produce that enchantment—can be replicated by foregrounding the social interests of the prostitute against the bourgeois fantasies that overwrite her labor. But the retrieval of the perspective of prostitutes is inherently difficult because of their own complex theatricalized role ("painted women") and that of the brothel. As a scene that couples sexual intimacy with emotional impersonality, social conviviality with social estrangement, the domestic bedroom with the commercial shop, the brothel is a contradictory, self-masking space. In "Circe" the brothel's intersected, theatricalized functions are further occluded by the chapter's expressionistic technique that superimposes one theatrical *mise en scène* over another: an interiorized fantasyscape obscures the already scripted and conventionalized social intercourse between the men and women at 82 Tyrone Street in Dublin. Retrieval of the female perspectives of the prostitutes—and I use the plural to suggest that they will themselves be doubled and heterogeneous—is finally abetted by an outside "gaze," a perspective imported from outside the chapter, the perspective of the ultimate "outsider," the woman in the black straw hat who in "Eumaeus" literally peers into the space of a society that excludes her even from its dregs.

But before importing the perspective of prostitution into the discourse of feminism—to abet by troubling it—I will return to sort out the multiple tropes I have invoked as arms for the critical voyager who approaches "Circe"'s magical glen as female. Theater is the *pharmakos* that will serve as my moly chiefly because it exemplifies a model of a disenchanting enchantment—a masking system obliged to unmask itself. The concept of the theatrical is therefore a useful theoretical weapon for training upon the artifice of doubled constructions such as gender itself. This way of using the theatrical is intended to resonate to the use of masquerade to expose and explore femininity in the writings of Joan Riviere.[10] But the theatrical allows me to broaden my focus on gender beyond the ontological, to comprehend the social systems, institutions, and cultural forms that function as the technologies for its production. I will therefore begin with what is best described as the social imbrication in the chapter: the layering or overlapping of discourses from a variety of social systems (including the court, commerce, the circus) that are theatrically inscribed into the discourses and institutions of the erotic—pornography and prostitution.

"Circe" follows the logic of pornography's etymology when its prostitutional setting evokes the Greek *pornographios,* or writing about harlots. Pornography in "Circe" participates in a series of overlapping social technologies with similar strategies for social control that rely on forcing sexuality, which is hidden and silent, into publicity and into speech. The larger circles of surveillance that shadow Nighttown politically—the watches, soldiers, constables, and imagined spies—define the overdetermination of the paranoid affect produced by forcing sexuality into exhibition to a hostile and punitive gaze. But a funny thing happens to Bloom on the way to Bella Cohen's. The slippage of real into imagined surveillance—for example, the watch's routine request for identification conjuring the guilty aliases and alibis of the Martha Clifford correspondence—drifts into the discourse of pornography and is pressed into service as part of its mechanism. The fantasy of an imagined accusation for his pornographic correspondence—"He wrote me an anonymous letter in prentice backhand when my husband was in the North Riding of Tipperary on the Munster circuit, signed James Lovebirch" (15.1016–18)—allows him to substitute an accomplished dominatrix, "Mrs Yelverton Barry," for the incompetent Martha Clifford and lets her use his indecent letters as pretext for the language of erotic discipline he craves. In the process other maneuvers and reversals come into play. Bloom's earlier fantasies of aggression toward high-born women ("Like that haughty creature at the polo match. . . . Possess her once take the starch out of her" [5.103–6]) are transformed into masochistic pornography, as the haughty creature is given an inflated name ("The Honorable Mrs Merwyn Talboys"), an amazon costume complete with hunting crop, and the sadistic language ("Take down his trousers without loss of time. Come here, sir! Quick! Ready?" [15.1118–19]) that even his intense coaching of Martha Clifford has failed to produce ("Go further next time. Naughty boy: punish: afraid of words, of course" [5.272–73]). By pre-texting the pornographic episodes of "Circe" with other pornography—for example, citing *Venus in Furs* as the incitement for mimicking its language ("He addressed me in several handwritings with fulsome compliments as a Venus in furs and alleged profound pity for my frostbound coachman Palmer" [15.1045–47])—Joyce doubles the transgressive position of pornography by allowing it to mock, exploit, and resexualize its own censorships and suppressions.

In the process of this pre-textualization a series of larger theoretical points are made explicit by being dramatized. The first is that the structure of pornography resides in what Roland Barthes called "a reversion of texts: the image appears to originate a program, the program a text, and the text a practice; however, this practice is itself written, it returns (for the reader) to program, to text, to fantasy."[11] The pleasure of pornography resides in certain relations of textuality, and what is sexualized is always language and discourse. Joyce enacts this insight in "Circe" on the level of plot by having the brothel produce little eroticism and less sex—or, as Joseph Boone puts it, "'sex' in Nighttown occurs almost exclusively as a textual-narratological experience."[12] Pornography, in turn, produces its pleasures by importing, mocking, hyperbolizing, subverting, and exploiting rhetoric found elsewhere, in social discourses with powers of enactment that make it far more menacing and dangerous: for example, the moral inquisition ("Say! What was the most revolting piece of obscenity in all your career of crime" [15.3042–43]); the accusation ("And showed off coquettishly in your domino at the mirror . . . your unskirted thighs" [15.2990–92]); the demonstration ("[*he bares his arm and plunges it elbowdeep in Bloom's vulva*] There's fine depth for you! What boys?" [15.3088–90]); and the threat of juvenile discipline ("You will dance attendance or I'll lecture you on your misdeeds, Miss Ruby, and spank your bare bot right well, miss, with the hairbrush" [15.3076–77]). Evoking Circe's animal transformations, the Bello section pornographically glosses other cruel or degrading systems of human domination, including slavery, but particularly animal domestication: breaking in riding horses, slaughtering pigs, milking cows, and the like.

Curiously, the figure of animal abuse, which haunts Bloom all day, was itself triggered by his strangely correct-mistake of the morning, when he looks at a novel on circus reform, *Ruby: the Pride of the Ring,* that—much to Molly's disappointment ("There's nothing smutty in it" [4.355])—he had mistaken for a pornographic novel:

> *Ruby: the Pride of the Ring.* Hello. Illustration. Fierce Italian with carriagewhip. Must be Ruby pride of the on the floor naked. Sheet kindly lent. The monster Maffei desisted and flung his victim from him with an oath. Cruelty behind it all. Doped animals. Trapeze at Hengler's. Had to look the other way. (4.346–50)

Bloom's thoughts here slip from the pornographic to the humanitarian, and although he apparently mistook the novel of circus abuse for pornography,[13] the theme of the circus conjures for him thoughts of its hidden cruelties. Joyce demonstrates here the rigid separation between Bloom's perception of enacted, real-life cruelties—which pain and disgust him ("Had to look the other way")—and his titillation by them in the form of erotic fantasy ("I'll lecture you on your misdeeds, Miss Ruby, and spank your bare bot right well"). Bloom's double maneuver of textual confusion takes contradictory directions: in the morning the putative pornographic book stimulates humanitarian impulses; in Nighttown, he pornographically rescripts the earlier images of animal and female abuse and casts himself erotically as their masochistic victim. But Joyce's overlapping of the circus reform book with a pornographic fantasy double allows two further theoretical points to emerge. First, pornography's power to appropriate, parody, and sexualize social institutions and discourses—for example, infantile toilet training ("If I catch a trace on your swaddles" [15.3024]) and socialization ("Come, ducky dear, I want a word with you, darling, just to administer correction" [15.2882])—exposes their own hypocritically masked libidinal aims. Second, the circus, like the brothel, is particularly vulnerable to pornographic misprision because both institutions represent already theatricalized and self-concealing spaces in which layers of coercion and brutality are masked and sanitized for public, bourgeois consumption while remaining available as a resexualizable trace or residue.

By bringing the pornographized circus into the brothel, Joyce makes visible the extent to which the brothel is itself capable of being pornographized. Both circus and brothel are institutions which fail to speak for themselves, and whose mutism amidst much theatrical noise is a constitutive trait. They are therefore liable to various cultural encodings of which three might be isolated as made visible in *Ulysses:* in descending order of realism we find the circus and brothel as space of exploitable and often brutalized labor, circus and brothel as space of pleasurable bourgeois entertainment, and circus and brothel as space of pornological fantasy—the modern counterpart to the Homeric Circean enchantment. The twin fascination of avant-garde art in the late nineteenth and early twentieth centuries with both the circus and its denizens, and with the bordello and its denizens,[14] revolves around these perspectival slippages, and around their theatrical pressure against ontological categories—including those of gender. As a "writing about harlots," pornography is neither mimetic nor representational but purely speculative—a depiction not of what the brothel is, or what the harlot is, but a fantasy of how their figurations might be constructed to gratify both libidinal and textual desires. Bloom as harlot is a rhetorical creation or exhortatory discourse that scripts and anticipates transformations that the text declines to represent so that the language can draw attention to its own artifices ("fluescent") and conceits ("knees modestly kissing"): "Learn the smooth mincing walk on four inch Louis Quinze heels, the Grecian bend with provoking croup, the thighs fluescent, knees modestly kissing. Bring all your powers of fascination to bear on them. Pander to their Gomorrahan vices" [15.3119–22]). The pornographic harlot is not only a costume, but a language of costume that suspends itself in speculation and prolepsis in order to draw attention to its theatrically seductive and sadistic effects: "You will be laced with cruel force into vicelike corsets of soft dove coutille and whalebone busk to the diamondtrimmed pelvis" (15.2975–77). As an oxymoronic and hyperbolic extreme of the language of fashion,[15] the discourse of Bello in "Circe" is language as harlot.

John Gordon, in arguing for the mimetic function of the language of "Circe," sets himself against the long tradition articulated most prominently by Karen Lawrence, that views the style of *Ulysses* as developing in the direction of "flaunted artifice" with a culmination of virtual textual freeplay in "Circe": "The above instances do not exemplify pieces of text coming together; they exemplify an individual's sensations, memories, and associations coming together."[16] By renaming Lawrence's notion of the rhetorical performativity of *Ulysses* in terms of its generic and cultural functions as a theatrical *pharmakos,* I stress the pre-textuality that both conjures and disenchants a variety of sexual, erotic, and gender illusions in "Circe." In this way the psychological "realism" of the chapter (in Gordon's sense) can be anatomized as itself constructed by certain traditions of writing (pornography) and thinking about sexuality and gender. By renaming the rhetorical functions of the chapter's language in terms of active grammatical forms as verbs, "Circe"'s style can be transformed from a writing about sexuality, or about men and women—that is, a *mimetic* writing in John Gordon's sense—into a writing that makes men and women what culture tends to think they are. *Pornographizing, harlotizing, theatricalizing* are awkward linguistic constructions intended to locate the relationship between language and sexuality and gender in exercises of creation and construction rather than in representation. In describing the theatrical style of "Circe" as a brothel of language, I intended to stress not only its production of roles and relations of sexual power and being, but its exposure of those roles and relations as something *written* (produced by discourse) rather than as something *written about.*

"Circe" quite literally infuses the image of femininity as masquerade with an erotic politics of coercion and cruelty. Gilbert and Gubar identify the pornographic pre-texts for this fantasy as the Victorian transvestite pornographies *Miss High Heels* and *Gynecocracy.*[17] Bloom himself, as usual, gets the text wrong ("It was Gerald converted me to be a true corsetlover when I was a female impersonator in the High School play *Vice Versa*" [15.3009–11]) since *Vice Versa* is Anstey's play about a father-son metempsychosis rather than about cross-dressing. By making the masquerade of cruel femininity an instance of transvestism, Joyce doubly theatricalizes the construction, and deconstruction, of gender and sexuality.[18] I emphasize the foregrounding of the theatrical in both the Circean text, and Anstey's intertext, because keeping an eye on the technology of gender production makes it possible to avoid the essentializing of gender that Gilbert and Gubar see as the product of this section of "Circe": "For Joyce's parodic narrative implies that to become a female or to be like a female is not only figuratively but literally to be de-graded, to lose one's place in the preordained hierarchy that patriarchal culture associates with gender. If this is so, however, Joyce is also hinting that to be a woman is inevitably to be degraded, to be 'a thing under the yoke.'"[19] I would rather argue that Joyce exposes pornography as not a writing about harlots—that is, a writing with anything to say about woman—but precisely as a harlot-making or harlotizing writing. The harlot is unmasked in "Circe" as a linguistic figment, the product of a writing that the text in turn complicates by overlapping it, within the chapter, with a nonpornographic, non-erotic writing about harlots. In the process, *Ulysses* unmasks the prostitute as a doubled body, or a palimpsestic body—a body of woman with multiple writings on it of her imagined essences and functions. The text thereby introduces a complex notion of gender, by multiplying and intersecting even this subcategory of woman, by exploring differences within the prostitute, and among prostitutes.

Explaining why "the real" is rapidly left behind in his study of prostitution in nineteenth-century French art, Charles Bernheimer writes, "such a description would in any event be very difficult to establish, since, with the exception of a few autobiographical writings by the great courtesans of the period, we have no nineteenth-century accounts written by French prostitutes themselves."[20] Prostitutes may not write; but in "Circe" they do (fictionally) speak, although the difficulty of sorting out the textually constructed harlot from the woman is complicated by the fact that even the unpornographized space of the brothel is still theatricalized, and the prostitute costumed and scripted for a role. But the four women who work at 82 Tyrone Street in Monto—labeled by the 1885 Encyclopedia Britannica as "the worst slum in Europe" (*JJ* 366)—neither dress nor speak as Bello appears to describe them in her threat to Bloom: "As they are now so you will be, wigged, singed, perfumesprayed, ricepowdered, with smoothshaven armpits" (15.2972–73). The three young women who work for Bella Cohen, two of whom may have been patterned after the well-known historical Dublin prostitutes Fleury Crawford and Becky Cooper (*JJ* 368), are sketchily but pointedly differentiated in dress, appearance, speech, and personality. Zoe Higgins, the boldest and most playful of the trio (whom Virag in fantasy characterizes as a "flapper"), wears a *"sapphire slip, closed with three bronze buckles"* and a black odalisque fillet around her neck (15.1279–80); she is naked under the slip above her garters. In contrast, Kitty Ricketts, who likes to go abroad with her clients and has spent the day outdoors with Lynch, wears a tight corset and petticoat under her outdoor clothes, or "walking costume," as Virag calls it: *"navy costume, doeskin gloves rolled back from a coral wristlet, a chain purse in her hand"* (15.2050–52), complete with sailor hat on her henna hair, and a boa around her neck. Florry Talbot, blonde, overweight, and unattractive, wears a comfortable, sloppy, and loose-fitting garment—*"a tatterdemalion gown of mildewed strawberry"* (15.2074–75). Joyce uses the language of Virag to repornographize the three women and their appearance—"on her rere lower down are two additional protuberances, suggestive of potent rectum and tumescent for palpation" (15.2358–60)—but his lewd embellishments, failing to obliterate their identities or particularities, serve actually to reinforce them. The working women of "Circe" thus elude both the pornographizing that essentializes them into a single type of the harlot, and the rhetorical cutting up of the prostitute's body into the many interchangeable parts and fragments that would make it a mere erotic machine.

If the brothel is overwritten by pornography, it is underwritten by bourgeois desire. As a result, its erotic theatricalizations in "Circe" are doomed to the same halfheartedness we find in Martha Clifford's letter—with its inept and insincere efforts to produce Bloom's alien erotic language irrupted by desire to utter a conventional language of romance and love. Each woman's personality is inscribed with a gap between her professional role and her social background, aspirations, or interests, and she is thus within herself an incongruous and intersected text. Zoe, the Yorkshire girl, whose origins may be both rural ("Hog's Norton where the pigs plays the organs" [15.1983]) and industrial (Cheryl Herr calls her "an uprooted, imported part of the British working class")[21] is most adept at maintaining a role constructed of conventional proverbs and playful clichés: "What the eye can't see the heart can't grieve for" (15.1998); "Silent means consent" (15.2011); "Ladies first, gentlemen after" (15.2030); "Those that hides knows where to find" (15.3525–26). Kitty Ricketts, who spends more time looking at her reflection in the mirror than looking at the men, betrays a desire for social glamour as childish and fatuous as that of Mangan's sister in "Araby." She cannot stop talking about her recent visit to the Mirus bazaar—"The engineer I was with at the bazaar does have lovely ones. Full of the best liqueurs. And the viceroy was there with his lady. The gas we had on the Toft's hobbyhorses. I'm giddy still" (15.2717–19)—and her delight at a ride on the merry-go-round horses marks a dramatic contrast to the sadistic equestrian scenario Bloom scripts for "The Honorable Mrs Merwyn Talboys"'s language: "He implored me ... to bestride him and ride him, to give him a most vicious horsewhipping ... I'll dig my spurs in him up to the rowel" (15.1070–73, 15.1116). Although Florry is introduced with a patent insult—*"With obese stupidity Florry Talbot regards Stephen"* (15.2127)—her behavior is focused on conducting a peculiarly metaphysical flirtation with Stephen that contrasts nicely with Zoe's more conventional parlor-game palmestry. She reads the newspaper ("Well, it was in the papers about Antichrist" [15.2135]), and her opening gambit is eschatological—"They say the last day is coming this summer" (15.2129)—and betrays a spiritual disposition that recognizes affinities with Stephen, whom she mistakes for a lapsed Maynooth seminarian ("I'm sure you're a spoiled priest. Or a monk" [15.2649]). The undertow of bourgeois desire to produce a language of wit, decency, or intellectuality (Harry Blamires describes Florry as "one of the whores" who "tries to rise to the level of Stephen's intellectual conversation")[22] makes the women's speech doubled and troubled, and curiously inadequate to its role as seductive harlot talk.

If the enchantment of pornography throws a mesmerizing erotic articulation over the brothel, its immanent powers of disenchantment, of exposing the technologies that create the spell that conceals social and cultural constructions, is never so apparent as in the construction of the "massive whoremistress," Bella Cohen. As the fascinating dominatrix, Bello, endowed with all the false phallic appurtenances only the most vulgar pornography can muster, Bella Cohen's Circe reverses not only her Homeric image as the goddess with the golden braids who sings beautifully and tends a great web, but also her quotidian image as the brothel madam: her first words articulate the physical labor of prostitution—"My word! I'm all of a mucksweat" (15.2750). Bloom's fantasy gives her a highly operatic entrance—she "*cools herself flirting a black horn fan like Minnie*

Hauck in Carmen" (15.2744–45)—whose social subtext of Bizet's factory lass as temptress romanticizes the quotidian commercialism of Bella Cohen's enterprise: "Who's paying here?" (15.3529). Bloom's perspectival distortions of Bella Cohen in this instance anticipate similar ones he produces about the Italian language in "Eumaeus"—"A beautiful language. . . . Why do you not write your poetry in that language? *Bella Poetria*! It is so melodious and full. Belladonna. Voglio"—to which Stephen replies, "They were haggling over money" (16.345–50). In Bella Cohen's brothel, too, the pornologizing of the language conceals that there is much more haggling over money than either eroticism or sex ("Do you want three girls? It's ten shillings here"; "The gentleman . . . ten shillings . . . paying for three . . . allow me a moment . . . this gentleman pays separate" [15.3542–43, 15.3356–57, Joyce's ellipses]). Indeed, the only sexual intercourse, if any, occurs offstage between Bella Cohen and a veterinarian: "She's on the job herself tonight," Zoe Higgins tells Bloom, "with the vet her tipster that gives her all the winners and pays for her son in Oxford. Working overtime but her luck's turned today" (15.1288–90). This rumpled, domesticated veterinarian is an utterly unprepossessing figure in a place of pleasure—*"A man in purple shirt and grey trousers, brownsocked, passes with an ape's gait, his bald head and goatee beard upheld, hugging a full waterjugjar, his twotailed black braces dangling at heels"* (15.2035–38). But in spite of Bello's oath on reading the racing news—"And that Goddamned outsider *Throwaway* at twenty to one" (15.2935)—Bella Cohen may be the only gambler in Dublin to have bet on *Throwaway* on a professional tip from a turf insider.

This brief glimpse into Bella Cohen's working world sketches out the economic system of the brothel as one that parodies capitalistic enterprise at the same time that it exposes the role of the figure of business in the construction of gender. Bella Cohen deploys procurement into investment capital, and her own sexual activity into information, in order to play her version of the stock market (betting on races) with the help of her version of insider trading—a veterinarian's tip. Her commercial enterprise can only parody the world of business, but as a business woman, Bloom transmogrifies her in his pornological imagination (along with her postmenopausal moustache) into a bloated masculinized capitalist sadist:

> I shall sit on your ottoman saddleback every morning after my thumping good breakfast of Matterson's fat hamrashers and a bottle of Guinness's porter. (*he belches*) And suck my thumping good Stock Exchange cigar while I read the *Licensed Victualler's Gazette*. . . . and by the by Guiness's preference shares are at sixteen three quarters. Curse me for a fool that didn't buy that lot Craig and Gardner told me about. (15.2894–98, 15.2933–35)

This pornographized distortion of Bella Cohen masks both her bourgeois and maternal desire for legitimacy and respectability for her son—whom she labors to turn into an Oxford gentleman by the mucksweat of her body. Bella Cohen's aspirations for her son mirror Bloom's own for Rudy—"I could have helped him on in life. I could. Make him independent" (6.83). Like Ibsen, who glosses the homologies of marriage and prostitution in *A Doll's House,* Joyce glosses the homologies of the Oxfordian parents, the brothel madam and Haines's father, the imperialist who "made his tin by selling jalap to Zulus or some bloody swindle or other" (1.156–57). In her disenchanted form, Bella Cohen's corruptions resemble white-collar swindles more than Sadean criminality; her concerns are utterly bourgeois: to curtail obscenity ("None of that here. Come to the wrong shop" [15.3871]) and to preserve real estate ("Here. This isn't a musical peepshow. And don't you smash that piano" [15.3528–29]; "Who pays for the lamp? . . . Here, you were with him. The lamp's broken" [15.4268–69]).

The pornologized cruelty of Bella Cohen's sadistic Bello distorts and conceals the non-erotic cruelties she may visit on the women who work for her—not in the form of physical abuse, but in neglect and exploitation. The palimpsestic body of the prostitute, costumed for her work, but further pornologized in Bloom's atavistic imagination (through Virag), writes its own narrative of medical peril and neglect. In its unfetishized form, the body of the prostitute bears the marks and signs of the body's vulnerability to decay and disease. Zoe, who bears vaccination marks on upper arm and thigh, seems to live on cigarettes, which have poisoned her breath, and chocolates, which have rotted her teeth *("She bites his ear gently with little goldstopped teeth, sending on him a cloying breath of stale garlic"* [15.1339–40]). Kitty is described as bony and pallid, and prone to hiccoughs. Florry is obese, torpid, and prone to infection—the sty on her eye perhaps a sign of an upward displacement of a downward infection, like the catarrh of Freud's Dora. The threat of venereal disease decodes their seeming foreplay ("Has little mousey any tickles tonight? . . . *A hand glides over his left thigh*") into covert medical inspections ("[*in sudden alarm*] You've a hard chancre" [15.1295–1304]). Neither the chapter text, nor its critics, remark on the offhand but telling utterances, in which the prostitutes voice the horrific consequences of failure to protect against syphilis. Kitty Ricketts's brief comment is usually read by critics as the text seems to read it, as an obscene gloss on the Virgin Mary: "And Mary Shortall that was in the lock with the pox she got from Jimmy Pigeon in the blue caps had a child off him that couldn't swallow and was smothered with the convulsions in the mattress and we all subscribed for the funeral" (15.2578–81). The "blue caps" Kitty refers to were soldiers who, according to Richard Ellmann, frequented Monto and whom Bloom stereotypes, as the press did, as "an army rotten with venereal disease" (5.72). The "lock" which interns Mary Shortall with the pox was the Westmoreland National Lock Hospital on Townsend Street. Gifford and Seidman write, "The Contagious Diseases Acts of 1864, 1866, and 1869 made the lock hospitals virtual prisons for women suffering from venereal diseases."[23] The small vignette of Mary Shortall is, in a sense, the "other" of pornography—the unerotic sociology of prostitution that remains untold if the prostitute does not speak. Does it speculatively inscribe other horrors: the diseased and demented woman driven to infanticide by the hopelessness of the deformed newborn? The image of a community of prostitutes, themselves on the edge of subsistence, subscribing to the funeral of a syphilitic infant, is a disenchanted scene not encompassed by pornography's eye.

Bloom, who provides the pornological perspective I have coded as the enchantment of "Circe," provides in "Eumaeus" a retrospective antipornographic coda to his experience in the brothel that seals its disenchantment. When the streetwalker "glazed and haggard under a black straw hat" (16.704–5) peers into the cabman's shelter looking for customers, Bloom takes on the hypocritical censoriousness of a Victorian guardian of morals:

> The elder man, though not by any manner of means an old maid or a prude, said it was nothing short of a crying scandal that ought to be put a stop to *instanter* to say that women of that stamp . . . a necessary evil, were not licensed and medically inspected by the authorities, a thing, he could truthfully state, he, as a *paterfamilias,* was a stalwart advocate of from the very first start. (16.739–45)

Aligning himself explicitly with the Contagious Diseases Acts, Bloom takes a pointedly patriarchal position ("as a *paterfamilias*") that the prudish rhetoric (in spite of its disavowals) manages to mock. Bloom, who earlier pornographized the brothel, now advocates submitting the bodies of its workers to an oppressive regime of governmental control that only the organized feminist activism led by Josephine Butler had managed to repeal eight years before, in 1896. He seems scarcely aware that his program of coercion and control over the female body functions as the hypocritical double of the eroticized disciplines projected by his imaginary Bello. Furthermore, the object of this powerful oppression is a figure of nearly total abjection, who could easily be Mary Shortall herself: "It beats me, Mr Bloom confided to Stephen, medically I am speaking, how a wretched creature like that from the Lock hospital reeking with disease can be barefaced enough to solicit" (16.728–30). The figure of the woman in the black straw hat dramatizes that the brothel has an "outside," a margin incapable of being pornographized or eroticized, and therefore unspoken, unrepresented, mute. The outside of the brothel is a social abyss for an untouchable caste of diseased or demented women who live without madams or their houses to shelter them, reduced to futile beggary for dirty washing ("Psst! Any chance of your wash" [11.1255–56]). If gender is defined as a position in the symbolic or social order, then the woman in the black straw hat is so thoroughly degraded and declassed as to become unsexed in the sense of negatively sexed, a repulsively sexually marked thing. Nighttown is haunted by the prostitutes that escape for good or ill: on the one hand, the Georgina Johnsons, rescued into respectability by marriage to a traveling salesman; on the other, the syphilitic women, turned literal streetwalkers, who are extruded from its fragile and ephemeral social cohesions.

In receiving the multiple perspectives of "Circe," the reader is subjected to the same shifting and multiple gender constructions as the figures in the text: not only male and female, but many kinds of male, many kinds of female, male and female combined, or sexually overwritten, or unsexed by being oversexed, and so on. As such, the reader is subjected to the shifting and multiple perceptions and illusions generated by the carnival of discourses that speak the figures in the text in so many rhetorical registers, and thereby in so many social and symbolic gender positions. Furthermore, just as the languages of "Circe" are pretexted and ventriloquized—that is, just as Bloom contains within himself knowledge of discourses, many of which are never uttered in real life—so readers too are pretexted and (in what may be the opposite of ventriloquism) capable of distinguishing and recognizing theatrical overwritings and overspeakings (as well as the silences of voices that are thereby suppressed). As a result, the reader is as implicated in the pornography and other transgressive languages of the chapter as are Bloom and the prostitutes. In Odyssean terms this genders the reader as the ingenue male, the sailor fascinated by the erotic extremes of the pornological fantasies and their language, while—like Odysseus—remaining capable of resistance and defense against their illusions. The reader's implication may be figured otherwise, too—for example, as made vulnerable to exposure and blackmail by the doubleness we are obliged to maintain when enjoying "Circe," like Bella Cohen wishing her son's respectability to remain uncontaminated by its disreputable source in her brothel—"You don't want a scandal. . . . And if it were your own son in Oxford? (*warningly*) I know" (15.4299–306). The defense against this blackmail was devised by Judge Woolsey, when he implicitly exonerated readers of *Ulysses* (but tacitly more pointedly of "Circe") as long as the text made them nauseous rather than excited: "But my considered opinion, after long reflection, is that whilst in many places the effect of *Ulysses* on the reader undoubtedly is somewhat emetic, nowhere does it tend to be an aphrodisiac."[24] Readers and critics alike can defend themselves against implication by contending that reading "Circe" makes them sick. But there are better alternatives than following the hypocrisy of Bloom in denying the excitement of the brothel by arguing sternly ("as a *paterfamilias*") for its licensing, inspection, censorship, and moral disapprobation. This alternative is the use of the *pharmokos* of the theatrical, the refusal of total enchantment and fascination by remembering the artificiality and doubleness of everything that transpires in "Circe," remembering particularly that the women who serve as the pretext for pornography are working women caught in a bad business, as even Stephen recognizes—"She is a bad merchant. She buys dear and sells cheap" (16.738). Recognizing the multiple theatricalizations of the brothel could save us, as readers, from the superiority of the sociologist, or the sanctimoniousness of the philanthropists—like the board ladies of *Dublin by Lamplight* laundry in "Clay"—who gather up the women in black straw hats and give them a proper laundry in which to take in washing, but without acknowledging their own implication in their plight.

16

The Double Life of "Eumaeus"

COLLEEN LAMOS

"Eumaeus" is famous for its mistakes. The proliferation of grammatical, syntactical, and rhetorical errors in the episode has given it a long-standing reputation as the stylistic black sheep of *Ulysses.* Since Joyce told Carlo Linati that the episode signified "The Ambush at Home" and that the ambushing sailor played the part of "Ulysses Pseudoangelos" (the false messenger), and since Frank Budgen, apparently with Joyce's approval, described its language as that of "tired men," "Eumaeus" has been viewed as the site of duplicity and exhaustion, of seedy characters and of worn-out language.[1] Gerald Bruns's remarks on its "deadly language" and Hugh Kenner's criticism of the "falsity" of its diction have contributed to the general consensus that "Eumaeus" is the nadir of *Ulysses.*[2] The episode is typically read as, at best, an exemplar of bad style, vulgar commonplaces, and downright fraudulence.

To make matters worse, "Eumaeus" is rife with textual errors. According to Hans Walter Gabler, it contained the greatest number of textual mistakes of any episode in the 1922 edition of *Ulysses.*[3] Gabler's reconstruction of the text restored many of the original "errors," especially punctuation lapses, that appeared in Joyce's manuscripts and hence, in a sense, rendered "Eumaeus" even more erroneous. The Gabler edition permits and even encourages what Fritz Senn calls "misreadings," as the reader attempts to make sense out of the episode's now more garbled syntax.[4] The *Evening Telegraph*'s "usual crop of nonsensical howlers of misprints" (16.1262–67) seems an even more apt metatextual commentary on "Eumaeus"'s graphic lies and errors.

To whom are these mistakes attributable, and why? The dilemmas posed by the error-ridden language of "Eumaeus" have often been understood as narratological; that is, many critics have addressed the episode's egregiously errant style as a problem of the status of an anonymous narrator and his relationship to Bloom. Yet these errors raise broader epistemological questions that are also, and especially, sexual questions. The difficulty that so many readers have locating the source of the errors in Eumaean discourse and specifying who is speaking—whether Bloom or the narrator—suggests that the problem of error is bound up with a generalized epistemological anxiety which exceeds any single character or voice. "Eumaeus" is pervaded by a sense of uncertainty and deception that is particularly acute on the issue of homosexual knowledge; indeed, the episode is suffused with an atmosphere of paranoia that, while often focusing upon D. B. Murphy, has the ubiquitous character of homosexual panic. A brief consideration of the problem of the narrative voice may show how it is involved with these larger concerns.

It has become a critical truism that the discourse of "Eumaeus" comprises hackneyed phrases and equally clichéd ideas. It is almost as much of a commonplace to attribute this discourse to an unnamed narrator or, more broadly, to a collective "voice of culture" who, as Karen Lawrence puts it, is "a transpersonal repository of received ideas."[5] For many readers, Bruns's approach, although dated, remains influential: after arguing that the lexicon of the episode "is situated less in a specific consciousness (the narrator's, Bloom's) than in the already given world of worn expressions," so that "the narrator exists as a mind fabricated out of other minds," Bruns nonetheless describes the narrator as "a figure of impoverished sensibility" who occasionally emerges as an "individual consciousness." Bloom, however, escapes the narrator's "world of banal locutions" and pursues his "authentic role" of exposing the narrator's posturing and Eumaean imposture in general.[6]

Distinguishing between the narrative voice and that of Bloom is important for critics with a variety of interpretive aims, ranging from Bruns's existentialist claim that the narrator speaks in the unauthentic voice of the "tribe" to Lawrence's neo-Marxist argument that "the dominant cultural 'voice' of 'Eumaeus' mimes the hegemony of middle-class ideology."[7] These divergent critical projects converge insofar as they rescue Bloom from the gross rhetorical errors putatively characteristic of the man on the street or the bourgeoisie. Whether presenting Bloom as an ethically sound or a politically sensitive character, such readings save Bloom from the discourse of "Eumaeus" by attributing the latter to an anonymous and more or less subjectified narrator. Insofar as they displace errancy in its many forms onto an invariably vilified other, these critics repeat the move made *within* "Eumaeus" in which sexual errancy—especially homosexual desire—is displaced from Bloom onto the episode's most prominent figure of alterity, D. B. Murphy.[8]

This move is very common in Eumaean criticism. For example, Alistair Stead argues that, despite the "blurring of distinctions between the narrator and the protagonist in the method of free indirect speech," and despite Bloom's "relentlessly formulaic" and "paralyzing language of the newspaper," Bloom is nonetheless the victim of the narrator's cruel or stupid "treatment." Likewise, the episode is a "comedy of errors" in a larger sense because its many linguistic mistakes point to "the correct word or phrase." Just as the narrator's faults ultimately exculpate Bloom, so, according to Stead, "most of the errors in the book can only be appreciated if the reader acknowledges . . . standards of correctness"; indeed, "the postulate of correctness" is "indispensable to the comic effect" of the episode.[9] By thus assuming that the errancy of "Eumaeus" is governed by the truth that it violates and that its representation of Bloom's errors finally serves to satirize the narrator and not the hero, Stead is able to read the episode as a temporary trespass of grammatical and, at bottom, moral boundaries.

Stead's argument is reiterated in a somewhat different fashion by other critics who appeal to a ground of authenticity or seriousness beyond the corrosive irony of Eumaean discourse. Hence, for instance, Barbara Stevens Heusel urges that ultimately "Joyce maintains . . . moral and linguistic values" in the episode, despite its "obfuscating language,"[10] while Mark Osteen claims that "most readers detect some stable foundation in 'Eumaeus' beneath the play of counterfeits."[11] The episode seems to elicit a salvational impulse from its critics, even if such redemption merely takes the form, as John Henry Raleigh argues, of the "three smoking globes of turds" (16.1876–77) dropped by the horse at the end of "Eumaeus," which Raleigh interprets as a "countersign" to the "downward drift" of the world represented in *Ulysses.*[12]

Reading "Eumaeus" as a commentary on contemporary Irish society and politics rather than a reflection of the consciousness of Bloom or of the narrator offers a fresh perspective on the problem of errancy in "Eumaeus," including the linguistic mistakes, fraudulent identities, and other sorts of misunderstandings and misrepresentations in the episode. Like Raleigh, Andrew Gibson argues that its cliché-ridden style, "strewn with [verbal] flotsam and jetsam," mimes the disintegration of its subjects, the human "wreckage" of Dublin. Dismissing the long-standing problem of the narrator, he claims that "there is no single narrative . . . voice" but only "a loose assemblage of bits and pieces" of discourse; therefore, "the irony of 'Eumaeus' has no foundation" since there is no superior, nonironic vantage point within the episode.[13] However, this irony "lures" readers "into a fellowship with brokenness," Gibson urges, eliciting their sympathy for the victims of turn-of-the-century Irish society but without generating a sense of epistemological uncertainty.

Karen Lawrence offers a more sophisticated analysis of the political implications of what she calls "the ludic drama of language" in "Eumaeus." Its errant rhetoric works against itself: while "the dominant cultural 'voice' of 'Eumaeus' mimes" the idioms and ideology of the middle class, the manifest errors of this style indicate the failure of the values it espouses. According to Lawrence, the language of the episode "abounds in gestures of prudence, punctiliousness, and regulation, as if to maintain a boundary between vulgarity and bourgeois gentility," but such language, despite its "attempts at beautification, sanitation, and productivity," is fraught with waste matter, including verbal dung ("excess, superfluity, and accident") as well as references to literal dung.[14] Although Joyce allows neither transcendence of the values of the bourgeoisie nor "escape" from its notorious banalities, Lawrence holds out the hope that the errant language of the episode provides some "resistance" to them.

In keeping with the practice of opposing the narrative voice to that of Bloom, Lawrence asserts that the latter, despite his participation in the "bourgeois imaginary" of the narrative, sometimes displays "solidarity with the working class." Yet the originality of her argument lies in her claim that the rhetoric of "Eumaeus" undermines its own labors at respectability by virtue of its very erroneousness. Thus, she argues that the linguistic excesses of "Eumaeus" are not just verbal garbage but may be reclaimed as truly meaningful.

> Despite the fact that there are all sorts of errors, mistakes, and, on the linguistic level, semantically vacuous connections, the chapter does produce unlikely doublings that create significances and breed a sense of . . . faith in the meaning of randomness. What is viewed as waste . . . produces meaning.[15]

The semantic productivity of apparent nonsense or plain stupidity, the conversion of waste to profit, the harnessing of verbal play for the work of meaning—by such means, the errors of "Eumaeus" are again redeemed and its pervasive errancy once more rectified.

In the spirit rather than the letter of Lawrence's essay, we might take waste seriously as such and not as an indirect route to linguistic or literary utility. In a parenthetical aside, Lawrence offers a direction for such a reading: referring to the union of Stephen and Bloom at the end of the episode, she notes that "perhaps the homoerotic implications of this 'marriage' here suggest . . . a connection that exists outside the classical economy of *reproduction,* which might provide another significance to the puns on anality in the chapter."[16] Although homosexual relations are surely not fully external to heterosexuality or to classical economies of semantic or biological (re)production, Lawrence's remarks provoke a consideration of "Eumaeus" in terms of a mutually implicated and enforcing *double economy* and a *double life.*

Just as homosexuality has, in modern times, existed as an open secret, concealed as the shadowy, reverse side of the fabric of public heterosexuality, so, too, in "Eumaeus" male homosexuality represents the underside of middle-class values and its language of respectability. However, the trashy and irredeemable errancy of Eumaean discourse lies not in same-sex desire, as such, but in the deceit of a culture that whispers under its breath, that both knows and refuses to know, and that admits only by means of error (and only *as* error) homoerotic desires. Eumaean discourse is marked by such dubious acknowledgments and anxious denials.

In all sorts of ways, "Eumaeus" trades upon duplicity. It has been frequently noted that the identities of most of the major and minor characters in this episode are provocatively mysterious. The cabman's shelter, while serving as a refuge for men during the night, may also be—and the uncertainty is precisely the point—a site of homosexual cruising and political subversion. It is the place where Bloom concocts his illusory vision of Stephen's future in his household, thereby misinterpreting the young man's wishes as well as apparently misrecognizing his own desires. Finally, the sailor, D. B. Murphy, is the embodiment (specifically, the bottom) of the double life of "Eumaeus," bearing in his person the vagrancy that is displayed in the episode's errant locutions. His enigmatic sexual identity incites homosexual paranoia and elicits the impulses toward correctness and decorum characteristic of both Bloom and the discourse of the episode in general.

To a surprising degree, what Jennifer Levine calls the "hermeneutical anxiety" depicted in and invited by "Eumaeus" is traceable to pervasive homosocial desires. With exacting precision, Levine scrutinizes the densely coded, homophobic representation of such desires. One of the curious effects of this fear is evident in the recurrent "hesitation about . . . acts of naming" in the episode, along with the narrative's urgency to name Murphy and Murphy's insistence upon naming himself.[17] This suspicion as to "What's in a name" (16.364), concomitant with the host of changing names attributed to Murphy, a Morpheus figure, not only suggests the amorphous and nightmarish character of (homo)sexual paranoia, as Levine notes,[18] but, to extend her argument, also implies the extensive linguistic and epistemological ramifications of a phenomenon that, paradoxically, must and cannot be designated. As well as posing a thematic problem, male same-sex desire is an inducement to discursive errancy.

In "Eumaeus," representing homosexuality compels evasion and duplicity: these strategies are proximate and interior to the normality that they defy, rendering any attempt to name them a forgery. As Derek Attridge points out, "Eumaeus" demonstrates "the impossibility of fixed . . . significations when the structures of language are permeated by the dissolving energies of erotic desire." Although he offers a subtle, detailed anatomy of the various kinds of linguistic error in the episode, demonstrating how its language "permits slippage and uncertainty, deception and detour,"[19] he stops short of articulating the homoerotic forces that elicit the episode's linguistic errancy.

The textual and discursive errors in "Eumaeus" are thus involved with the broader question of errant knowledge, especially homosexual knowledge. The central problem of "Eumaeus" is how to put together fragmentary and dubious bits of information, or, in Bloom's words, "pieces of intelligence," into a body of knowledge. Nearly every source of information in the episode is corrupt. The newspaper is as unreliable as the numerous accounts purporting to explain various characters' identities. The rumored genealogy of Lord John Corley, allegedly descended in an irregular fashion from the Lords Talbot de Malahide, is an early example of a pattern, repeated throughout the episode, in which knowledge of a character is based upon gossip, doubtful "facts," and possibly fraudulent documents. These problems are typically presented in the narrative as Bloom's, yet his judgment also comes under suspicion, particularly in regard to sexual matters. Intrigued by Murphy, Bloom plays the detective; "Sherlockholmesing him up" (16.831), he tries to figure out who Murphy is, yet he plainly avoids reading the homosexual clues that surround the sailor. The conclusions that Bloom draws about Murphy, and his knowledge in general, are as questionable as those of other characters.

The epistemological dilemmas of "Eumaeus" focus on the enigmatic sailor whom Bloom tries to decipher but include the keeper of the shelter and other minor figures. "[S]aid to be the once famous Skin-the-Goat, Fitzharris," a member of the invincibles (16.323–24), the keeper is the mouthpiece for nationalist polemic and is therefore the representative of what one may call political perversion. However, it is Murphy who dominates the scene and whose tall tales of his exploits across the seas magnetize his audience, while the crux of his mystery lies not in his salty yarns but in his obscure sexuality. Although he is the locus of sexual perversion in the episode, the latter extends beyond him to touch other characters, especially Stephen and Bloom.

Knowledge circulates in "Eumaeus" by means of indirection and innuendo, as the possession of insiders, concealed like a dangerous weapon and revealed through circumlocutions, oblique clues, or inadvertent slips of the tongue. Both sexual perversion and subversive political conspiracy function as open secrets, officially nonexistent and privy only to the initiated. An amusing and telling example of this paranoid epistemology occurs early in the episode, following Murphy's story about the man whom he saw knifed in the back in Trieste by "an Italian chap" (16.576). One of the other men in the shelter puts in that the Italians are "great for the cold steel. . . . That was why they thought the park murders of the invincibles was done by foreigners on account of them using knives" (16.589–92). Bloom, who fancies that he knows about the Phoenix Park murders, enjoys a smug sense of superiority over this fellow, "who was evidently quite in the dark," and he draws Stephen into the circle of the supposed cognoscenti. "At this remark passed obviously in the spirit of *where ignorance is bliss* Mr B. and Stephen . . . both instinctively exchanged meaning glances, . . . of the strictly *entre nous* variety however, towards . . . Skin-the-Goat, *alias* the keeper," whose "inscrutable face . . . conveyed the impression that he didn't understand one jot of what was going on. Funny, very!" (16.593–600). The joke, of course, is on Bloom, but we as readers are nevertheless in the dark as to what, if anything, the keeper knows. Moreover, his inscrutability, as he stands "drawing spurts of liquid from his boiler affair" (16.597), is suggestively sexual, just as is Murphy's tale of the murder of the man in Trieste, killed by a knife that "went into his back up to the butt" (16.582), which Murphy tells while playing with his own "formidable *stiletto*" (16.585).

In contrast to his claim to have gotten Skin-the-Goat's number, Bloom is evasive regarding Murphy. Confident that he is "bogus," Bloom nonetheless does not seem to want to understand who Murphy is, and when insinuations of his sexuality arise, Bloom changes the subject, looks out the door, ignores the matter, or denies it. Yet Bloom's own version of "where ignorance is bliss," concerning homosexuality, coexists with his constant references to it, references often apparently innocent.

In "Eumaeus," error is a way of knowing. Neither an accident nor simply the effect of repression, it is productive and enabling. Thus, Bloom's mistakes and misjudgments comprise a knowing ignorance of sexual perversion which structures the episode and which sanctions and even sanctifies its concluding epithalamium: the putatively nonperverse union of Stephen and Bloom. His mistakes and moments of incomprehension permit him at once to know and not to know about homosexuality. The placement of the narrative voice at an indeterminate distance from Bloom is crucial to this double gesture of revealing and concealing his familiarity with same-sex desire. "Eumaeus" contains a startling number of off-the-cuff phrases with ambiguous connotations, such as "the genus *homo*" (16.328), to "fag out" (16.251), "queer sights" (16.464) and "queer things" (16.465–66), "a gay sendoff" (16.1247), and the "queer suddenly things" that Stephen pops out with, which "attracted the elder man" (16.1567–68).[20] The uncertainty of grasping precisely what these words mean—whether they are throwaway phrases or slips of the tongue that expose Bloom's covert cognizance of homosexuality, the overt awareness of which he avoids—reflects the epistemological instability of sexual knowledge in "Eumaeus" as a whole. This instability is itself "queer" in the sense that the signs of homosexuality function in the episode like a counterfeit, cheat or trick.[21]

This queer linguistic undercurrent contributes to the semiotic duplicity that pervades "Eumaeus," which, to a large degree, issues from what Eve Kosofsky Sedgwick calls homosexual panic.[22] The equivocal signs of homosexuality in "Eumaeus," rather than indicating the sexual orientation of any of its characters, indicate the fear of being thought homosexual. Moreover, this fear is not reducible to the personal anxiety of any particular character but operates on the discursive level to disrupt the certainty of sexual identity and to obscure the objects of desire. The proliferation of the signs of homosexuality in "Eumaeus" thus signifies not a determinate sexual orientation but the indeterminacy of homophobia.

The general structure of perverse knowledge in "Eumaeus" breaks down along the following lines: Murphy, the experienced outsider, possesses the dark, inner secrets of perversion, learned in the East and *non nominandum inter christianus,* yet inscribed enigmatically upon his chest; whereas Bloom, the domestic Dubliner, whose dreams of adventure consist of taking the ferry to Holyhead, tries not to, or at least pretends not to, know the unspeakable secrets symbolized by Murphy's tattoo. As a consequence, Murphy remains an internal exile in the episode, the great imposter, while Bloom, by virtue of his seeming innocence, is free to attempt to lure Stephen into a frankly homoerotic triangle with Molly.

"Eumaeus" thus comprises two, opposed and reversed, representations of homosexuality: on the one hand, the explicit, albeit mysterious, portrayal of perversion embodied by Murphy, who is, broadly speaking, the homosexual abject of "Eumaeus"; on the other hand, the implicit, domesticized portrayal of male same-sex affection embodied by Bloom and Stephen, who walk off arm in arm at the end of the episode *"to be married by Father Maher"* (16.1887–88), protected from homophobic retribution by their apparent ignorance. Indeed, Bloom's preoccupation with the issue of adultery in the second half of the episode serves as a screen that shields him from what Budgen observed was his "homosexual wish" to share his wife with other men.[23]

In the critical literature on "Eumaeus," Bloom and Murphy are usually opposed to each other, yet the episode constructs a series of parallels between the Odyssean Bloom and the pseudo-Odyssean Murphy that undermines one's certainty about which is the cheat and which is the genuine article. Bloom is often represented as amiable and bumbling but well meaning and kindhearted, the self-deprecating yet resourceful *eiron* of "Eumaeus," while Murphy is portrayed as a boastful fraud. Although he carries the burden of lowlife desires and has come to serve as a metonymy for the duplicitous significations of the episode, Murphy is simply the designated bearer of the secret of male same-sex desire that affects (and infects) all of the men gathered in the cabman's shelter, including Bloom.

The crucial moment in "Eumaeus" when Bloom and Murphy come face-to-face metaphorically is the tattoo scene. Elaborating on the "queer sights" and "queer things" that he has seen in his sailing career, Murphy pulls out a "picture postcard" which, he claims, "a friend of mine sent me," featuring "a group of savage women in striped loincloths . . . amid a swarm of infants," beneath which is printed the inscription *"Choza de Indios* [Indian huts]. *Beni, Bolivia"* (16.471–77). As many readers have noticed, the inscription does not correspond to the picture. Bloom's own doubts are raised when he turns over the card to find that it is addressed not to Murphy but to "*Señor A Boudin, Galeria Becche, Santiago, Chile,*" and that it contains no message (16.489–90). "[H]aving detected a discrepancy between his name (assuming he was the person he represented himself to be and not sailing under false colours . . .) and the fictitious addressee of the missive," Bloom "nourish[es] some suspicions of our friend's *bona fides*" (16.494–98). Along with other critics' suspicions, Levine's are raised by the fact that "'Boudin' is not just typically French; it is impossible in Spanish," while "Becche" is obviously Italian.[24] In short, the postcard points ostentatiously to Murphy's duplicity.

Murphy's questionable postcard parallels the photograph of Molly that Bloom later produces as his own bona fides for Stephen. Both show women in various stages of undress: the bare-breasted Indian women of the postcard pose, *National Geographic*–style, while Molly wears an "evening dress cut ostentatiously low . . . to give a liberal display of bosom" (16.1429–30). These pictures of women are passed around the group of men not only for sexual titillation but as a way of forming bonds with each other; the circulation of the postcard and photograph in the cabman's shelter is a time-honored, homosocial ritual of men exchanging women.[25] Bloom's exhibition of Molly's picture confirms his heterosexuality while serving to lure Stephen home with him. Although Bloom's gesture is designed to attest to his normality as well as to attract Stephen, Murphy's similar gesture provokes Bloom's anxiety.

Murphy's character takes on an explicitly sexual cast when he bares his "manly chest" (16.690) to reveal his tattoo. His self-exposure repeats the exposure of the chests of the Indian women and of Molly, with the crucial difference that the breast he bares for their viewing pleasure is a hairy, masculine one.

He does so to oblige the members of his audience, who—in the grip of his stories about crocodiles, magical Chinese pills, and a man knifed in Trieste—are so transfixed that they stare at his chest. "Seeing they were all looking at his chest he accommodatingly dragged his shirt more open so . . . they had a full view of the figure 16 and a young man's sideface looking frowningly rather" (16.673–76). Later in the episode, Bloom gazes at Stephen's "sideface," confirming the structural parallel between him and the sailor, and between Stephen and the "young man."

Murphy explains that the tattoo was done by "Antonio, . . . a Greek" (16.679). When asked "what's the number for?" he directs a knowing, "half smile" toward the questioner and answers, "A Greek he was" (16.695–99). Antonio is not a Greek name, suggesting that his emphatic Greekness has to do with nonracial characteristics associated with the number sixteen. Although Murphy never tells his secret, Don Gifford claims that sixteen signifies homosexuality in European slang.[26] Antonio's Greekness lies in the Greek vice, an identification that Levine pursues through a detailed discussion of the Italian phrase "la smorfia," translated as "to pull a face," which is etymologically connected to the name of Morpheus, the Greek god of dreams. In contemporary Italian folk numerology, dreams were identified with numbered cards in a game called "lotto," in which sixteen represented an artist, from which Levine concludes that Murphy, like Antonio, is linked to Morpheus in a "figuring of the artist as essentially an actor, a trickster, [and] a dream-worker."[27]

While all of the other men in the shelter congregate around Murphy, admiring his tattoo, Bloom remains detached. His inchoate awareness of the homosexual implications of Murphy's tattoo is deflected by his attention to a streetwalker who pokes her head into the door of the shelter at that moment, looking for business. She finds no takers, for all of the men are grouped around and gazing at "Murphy's nautical chest" (16.725–26).[28] Bloom is embarrassed by the fact that he had met her earlier that day and recalls she had once "begged the chance of his washing." Recalling the incident compels him to admit to himself that "he had washed his wife's undergarments when soiled" (16.712–17), and he is consequently relieved when she leaves. His coprophilic confession immediately induces a reverse discourse: a brief lecture to Stephen on the need for the regulation and medical inspection of prostitutes "by the proper authorities, a thing, he could truthfully state, he, as a *paterfamilias,* was a stalwart advocate of" (16.743–44).

The regulation and inspection of prostitutes was the primary purpose of the Criminal Law Amendment Act of 1885, which linked prostitution with male homosexual behavior, attributing both to unbridled male lust as the "corrupter of youth."[29] Section 11 of that act, which outlawed male homosexuality, recurs in Bloom's mind a few moments later, while ruminating over an incident involving O'Callaghan in a sexual indiscretion. He recalls how the latter "had to be spirited away by a few friends . . . so as not to be made amenable under section two of the criminal law amendment act" (16.1191–94), evidently misreading the Arabic numeral 11 as the Roman numeral II. Bloom's mistake, in keeping with the episode's errant style, sustains his putative ignorance and innocence of homosexuality and maintains the ambiguity that obscures the homosexual theme throughout *Ulysses*.[30] While reflecting on O'Callaghan, Bloom "put[s] two and two together" and comes up with "six sixteen," yet, as with Murphy, "he pointedly turned a deaf ear" to the conclusion of his own calculations (16.1195–96).[31]

Bloom's digression from Murphy's tattooed chest to the prostitute is overlaid by his preoccupations with women's soiled underwear and public hygiene. More importantly, the prostitute draws Bloom's attention away from Murphy's tattoo and its disturbing implications for his attraction to Stephen. In short, she serves as an alibi, allowing him to disavow (and to indulge) his homoeroticism. In a similar fashion, Bloom denies that Antonio, the Greek tattoo artist, bears any "relation to the dramatic personage of identical name who sprang from the pen of our national poet" (16.839–40). Many critics have noticed that the friendship between Antonio and Bassanio in Shakespeare's *Merchant of Venice* has a homoerotic aspect, which Bloom's disavowal merely underscores.[32]

Bloom's repeatedly voiced doubts about Murphy's veracity serve to cement, at least in Bloom's mind, the bond between himself and Stephen. Confiding *"sotto voce"* to the latter, Bloom remarks that "our mutual friend's stories are like himself. . . . Do you think they are genuine?" (16.821–22). Bloom's reference to Dickens's novel, which is laced with homoerotic themes, is ostensibly designed to draw Stephen into his confidence, allying them against the deceptive and sexually suspicious Murphy, yet it tacitly alludes to the homosexual aspect of their collusion. Murphy thus mediates the relationship between Bloom and Stephen, much as Molly does in the following episode.

In Bloom's account, Murphy possesses an imaginary strangeness and power. Like Sinbad the Sailor of *The Arabian Nights,* he is an exotic, fantastic figure, larger than life. The object of Bloom's projections of homosexual perversion and of an intimidating masculinity, Murphy urinates in epic proportions, awakening Gumley in the sentry box and a horse in the cabrank, as well as prefiguring Bloom's and Stephen's mutual micturition in "Ithaca" and exceeding theirs in its display of virility. Despite Bloom's scorn for his "sixchamber revolver anecdotes" (16.1632), Murphy commands authority in the shelter as a man's man, especially through his abilities as a raconteur. Bloom's admiration for him is evident when he tries to compete with Murphy through repeated references to his own witty repartee in Barney Kierney's pub.

Most of all, Murphy is charged with the allure of the hidden knowledge of homosexuality. His status as the subject who knows secrets is confirmed late in the episode when he puts on "greenish goggles" to read the newspaper (16.1672). These green eyeglasses, resembling those of Joyce, render him an author surrogate.[33] His esoteric and heterogeneous reading habits bear a curious similarity to those of Joyce. Murphy's favorite books are *The Arabian Nights,* a collection of stories whose English translation included Sir Richard Burton's notorious "Terminal Essay" concerning Eastern homosexual practices among men, and *Red as a Rose Is She* by Rhoda Broughton, a sentimental novel laced with moral commonplaces. Burton's translation of *The Arabian Nights* served as a metonymy in late Victorian culture for perverse sexuality in general, contributing to the widely held belief that the Orient was the seat of sexual license and the origin of corrupting—or liberatory—homosexual practices.[34] By contrast, Broughton's romance upholds Victorian conventions of heterosexual love and decency. Poised between Burton and Broughton, Murphy occupies a strange position of both depravity and ordinariness, as though Joyce wished, at the end of "Eumaeus," to ameliorate or complicate the portrait of his author-surrogate.

The numerous associations between Murphy and Joyce cast into a different light the long-standing problem of the errancy of the narrative voice in "Eumaeus" and its relation to Bloom. If, as Raleigh claims, "Murphy is a persona for Joyce himself," and if, like the "Morphios" in *Finnegans Wake,* he is a figure for "the Greek Irishmen, all the Murphys, exiled writers, returning sailors, . . . [and] buried and life-giving murphies," in Susan Brienza's words,[35] then Murphy is the apotheosis of the artist as a shape-changing forger. As such, he is aligned with the narrative voice of the episode. Indeed, Robert Bell calls the narrator "the Penman," based upon his resemblance to the forgers James Townsend Saward, a.k.a. Jim the Penman, and Richard Pigott, arguing that the narrator is an early version of Shem the Penman.[36]

Instead of rescuing Bloom from the contaminating voice of the narrator, we might reverse the line of vision and see him as the straight man of the episode. Likewise, rather than simply opposing him to Murphy, we might understand this pair as joined in the way that Shem and Shaun are, as two of a kind. As Bloom's abjected alter ego, Murphy is his queer other. Finally, instead of correcting the errant discourse of "Eumaeus," such a queer reading revalues the play of error, including errant desires and the desire for error. Yet a surprising number of critics resist Murphy. Osteen, for instance, grudgingly allows that "the sailor's counterfeit tales are a paradigm for all those in the episode, including those of the narrator," but insofar as he wishes to believe that "beneath all copies lies something that is not a copy"—an original—Osteen tries to distinguish Bloom's stories from the narrator's Murphy-like counterfeits.[37]

Like Nietzsche's figure of woman as the untruth of truth, Murphy gives the lie to straight narratives and straight desires. It is therefore difficult to say what, exactly, "Eumaeus"'s errant prose or Murphy's errant sexuality signifies. Instead of producing meaning, the verbal wastefulness of the text does not finally turn a profit, just as the homoeroticism that pervades the cabman's shelter does not lead to a conclusion about the determinate sexual orientation of any of its denizens or even to a specifically homosexual theme. In short, "Eumaeus" represents neither Murphy nor anyone else as really gay, nor is homosexuality its interpretive key. Rather, the fear and fascination of male same-sex desire, generalized through the episode's paranoid epistemology, generates a systematic and unstable duplicity of sexual signs—a textual "double economy" correlative to the potential "double lives" of its characters.

Finally, "Eumaeus" suggests that errancy is a pseudo-liberatory ploy. In much the same way that the notion of "the feminine" seemed to many male modernist writers, including Joyce, to offer an escape from nominatively masculine logic and language, so homosexual desire in "Eumaeus" appears as an alluring secret, plumped with the dangers and thrills of a double life, of duplicitous meanings, and of an outlaw pleasure, as Lawrence puts it, "outside the classical economy of reproduction." But Joyce never completely swallows the bait; instead, he leaves his readers with the erratic logic of guesswork.

At one point in the episode, Joyce shows his hand, presenting Murphy not as an imaginary figure of Bloom's fears and desires but as a sailor whose wanderings have worn him out. In a non sequitur to Bloom's question about Gibraltar—the locus of his cherished fantasies—Murphy responds, "I'm tired of all them rocks in the sea. . . . Salt junk all the time" (16.622–23). For a single moment, Murphy seems to reply to his creator, like Molly crying, "O Jamesy let me up out of this" (18.1128–29), asking to be freed from his role as the abjected and inflated projection of another's passions, giving the lie to the longing for errancy in a queerly tender way that makes Bloom, the straight paterfamilias, seem like just a homeboy.

17

Sidereal Writing

Male Refractions and Malefactions in "Ithaca"

VICKI MAHAFFEY

The average reader hopes to find in "Ithaca" a final destination, a climax and anchor of the reading experience. Instead of the seasickness produced by constant change—of style, time of day, character, organ, and symbol—the Odyssean word-voyager longs for a stable rock on which to rest, a rock that is also "home": an equivalent to the unmoving, deep-rooted olive tree that Odysseus shaped into his marriage bed.[1] But "Ithaca" both is and is not the home for which the reader has been seeking. It is a chapter of homecoming that highlights the impossibility of actual return; even if the traveler returns in space, time is irreversible, so that home will always, at least in part, be *"unheimlich."*[2] By this point in the journey, Bloom—like Odysseus—has become multiply other: alienated, fractured, adulterated. Moreover, Bloom's story is so crossed with other narratives, his character so haunted by other written characters, that the associations of the home he reaches are tied to much more than the island Odysseus once ruled. In *Ulysses,* the rock of Ithaca is also Mount Pisgah, and Bloom a constellation of Jewish Moseses,[3] none of whom may actually enter the promised land although they are brought far enough to glimpse it. *Ulysses* draws its readers toward an end that lacks closure, or where closure is produced by a conspiracy between fatigue and the driving logic of grammar, which demands the episode's final engorged period. Like Bloom, we "end" in a context that is both familiar and strange, where known and unknown commingle, where the "rock" of certainty metamorphoses into a huge and fantastic roc, the bird that carries Sinbad from a deserted island into another round of voyages.

Readers tend to find "Ithaca" hopelessly boring or emotionally devastating. What produces both reactions is Joyce's use of the complex machinery of human knowledge to bring into sharp relief the vastness and power of the unknown.[4] "Ithaca" presents its readers with a self-evident enigma like the one Bloom suddenly comprehends when he effects "natural obscurity by the extinction of artificial light" (17.2068–69). Having been puzzled for thirty years by the riddle, "Where was Moses when the candle went out?" (17.2070), Bloom immediately realizes that Moses—like himself—was in the dark. "Ithaca" uses all the artificial light of human scientific and mathematical knowledge to make the reader see that she too is "in the dark," but then it shows that the dark is shot through with sidereal light. The most important working of the episode is to show how, in the "fabulous formless darkness" of the unknown and the unknowable, we variously transform that sidereal light into the impossible cause and fulfillment of our desires.

"Sidereal" light is, of course, starlight; its association with desire is supported by at least one of the possible etymologies of "desire" as "*de-sider,*" from the stars (*Webster's Collegiate Dictionary*). Desire, then, is a longing for something impossibly remote, something that may have ceased to exist by the time we apprehend it. In "Ithaca," Joyce uses the stars as a kind of writing, which human characters "read" as signs of the simultaneous remoteness and fulfillment of their wishes. When Bloom and Stephen leave "the house of bondage" (17.1022) and step into the garden, the spectacle that confronts them is a heavenly image of their desire for a newly Edenic beginning: a "heaventree of stars hung with humid nightblue fruit" (17.1039).[5] But Bloom, after considering the massive movements of evolution and involution, logically concludes that the night sky

> was not a heaventree, not a heavengrot, not a heavenbeast, not a heavenman. That it was a Utopia [literally, "no place"], there being no known method from the known to the unknown: an infinity renderable equally finite by the suppositious apposition of one or more bodies equally of the same and of different magnitudes: a mobility of illusory forms immobilised in space, remobilised in air: a past which possibly had ceased to exist as a present before its probable spectators had entered actual present existence. (17.1139–45)

Like writing, or like *Ulysses* itself, the sky sends a reminder from the past of an infinity that we render finite by selection and arrangement. What the stars allow us to see are the tracings of our own desire upon the void of "no place," and at the same time they gently remind us that such desires are both achingly precious and futile, for "at the termination of any allotted life only an infinitesimal part of any person's desires has been realised" (17.1761–63). As the narrator explains, we paradoxically render something desirable by *obviating* desire (17.2033); by definition, desire precludes relation, like the statue of Narcissus that sits erect in the center of Bloom's table. The stone image offers various consolations—of "candour, nudity, pose, tranquility, youth, grace, sex" (17.1427), but it will produce no Echo (Narcissus having spurned her). Like Narcissus, desire desires itself: "sound without echo, desired desire" (17.2034).

Although Bloom understands the pragmatic function of desire as a compensatory illusion, he nonetheless writes (and reads) his desires in the night sky in a way that is strangely amplified and made more complex by his scientific knowledge. Bloom's ambivalence about returning home, for example, is writ large in his identification with a comet, which Joyce in his schema identifies as the symbol of the episode. When Bloom is pointing out features of the night sky to Stephen, shortly after their emergence into the penumbra of the garden, he considers "the almost infinite compressibility of hirsute comets and their vast elliptical egressive and reentrant orbits from perihelion to aphelion" (17.1112–13). By referring to the comets as "hirsute," the narrator signals an awareness that the word "comet" comes from the Greek, meaning "wearing long hair." The comet, then, serves as a heavenly correlate for the Odyssean voyager, who travels far in time and space and returns unkempt and unrecognized.

What the Greeks called the "hair" of the comet is actually its tail, which behaves in a way that dramatizes the comet's gravitational ambivalence toward the sun. As the comet returns toward the sun, the different parts of the comet react in opposite ways, which produces the magnificent beauty of the comet and makes it visible in the sky. If we refer to a book that Bloom has on his shelves, Sir Robert Ball's *The Story of the Heavens* (see 17.1373), we find that Ball stresses the gravitational ambivalence of comets:

> That the comet as a whole is attracted by the sun there can be no doubt whatever. The fact that the comet moves in an ellipse or in a parabola proves that the two bodies act and react on each other in obedience to the law of universal gravitation. But while this is true of the comet as a whole, it is no less certain that the tail of the comet is repelled by the sun.[6]

Since the tail is repelled by the sun, it grows longer as the comet approaches nearer, and it catches the sunlight in the expanding glory of its "hair." The beauty of the comet is thus produced by its ambivalent attraction/repulsion to its "home," and the ambivalence of the comet itself was reproduced in the reactions of the observers who witnessed it. Comets were not only perceived as glorious, they were also perceived as harbingers of destruction (Ball writes that "they rapidly swell in size to an extent that in superstitious ages called forth the utmost terror").[7]

A cometary return in power and glory is the ultimate fantasy of the outsider, as Bloom shows when he is imagining his own departure from home:

> Ever would he wander, selfcompelled, to the extreme limit of his cometary orbit, beyond the fixed stars and variable suns and telescopic planets, astronomical waifs and strays, to the extreme boundary of space, passing from land to land, among peoples, amid events. Somewhere imperceptibly he would hear and somehow reluctantly, suncompelled, obey the summons of recall. Whence, disappearing from the constellation of the Northern Crown he would somehow reappear reborn above delta in the constellation of Cassiopeia and after incalculable eons of peregrination return an estranged avenger, a wreaker of justice on malefactors, a dark crusader, a sleeper awakened, with financial resources (by supposition) surpassing those of Rothschild or the silver king. (17.2013–23)

For Bloom, however, unlike Odysseus, his return as a dark avenger is pure fantasy. He rejects the option of departure, just as he refused to slay his rivals, justifying his sentiments to himself by reflecting upon "the futility of triumph or protest or vindication: the inanity of extolled virtue: the lethargy of nescient matter: the apathy of the stars" (17.2224–26).

Although Bloom knows himself to be "in the dark," alternately self-compelled and sun compelled as he orbits through the vast waste of the known, he always returns "home," and even in his darkest travels he is guided by luminous signs—by the polestar at sea and by "a bispherical moon" on land (17.1992–96). Moreover, the idealized lights that guide him are invariably gendered female: the sun that pulls him home is personified as "an invisible luminous body," perceptible at dawn through its "first golden limb . . . low on the horizon" (17.1267–68). Earlier in the day Bloom envisioned the sun as "a girl with gold hair on the wind," in slim sandals, running to meet him (4.240–42). With consummate delicacy, Joyce connects this golden girl with Milly, his surprisingly blonde daughter ("born of two dark" [17.868]). However, in Bloom's mind and emotions, Milly is also a revised version of Molly as she was in 1888. The inexorable gravitational force that brings Bloom home, then, is the "sun" of memory, his memory of Molly as he first knew her, resurgent as his (absent) daughter.

Molly as she is now gains her brightness from the reflected light of that remembered and re-arising sun: she is the moon, alternately seen as coldly dependent, the frigid "satellite of their planet" (17.1149–50), and omnipotent, a deity in the form of a rump leading him from bondage to the promised land. The bispherical moon that guides Bloom's travels is relocated inside a woman's skirt, "revealed in imperfect varying phases of lunation through the posterior interstice of the imperfectly occluded skirt of a carnose negligent perambulating female, a pillar of the cloud by day" (17.1996–99). This "moon" undergoes one more transformation: it becomes, at the end of the chapter, the terrestrial hemispheres of the earth, Bloom's promised land, which with ambivalent gravitational attraction draws him home. When Bloom is in bed, his antagonistic sentiments and reflections converge in a simple, final satisfaction "at the ubiquity . . . of adipose anterior and posterior female hemispheres, redolent of milk and honey and of excretory sanguine and seminal warmth" (17.2229–33). His satisfaction culminates in his "obscure prolonged provocative" kissing of "each plump melonous hemisphere, in their mellow yellow furrow" (17.2241–43). The end of Bloom's travels is finally troped as a return to earth, the warmth and the "mute immutable mature animality" of a woman's body (17.2235–36).

Bloom's ability to come "down to earth" in the moments before he falls asleep may be a kind of triumph for him, but Joyce is careful to stress how little it means to Molly, who reflects,

> its a wonder Im not an old shrivelled hag before my time living with him so cold never embracing me except sometimes when hes asleep the wrong end of me not knowing I suppose who he has any man thatd kiss a womans bottom Id

> throw my hat at him after that hed kiss anything unnatural where we havent 1 atom of any kind of expression in us all of us the same 2 lumps of lard (18.1399–1404)

Bloom's imagined space odyssey is not a model of relation but a tracing of desire, which renders relation both immaterial and overly material. For Bloom, Molly is both the moon and two lumps of lard, a luminous sign and a corpulent Gea Tellus, a remote deity and a paragon of fleshy animality. It is Bloom's inability to see her without the telescope of idealization or a microscope for examining her biologically that causes Molly to experience him as "cold"; for him, Molly is always behind glass or partially screened from view.

Bloom's most typically idealized view of Molly is as a light in darkness, whether natural (the moon) or man-made (a lamp). Bloom's propensity to substitute a moon goddess for Molly is highlighted in "Circe," when his first actions as "serene and potent and very puissant ruler" of the realm (15.1472) are to choose his horse, Happy Copulation (Copula Felix), as grand vizier and to repudiate his former spouse in favor of "the princess Selene, the splendour of night," *"in moonblue robes, a silver crescent on her head"* (15.1504–10). In "Ithaca," Bloom enumerates the affinities between the moon and woman at some length, and his list includes

> her nocturnal predominance: her satellitic dependence: her luminary reflection: her constancy under all her phases, rising and setting by her appointed times, waxing and waning: the forced invariability of her aspect: her indeterminate response to inaffirmative interrogation: her potency over effluent and refluent waters: her power to enamour, to mortify, to invest with beauty, to render insane, to incite to and aid delinquency: the tranquil inscrutability of her visage: the terribility of her isolated dominant implacable resplendent propinquity: her omens of tempest and of calm: the stimulation of her light, her motion and her presence: the admonition of her craters, her arid seas, her silence: her splendour, when visible: her attraction, when invisible. (17.1160–70)

As the moon, woman is both sublime and dependent, inspiring love and lunacy; she stimulates, embarrasses, admonishes, terrifies, and attracts, dominating the nighttime sky of Bloom's desires. Although she is changeable, Bloom detects a consoling "constancy under all her phases."

Bloom's vision of Molly as moon goddess metamorphoses into a related apprehension of her as a less remote, man-made mechanism for illuminating darkness and mediating relations among men: a lamp behind a blind. Shortly after Bloom contemplates the similarity between woman and the moon, his attention is attracted to a "visible splendid sign" denoting "the mystery of an invisible attractive person," Molly (17.1177–78). The sign is produced by "the light of a paraffin oil lamp with oblique shade projected on a screen of roller blind" (17.1173–74). So seen, Molly represents a felicitous cooperation of extremes (light and shade) that like fortune is also blind, as blind as an image upon a screen. Joyce uses the image of projection not only to suggest that Bloom projects his desires onto Molly, and to show that he does it in "old high way of love"; Joyce also shows that in Bloom's world, Molly is the equivalent of a screen star: her light shines from above, projected onto the quotidian equivalent of a movie screen. Bloom's desire constructs her image as one that is visible to him, and as one that allows him to see other men by its light, but also as one that is not itself sighted; Molly as Bloom worships her was designed to be seen rather than to see. It is by the elevated light of Molly that Bloom and Stephen silently contemplate their similarities and differences "in both mirrors of the reciprocal flesh of theirhisnothis fellowfaces" (17.1183–84), and it is at this "projected luminous and semiluminous shadow" (17.1189–90) that they gaze when urinating together in the dark. Comically, Joyce suggests through this pragmatic united activity that the "union" of Bloom and Stephen is a waste. Relation between them is impossible because of the same mediating light that allows them to see one another in the dark—the luminous sign of desire.

For a brief moment, the apparition of Molly seems to bring Stephen and Bloom together, but what is less immediately apparent is that she—or what she represents to Bloom, the shared principle of glass, luminosity, and water—also drives them apart. For Bloom, Molly is both transparent and a screen for his desire; he has enshrined her, elevated her, placed her behind the glass of the window, offering her as "light to the gentiles." She is to him the principle of luminosity, but also of glassy aquacity, an aquacity that he, "waterlover, drawer of water, watercarrier," admires (17.183). As the moon, she has "potency over effluent and refluent waters" (17.1163–64); with water she shares qualities of independence, variability, profundity, persevering penetrativeness, buoyancy, and its variety of forms (see 17.185–228). Molly, as the combined principle of both luminosity and clarity, is for Bloom both mysteriously remote and utterly legible; she is ancient and ubiquitous and at the same time fragile; she is the glass in which he sees himself and through which he sees the world, the glass that now reflects his image as that of a horned cuckold. Joyce presents the clearness of glass and water and the luminosity of heavenly light as versions of one another, a conjunction that may be etymologically motivated. According to the *Oxford English Dictionary,* the word "glass" is related to "glow," especially in its relation to amber, which was believed to glow when rubbed (the word "lamp" has a similar etymology, deriving from a word meaning "to shine").

In his search for illumination, guidance, and self-knowledge, Bloom has tautologically constructed Molly in the way that patriarchal society at large constructs women: Molly is Jacques Lacan's *l'objet a;* she is both the source of and the answer to a man's desire. This is why it can be said that for Bloom, as for Lacan, "*la femme n'existe pas.*"[8] As a sign of Bloom's desire, Molly does not exist for him as a true other, but as the alienated parts of himself for which he continues to long. Bloom's nostalgic and quixotic desire is for a wholeness he imagines as lost, for the restoration of a once-integrated self that was always a delusion, which explains why his desire narcissistically precludes reciprocal relation. Stephen, in apparent contrast, perceives himself as having preserved his wholeness, and he holds onto his mental and emotional virginity with fierce integrity. He fears fragmentation, directing his fear at women and Jews as those he believes most likely to disintegrate or symbolically castrate him. His comic concern with whether Christ circumcised has retained his sacerdotal integrity (17.1203–5) and his sympathy with Shakespeare as a man unmanned by Anne Hathaway are just two examples of his anxiety over the prospect of self-division at the hands of women or Jews.

Stephen's hatred of water, glass, and women is an extension—perhaps a projection—of his fear of being fractured: he fears not only the fragility of glass and the power of water to overwhelm and inundate, but also the division (and multiplication) of the self through mirrored reflections. He declines Bloom's offer to wash on the grounds that he is "hydrophobe, . . . disliking the aqueous substances of glass and crystal, distrusting aquacities of thought and language" (17.237–40). Stephen's attitude is the shadow or mirror image of Bloom's; it exposes the gynephobia behind the idealization of women and confesses in code the interdependence of fear and worship, both in men's attitudes toward women and in the pervasive anti-Semitism that paradoxically haunts a religion in which a Jew is worshiped as one hypostasis of a threefold godhead. For Bloom, loss is retrospective, which accounts for his idealization of women, but for Stephen it is prospective, taking the form of gynephobia. When Stephen and Bloom are together, each senses the opposite temporal orientation of the other: Stephen hears "in a profound ancient male unfamiliar melody the accumulation of the past," and Bloom sees "in a quick young male familiar form the predestination of a future" (17.777–80). What neither male questions, however, is the assumption that the experience of loss—whether retrospective or prospective—is initiated by a woman.

A capsule illustration of how Bloom and Stephen diverge in their attitudes toward women as provocateurs of desire is apparent in their sharply different attitudes toward the mystery of women writing. Bloom's proposal for the ultimate advertisement is to seat two smartly dressed girls in a traveling, illuminated showcart, and to have them writing (17.608–10). For Bloom, the invisible writing of attractive girls is an irresistible magnet for curiosity and desire. Stephen, however, counters Bloom's implied assertion with a very different story about the "mystery" of what women write. He sets the stage for a dramatic revelation:

> Solitary hotel in mountain pass. Autumn. Twilight. Fire lit. In dark corner young man seated. Young woman enters. Restless. Solitary. She sits. She goes to window. She stands. She sits. Twilight. She thinks. On solitary hotel paper she writes. (17.612–17)

But when the woman hurries out and the young man rushes to read what she has written in a fever of curiosity, he finds that it is just the name of the hotel repeated over and over in different styles: "Queen's Hotel, Queen's Hotel, Queen's Hotel, Queen's Ho . . ." (17.619–20). Like Oscar Wilde in his most urbane guise, Stephen sees women as "sphinxes without secrets"; according to him, their thoughts are shallow, derivative, and not worth wondering about. Interestingly, though, unbeknownst to Stephen the woman's writing does have meaning for Bloom, a meaning that Bloom attributes to coincidence: she writes the name of the hotel where Bloom's father committed suicide. There *is* in fact a mystery attached to her writing, but neither she nor Stephen is in control of it; it is the mystery attendant upon the unpredictable recirculation of signs—sounds, words, and names.

Despite their differences about the iconic power of women, when Stephen and Bloom are conversing over cocoa they seem to discover numerous points of connection linking their Irish and Jewish heritages, respectively. They cite fragments of verse from Irish and Hebrew; they compare the written symbols of the two languages, writing selected characters on the penultimate blank page of *Sweets of Sin;* they pinpoint a common ancestor linking the Gael and the people of Israel, Fenius Farsaigh;[9] and they compare the desire to restore Zion with the "possibility of Irish political autonomy or devolution" (17.760). Bloom even begins to sing the Hatikvah, which is now the national anthem of Israel, but which was then a Zionist song expressing the hope for nationhood.[10] Immediately after these sparks of connection have been struck, Stephen strangely, inexplicably proposes to sing an anti-Semitic song, "Little Harry Hughes." As he listens to Stephen "chant in a modulated voice" this "strange legend on an allied theme" (17.795–96), Bloom's smile gradually fades and his feelings become mixed (17.830). Stephen's singing of the song is a hostile gesture that disrupts the atmosphere of mutual comprehension, triggering in Bloom memories of his daughter, and finally culminating in Stephen's refusal of asylum: "Promptly, inexplicably, with amicability, gratefully it was declined" (17.955). This song and its history symptomatically show how the connections between Bloom and Stephen are also points of rupture. They are divided by the same worry that unites them: womanhood, or as the narrator of "Ithaca" puts it near the beginning of the episode, by "a matutinal cloud (perceived by both from two different points of observation, Sandycove and Dublin) at first no bigger than a woman's hand" (17.40–42, referring to 1.248–83, 4.218–42).

The song Stephen sings to Bloom, "Little Harry Hughes," is on one level a sexist and anti-Semitic account of how a Jew's daughter seduces and decapitates an innocent Christian boy. The song recounts an incident in which little Harry Hughes fractures all of a Jew's windows while playing ball. The Jew's daughter comes out, dressed all in green, and takes a lethal revenge with her penknife. The background for the song, which Joyce undoubtedly knew from Sir Francis Child's annotations to *The English and Scottish Popular Ballads,* provides additional evidence of its anti-Semitic function. The source of the ballad is supposedly a record of the "crucifixion" of Hugh of Lincoln in 1255 by a group of Jews. Child unequivocally condemns the circulation of stories such as this one, which alleged that "the Jews crucified a boy every year, if they could get one," and which served as a pretense for plundering Jewish neighborhoods or expelling Jews from the country (such stories figured in the expulsion of Jews from Spain under Ferdinand and Isabella). Child asserts that "these pretended child-murders, with their horrible consequences, are only a part of a persecution which, with all moderation, may be rubricated as the most disgraceful chapter in the history of the human race." Child also gives numerous examples of more recent incidents in which Jews were accused of murdering children for their blood, accusations that prompted massive reprisals. One of the more chilling instances he cites was reported in the 1880s, when a Greek child was murdered by being punctured with thousands of pins. The boy's mother blamed the Jews for the crime, and the Christian population promptly went to the Jews' quarter and massacred more than six hundred Jews.[11]

Especially in view of the history on which it is based, "Little Harry Hughes" is an aggressively anti-Semitic ballad for Stephen to sing, especially after a pleasant discussion of the many correspondences between Irish and Hebrew. The implications of the ballad grow even more complex when the Jew's daughter is introduced as the perpetrator of the crime (replacing the Jew variously named Jopin, Copin, and Peitevin in the annals). Versions of the story are recorded in the *Annals of Waverly*, in Matthew Paris's *Chronica Majora*, and in the *Annals of Burton*. Although these versions give no mention of a Jew's daughter, several do emphasize the important role played by the boy's mother in prosecuting the Jews. It is the mother (who Child argues was known to be named Beatrice) who accuses the Jews of having crucified her son, and who is therefore responsible for their massacre. When the versions in the annals are superimposed onto the ballad versions and reset in the context of "Ithaca," it is clear that still another rivalry is fueling the destructive events that the story describes: a generational rivalry between the boy's mother and the young girl who "kills" him. Most versions of the ballad structure a tension between the "pure" Christian mother and the "deadly" Jewish daughter that is a thinly disguised battle for the body of the son. Although Stephen is probably not aware of this, his fear of the Jew's daughter is produced and sustained by his ambivalent identification with his (dead) mother.[12]

In the context of "Ithaca," "Little Harry Hughes" is not only about racial conflict and an intergenerational tension between women; it also superimposes these conflicts onto sexual antagonism in a way that highlights Stephen's own fearful prejudices. When little Harry Hughes breaks *"the Jew's windows all"* (17.807), it expresses Stephen's own instinctual animosity to "aqueous substances of glass and crystal" and to constructions of women as elevated (often luminous) sites of access to interior mysteries; it is a sexual as well as a racial assault, disguised (and defended) as boyish play. As elaborated by Stephen's commentary, the song expresses his private hope and fear that a young girl who seems to be "an apparition of hope and youth" (17.835) will unman and immolate him, with his reluctant consent. It is as if Stephen has sensed Bloom's hope of "a permanent eventuality of reconciliatory union between a schoolfellow and a Jew's daughter" (17.941–42), and he is trying to explain his ambivalence about such a possibility.[13] Some of Stephen's ambivalence is linked to his perception of Bloom as someone who has already undergone such castration at the hand of a Jew's daughter: the narrator's questions suggest that Little Harry Hughes is not only Stephen but also Bloom (in his role as Christ). The narrator first identifies the host (Bloom) as the "victim predestined" (17.838), which is the term Stephen used in his commentary to describe Little Harry Hughes, and describes him as "reluctant" and "unresisting" (17.841); the next question, however, associates him with the "secret infidel" who immolates Hughes (17.843). By implication, Bloom can play either role, depending upon whether he is acting as lover or father. As lover, he is—like Shakespeare—overborne (and "unmanned") by a girl; as father, he (like the mother of the Christian boy) is seen as controlling his daughter's actions, prompting her to unman any rival by reenacting upon his body the history that divides them (the crucifixion of Christ). Not only are Stephen and Bloom candidates for the role of Little Harry Hughes; even Hugh Boylan is written into the part, as his name suggests—he too is a "Boy" named "Hugh" who is seduced and overborne by an irresistible woman. In short, Little Harry Hughes can be seen as a cipher for all boy-men in their vulnerability to the wiles of women. As men see him, Little Harry Hughes is a totally innocent, unjustly martyred victim.

Although "Little Harry Hughes" may seem to designate the male Christian child rather self-righteously as the "victim predestined," the framing of the child as innocent victim is undermined by the fact that he instigates the steady escalation of events by breaking *"the jew's windows all"* (17.807). He treats his transgression as mere play, but glass, in "Ithaca," has come to take on more serious symbolic connotations as an image of how men construct women by emphasizing "the preordained frangibility of the hymen" (17.2212). Glass represents not only the precariousness of a woman's virginity but also the fragility of men's idealization of women. Seen this way, Hughes's breaking of the windows suggests not only that he has—literally or metaphorically—assaulted the Jew's daughter, but also that by so doing he has destroyed her father's idealized image of her. The act of breaking windows therefore triggers a series of reflections on what it means for males to fracture and refract glass, which is simultaneously a representation of a woman's sexuality and her idealized image. Joyce positions the song so that the gender conflict is superimposed onto a racial parable about how Christians distort the image of Jews; it is through this distortion, or breaking of *"the jew's windows all,"* that the Christian invokes his own immolation, to which he submits, "consenting" (17.837). The Jews' reprisal against the Christian licenses further reprisals, forging an unbroken chain of animosity along the lines of gender and race.

When Bloom meditates on the possible arguments for and against such murder, one of the motivations he considers is the "continued fraction of veridicity" (17.846). It is the fraction of veridicity that "Ithaca" simultaneously parodies and deplores. Joyce depicts the analytical fraction and multiplication of human beings as operations that are perpetually in process. He implies that such fracturings of truth solicit the immolation or castration or betrayal of the viewer by the viewed; they set up an inversion, conversion, and perversion, a "turning" that is epitomized in the color green worn by the Jew's daughter. The word *vert,* meaning both green and a turning, derives its different meanings from two different roots which have grown into the same word. The association of *vert* with green comes from the Latin word for green, *viridis* (which also contains within it the Latin words for man, *vir*). The use of *vert* to mean *turning,* as in *convert, invert,* and *pervert,* is related to both *verse* and *versatility.* It is tempting to associate such turning with *veritas,* which would produce truth as a series of turns, a perpetual movement of fracturings and reversals reflected in the con*vers*ation of question and answer that structures the chapter. Through "Little Harry Hughes," Stephen suggests that the fracturings or refraction of vision instigates a reversal that constitutes a kind of "poetic" justice, but that poetic justice is both predictable and mutually destructive. What Joyce offers in its place is the reciprocal unlikeness of a flesh mirror, which works through mutual recognition of sameness and difference rather than through constructing an other as clear, pure, and fragile in order to fracture it in a series repeated to infinity. An example of mutual recognition through difference is the moment when Bloom and Stephen regard each other as both familiar and strange, when they see in each other the outlines of the *"unheimlich":* "each contemplating the other in both mirrors of the reciprocal flesh of theirhisnothis fellowfaces" (17.1183–84). The lonely beauty of mutual acceptance is also expressed auditively as a musical echo, when Bloom, alone, hears "the double reverberation of retreating feet on the heavenborn earth, the double vibration of a jew's harp in the resonant lane" (17.1243–44). It is the fictional rendering of women as familiar—as personifications of home (Bloom)—and the equal and opposite rendering of them as hostile and alien (Stephen) that perpetuates disappointment, preserves narcissistic solitude, and encourages violence. Only a complex apprehension of the interdependence of the alien and the familiar allows us to imagine the union of image and echo, producing a possibility of reciprocal relation that must be constantly readjusted from person to person and moment to moment.

Driven by relentless mathematical operations, "Ithaca" constantly changes the material value of the self—both alone and in relation to other variables. Joyce described it as "written in the form of a mathematical cathechism" (*Letters I* 159), and the point of its numerical variability is to remind readers near the end of their journey of the endless recombinations that are not only possible but always in progress. When we read Bloom's name from left to right, with the letters always in the same order, we lose our apprehension that he is also, potentially, "Old Ollebo, M.P." (which contains the name "Bello" spelled backward), "Molldopeloob" (a moll, or whore, Molly's dope, and even Molly herself), and "Ellpodbomool" (his mother, Ellen's, "pod," or seedcase [17.405–9]). If we substitute Stephen for Bloom we can get "Stoom," and substituting Bloom for Stephen we can make "Blephen" (17.549–51). Bloom can be reduced by "cross multiplication of reverses of fortune . . . and by elimination of all positive values to a negligible negative irrational unreal quantity" (17.1933–35), and he can be projected 83,300 years into the future through the multiplication of his age (17.460). Bloom's sense of potential abundance is reflected even in the name of his daughter, Millicent, whose name is built out of the numbers one thousand and one hundred. Transformation is constantly taking place, often at an imperceptibly slow pace; even the coal that Bloom uses to light the fire contains "in compressed mineral form the foliated fossilised decidua of primeval forests" (17.260–61). In a universe wrought by constant complex calculations, some inaccuracy of apprehension is inevitable, as Joyce has been careful to show.[14] But a universe of constant movement demands a more flexible and precise attitude toward relation, as the narrator implies when interrogating Bloom's jealousy:

> Because a nature full and volatile in its free state, was alternately the agent and reagent of attraction. Because attraction between agent(s) and reagent(s) at all instants varied, with inverse proportion of increase and decrease, with incessant circular extension and radial reentrance. Because the controlled contemplation of the fluctuation of attraction produced, if desired, a fluctuation of pleasure. (17.2163–68)

The model of a mathematically varied conception of relation that Joyce introduces in "Ithaca" demands not only precision and flexibility, which produces pleasure, but also a willingness to experience "lonechill," "the cold of interstellar space," which the narrator exaggerates as "thousands of degrees below freezing point or the absolute zero of Fahrenheit, Centigrade or Reaumur" (17.1246–48).[15] The fear of loneliness makes space seem colder and emptier than it is, and it reminds Bloom of dead companions, which propels him toward Molly's animal warmth rather than her human complexity. And his last coherent thought after he has reverently climbed into bed, "the bed of conception and of birth, of consummation of marriage and of breach of marriage, of sleep and of death" (17.2119–21), is about the limitation of his activity by "various reiterated feminine interrogation concerning the masculine destination" (17.2294–95). Bloom himself wants to know, but not be known: like Turko the Terrible, he is *"the boy / That can enjoy / Invisibility"* (1.260–63). However, he would like for Molly's desire to be the inverse of his; he desires her to be transparent and legible, but he does not want to be subject to her interrogations and readings. After all, he experiences her desire to know his whereabouts as an infringement of his liberty.

As "Ithaca" segues into "Penelope," the downwinding narration gently chides its "childman weary, the manchild in the womb" (17.2317–18) for his childlike insistence on seeing women as something to be looked at, seen through, or gazed into in order to behold a reflected self-image, since the narrative has clearly shown that when men regard women as fragile, reflective, or transparent media, women are capable of powerful reprisal. The narrator at long last closes Bloom's weary eyes, and it is only when he is no longer looking—when he has begun his Arabian night voyages with "Sinbad the Sailor and Tinbad the Tailor and Jinbad the Jailer" (17.2322)—that Molly begins to speak. For the first time, we hear Molly instead of seeing her through the lens of someone else's desire or fear. Joyce presents her to us not as naked, as she would be if she were transparent and vulnerable (the embodiment of male desire), but as complexly and dynamically clothed, and therefore always partly closed[16]—and the reader is prodded to realize that he has never known her this way before. Like Stephen in "Proteus" (3.10), we learn that we must close our eyes to hear.

18

Molly's Heavenly Body and the Economy of the Sign

The Invention of Gender in "Penelope"

CHRISTINE VAN BOHEEMEN

Id cut them off him so I would (18.998–99)

Molly Bloom

THE CONFESSING VAGINA

Walter Kendrick's definition of pornography in *The Secret Museum: Pornography in Modern Culture* does not address the common qualities of a group of texts or images but rather their social determination.[1] Pornography is what is, or once was, censored. Today, toward the end of the century, we may have become immune to the violent novelty of Joyce's obsessively voyeuristic representation of Molly Bloom. Television and video clips bring sexual fantasy into the sanctity of the home, and familiarity has attenuated the shock effect of her polymorphous perversity. To us, "Penelope" seems hardly obscene; our criticism tends to emphasize the positive values of Molly's affirmation and her endurance.

Contemporary reaction was markedly different from our polite acceptance. In February 1922, in a letter from Trieste, Stanislaus referred to "Penelope" as an "obscene ignorant scrawl" (*Letters III* 191); the *Daily Express* of March 25 found itself aggressively confronted with "all our most secret and most unsavoury private thoughts"; the *Sporting Times* called it a "glorification of mere filth," ultimately "supremely nauseous," while *To-Day* concluded simply, "most disgusting."[2] We cannot but believe that the censorship of *Ulysses* reflected accepted middle-class norms. Even the otherwise unsqueamish Stephen Dedalus of *Portrait,* who saw menstruation as women's "strange humiliation" and "dark shame" (*P* 222), would have found the vivid depiction of the frothing stream of Molly's urine and menstrual blood intrusively garish.

In fact, my association of "Penelope" with pornography derives from Joyce himself. Not only did he give his heroine a name denoting "whore," and emphasize the association through Molly's allusion to Moll Flanders as a "whore,"[3] in September 1921, in a letter to Frank Budgen, he had asked his friend for "Fanny Hill's Memoirs (unexpurgated)" (*Letters I* 171).[4] This specific request allows me to shift from Kendrick's sociological perspective on *Ulysses* as pornography to the rhetoric of pornography. "Penelope" belongs to an ancient tradition of texts in which women speak the secret of their sexuality, revealing its truth, staging its "true" nature. Molly Bloom confesses her pleasure in sexual intercourse, describing her physical response even more emphatically than John Cleland's Fanny Hill. Linda Williams begins her study of pornography in film with pointing to Diderot's 1748 fable *Les byoux indiscrets* (*The Indiscrete Jewels*).[5] A genie tries to satisfy the sultan's wishes to hear women speak of their experience and gives him a ring which will facilitate this wish. The women will speak of their adventures loudly and explicitly whenever he turns the stone of this ring. The genie adds that the sultan should not be misled and believe that the women will speak with their mouths. The astonished sultan learns that they will instead use the organ which is most knowledgeable on the subject of sex, their "jewel." We might see "Penelope," in its sexual explicitness, as an avatar of *Fanny Hill,* spoken not through the mouth, but through Molly's "jewel."[6]

THE DARK CONTINENT OF FEMININITY

In the following pages, I shall focus on the implications of Joyce's obsessively voyeuristic use of sexual difference in relation to representation and its media.[7] My focus is the cultural-historical psychodynamic of his transformation of Molly Bloom into a "star," an image of transcendent and invulnerable physicality, and its place in the history of modernity. In fact, I shall argue that the last chapter of *Ulysses,* characterized by its unpunctuated flow of feminine speech, is the *locus* of the invention of what we now call "gender," the understanding of sexual difference as inscription and style, rather than an ontological essence. At the same time, my analysis aims at revealing the political unconscious of this move.

If Joyce participates in the drive to speak about sexuality, which, according to Foucault in *The History of Sexuality,* has been the discursive characteristic of Western culture of the last century, he is even more specifically engaged in the effort to lift the hem of the secret of femininity, which preoccupied not only pornographers but also medical science. From Charcot, through Freud to Lacan,[8] the impetus of the work of psychiatry seems to have been to fill in the map of the "dark continent" of female sexuality, to answer its riddle. Thus the mystery of the feminine became the motor of textuality. The enigma of a living body—in contrast to the generic convention of the detective story which makes a dead body the engine of the plot—provides the hermeneutic drive for medical science. It might even be argued that a certain train of philosophy plays upon its privileged insight into the "truth" of the feminine. Nietzsche's words in *Ecce Homo* suggest as much: "May I here venture the surmise that I *know* women? That is part of my Dionysian dowry. Who knows? Perhaps I am the first psychologist of the eternally feminine."[9]

Apparently, understanding this secret entailed social and cultural prestige, as it probably also did for Joyce—who had always wanted to become a medical doctor himself. Thus he praised his venerated example, Ibsen, for his portrayal of women: "he seems to know them better than they know themselves" (*CW* 64). When he read Jung's comments on *Ulysses,* he could not but have taken pride in this confirmation of his own intellectual stature and avant-garde importance: "The 40 pages of non stop run in the end is a string of veritable psychological peaches. I suppose the devil's grandmother knows so much about the real psychology of a woman. I didn't" (*Letters III* 253). Although Joyce vented his disappointment at Jung's unsmiling reading of *Ulysses,* he was eager to have this authoritative opinion of his superior insight broadcast. He must have taken it as a compliment.

More recently, we have come to query the truth value of this filling in of the map of the other. Woman as the defining limit, the horizon of man, will remain and cannot but remain behind the veil.[10] As Stephen Heath writes in *Men in Feminism,* "All representation, we know, is transferential. Representation is at once an image given, an argument made and a deputation established, a construction of object, me and other. Representation, to put it another way, includes my position, my desire and its vicissitudes."[11] This implies that "Penelope" is not to be seen as the presentation of an objective truth about female sexuality (not even of Nora Joyce, who supposedly sat for this portrait). The chapter is the projection upon the screen of representation of the unconscious content of the masculine mind. Seen thus, Joyce *ventriloquizes* his own notion of what femininity is through the textual construction of "Penelope."[12]

In this context it is interesting to note that Joyce, according to Budgen, complained loudly about the "invasiveness" of women, and their "perpetual urge to usurp all the functions of the male."[13] Here we see Joyce accusing women of what he practices himself: usurpation of the functions of the other sex. This transferential projection was possible, of course, owing to a natural, culturally accepted habit of colonialism, which treated women as occupied countries. It should not come as a total surprise, then, that the notesheets in the British Museum give us the following specification of Molly's "jewel": "her cunt, darkest Africa."[14] Thus the organ which "speaks" "Penelope" is not only obscenely sexual, it is also explicitly named as the dark continent—where dark probably does not only connote "unknown" or "uncharted" but also attractively "mysterious" in its foreignness. Joyce's orientalism does not only betray the ideological climate of the beginning of the century. In emphasizing the "foreignness" of Molly's jewel, he also underscored his own magical powers. He could make this "heart of darkness" speak. He could go down there and return unharmed like Orpheus.[15]

In *Playing in the Dark: Whiteness and the Literary Imagination,* Toni Morrison addresses the question, "How does literary utterance arrange itself when it tries to imagine an Africanist other?" Not only does she, like Stephen Heath quoted above, realize that "the subject of the dream is the dreamer," but she also provides a metaphor to denote the invisible structure of force lines which keeps representation in place by lending it naturalness, truth and lifelikeness. "It is as if I had been looking at a fishbowl—the glide and flick of the golden scales . . . the barely disturbed water . . . the tranquil bubbles traveling to the surface—and suddenly I saw the bowl, the structure that transparently (and invisibly) permits the ordered life it contains to exist in the larger world."[16] Morrison's "structure" is the way in which Americans "choose to talk about themselves" by means of a repression of an "Africanist presence." Adopting her metaphor, I would like to focus this discussion on the "structure" of "Penelope," the invisible lines of ideological force which hold the representation in place. The way the chapter chooses to talk about women is not merely in the service of masculine identity formation, but, as I hope to show, intended as proof that Joyce was "capable of engendering the cultural domain"[17] by giving the world an apotropaic image of femininity of such seeming naturalness and force that it could and would contain not only personal but also collective fears of extinction or castration in removing the sting of ontological difference.

THE THREAT OF AN ENDING

Like "The Dead," "Penelope" was a pivot in Joyce's work, but of a different order. If the completion of the short story facilitated the writing of *A Portrait* and *Ulysses,* the flow of "Penelope" prepared the relinquishing of the representational imperative in *Finnegans Wake.* Just as Picasso's *Les Desmoiselles d'Avignon* (1907), a representation of the female body (girls in a brothel), initiated the Cubist movement, "Penelope" marks the beginning of "the revolution of the word," the belief—still prevalent in French theory and writing of the sixties and seventies—that writing could transform the world, constitute a new reality. Just as Picasso permanently changed our perception of visual space, "Penelope" added a new dimension to linguistic representation, to the function of the literary sign.

What unites "The Dead" and "Penelope" is their status as endings. They are conclusions to a body of text. If the ending of "The Dead" is notoriously ambivalent, Joyce himself was ambivalent about the ending of *Ulysses.* He sent "Penelope" to the printer before the completion of "Ithaca," and wrote Harriet Weaver that the penultimate episode was "in reality the end of *Ulysses*" since "Penelope" has no "beginning, middle or end" (*Letters I* 172). Not only was Joyce unable to separate himself emotionally from his work and declare it finished (he kept reworking the text of *Ulysses* as long as possible), he was unable to name the ending the end, to think of it as final. It is as if finality generated a certain anxiety in Joyce and had to be precluded. It evidently was related to the threat of death. In one of his letters to Harriet Weaver he refers to the writing of "Penelope," concluding: "Bloom and all the Blooms will soon be dead, thank God. Everyone says he ought to have died long ago" (*Letters I* 168). It is as if in not ending he were keeping his protagonist alive, perhaps even at personal cost, as if Joyce identified with Bloom.

All his major works connect the end with the beginning, bending the linearity of narrative into the circularity of myth. "The Dead" finishes when Gabriel's consciousness merges with the dream of an Ireland unified by snow, awaiting a new dawn. *A Portrait* recirculates itself as textual system, enclosing experience and identity, in framing beginning and end as fairy tale and diary—anticipating the recirculation of *Ulysses* (through the initial and final "s" of "stately" and "yes") and that of *Finnegans Wake* (where the incomplete final sentence runs on to join the opening words). Joyce literally refuses to come to the point, as if the finality implied in ending a piece of writing entailed the finality of the writing self. If Leopold Bloom is accused of not being able to "put it out of sight" (12.1655), Joyce cannot "put it out": hand over his text to the publisher and declare it finished, as if concluding were *"un petit mort,"* "a little death" like the surrender to orgasm.

In fact, the figure of Molly herself seems identified with the threat of death in Joyce's unconscious. Ellmann relates Joyce's dream about Molly, in which she picks up a "snuffbox, in the form of a little black coffin" and throws it at Joyce with the words, "I have done with you too, Mr. Joyce" (*JJ* 549). Here the term "snuff" bears associations with extinction, while Molly's "box" also has the shape of a coffin. Looking at the other dreams Ellmann mentions in these pages, I am struck by how many are associated with death: female mourners, the imprisoning effect of boxes, the threat of extinction by "little beasts," women in black clothes. Joyce's dreams seem to breathe a general tone of anxiety about death and the feminine. The pattern of association fits Freud's suggestion that the fear of death should be seen as analogous to the fear of castration.[18]

In Ellmann's biography, these dreams are immediately followed by a parodic ballad which fuses the characters of Molly Bloom and Anna Livia as "flowers." Interesting to me is not only the extreme promiscuity which it attributes to Molly, but its conjunction with a refrain echoing the threat of death: "She's left me on the doorstep like a dog for to die" and "O Molly, handsome Molly, sure you won't let me die?" (*JJ* 550). The image of Molly Bloom seems composed of two ingredients, rampant sexuality and the threat of extinction. She has the power of Medusa to petrify those who behold her. In Greek myth, Medusa's horrible aspect was the result of her rivalry with Minerva, who turned her beautiful hair into writhing serpents and made her face gruesomely ugly. In our century, this image of a horrifying center surrounded by snakes has received a sexual interpretation. According to Freud, the horror of Medusa was the effect of the son's vision of the mother's genitals, and his realization that she was castrated; and this, in turn, implied that he might lose his penis too. Henceforth "the Medusa's head" was associated with the fright at the notion of castration, the fear of extinction. More recently, feminist critics, pointing out that the mother is not castrated and does not have an ugly wound where a penis ought to have been, have interpreted Freud's reading of the image of Medusa as the product of the masculine inability to recognize female otherness.[19]

The masculine repression of the possibility of difference is so strong, as Cixous and others suggest, that patriarchy prefers to be petrified by the self-projected threat of castration rather than relinquish its unique superiority. "Too bad for them if they fall apart upon discovering that women aren't men, or that the mother doesn't have one. But isn't this fear convenient for them? Wouldn't the worst be, isn't the worst, in truth, that women aren't castrated?"[20] It is not my intention to present another feminist deconstruction of the image of Molly as Medusa. What strikes me is that Freud should have reinterpreted the ancient myth, and given it a psychosexual reading, around the time of the publication of *Ulysses,* as if both Freud and Joyce, each in their own way, were addressing the problem of a threat of diminishment, the fear of death. But if Freud suggested that following Oedipus is the normal way for a boy to cope with castration anxiety, Joyce's solution is very different.

POISON CURES

If Joyce saw Molly Bloom as a castrating female who threatens to "cut them off him so I would" (18.998–99), not so different in the end from the other female monsters (a Calypso, a Siren, a Scylla, a Charybdis, or a Circe) who had beset his Odysseus, he also saw the figure of Molly as the instrument of escape from this threat of finitude. Writing to Budgen, he named "Penelope"—not the figure of Molly, but the text of the chapter—also "the clou" of *Ulysses* (*Letters I* 170). The French dictionary suggests that the word "clou" can bear several interpretations: we can see "Penelope" as the crowning moment of the novel, but also as the rivet of the text. Moreover, *"clouer"* means "to fix with a pointed instrument," such as a dagger (or a pen), and to reduce to silence. As "clou," "Penelope" may have more than just a textual or formal function. In addition to ending the narrative, the chapter may have the psychosexual task of nailing the threat of finality, "fixing" Medusa, and reducing to silence the castration fear generated by the act of ending. As "clou," "Penelope" transforms the anxiety related to a break in the forward flow (of ink rather than sperm) into a "passport to eternity" (Joyce's own words about "Penelope").

The text of *Finnegans Wake* suggests as much when it refers to "Penelope" toward the end of I.5 (in a passage suggesting the narrator's weariness at the objections which had been raised to the episode, while highlighting the difficulty of ending):

> and, eighteenthly or twentyfourthly, thank Maurice,[21] lastly when all is zed and done, the penelopean patience of its last paraphe, a colophon of no fewer than seven hundred and thirtytwo strokes tailed by a leaping lasso—who thus at all this marvelling but will press on hotly to see the vaulting feminine libido of those

> interbranching ogham sex upandinsweeps sternly controlled and easily repersuaded by the uniform matteroffactness of a meandering male fist. (*FW* 123)

In choosing the word "paraphe," Joyce denotes the chapter as the flourish added to a signature as a protection against forgery, labeling it as a supplement but also as a safeguard against imitation. The term "colophon" proves even more complex. The *Oxford English Dictionary* gives "tail-piece . . . often ornamental." Joyce seems here at his ambivalent best. "Colophon"—which may be read as "culophone" (*cul* is French for "arse") in another variant of the "speaking jewel"—conflates the last part of a book (added as supplementary afterword and ornamental flourish) with the nether part of the body. But Joyce's favorite etymological dictionary, *Skeat's,* tells us that "colophon" derives from the Greek word *kolophoon,* which has the meanings "pinnacle" and "crown," suggesting rather the opposite. Thus the obscene afterpiece of "Penelope" is also the crowning highlight of the text. In fact, the colophon is the part of the book which inscribes the name of its maker; so that in choosing this word Joyce denotes this "speaking jewel" as the "passport to eternity" of his writerly immortality. Moreover, this "tail-piece" (also piece of tail) reconfirms the superiority of his masculine authority. It is "tailed by a leaping lasso" in 732 phallic "strokes," thus containing the threat of a "vaulting feminine libido" through the agency of writing, of the "meandering male fist." In short, "Penelope," stylistically a "leaping lasso" of a chapter, is characterized as the triumph of the male writer's fist over feminine libido (personified as the unruly interlocking branches of the letters/trees of the Irish alphabet), constituting the imprint of its author's immortality. If there is a threat of death implied in the figure of Molly (or in femininity in general) it is—and can be—undone (in Joyce's psychodynamic) by his *writing the feminine.*

Placing this passage in its context in *Finnegans Wake,* it proves the conclusion of a long discussion of the *Tunc* page of the *Book of Kells,* where *Tunc* is the first word of the text of Matthew 27:38: *"Tunc crucifixerant XPI cum eo duos latrones"* (Then were there two thieves crucified with him). The Latin text differs from the English in that it clearly places Christ as object: "Then they crucified Christ and with him two thieves." Even this passage, so seemingly concerned with writing and the representation of writing, predicates itself upon a dead body in another conjunction of death and signification.

One lesson from these pages in *Finnegans Wake* is that the writing of the feminine in "Penelope" should not—or should no longer—be seen as the copying translation into language of a real female person or identity. Joyce here presents a Molly Bloom whose sexuality is already mediated through the letters of the Irish alphabet, which in turn are named after trees—those "interbranching ogham sex upandinsweeps" (an image which transforms the snakes on Medusa's head into phallic symbols). Joyce triggers a spinning process of reversals of nature and culture, matter and sign, which turns around the dead body of Christ or HCE. This implies that it must have been the act of writing "Penelope" itself which neutralized the threat of castration implied in her Medusan figure, and which made it possible for Joyce to move on from the feminine threat of death, which haunts all of *Ulysses,* to the triumphant display of the prostrate presence of an unthreatening masculine-paternal dead body in *Finnegans Wake.* The idea of a Molly Bloom was her author's "moly" (Odysseus's magic preservative guaranteeing survival).

THE FLIP OF THE COIN

One suggestion is presented by Joyce's notes for the chapter in the British Museum, where we read "she weaves a deathshroud for *R* {Laertes which is Ul. coronation robe}."[22] Penelope's texture can reverse itself from a tissue enveloping a corpse into the token of royal power. Is "Penelope" itself the magic integument, the agency which transforms the penis into the crowning scepter of a phallus? At any rate, "Penelope" as conclusion of the text would seem to function apotropaeically as a strategy of coping with ending in the act of ending.

Let us have a closer look at "Penelope" itself. The first thing which strikes me upon rereading it is its reversibility. On the one hand we have extreme obscenity: "if he wants to kiss my bottom Ill drag open my drawers and bulge it right out in his face as large as life he can stick his tongue 7 miles up my hole as hes there my brown part" (18.1520–22). This, as if by the flip of a coin, goes over into the lyricism of what Derrida has called Joyce's "perfumative":[23] "I love flowers Id love to have the whole place swimming in roses" (18.1557–58); "I was a flower of the mountain yes so we are flowers all a womans body yes that was one true thing he said in his life and the sun shines for you today yes" (18.1576–78).

This flipping reversal of tone and mood seems related to another reversal having to do with age and youth. Joyce places in Molly's mouth a string of criticisms of older or aging women—Mrs. Rubio, Mrs. Riordan, Josie Powell, Fanny McCoy, Mrs. Fleming "sneezing and farting into the pots well of course shes old" (18.1083). She calls them "old faggot," "ugly," "vain," "filthy bitches"; she notices the signs of age on their faces; she accuses them of the desire "to be born all over again" (18.1268). She worries that Bloom when he is out with "those medicals" will "imagine hes young again" (18.926) and behave like the "old fool" he is. She notices that Bloom may be experiencing a midlife crisis: "all men get a bit like that at his age especially getting on to forty he is now" (18.51). She also tries to deny her own approaching sexual redundancy: "I suppose he thinks Im finished out and laid on the shelf well Im not no nor anything like it well see well see" (18.1022–23). As is all of *Ulysses,* Molly's soliloquy is suffused with the presence of death: she mourns Gardiner, who died in the Boer War, and Mulvey, who may be dead or killed; she thinks of the late Paddy Dignam, Nancy Blake, Mr. Dillon, and especially her dead son, Rudy. She had "heard the deathwatch too ticking in the wall" (18.1309) and senses the encroachment of nothingness as she lies awake: "I suppose theyre all dead and rotten long ago besides I dont like being alone in this big barracks of a place at night I suppose Ill have to put up with it" (18.977–79). When a thunderclap wakes her, it is as if "the world was coming to an end" (18.136–37).

THE ASTRAL BODY

But just as obscenity can flip over to lyricism, so the cruel theme of old age and death can reverse into youth and poetry, making the text "Bloom," letting its hero return as a flower of rhetoric, immortal language, "the word that shall not pass away" because it is part of the endless diachronic chain of signification.[24] The central pivot in the text is the end of the fourth "period," where Molly herself makes a radical turn from evening to morning, old age to youth:

> but as for being a woman as soon as youre old they might as well throw you out in the bottom of the ashpit.
>
> Mulveys was the first when I was in bed that morning. . . . (18.746–48)

I am grateful to Hans Walter Gabler for restoring the period which concludes this middle sentence. Apart from the one following the final "Yes." (18.1609), it is the only one in the soliloquy, and it marks the pivotal point of symbolic reversal, where death turns into return and renewal, old age into blooming youth. In that sense its significance seems related to the large dot at the end of "Ithaca," which marks the *locus* of Bloom's escape as heavenly body from text and print into eternity and starry night. In fact, the period in "Penelope" is its counterpointing confirmation, the repetition which seals and guarantees authenticity, its "paraphe."

If anything, it is the turning, recirculating movement of "Penelope," which according to its author traces the figure of the lemniscate, symbol of eternity, spinning "like the huge earthball slowly surely and evenly round and round," which would seem the clou to the resurrective power of the text (*Letters I* 170). It is its "spinning" in this sense (and not its "weaving") which brings the text to Bloom as its finale, taking the sting out of finality and death, tracing a moebius strip of renewal, rewriting "conclusion" as "metempsychosis." The movement of the heavenly body, the star, makes the femininity of Molly prehuman and "posthuman" (*Letters I* 180). Thus "Penelope" incarnates what "Ithaca," in its association of Bloom and Stephen with stars and "interstellar spaces," has already claimed. "Penelope" is the performative of "Ithaca"'s constative.

Of course, on one level, this figuration of "Penelope" as instrumental symbol of eternal rebirth might be read as the displacing projection of Joyce's own concern with approaching middle age upon the screen of the text. He wanted the novel published on his fortieth birthday (as Molly's words suggest, the typical age for a midlife crisis at that time);[25] and *Giacomo Joyce* records such a crisis between late 1911 and mid-1914, when Joyce was beginning *Ulysses*. *Giacomo Joyce* ends its dream of renewal through the fountain of youth with renunciation: "It will never be. You know that well. What then? Write it, damn you, write it!" (*GJ* 16). At first sight this seems a different strategy of coping than that of "Penelope." *Giacomo Joyce* suggests sublimation, turning experience into art, drive into secondary process. But Joyce's words are not "write it down" in the sense of make a record of it, turn it into a story; he speaks of "writing it," where writing takes the place of experience and substitutes for it without the *Aufhebung* of sublimation. In this connection there is another aspect of *Giacomo Joyce* which draws our attention. If Joyce describes "Penelope" as a heavenly body, the earth turning indifferently and transcendently, there is in *Giacomo Joyce* a similar tendency to turn Amalia Popper into a heavenly body: "She speaks. A weak voice from beyond the cold stars"; she has "starborn flesh"; and she is figured as a transcendent image of inhuman evil—"A starry snake has kissed me: a cold nightsnake. I am lost" (*GJ* 15). The similarity in gesture, transforming Molly and Amalia into "stars," astral bodies, suggests that this metaphor has special meaning, even more so because Joyce, in the dream referred to above, recounts a long speech to Molly which he ends on an "astronomical" climax, while the ballad compares her to "this gaily spinning earth of ours."[26]

What Joyce may have had in mind with this "astral" quality is perhaps suggested in Jean Baudrillard's *America:*

> I went in search of *astral* America [*l'Amérique sidérale*] . . . the America of the empty, absolute freedom of the freeways, . . . of desert speed, of motels and mineral surfaces. I looked for it in the speed of the screenplay, in the indifferent reflex of television, in the film of days and nights projected across an empty space, in the marvelously affectless succession of signs, images, faces, and ritual acts on the road.[27]

This evocation of the detachment from origin, and the transcendent rootlessness of modernity (a system of signification without objective referent), which Baudrillard locates in the United States, suggests to me that Joyce's emphasis on the astral detachment of Molly Bloom and, in a literal sense, the "detachment" of "Penelope" from the body of the text, are in the first place related to this notion of modernity (and have to do with his understanding of and place in cultural history), rather than to the psychodynamics of Joyce, the fin-de-siècle man, and his primary focus on a type of Medusa. "Darkest Africa" here turns into "America, my new-foundland."[28]

PEN IS CHAMP

As several critics have suggested, Joyce's figuration of Molly Bloom seems implicated in the economy of fetishism.[29] The threat of castration is disavowed by the phallic attributes or qualities of the heroine. She seemingly denies the lack patriarchy projects upon women. As "heavenly body" or "star," Molly, indifferent, autonomous to the point that she can talk back to her creator and throw coffins at him, stands as "token of triumph over the threat of castration and as protection against it."[30] It is not accidental that in the notesheets and notebook V.A.2, Molly should be associated with Queen Victoria.[31] But we are here not talking about Molly Bloom, a character in a fiction or a representation of womanhood, we are talking about "Penelope," a chapter in Joyce's work, a piece of writing. It is not just the figure of Molly Bloom as the novelistic representation of a phallic mother which is pivotal, it is her soliloquy, Joyce's text. The question is: how can a chapter, or a piece of text *itself* function as fetish?

In his notes for "Penelope," Joyce had the habit of referring to Molly as "Pen."[32] He also did so in the text of *Ulysses* itself. In "Aeolus" the Ithacans vow "PEN IS CHAMP" (7.1034). In the passage following, the text refers to "a book . . . which [takes] away the palm of beauty from Argive Helen and hand[s] it to poor Penelope" (7.1038–40). Since Helen was not only the incarnation of beauty but also the instrument of massive death, the shift from Helen to Penelope as "PEN" suggests that Joyce transfers his authorial favor from the beauty of mortal and lethal flesh to textuality personified as the (phallic) instrument of writing. The "clou" of "Penelope" is that it shifts the object of representation from the image which it creates to the process of writing itself. It favors style over message, textuality and code over a referent, the sign over the body, the masquerade of gender over the ontological difference of sexuality. In addition to notes like "Pen-stupid" or "Pen-remote," we find "odyss of Pen," as if the "true" epic plot of *Ulysses* were not the homecoming of its hero, but the transformation of the heroine into a "pen"—mightier than the sword, and victorious over all the author's rivals. It is this "pen," as a maternal phallus, which produces the flowers of rhetoric which let the text "Bloom," and which generates the flow of textuality which in its endless circular movement guarantees immortality.

It seems to me that Joyce, in a curious but not incomprehensible displacement, transferred the libidinal cathexis from sexuality onto the flow of writing, or, at any rate, refused to channel his energy solely as sexuality. Writing and sex are closely related throughout the oeuvre. Stephen Dedalus thinks of sex as writing, as does Bloom ("Blank face. Virgin should say: or fingered only. Write something on it: page" [11.1086–87]), and in *A Portrait* the flood of language and soft liquid joy of sexuality are indistinguishable. The conflation of textuality and sexuality in *Finnegans Wake* needs no illustration. Even the pen is rendered in sexual terms as a "selfraising syringe and twin feeders" (*FW* 188). The notoriously obscene letters to Nora are not only the substitute for her absence, they are also an expression of the sexiness of writing itself.[33] Again I see a curious resemblance to Picasso, who, like Joyce, never underwent a sexual latency period during which "reaction-formations, or counterforces, such as shame, disgust and morality, are created in the mind."[34] For Picasso, painting *was* like sexual intercourse, the activity and rhythm of artistic expression would eventually even take the place of sexual expression; and a painting like *La Pisseuse* (1965), which gives the shocking frontal image of a urinating woman, is the impotent product of his declining years. If "Penelope" is Joyce's "Pen," this suggests the transferal of the *locus* of his vital selfhood from body onto text, the displacement of *cathexis* from the productivity of sperm to the activity of signifying, from penis to pen, from history to textuality, from the mortality of the body to the immortality of the signifier.

It is only from the position of such a displacement that the text can perform the metamorphosis of its author, penning his immortal body as words that "shall not pass away." In a chapter entitled "The Unstable Symbolic. Substitutions in the Symbolic: Fetishism," Kristeva suggests that the writer, "negating or denying the symbolic, without which he would be incapable of doing anything," "may imagine the thetic at the place of an object or partner. This is a fetishistic mechanism, which consists in denying the mother's castration, but perhaps goes back even further to a problem in separating an image of the ego in the mirror from the bodily organs invested with semiotic motility."[35] I have written elsewhere about the body image of Joyce's textuality;[36] my point here is that the only way to explain the transformative power of Joyce's textuality is to see it as an achieved perverse jump into the objectivity of the text, so foolproof that it can even allow what fetishism by definition cannot engage: the description of woman's genitals and the threat they represent. *Finnegans Wake* outperforms even "Penelope" in this respect. It drafts a geometrical ("geomatric" as earth-mother) diagram of the mother's vulva (*FW* 293), thus exhibiting the secret of her "darkest Africa" as if it were the map to John Donne's "O my America! my new-found land." Similarly, it is only from the point of achieved transcendence of the threat of castration that Joyce can refer to his novel as *Ulysses* or "your bitch of a mother" (*Letters I* 154).

But how did "Penelope" get transformed into the phallus? Let us focus on the text as if it were a female body. Everywhere around us we see that the phenomenology of the contemporary female body is its demarcation and division, in a subjection to its inscription as fetishistic sign. Whether in the theater, advertising, fashion, or striptease, "the playscript of erection and castration" is all-pervasive, as Baudrillard argues in *Symbolic Exchange and Death*. The high boots, the short skirt under a long coat, the horizontal line of the top of the stocking, belts, chains, the stripper's G-string—all suggest,

> the scenario is the same everywhere: a mark that takes on the force of a sign and thereby a perverse erotic function, a boundary to figure castration which *parodies* castration as the symbolic articulation of *lack,* under the structural form of a bar articulating two *full* terms (which then on either side play the part of the signifier and the signified in the classical economy of the sign). The bar makes a zone of the body work as its corresponding terms here. This is not an erogenous zone at all, but an erotic, eroticized zone, a fragment erected into the phallic signifier of a sexuality that has become a pure and simple concept, a pure and simple signified.[37]

We have moved outside of a world of real (even if sometimes invisible) presences into a realm where difference is no longer absolute or oppositional, but differential, relative, distributive, and variable, and where castration has lost its bite. Modern culture has substituted the stroke of demarcation between the elements in a sign system for the absolute dividing line of castration. Thus the significant difference, the formal division between signs, has replaced "the irreducible ambivalence," "the symbolic split (*écart*)."[38] Consequently, the mark or the bar dividing the body transforms the nakedness of the thigh not into the frightening absence of Medusa's face, but into sexual plenitude: "the naked thigh and, metonymically, the entire body has become a *phallic effigy* by means of this caesura, a fetishistic object to be contemplated and manipulated, deprived of its menace." What makes the fetish functional is this phantasmic cut that lends it the quality of erection, the bar which makes it autonomous and phallic. "Everything beyond this bar is the phallus, everything is resolved into a phallic equivalent, even the female genitals, or any gaping organ or object traditionally listed as a symbol of the feminine." Moreover, any part of the body may take on this structural function, provided it is "as closed and smooth as possible"; and this, to Baudrillard, is modern culture's "real castration" of the feminine.[39]

From this point of view the ritual of striptease is the slow ritual of transubstantiation of the body into a simulacrum of the phallus. Instead of revealing depth, a hidden truth, a "darkest Africa," the process of revelation proves a construction of a simulacrum. There is no depth. Every piece of clothing which falls increases the constructive transformation of body into phallic autonomy. Hence the striptease must not only be slow, the best stripper is herself as transcendently aloof and "astral" as a goddess, a star. From this perspective, Joyce's "detachment" of "Penelope" from the body of the text, his insistence that this chapter did not belong to its story, and that it be marked off by the dot at the end of "Ithaca," in combination with its oddly unpunctuated, "smooth and closed" textual structure, makes the detachment function as the horizontal mark of the top of the stocking. It transforms the chapter, and by extension the whole text, not into a symbol of lack or castration, but into the plenitude of the phallus.

In addition to calling it "the clou" to *Ulysses,* Joyce also called "Penelope" *"le dernier cri"* (*Letters I* 169). That he was fully aware that this expression related to the world of fashion is proved by its occurrence in *Ulysses* in the following context: "Henry and James's wax smartsuited freshcheeked models, the gentleman Henry, *dernier cri* James" (10.1215–16). Even if we did not know that in his later years Joyce pronounced himself more interested in women's clothes than their bodies, we might come to the conclusion that Joyce was not unaware of the fashionable implications of his fetishistic textuality (which substitutes the imaginary for the symbolic, as do cinema, glossy magazine, glamour photography, soap opera, and fashion show). Like Joyce's textuality (which, as I said, transforms the irreducible difference between the sexes into the difference between signs), fashion transforms body or clothing into sign or image, depriving it of presence or depth and linking it into an infinite chain of substitution. In calling "Penelope" *"le dernier cri,"* Joyce signals his consciousness of the modernity of his own procedure of understanding sexuality as if it were a system of signs. In using it in turn as a model of signification, creating an object which frustrates the search for symbolic meaning and depth, fixing the gaze to the glaring details of aesthetic surface, Joyce practices the opposite of what Carlyle, in *Sartor Resartus,* called his clothes philosophy. If Carlyle pointed to the illusion of appearance, Joyce emphasizes the truth of the image, the power and presence of appearance. It is as if Joyce, living in the age of the rise of cinema and the flowering of photography, saw his own textuality in the light of those art forms. The photographic image *is* its object of representation. It seems transcendently autonomous, freed from the conditions of time and space which constrict it. It does not "represent," like language, but it "re-presents." Its semiotic status of icon suggests that it does not resemble the world, but it *is* the world owing to the objectivity of its registration of a slice of life on a reel of celluloid. The extreme—obscene—realism of "Penelope" would seem to have a function in this constitution of the chapter as *"le dernier cri"*—a piece of literature which approaches the power of the new media owing to its seeming vividness and extreme concreteness of representation. In another way, too, the creation of the figure of Molly Bloom as "star" would seem related to the world of cinema. Like Marlene, Mae, Marilyn, or Madonna after her, Molly is an image of the transcendently feminine, a female (bitch) goddess, a fetishized heavenly body made to seem immortal by the optical illusion of the screen of representation. Even more pertinently perhaps, Molly incarnates the qualities of the consumer fetish, she is infinitely available (indiscriminatingly willing to engage any passerby in Joyce's ballad), and infinitely desirable (even to herself, so that she vicariously identifies with men who have the privilege of making love to such desirable creatures as women).

As we know, the fetish is an object of fascination in order not to see, not to look. In the Freudian version of fetishism, what had to be avoided was the look at the wound of castration. Almost a hundred years later, the occurrence of fetishism would no longer seem limited to individual psychopathology; modern consumer culture, turning everything into sign, skating on a void of meaninglessness without daring to look down, thrives on the fetish of the female body as its propelling mechanism. In relating Joyce to the new media technology of his age, I am trying to suggest that Joyce's fetishistic understanding of "Penelope" should be seen as the reflection of his crucial participation in this modernity of our century. Joyce invented "gender" long before philosophy caught up with it, or consumer culture and the power of the media made the re-inscription of sex as gender seem natural to us.

Concluding this reading of "Penelope," I shall refrain from attempting what we have seen Nietzsche, Freud, or Joyce do: claiming or summing up "the truth" of or behind "Penelope," a "truth" which Joyce might have missed or denied in his revisionary rewriting of sexual difference as a triumph over castration and a protection against it, or a "truth" which might return after repression has been lifted. As Baudrillard cautions,

> There is nothing behind this succession of veils, there has never been, and the impulse which is always pressing forward in order to discover this is strictly speaking the process of castration; not the recognition of lack, but the fascinating vertigo of this nihilating substance. The entire march of the West, ending in a vertiginous compulsion for realism, is affected by this myopia of castration.[40]

Instead of asking what is behind the veil, I would like to conclude with pointing to what is on this side of it, to the *effect* of Joyce's invention in "Penelope." The name of Molly Bloom has itself entered the chain of signification as signifier for adulterous dalliance. In an ad in the "Personal" column of the *New York Review of Books* of February 1, 1990, we note the following text: "YES I WILL YES. Male Molly Bloom, fit fiftyish, married, wants to go Blazes in afternoon with male friend. Box 165, 1202 Lexington Avenue, NY 10028." The affirmation of Molly's surrender to life, "yes I will," is here trivialized into consent to both extramarital and homosexual activity, motivated by midlife panic ("fiftyish" but "fit"). The name of Molly Bloom as a signifier refers to afternoon escapades; it functions here to bring together two men. We seem to be back at the familiar structure of kinship in which a woman (deprived of subjectivity) is only the *trait d'union* between male subjects. (The male bonding in "Eumaeus" and "Ithaca" prefigures this; and long before Joyce called his Penelope "Molly," the "molly house" was the eighteenth-century name for the clubs where sodomites met to have fun). Inadvertently, the advertisement in the *New York Review of Books* would seem to reveal the ideological structure of "Penelope," and the effect of rewriting sexual difference as gender. We have arrived at Toni Morrison's "fishbowl."

Notes

INTRODUCTION

1. See "Joyce and Homosexuality," a special issue of *James Joyce Quarterly* 31 (spring 1994), ed. Joseph Valente.

2. We would cite in particular *Molly Blooms: A Polylogue on "Penelope" and Cultural Studies,* ed. Richard Pearce (Madison: University of Wisconsin Press, 1994); Karen Lawrence, "Joyce and Feminism," in *The Cambridge Companion to Joyce Studies,* ed. Derek Attridge (Cambridge: Cambridge University Press, 1990); and "Feminist Readings of Joyce," a special issue of *Modern Fiction Studies* 35 (autumn 1989), ed. Ellen Carol Jones. Freud's influence is most recently evident in *Joyce: The Return of the Repressed,* edited by Susan Stanford Friedman (Cornell: Cornell University Press, 1993). Though neither feminism nor gender is the primary focus of this particular essay collection, both topics are omnipresent through the emphasis on the maternal. Lacanian readings of Joyce's works are provided in "Joyce Between Genders," a special issue of the *James Joyce Quarterly* 29 (fall 1991), ed. Sheldon Brivic and Ellie Ragland-Sullivan.

3. Robert Boyle, S.J., "Penelope," in *James Joyce's "Ulysses": Critical Essays,* ed. Clive Hart and David Hayman (Berkeley: University of California Press, 1974), 418.

"A LITTLE TROUBLE ABOUT THOSE WHITE CORPUSCLES"

1. Peter Middleton, *The Inward Gaze: Masculinity and Subjectivity in Modern Culture* (New York: Routledge, 1992), 51, 48.

2. Of course I do not wish to argue that Mulligan *is* Gogarty, but it seems worth noting that the persistent theme of Ulick O'Connor's biography, *Oliver St. John Gogarty* (London: Mandarin, 1963), is how his subject made himself into the current paradigm of what a "real man" was. I select, almost at random, one excerpt: "He was fastidious about his clothes on the track [as a bicyclist] as he was off of it. He had his cycling singlet, with full-length sleeves which were compulsory in those days, made to order by a tailor and it fitted him like a glove. . . . His racing shoes were scarlet in colour to match the pedal blocks on which the shoes were fitted" (25).

3. Kimberly J. Devlin, "Castration and Its Discontents: A Lacanian Approach to *Ulysses,*" *James Joyce Quarterly* 29 (fall 1991): 132.

4. Garry Leonard, *Reading "Dubliners" Again: A Lacanian Perspective* (Syracuse: Syracuse University Press, 1993), 37.

5. Judith Butler, *Gender Trouble* (New York: Routledge, 1990), 3.

6. Jacques Lacan, *Feminine Sexuality,* ed. Juliet Mitchell and Jacqueline Rose (New York: Norton, 1982), 159.

7. Wayne R. Dynes, *Encyclopaedia of Homosexuality: Volume I* (New York: Garland

Press, 1990), 189. As Cheryl Herr and others have made clear, Joyce was familiar with the music halls in Dublin and London, as well as the cabarets in Paris (*Joyce's Anatomy of Culture* [Urbana: University of Illinois Press, 1986]).

8. Carole-Anne Tyler, "Boys Will Be Girls: The Politics of Gay Drag," in *Inside/Out: Lesbian Theories, Gay Theories,* ed. Diana Fuss (New York: Routledge, 1991), 32.

9. Susan Sontag, "Notes on Camp," in *Against Interpretation* (New York: Farrar, Straus, & Giroux, 1966), 288.

10. Andrew Ross, *No Respect: Intellectuals and Popular Culture* (New York: Routledge, 1989), 139.

11. For a more complete discussion of how Lacan views the relationship between history and identity, and how Stephen seems to ruminate on similar issues in "Nestor," see my essay, "Joyce and Lacan: The Twin Narratives of History and His[S]tory in the 'Nestor' chapter of *Ulysses,*" in *Joyce in Context,* ed. Vincent J. Cheng and Timothy Martin (Cambridge: Cambridge University Press, 1992), 170–83.

12. Dynes, *Encyclopaedia of Homosexuality,* 190.

13. Butler, *Gender Trouble,* 29.

14. Oscar Wilde, *The Picture of Dorian Gray* (New York: Norton, 1988), 10.

15. Butler, *Gender Trouble,* 9–10.

16. Devlin, "Castration and Its Discontents," 133.

17. Wayne Kostenbaum, *Doubletalk: The Erotics of Male Literary Collaboration* (New York: Routledge, 1989), 3.

18. Richard Dellamora, *Masculine Desire: The Sexual Politics of Victorian Aestheticism* (Chapel Hill: University of North Carolina Press, 1990), 1, 5.

19. Elizabeth Grosz, *Jacques Lacan: A Feminist Introduction* (New York: Routledge, 1990), quoted (but not cited) on the frontispiece.

20. Dellamora, *Masculine Desire,* 7.

21. Ibid.

22. Ibid., 69.

23. Dynes, *Encyclopaedia of Homosexuality,* 521.

GENDERS OF HISTORY IN "NESTOR"

1. Charlotte Perkins Gilman, *The Yellow Wallpaper* (New York: The Feminist Press, 1973), 22, 30.

2. Homer, *The Odyssey,* trans. Robert Fitzgerald (New York: Doubleday, 1963), 192.

3. Jacques Derrida, *Specters of Marx: The State of the Debt, the Work of Mourning, and the New International,* trans. Peggy Kamuf (New York: Routledge, 1994), 74.

4. On the female personification of Ireland, see Elizabeth Butler Cullingford, "'Thinking of Her . . . as . . . Ireland': Yeats, Pearse and Heaney," *Textual Practice* 4 (1990): 1–21.

5. "The Rose of the World," in *The Poems of W. B. Yeats,* ed. Richard J. Finneran (New York: Macmillan, 1983), 36.

6. "Lullaby," in Finneran, *The Poems of W. B. Yeats,* 264–65.

7. For a sustained discussion of the artist's oedipal relation to the maternal body, see Christine Froula, "History's Nightmare, Fiction's Dream: Joyce and the Psychohistory of *Ulysses,*" *James Joyce Quarterly* 28 (summer 1991): 857–72. Froula finds special sig-

nificance in Joyce's invention of Molly Bloom, his "wish not to love a woman in all the specificity of her real, historical, human otherness, but to *be,* to act out, the female repressed within his masculine self; to be himself his own 'mother' and 'other'—in writing, because not in history" (868–69). Although it is beyond the scope of an essay focused on "Nestor," Joyce's use of Molly and her monologue as a ground which, outside the time and structure of the rest of *Ulysses,* somehow sustains and justifies the novel, is not unrelated to Stephen's meditation on the nurturing maternal body that is ultimately trampled by the son.

8. Quoted in Alessandro Francini Bruni, "Joyce Stripped Naked in the Piazza," in *Portraits of the Artist in Exile: Recollections of James Joyce by Europeans,* ed. Willard Potts (Seattle: University of Washington Press, 1979), 29.

9. Robert Spoo, *James Joyce and the Language of History: Dedalus's Nightmare* (New York: Oxford University Press, 1994), ch. 1, 4.

10. Derrida discusses the historico-philosophical valences of spirit, specter, and nightmare in the writings of Hegel, Marx, and Max Stirner, in *Specters of Marx,* especially 99–124 and 136–37.

11. *Ghosts,* in *The Collected Works of Henrik Ibsen,* trans. William Archer (1906; reprint, London: William Heinemann, 1909), 7:225.

12. See Robert Spoo, "'Nestor' and the Nightmare: The Presence of the Great War in *Ulysses,*" in *Joyce and the Subject of History,* ed. Mark Wollaeger, Victor Luftig, and Robert Spoo (Ann Arbor: University of Michigan Press, 1996).

13. *The Letters of Henry James,* ed. Percy Lubbock (London: Macmillan, 1920), 2:398, 406.

14. "The Mark on the Wall," reprinted in *The Complete Shorter Fiction of Virginia Woolf,* ed. Susan Dick (New York: Harcourt Brace Jovanovich, 1989), 86, 88.

15. Terry Eagleton, *Literary Theory: An Introduction* (Oxford: Blackwell, 1983), 30.

16. See Hayden White, "The Burden of History," in *Tropics of Discourse: Essays in Cultural Criticism* (Baltimore: Johns Hopkins University Press, 1978), 33.

17. W. J. McCormack, "Nightmares of History: James Joyce and the Phenomenon of Anglo-Irish Literature," in *James Joyce and Modern Literature,* ed. W. J. McCormack and Alistair Stead (London: Routledge & Kegan Paul, 1982), 90.

18. Derek Attridge, "Joyce, Jameson, and the Text of History," in *James Joyce 1: "Scribble," genèse des textes,* ed. Claude Jacquet (Paris: Minard, 1988), 184.

19. S. L. Goldberg, *The Classical Temper: A Study of James Joyce's "Ulysses"* (New York: Barnes & Noble, 1961), 198.

20. Giorgio Melchiori, "Joyce, Eliot and the Nightmare of History," *Revue des langues vivantes* 40 (1974): 598.

21. Mircea Eliade, *The Myth of Eternal Return or, Cosmos and History,* trans. Willard R. Trask (1954; reprint, Princeton: Princeton University Press, 1971), 153. I refer also to Joseph Frank's famous essay, "Spatial Form in Modern Literature" (1945), reprinted in *The Widening Gyre* (New Brunswick: Rutgers University Press, 1963).

22. Vincent John Cheng, *Shakespeare and Joyce: A Study of "Finnegans Wake"* (University Park: Pennsylvania State University Press, 1984), 22.

23. Colin MacCabe, "An Introduction to *Finnegans Wake,*" in *James Joyce: New Perspectives,* ed. Colin MacCabe (Bloomington: Indiana University Press; Sussex: The Harvester Press, 1982), 35.

24. Froula, "History's Nightmare, Fiction's Dream," 857.

25. Spoo, *James Joyce and the Language of History,* 88.

26. Cheryl Herr, *Joyce's Anatomy of Culture* (Urbana: University of Illinois Press, 1986); R. B. Kershner, *Joyce, Bahktin, and Popular Literature: Chronicles of Disorder* (Chapel Hill: University of North Carolina Press, 1989); and Stephen Watt, *Joyce, Casey, and the Irish Popular Theater* (Syracuse: Syracuse University Press, 1991).

27. Ernest Jones, *On the Nightmare* (1931; reprint, London: Hogarth Press, 1949), 47–75.

28. Stephen uses "beldam," significantly, in the sense of "mother." It also has the obsolete sense of "grandmother."

29. For an extended discussion of Stephen's attitudes toward women and his use of Anne Hathaway in his Hamlet theory, see Jeri Johnson, "'Beyond the Veil': *Ulysses,* Feminism, and the Figure of Woman," in *Joyce, Modernity, and Its Mediation,* ed. Christine Van Boheemen (Amsterdam: Rodopi, 1989), 201–28.

30. Jones, *On the Nightmare,* 276.

31. "I hear an army charging upon the land" was clearly influenced by Yeats's poem, "He bids his Beloved be at Peace" (1899), which begins, "I hear the Shadowy Horses, their long manes a-shake, / Their hoofs heavy with tumult, their eyes glimmering white" (Finneran, *The Poems of W. B. Yeats,* 62). Like Joyce's, this poem about the "Horses of Disaster" records, with implicit punning, an experience of nightmare.

32. *Joyce's Notes and Early Drafts for "Ulysses": Selections from the Buffalo Collection,* ed. Phillip Herring (Charlottesville: University Press of Virginia, 1977), 244.

OLD WIVES' TALES AS PORTALS OF DISCOVERY IN "PROTEUS"

1. Eileán Ní Chuilleanáin, *The Second Voyage* (Dublin: Gallery Press, 1986), 14.

2. Robert Edward Hurley, "The 'Proteus' Episode of James Joyce's *Ulysses:* A Study" (Ph.D. diss., Columbia University, 1963).

3. Thomas Molnar, *God and the Nature of Reality* (New York: Basic Books, 1973), 198–209.

4. *Joyce's Notesheets in the British Museum,* ed. Phillip Herring (Charlottesville: University Press of Virginia, 1972), 455.

5. Phyllis Rooney, "Gendered Reason: Sex Metaphor and Conceptions of Reason," unpublished essay, 1989.

6. Bonnie Kime Scott, *Joyce and Feminism* (Bloomington: Indiana University Press, 1984); Scott, *James Joyce* (Atlantic Highlands: Humanities Press International, 1987); Scott, "Feminist Approaches to Teaching *Ulysses,*" in *Approaches to Teaching Joyce's "Ulysses,"* ed. Kathleen McCormick and Erwin R. Steinberg (New York: Modern Language Association of America, 1993), 49–58.

7. Homer, *The Odyssey,* trans. Albert Cook (New York: Norton, 1974), 51.

8. Vrinda Dalmiya and Linda Alcoff, "Are 'Old Wives' Tales' Justified," in *Feminist Epistemologies,* ed. Linda Alcoff and Elizabeth Potter (New York: Routledge, 1993), 217.

9. *Plato: Theaetetus,* trans. John McDowell (Oxford: Clarendon Press), 149a-151d. I am indebted to David G. Stern for directing my attention to Joyce's use of the *Theaetetus.*

10. Note that when Stephen seeks the ultimate word, he does so as part of an imaginary scene involving an unknown woman: "She, she, she. What she?" (3.426), Stephen asks himself. If we were to attend to the phonotextual side of this episode, the repeated word "she" might be mistaken as the Irish word designating the world of fairy, "sidhe"

(pronounced *shee*). In terms of its oral dimension, then, the episode thus leads us toward alternative forms of knowing.

11. Jean Towler and Joan Bramall, *Midwives in History and Society* (London: Croom Helm, 1986), 35–37. It is worth noting here that the counterpoint to the midwife's role in Irish traditional life is the laying out of the dead body under the sound of women's ritual keening, a staple of "soundsense" in *Finnegans Wake;* in many ways, "Proteus" reaches out the *Wake.*

12. Jo Murphy-Lawless, "The Silencing of Women in Childbirth or Let's Hear It from Bartholomew and the Boys," *Women's Studies International Forum* 11 (1988): 293–98. For a more celebratory view of the work done at the Rotunda and for an overview of maternity care in Dublin, see Davis Coakley, *The Irish School of Medicine: Outstanding Practitioners of the 19th Century* (Dublin: Town House, 1988), 115.

13. Murphy-Lawless, "The Silencing of Women in Childbirth," 295–96.

14. See the chapter on lying-in hospitals in Coakley, *Irish School of Medicine.* Another useful resource on the history of maternity care in Ireland is John Fleetwood's *The History of Medicine in Ireland* (Dublin: Skellig Press, 1983).

15. Scott, "Feminist Approaches to Teaching *Ulysses,*" 56.

16. Luce Irigaray, *Marine Lover of Friedrich Nietzsche,* trans. Gillian C. Gill (New York: Columbia University Press, 1991), 3.

17. Irigaray, *Marine Lover,* 11–13, 20.

18. Ibid., 28, 31, 37.

MILLY, MOLLY, AND THE MULLINGAR PHOTO SHOP

1. This article, which originally appeared in Dickens' magazine *Household Words* in 1853, is reprinted in *On Photography: A Source Book of Photo History in Facsimile,* ed. Beaumont Hall (Watkins Glen, N.Y.: Century House, 1956), 82–90. Hall notes, "It is not known who wrote [the article]; if it is not from the pen of Dickens himself, it is worthy of it" (82).

2. Michael Seidel, *Epic Geography: James Joyce's "Ulysses"* (Princeton: Princeton University Press, 1976), 151.

3. Michel Foucault, *Power/Knowledge: Selected Interviews and Other Writing: 1972–1977,* ed. Colin Gordon (New York: Pantheon, 1980).

4. Michel de Certeau, *The Practice of Everyday Life,* trans. Steven Rendall (Berkeley: University of California Press, 1984), 70.

5. Ibid., 48.

6. After I presented a shorter version of this essay as a lecture in Seville in June 1994, Murray Beja told me he was looking forward to my work on Leopold Bloom. His point is well taken: masculinity is similarly constructed in *Ulysses* and can require similar tactics of disruption if old patterns are not to be repeated. I've chosen in this essay to focus on the daughter, the figure only textually present in "Calypso"—in her letter and card—and to foreground what Marianne Hirsch calls "the mother/daughter plot," as it is discernible primarily in "Calypso" and "Penelope" (*The Mother/Daughter Plot: Narrative, Psychoanalysis, Feminism* [Bloomington: Indiana University Press, 1989]). I realize that this kind of writing is not balanced or inclusive. I see it instead as an act of restitution, intended to revise or challenge or add to our understanding of conventional plot structures (and conventional ways of reading) in which men are seen as central agents while

women serve as markers of male achievement—either their obstacle or their desired object.

7. Walter Benjamin, "The Work of Art in the Age of Mechanical Reproduction," in *Illuminations* (New York: Schocken, 1968), 220. As Benjamin argues, "technical reproduction can put the copy of the original into situations which would be out of reach for the original itself. . . . And in permitting the reproduction to meet the beholder or listener in his own particular situation, it reactivates the object reproduced. These two processes lead to a tremendous shattering of tradition . . ." (221).

8. This gesture contrasts with one of Bloom's salient memories of Milly's adolescence: "On the duke's lawn, entreated by an English visitor, she declined to permit him to make and take away her photographic image (objection not stated)" (17.876–78). Did she (a "tomboy" [6.87]) originally resist this inscription as image, object of the male gaze?

9. Hirsch points out, "western culture represents the mother's position in a familial and social configuration [as one in] which women carry children in their bodies, give birth to them, and then relinquish them to a world in which they themselves are powerless to determine the course of their children's development" (*The Mother/Daughter Plot,* 36).

10. Nancy Chodorow, *The Reproduction of Mothering: Psychoanalysis and the Sociology of Gender* (Berkeley: University of California Press, 1978), 7.

11. See especially Melanie Klein, *The Psychoanalysis of Children* (London: Hogarth Press, 1932); D. W. Winnicott, *The Family and Individual Development* (New York: Basic Books, 1965); and D. W. Winnicott, *The Maturational Processes and the Facilitating Environment* (New York: International Universities Press, 1965).

12. Chodorow, *The Reproduction of Mothering,* 50, 78, 83. In our own time, it is easy to challenge Chodorow by observing that many men play nurturing roles in the lives of their infants; but since her generalization by-and-large describes the organization of Dublin family life in 1904, I will simply let it stand in this context.

13. Chodorow, *The Reproduction of Mothering,* 38, 39, 86.

14. It is also interesting—extraordinary really—that in the recent book *Molly Blooms: A Polylogue on "Penelope" and Cultural Studies,* ed. Richard Pearce (Madison: University of Wisconsin Press, 1994), not one of the twelve essays about Molly is about mothering. The word "mother" does not even appear in the index.

15. See Sandra Gilbert, "Life's Empty Pack: Notes toward a Literary Daughteronomy," in *Daughters and Fathers,* ed. Linda Boose and Betty Flowers (Baltimore: Johns Hopkins University Press, 1989), 256–77.

16. Adrienne Rich, *Of Woman Born* (New York: Norton, 1976), 225–26.

17. Michel de Certeau argues, "The wild is transitory. . . . it alters a place (it disturbs), but it does not establish a place" (*The Practice of Everyday Life,* 155).

18. For an excellent reflection on the relation of photographs to death (and in particular the death of mothers), see Roland Barthes, *Camera Lucida* (New York: Hill & Wang, 1981).

19. de Certeau, *The Practice of Everyday Life,* 26, 30, 32, 40. De Certeau is referring to the Renault automobile factory in Billancourt (on the outskirts of Paris), which employs many immigrants from North Africa.

20. In thinking about this furtive commerce between lovers in this section, it is especially interesting to recall that the name *calypso* is derived from the Greek *kalupto* meaning "I hide, veil." As Stuart Gilbert further notes, "the Semitic root s-p-n-I is the

exact translation of the Greek *kalupto.* I-spania, Spain is the *land-of-the-hiding-place*" (*James Joyce's "Ulysses"* [New York: Vintage, 1952], 142).

21. All of the Blooms, including Leopold, engage in these practices, and it is here, in secrets and in clandestine writing between lovers, that we can see a male version of the resistance that I call attention to in the representation of Molly and Milly. In "Calypso," Bloom dreams of the Orient; he checks the card in his hatband that plays a part in his secret correspondence; he furtively watches the nextdoor girl on his errand outside the house; he hides his anxiety about Boylan.

22. As Carroll Smith-Rosenberg argues, "groups who experience themselves as marginal to or inferior within a social structure, or who are in revolt against that structure . . . will seize upon the body as a vehicle expressive of their revolt against structure. . . . All had enveloped the body politic within the carnal body" (*Disorderly Conduct: Visions of Gender in Victorian America* [New York: Oxford University Press, 1985], 49, 51).

23. This translation of *The Odyssey* that I am re-gendering is quoted in Gilbert, *James Joyce's "Ulysses,"* 140.

SKINSCAPES IN "LOTUS-EATERS"

1. *James Joyce in Padua,* trans. and ed. Louis Berrone (New York: Random House, 1977), 21.

2. *The Odyssey of Homer,* trans. Richard Lattimore (New York: Harper and Row, 1975), 140.

3. See Richard le Gallienne, "The Boom in Yellow," in *Prose Fancies* (Second Series) (London: John Lane, 1896), 79–89; reprinted in *Aesthetes and Decadents of the 1890's,* ed. Karl Beckson (Chicago: Academy Chicago Publishers, 1982), 128–33.

4. The Gilbert and Linati schema are reproduced in *Ulysses,* ed. Jeri Johnson (Oxford: Oxford University Press, 1993), 734–39.

5. Sigmund Freud, *The Interpretation of Dreams,* in *The Complete Psychological Works,* trans. James Strachey (London: Hogarth Press, 1953–74), 5:375–76.

6. "Castration" is a symbol in the Linati schema; "Eunuchs" a correspondence in the Gorman plan.

7. Don Gifford notes that Edward Payson Vining (1847–1920), in *The Mystery of Hamlet; An Attempt to Solve an Old Problem* (Philadelphia, 1881), theorized that Hamlet was a woman, educated and dressed as a man in a plot to secure the throne of Denmark for her family's lineage. The idea that Hamlet's sex was the reason why Ophelia killed herself, however, is pure Bloom. See Don Gifford with Robert J. Seidman, *"Ulysses" Annotated: Notes for James Joyce's "Ulysses"* (Berkeley: University of California Press, 1988), 88, 225.

8. Freud, "The 'Uncanny,'" in *Complete Psychological Works,* 17:235.

9. See *"Ulysses": A Facsimile of Placards for Episodes 1–6,* ed. Michael Groden (New York: Garland, 1978), 85, 90, 91, 180, 187, 199.

10. Paul Valéry, *L'Idée fixe, ou Deux hommes à la mer* (1932), in *Oeuvres,* Pleiade Edition, ed. Jean Hytier (Paris: Gallimar, 1960), 2:215.

11. See Didier Anzieu, *The Skin Ego,* trans. Chris Turner (New Haven: Yale University Press, 1989), 14–15.

12. Valéry, *L'Idée fixe,* 216: "marrow, brain, all these things we require in order to

feel, to suffer, to think . . . are inventions of the **skin** . . . . We burrow down in vain, doctor, we are . . . ectoderm."

13. Anzieu, *Skin Ego,* 9.

14. Freud, *The Ego and the Id,* in *Complete Psychological Works,* 19:26.

15. Ashley Montagu, *Touching: The Human Significance of the Skin* (New York: Columbia, 1971), especially 5–25.

16. See Montagu, *Touching,* 7; and Barrie M. Biven, "The Role of Skin in Normal and Abnormal Development with a Note on the Poet Sylvia Plath," *The International Review of Psycho-analysis* 9 (1982): 213.

17. Sylvia Plath, "Tulips," discussed by Biven, "The Role of Skin," 217.

18. Anzieu, *Skin Ego,* 31–46; and Victor V. Weizsacher, "Dreams in Endogenic *Magersucht,*" in *Evolution of Psychoanalytic Concepts: Anorexia Nervosa: A Paradigm,* ed. M. Ralph Kaufman et al. (London: Hogarth Press, 1964), 189–90.

19. Plath, "Face Lift," cited by Biven, "The Role of Skin," 218.

20. See Andrew Strathern, "Why Is Shame on the Skin?," *Ethnology* 14 (1975): 347–56.

21. Thomas Carlyle, *Sartor Resartus* (1833–34), ed. Kerry McSweeney and Peter Sabor (Oxford: Oxford University Press, 1987), 48.

22. Terence S. Turner, "The Social Skin," in *Not Work Alone: A Cross-Cultural View of Activities Superfluous to Survival,* ed. Jeremy Cherfas and Roger Lewin (London: Temple Smith, 1980), 136–37.

23. See Emmanuel Levinas, *Ethics and Infinity: Conversations with Philippe Nemo,* trans. Richard A. Cohen (Pittsburgh: Duquesnes University Press, 1985), 86; and Levinas, "Language and Proximity," in *Collected Philosophical Papers,* trans. Alphonso Lingis (Dordrecht: Marinus Nijhoff Publishers, 1987), 120–21.

24. See Marilyn Strathern, "The Self in Self-Decoration," *Oceania* 49 (1979): 241–57.

25. Alfred Gell, *Wrapping in Images: Tattooing in Polynesia* (Oxford: Clarendon Press, 1993), 24.

26. Cited by Joseph O'Brien, *"Dear, Dirty Dublin": A City in Distress, 1899–1916* (Berkeley: University of California Press, 1982), 103.

27. Cited by James Delaney, *James Joyce's Odyssey: A Guide to the Dublin of "Ulysses"* (London: Hodder and Stoughton, 1981), 50.

28. H. G. Wells, "James Joyce," *New Republic* 10 (March 10, 1917): 159.

29. O'Brien, *"Dear, Dirty Dublin,"* 110–12, 118. Bloom alludes to Griffith's invective against the army: see 5.71–72.

30. See Barbara Maria Stafford, *Body Criticism: Imaging the Unseen in Enlightenment Art and Medicine* (Cambridge, Mass.: MIT Press, 1991), 281–83.

31. See Daniel Pick, *Faces of Degeneration: A European Disorder, c. 1848–1918* (Cambridge: Cambridge University Press, 1989), 117.

32. Max Nordau, *Degeneration* (London: Heinemann, 1913), 540, 27.

33. See J. B. Lyons, *James Joyce and Medicine* (Dublin: Dolmen Press, 1973), 29. Stanislaus Joyce observed that "many human lives were saved" by his father's having given up the study of medicine in 1867 (19).

34. Joshua Reynolds, *Discourses on Art,* ed. Robert Wark (San Marino: Huntington Library, 1959), 44; and William Blake, *Complete Writings,* ed. Geoffrey Keynes (London: Oxford University Press, 1966), cited by Stafford, *Body Criticism,* 318.

35. The whole passage, as Vicki Mahaffey has pointed out (*Reauthorizing Joyce*

[Cambridge: Cambridge University Press, 1988], 145–46), comes from Pater's conclusion to *The Renaissance* (1873/1893; Oxford: Oxford University Press, 1986), especially 152.

36. Stafford, *Body Criticism,* 329.

37. Cited by Harry Levin, *The Gates of Horn: A Study of Five French Realists* (New York: Oxford University Press, 1963), 186.

38. William Thayer, "The New Story-Tellers and the Doom of Realism," *Forum* 18 (December 1894): 470–80; reprinted in *Realism and Romanticism in Fiction: An Approach to the Novel,* ed. Eugene Current-García and Walton R. Patrick (Chicago: Scott, Foresman and Co., 1962), 157–58.

39. Emile Zola, *Germinal,* trans. Leonard Tancock (London: Everyman, 1991), 121, 162, 189.

40. Charles Baudelaire, "In Praise of Make-up" (1863), in *The Painter of Modern Life and Other Essays,* trans. Jonathan Mayne (New York: Da Capo Press, 1964), 33.

41. Max Beerbohm, "A Defence of Cosmetics" (1984), in *Aesthetes and Decadents,* 52–53.

42. See F. Scott Fitzgerald, *Tender Is the Night* (1934; reprint, New York: Macmillan, 1982), 183, 240–41.

43. Ernest Jones, "A Psycho-Analytic Study of the Holy Ghost Complex," in *Essays in Applied Psycho-Analysis* (London: Hogarth Press, 1951), 358–73.

44. *Leah, the Forsaken,* trans. Augustin Daly, from Salomon Hermann Mosenthal's *Deborah* (1850) (London and New York: Samuel French, n.d.), 25.

45. Similarly, Odysseus is recognized by Eurycleia in his bath when she reads his scar with her massaging fingertips. In all these stories, the fingers do the seeing. In *Leah, the Forsaken,* though, hearing also plays a part in identification, since Abraham recognizes Nathan's father through the voice, as well as through the facial features, of the son.

46. "Legal Action for Personal Injury Caused by the Use of Roentgen Rays," *Lancet* (February 20, 1904): 545.

47. Dinora Pines, "Skin Communication: Early Skin Disorders and Their Effect on Transference and Countertransference," in *A Woman's Unconscious Use of her Body: A Psychoanalytical Perspective* (London: Virago, 1993), 8–25.

48. Gifford, *"Ulysses" Annotated,* 100.

49. Robert Graves, *The Greek Myths* (Harmondsworth: Penguin, 1961), 2:165–67.

50. James Joyce, "Epiphany 19" (March 1902), in *The Workshop of Daedalus: James Joyce and the Raw Materials for "A Portrait of the Artist as a Young Man,"* ed. Robert Scholes and Richard M. Kain (Evanston, Ill.: Northwestern University Press, 1965), 29.

VISIBLE SHADES AND SHADES OF VISIBILITY

1. Homer, *The Odyssey,* trans. Samuel Butler (London: Longmans, Green, and Co., 1900), 144–53, emphases added. As Hugh Kenner points out, "Stannie recalled Jim using only two translations, Cowper's and Butler's (the latter published in 1900, hence the most up-to-date version available when *Ulysses* was being thought out)" (*Joyce's Voices* [Berkeley: University of California Press, 1978], 111).

2. R. M. Adams, "Hades," in *James Joyce's "Ulysses": Critical Essays,* ed. Clive Hart and David Hayman (Berkeley: University of California Press, 1974), 95. Adams lists five statues "in order": Sir Philip Crampton (6.191), Smith O'Brien (6.226), Daniel O'Connell (6.249), Sir John Gray (6.258), and Lord Nelson (6.293). Don Gifford notes a sixth, in close proximity to the foundation stone for Parnell (see 6.319–20): "The procession

passes a statue of the Reverend Theobald Mathew (1790–1861), the 'Apostle of Temperance,' famous for his work in the cholera epidemic of 1832 and the Great Famine" (*"Ulysses" Annotated: Notes for James Joyce's "Ulysses"* [Berkeley: University of California Press, 1988], 111).

3. Gifford, *"Ulysses" Annotated,* 105.

4. Bloom's conception of the eye as inherently vulnerable is shared by Stephen Dedalus: in *Portrait* the young sinner thinks to himself, "He was in mortal sin. Even once was a mortal sin. It could happen in an instant. But how so quickly? By seeing or by thinking of seeing. The eyes see the thing, without having wished first to see. Then in an instant it happens" (*P* 139).

5. See Gifford, *"Ulysses" Annotated,* 122.

6. Paul van Caspel, *Bloomers on the Liffey* (Baltimore: Johns Hopkins University Press, 1986), 97–98.

7. Butler, *The Odyssey,* 141.

8. For a more detailed analysis of burial as repression—both personal and historical—see Robert Spoo's contribution on "Nestor" in this volume.

9. For a more elaborate discussion of this point, see Carol Shloss's provocative essay on "Calypso" in this volume.

10. The connection between these two phrases was pointed out to me by Elizabeth Nicholas, a student of mine in an undergraduate course on *Ulysses* at the University of California, Riverside, in spring 1995.

11. Compare with Michel Foucault's contention that "traditionally, power was what was seen, what was shown and manifested"; he contrasts this with disciplinary power, which, "on the other hand, is exercised through its invisibility" (*Discipline and Punish: The Birth of the Prison,* trans. Alan Sheridan [New York: Vintage, 1979], 187).

12. For a thorough roster of these ghosts, see Adams, "Hades," 100.

13. One possible source for Joyce's representation of the relationship between Simon and his daughters is his father's correspondence (the dominant theme of which strikes me as self-pity). In a letter of 1907, John Stanislaus Joyce complains of Poppie's insolence (*Letters II* 222), in another of 1911, he writes of "the callous, unnatural treatment I am receiving from my three daughters" (*Letters II* 290), and in 1914 he modifies this slightly by harping again on "the cruel treatment I have received from my daughters" (*Letter II* 331). In *Portrait of the Artist* and *Ulysses,* Joyce at least hints at the daughters' side of the story, in marginal details I will discuss later.

14. Gifford, *"Ulysses" Annotated,* 469.

15. Zack Bowen places Dignam and his son in a list of fathers and sons that "all have comic associations" (*"Ulysses" as a Comic Novel* [Syracuse: Syracuse University Press, 1989], 9). May Dedalus is conspicuously absent from Bowen's argument. She is mentioned indirectly only twice, when Bowen notes that Stephen "like croppy failed to pray for his mother's rest" (53) and that his "anguish about his mother is real" (124–25). In Joyce's description of his own mother (Mary Jane 'May' Murray Joyce, the autobiographical source for May Dedalus), he underlines her tragedy by referring to her as a "victim" and by confessing to matricidal behavior: he identifies her cause of death as not only physical ("cancer") but also familial ("My mother was slowly killed, I think, by my father's ill-treatment, by years of trouble, and by my cynical frankness of conduct"). For the complete text, see this well-known letter to Nora Barnacle in *Letters II,* 48–50.

16. Vincent J. Cheng, "Stephen Dedalus and the Black Panther Vampire," *James Joyce Quarterly* 24 (winter 1987): 165, 170.

17. In "Hades" Bloom fantasizes the overturning of Paddy's coffin: "Bom! Upset. A coffin bumped out on to the road. Burst open. Paddy Dignam shot out and rolling over stiff in the dust in a brown habit too large for him. Red face: grey now. Mouth fallen open. Asking what's up now" (6.421–23). I am suggesting, however, that the real corpse escaping its confines in *Ulysses* is surely May. She returns metonymically in nearly every episode of the novel, and emotional reverberations of her passing also remain "at large." In the wee hours of June 17, the last thought of Stephen's that we are given access to (see 17.1230–31) records a fragment of a prayer for the dying, the auditory symptom of his filial guilt.

18. For a brief summary of the legal ambiguities, see Gifford, *"Ulysses" Annotated,* 339.

19. Seamus Deane, *Notes to "A Portrait of the Artist as a Young Man"* (New York: Penguin, 1992), 306.

20. For an elaboration of this particular example of an uncanny refiguration of the mother in the *Wake,* see my *Wandering and Return in "Finnegans Wake": An Integrative Approach to Joyce's Fictions* (Princeton: Princeton University Press, 1991), 21–22.

21. For an excellent discussion of laundrywomen in Joyce's fiction, see Margot Norris, "The Work Song of the Washerwomen in 'Anna Livia Plurabelle,'" chapter 7 of *Joyce's Web* (Austin: University of Texas Press, 1992), 139–63. Relying on evidence in Brenda Maddox's *Nora* (Boston: Houghton Mifflin, 1988), Norris explains the personal source of Joyce's familiarity with this particular form of female labor: Nora's probable experience as a laundress in Galway, and later, when married to Joyce, in Trieste—in both instances in order to contribute to precarious familial economies.

22. In *Stephen Hero,* Joyce is quite frank about Simon's childishness: "He was always interested in novelties, *childishly* interested and receptive, and this new name [Ibsen] and the phenomena it had produced in his house were novelties for him" (*SH* 87, emphasis added).

23. See Richard Ellmann, *Ulysses on the Liffey* (New York: Oxford University Press, 1972), appendix.

MACHINES, EMPIRE, AND THE WISE VIRGINS

1. Louis O. Mink, *A "Finnegans Wake" Gazetteer* (Bloomington: Indiana University Press, 1978), 429.

2. F. S. L. Lyons, *Ireland Since the Famine* (London: Fontana, 1973), 387. See also J. J. Lee, *Ireland, 1912–1985* (Cambridge: Cambridge University Press, 1989), 38–40.

3. D. George Boyce, *Nationalism in Ireland* (London: Routledge, 1991), 317.

4. Virginia Woolf, *Three Guineas* (New York: Harcourt, 1966), 13.

5. See David Cairns and Shaun Richards, *Writing Ireland: Colonialism, Nationalism and Culture* (Manchester: Manchester University Press), 42–57, and C. L. Innes, *Woman and Nation in Irish Literature and Society, 1880–1935* (Athens: University of Georgia Press, 1993), 9–25.

6. Don Gifford with Robert J. Seidman, *"Ulysses" Annotated: Notes for James Joyce's "Ulysses"* (Berkeley: University of California Press, 1988), 153.

7. Dominic Manganiello, *Joyce's Politics* (London: Routledge and Kegan Paul, 1980), 163.

8. Enda Duffy, *The Subaltern "Ulysses"* (Minneapolis: University of Minnesota Press, 1994), 1, 10.

9. Fredric Jameson, "Third-World Literature in the Era of Multinational Capitalism," *Social Text* 15 (1986): 76.

10. Antonio Gramsci, *An Antonio Gramsci Reader: Selected Writings, 1916–1935,* ed. David Forgacs (New York: Schocken Books, 1988), 351.

11. Edward W. Said, *Culture and Imperialism* (New York: Knopf, 1993), 223–24.

12. Frantz Fanon, *The Wretched of the Earth* (New York: Grove Weidenfeld, 1991), 203.

13. Duffy, *Subaltern "Ulysses,"* 155.

14. M. J. C. Hodgart, "Aeolus," *James Joyce's "Ulysses": Critical Essays,* ed. Clive Hart and David Hayman (Berkeley: University of California Press, 1974), 115.

15. Michael Groden, *"Ulysses" in Progress* (Princeton: Princeton University Press, 1977), 102.

16. David Pierce, *James Joyce's Ireland* (New Haven: Yale University Press, 1992), 21.

17. Duffy, *Subaltern "Ulysses,"* 84, 155.

18. Gifford, *"Ulysses" Annotated,* 145.

19. Ibid., 146.

20. See my comments in *Paperspace: Style as Ideology in Joyce's "Ulysses"* (Lincoln: University of Nebraska Press, 1988), 23–25.

21. Ira B. Nadel, *Joyce and the Jews: Culture and Texts* (Iowa City: University of Iowa Press, 1989), 85–107.

22. Groden, *"Ulysses" in Progress,* 101.

23. Nadel, *Joyce and the Jews,* 76, 83.

24. Ian S. Lustick, *Unsettled States, Disputed Lands: Britain and Ireland, France and Algeria, Israel and the West Bank-Gaza* (Ithaca: Cornell University Press, 1993), 187–88; Lyons, *Ireland Since the Famine,* 189.

25. Quoted in Edward Said, *The Question of Palestine* (New York: Vintage, 1980), 16–17, his emphasis.

26. Ibid., 81.

27. Theodor Herzl, "The Jewish State," in *The Zionist Idea: A Historical Analysis and Reader,* ed. Arthur Hertzberg (Garden City, N.Y.: Doubleday and Herzl, 1959), 222.

28. Seamus Deane, introduction to *Nationalism, Colonialism, and Literature* (Minneapolis: University of Minnesota Press, 1990), 8.

29. Bill Ashcroft, Gareth Griffiths, and Helen Tiffin, *The Empire Writes Back: Theory and Practice in Post-Colonial Literatures* (London: Routledge, 1989), 38–40.

30. Gifford, *"Ulysses" Annotated,* 46, 151.

31. Rosemary Cullens Owens, *Smashing Times: A History of the Irish Women's Suffrage Movement, 1889–1922* (Dublin: Attic, 1984), 28, 126, 128, 132.

32. E. J. Hobsbawm, *The Age of Empire, 1875–1914* (New York: Pantheon Books, 1987), 201–2.

33. Gayatri Chakravorty Spivak, "Can the Subaltern Speak?," in *Marxism and the Interpretation of Culture,* ed. Cary Nelson and Lawrence Grossberg (Urbana: University of Illinois Press, 1988), 308.

34. Duffy, *Subaltern "Ulysses,"* 164.

35. McGee, *Paperspace,* 23–24.

36. John Kidd, "An Inquiry into *Ulysses: The Corrected Text,*" *The Papers of the Bibliographical Society of America* 82 (December 1988): 495.

37. Jacques Derrida, "Ulysses Gramaphone: Hear say yes in Joyce," in *James Joyce: The*

Augmented Ninth, ed. Bernard Benstock (Syracuse: Syracuse University Press, 1988), 48–49.

LEGAL FICTION OR PULP FICTION IN "LESTRYGONIANS"

1. In Kant's *Anthropology,* as cited in Jacques Derrida, "Economimesis," *Diacritics* 11 (summer 1981): 23.

2. See J. Laplanche and J. B. Pontalis, *The Language of Psycho-analysis,* trans. Donald Nicholson-Smith (New York: Norton, 1973), 206.

3. See Sigmund Freud, *Totem and Taboo,* in *The Complete Psychological Works,* trans. James Strachey (London: Hogarth Press, 1953–74), 13:1–162. Two other key writings in which Freud develops the concept further are "Mourning and Melancholia," in *Complete Psychological Works,* 14:237–60, in which he speaks of incorporation as the subject identifying in the oral mode with the lost object, and *Group Psychology and the Analysis of the Ego,* in *Complete Psychological Works,* 18:67–143, in which he discusses the phenomena in more social terms related to a group identification with a powerful leader, based on an emotional common quality.

4. Derrida, "'Eating Well,' or the Calculation of the Subject: An Interview with Jacques Derrida," in *Who Comes after the Subject?,* ed. Eduardo Cadava, Peter Connor, and Jean-Luc Nancy (New York: Routledge, 1991), 113.

5. Julia Kristeva, "Joyce 'The Gracehoper' or the Return of Orpheus," in *James Joyce: The Augmented Ninth,* ed. Bernard Benstock (Syracuse: Syracuse University Press, 1988), 168.

6. See Henry Staten's excellent chapter, "How the Spirit (Almost) Became Flesh: The Gospel of John," in his *Eros in Mourning: Homer to Lacan* (Baltimore: Johns Hopkins University Press, 1995), 47–70. See also Staten's essay, "The Decomposition of *Ulysses,*" *PMLA* (May 1997): 380–92.

7. For a general "Feminist-Vegetarian Critical Theory" (which, however, wholly ignores the realm of the religious), consult Carol J. Adams, *The Sexual Politics of Meat* (New York: Continuum, 1990). See also Lindsey Tucker's helpful study, *Stephen and Bloom at Life's Feast: Alimentary Symbolism and the Creative Process in James Joyce's "Ulysses"* (Columbus: Ohio State University Press, 1984).

8. Richard Ellmann, *Ulysses on the Liffey* (Oxford: Oxford University Press, 1972), appendix.

9. Earlier, less charged moments anticipate this perception, for example at the very beginning of "Lestrygonians," when Bloom momentarily confuses his name with the "Blood of the Lamb": "Bloo. . . . Me? No. / Blood of the Lamb" (8.08–9). In "Aeolus," Bloom recalls with equanimity a Jewish account of the food chain, the chant *Chad Gadya* (One Kid) that closes the passover seder: "And then the angel of death kills the butcher and he kills the ox and the dog kills the cat. Sounds a bit silly till you come to look into it well. Justice it means but its everybody eating everyone else. That's what life is after all" (7.211–14). As Don Gifford puts it, "The kid [eaten by the cat], bottommost and most injured of all, is, of course, the people of Israel" (*"Ulysses" Annotated: Notes for James Joyce's "Ulysses"* [Berkeley: University of California Press, 1988], 133). The chant ends with God slaying the angel of death, avenging the victimization of the Jews.

10. Emer Nolan, *James Joyce and Nationalism* (New York: Routledge, 1995), 81.

11. Julia Kristeva, *Powers of Horror: An Essay on Abjection,* trans. Leon S. Roudiez (New York: Columbia University Press, 1982), 3–4, 109.

12. James McMichael, *"Ulysses" and Justice* (Princeton: Princeton University Press, 1991), 179–80, 181.

13. Gifford, *"Ulysses" Annotated,* 601.

14. Compare Bloom's thoughts earlier in the day about Milly: "Milly too. Young kisses: the first. . . . Lips kissed, kissing, kissed. Full gluey woman's lips" (4.444–50).

15. Frank Budgen, *James Joyce and the Making of "Ulysses"* (Bloomington: Indiana University Press, 1960), 106.

16. This image resembles Kristeva's description of those devotees of the abject who look for the "desirable and terrifying, nourishing and murderous, fascinating and abject inside of the maternal body" (*Powers of Horror,* 54).

17. Kristeva, "Joyce 'The Gracehoper' or the Return of Orpheus," 178.

THE PERILS OF MASCULINITY IN "SCYLLA AND CHARYBDIS"

1. Georges Borach, "Conversations with James Joyce," in *Portraits of the Artist in Exile: Recollections of James Joyce by Europeans,* ed. Willard Potts (Seattle: University of Washington Press, 1979), 70.

2. For this articulation, see Sigmund Freud, *An Outline of Psychoanalysis* (New York: Norton, 1969), 46.

3. Michel Foucault, *The History of Sexuality, Volume I* (New York: Pantheon, 1978), 43.

4. Ibid. For the historical currency of the inversion model, see Richard Dellamora, *Masculine Desire* (Chapel Hill: University of North Carolina Press, 1990), 199, and Alan Sinfield, *The Wilde Century* (New York: Columbia University Press, 1994), 110. I use the hybrid term sexual/gender inversion here advisedly. Although George Chauncey Jr. has argued that some distinction between sexual and gender inversion had evolved by the late nineteenth century (see "From Sexual Inversion to Homosexuality," *Salmagundi* 58–59 [1982–83]: 114–46), all of the contemporaneous studies that I have seen and will be citing exhibit a hopeless entangling or conflation of the two categories. One outstanding example of this tendency can be found in the influential nineteenth-century study, Albert Moll, *Perversions of the Sex Instinct* (Newark: Julian, 1931), 63–77. Moll was even known to quote a male homosexual as declaring, "We are all women" (see Havelock Ellis and J. A. Symonds, *Sexual Inversion* in *Studies in the Psychology of Sex* [London: Wilson & MacMillan, 1897], 1:119). Another outstanding example can be found in the work of Ellis and Symonds themselves, who proclaim, "There is a distinctly general, though not universal, tendency for sexual inverts to approach the feminine type, either in psychic disposition or physical constitution, or both" (*Sexual Inversion,* 119). Christopher Craft's recent critique of inversion theory captures this confusion of sexuality and gender precisely: "sexual inversion explains homosexual desire as a physiologically misplaced heterosexuality . . . referrable not to the sex of the body . . .but rather to a psychologized sexual center characterized as the 'opposite gender'" (*Another Kind of Love* [Berkeley: University of California Press, 1994], 77).

5. For a full theoretical articulation of homosexual panic, see Eve Sedgwick, *The Epistemology of the Closet* (Berkeley: University of California Press, 1990), 182–212.

6. Frank Budgen, *James Joyce and the Making of "Ulysses"* (Bloomington: Indiana University Press, 1960), 16.

7. Homer, *The Odyssey,* trans. Robert Fitzgerald (Garden City, N.Y.: Doubleday, 1963), 211–12.

8. Ibid., 212.

9. Ibid., 213, 218.

10. Ibid., 213.

11. Christine Froula, "History's Nightmare, Fiction's Dream: Joyce and the Psychohistory of *Ulysses,*" *James Joyce Quarterly* 28 (summer 1991): 862–64.

12. See Froula, "History's Nightmare, Fiction's Dream," 857–72, and her "Mothers of Invention / Doaters of Inversion: Narcissan Scenes in *Finnegans Wake,*" in *Joyce: The Return of the Repressed,* ed. Susan Friedman (Ithaca: Cornell University Press, 1993), 294–95.

13. For a definitive study of Shakespeare's phallic overcompensation and its place in *Ulysses,* see Kimberly J. Devlin, "Castration and Its Discontents: A Lacanian Approach to *Ulysses,*" *James Joyce Quarterly* 29 (fall 1991): 117–44.

14. Sigmund Freud, "On Narcissism," in *General Psychoanalytic Theory* (New York: Collier, 1963), 71–72.

15. Colleen Lamos, "Signatures of the Invisible: Homosexual Secrecy and Knowledge in *Ulysses,*" *James Joyce Quarterly* 31 (spring 1994): 341.

16. For "reverse discourse," see Foucault, *History of Sexuality,* 101.

17. For another account of homosexuality as a condition of heterosexual norms, see Judith Butler, *Gender Trouble* (New York: Routledge, 1990), 57–66.

18. The word "queer" began to connote homosexuality in the late 1880s according to Elaine Showalter, *Sexual Anarchy* (New York: Viking, 1990), 112.

19. David Weir speaks of Stephen's general suppression of homosexuality in his theory of Shakespeare in "A Womb of His Own: Joyce's Sexual Aesthetics," *James Joyce Quarterly* 31 (spring 1994): 220.

20. For the dynamics of negation, see Freud, "Negation," in *General Psychological Theory,* 213–17.

21. For the historical context of Joyce's use of sex/gender inversion, see Richard Brown, *James Joyce and Sexuality* (Cambridge: Cambridge University Press, 1985), 78–84. For Joyce's use of sex/gender inversion in *Portrait,* see Joseph Valente, "Thrilled by His Touch: The Aestheticizing of Homosexual Panic in *A Portrait of the Artist as a Young Man,*" in *Quare Joyce,* ed. Joseph Valente (Ann Arbor: University of Michigan Press, 1998).

22. For abjection in *Ulysses* and elsewhere in Joyce, see Joseph Valente, *James Joyce and the Problem of Justice: Crossing Sexual and Colonial Difference* (Cambridge: Cambridge University Press, 1995), 67–131, 192–201. For a theoretical account of abjection, see Julia Kristeva, *Powers of Horror* (New York: Columbia University, 1982), ch. 1.

23. Nowhere is this oppositional essentialism more baldly stated than in Freud's case study of the Wolf Man, which Joyce used in the composition of *Finnegans Wake.* See Freud, *Three Case Histories* (New York: Collier, 1963), 233. In Freud's study of da Vinci, which Joyce also read, he specifically equates male inversion with passivity. See Freud, *Leonardo da Vinci and a Memory of His Childhood* (New York: Norton, 1964), 36–37. Ellis and Symonds likewise equate feeling as a man in sexual relations with taking the active role, in *Sexual Inversion,* 63, a book with which Joyce was also familiar.

24. Sigmund Freud, *The Ego and the Id* (New York: Norton, 1960), 22.

25. Widely recognized as the father of the inversion metaphor, Karl-Heinrich Ulrichs is quoted in Sinfield, *The Wilde Century,* 110.

26. Ellis and Symonds, *Sexual Inversion;* Edward Carpenter, *The Intermediate Sex* (Manchester: Labour Press, 1896); Baron Richard Von Krafft-Ebing, *Psychopathia Sexualis* (London: F. G. Rebman, 1892), 186–294; Sigmund Freud, *Three Essays on Sexuality* (New York: Basic, 1962), 7. For Joyce's reading in this area, see Brown, *James Joyce and Sexuality,* 78–107. Brown claims that Joyce's sexological views most closely approximated those of Havelock Ellis, perhaps the most comprehensive exponent of sex/gender inversion.

27. Freud, *The Ego and the Id,* 23.

28. Ewa Ziarek, "'Circe': Joyce's *Argumentum ad Feminam,*" *James Joyce Quarterly* 30 (fall 1992): 61.

29. Vicki Mahaffey argues to similar effect about *Portrait* in "Père-version and Immère-sion: Idealized Corruption in *A Portrait of the Artist as a Young Man* and *The Picture of Dorian Gray,*" *James Joyce Quarterly* 31 (spring 1994): 193–96.

30. Don Gifford translates the Italian phrase as follows: "S. D.: his woman. Oh sure—his. Gelindo [a man's name] resolves not to love S. D." *("Ulysses" Annotated: Notes for James Joyce's "Ulysses"* [Berkeley: University of California Press, 1988], 245 [Gifford's bracket]).

31. Weir reads the poem as a straightforward homosexual fantasy involving Mulligan ("A Womb of One's Own," 226).

32. Weir shows an extended parallelism of Mulligan and Wilde throughout *Ulysses,* including their sartorial affinities ("A Womb of One's Own," 223–24).

33. Oscar Wilde, *The Works of Oscar Wilde* (Leicester: Blitz, 1990), 1089–90, 1094.

34. Wilde extends this element of father-son identification to the outer narrational limits of the mise en scène of *The Portrait of Mr. W. H.* by naming the mouthpiece of his Shakespeare theory, Cyril, after his own firstborn son. I am indebted to Vicki Mahaffey for this piece of biographical information.

35. Lamos, "Signatures of the Invisible," 341.

36. Chauncey, "From Sexual Inversion to Homosexuality," 125.

37. Craft, *Another Kind of Love,* 43.

38. Lamos comes to the same conclusion by a different path in "Signatures of the Invisible," 342.

39. Lamos, "Signatures of the Invisible," 340–41.

40. The most prominent work identifying the Jews with femininity was Otto Weininger's *Sex and Character* (London: Heinemann, 1906), with which Joyce was quite familiar according to Richard Ellmann (*JJ* 463). For a discussion of Joyce's use of Weininger, see Marilyn Reizbaum, "Weininger and the Bloom of Jewish Self-Hatred in *Ulysses,*" in *Jews and Gender,* ed. Nancy A. Harrowitz and Barbara Hyams (Philadelphia: Temple University Press, 1995), 207–14.

41. Of the many discussions of Stephen's "economy of heaven," two seem especially pertinent here: Froula, "History's Nightmare, Fiction's Dream," 862–70, and Jeri Johnson, "'Beyond the Veil': *Ulysses,* Feminism and the Figure of Woman," in *Joyce, Modernity and Its Mediation,* ed. Christine Van Boheemen (Amsterdam: Rodopi, 1989), 225.

42. I wish to thank Kimberly Devlin, Vicki Mahaffey, Marilyn Reizbaum, Molly Anne Rothenberg, and Joanne Slutsky for reading this essay at various stages and offering their comments and suggestions.

DIVERSIONS FROM MASTERY IN "WANDERING ROCKS"

1. A recent exception is Kathleen McCormick, who assesses reasons for its negative reception by readers as she sets out to reclaim it for pleasurable experience through reader response theory. See *"Ulysses," "Wandering Rocks," and the Reader* (Lampeter: Edward Mellen Press, 1991), 7.

2. Michael Seidel, *Epic Geography: James Joyce's "Ulysses"* (Princeton: Princeton University Press, 1976), 186.

3. Hugh Kenner, *"Ulysses"* (London: George Allen & Unwin, 1980), 98.

4. I take this term from E. D. Hirsch Jr., "Objective Interpretation," *PMLA* 75 (1960); reprinted in *The Critical Tradition: Classic Texts and Contemporary Trends,* ed. David H. Richter (New York: St. Martin's Press, 1989), 1392–1411.

5. In his footnote to this letter, Richard Ellmann suggests that this entr'acte "was not added," though arguably "Wandering Rocks" functions as a "pause," offers material of questionable relevance to what precedes and follows, and was the last episode to join his schema. The schema was mailed to Carlo Linati three days before the contemplated addition was mentioned in a letter to Budgen.

6. Both Frank Budgen and Richard Ellmann (*JJ* 452) have noted that Joyce was frustrating our access to major characters and concentrating instead on Dublin and Dubliners (*James Joyce and the Making of "Ulysses" and Other Writings* [Oxford: Oxford University Press, 1972], 125). By this means, Joyce struck a blow at hierarchical habits of reading.

7. For the Linati schema in its original Italian, followed by Ellmann's translation, see the appendix to his *Ulysses on the Liffey* (New York: Oxford University Press, 1972).

8. Budgen, *James Joyce and the Making of "Ulysses,"* 125.

9. "Christ and Caesar" are listed as the first item under the heading "symbol." Joyce follows "Errors" with "Homonyms, Synchronizations, and Resemblances," separating each of these with a colon.

10. Clive Hart, "Wandering Rocks," in *James Joyce's "Ulysses,"* ed. Clive Hart and David Hayman (Berkeley: University of California Press, 1974), 186.

11. Joyce demonstrated a personality at least as "difficult" as that of the "Wandering Rocks" narrator when he said that he had written *Finnegans Wake* "to keep the critics busy for three hundred years" (*JJ* 703).

12. Hart, "Wandering Rocks," 182.

13. See, for instance, Florence Walzl, "*Dubliners:* Women in Irish Society," in *Women in Joyce,* ed. Suzette Henke and Elaine Unkeless (Urbana: University of Illinois Press, 1982), 31–56.

14. See Margot Norris, *Joyce's Web: The Social Unraveling of Modernism* (Austin: University of Texas Press, 1992), and her "Not the Girl She Was at All: Women in 'The Dead,'" in James Joyce, *The Dead,* ed. Daniel R. Schwarz (Boston: St. Martin's Press, 1993), 190–204. Garry Leonard offers a combination of Lacanian and feminist interpretation of *Dubliners* in *Reading "Dubliners" Again* (Syracuse: Syracuse University Press, 1993).

15. Giles Deleuze, *The Deleuze Reader,* ed. Constantin V. Boundas (New York: Columbia University Press, 1993), 150.

16. Carol Gilligan, *In a Different Voice: Psychological Theory and Women's Development* (Cambridge: Harvard University Press, 1982), 8.

17. Budgen, *James Joyce and the Making of "Ulysses,"* 123.

18. Most notable in this category are Adaline Glasheen's census of *Finnegans Wake,* and, covering Joyce's preceding fictions, Shari and Bernard Benstock's *Who's He When He's at Home: A James Joyce Directory* (Urbana: University of Illinois Press, 1980), as well as Weldon Thorton's list of *Allusions in "Ulysses"* (Chapel Hill: University of North Carolina Press, 1961) and Don Gifford with Robert J. Seidman's *"Ulysses" Annotated: Notes for James Joyce's "Ulysses"* (Berkeley: University of California Press, 1988).

19. McCormick, *"Ulysses," "Wandering Rocks," and the Reader,* 17, 19.

20. Vicki Mahaffey, *Reauthorizing Joyce* (Cambridge: Cambridge University Press, 1988).

21. See Trevor Williams, "'Conmeeism' and the Universe of Discourse in 'Wandering Rocks,'" *James Joyce Quarterly* 29 (winter 1992): 267–79.

22. The asterisks present on Joyce's typescripts and page proofs had disappeared in the 1961 edition I first encountered, to be restored in the 1984 Gabler edition. They have for some reason been stretched into a straight line for the 1986 paperback, perhaps at the hands of the designer, John Ryder.

23. This has been memorably expressed by Cleanth Brooks in "Irony as a Principle of Structure," in *Literary Opinion in America,* ed. M. D. Zabel; reprinted in Richter, *The Critical Tradition,* 799–807.

24. McCormick, *"Ulysses," "Wandering Rocks," and the Reader,* 113; Joseph Boone, "Queer Sites in Modernism: Harlem/Paris/Greenwich Village," in *The Geography of Identity,* ed. Patricia Yaeger (Ann Arbor: University of Michigan Press, forthcoming).

25. Clive Hart and Leo Knuth, *A Topographical Guide to James Joyce's "Ulysses"* (Colchester: A Wake Newslitter Press, 1976), 27.

26. Gifford, *"Ulysses" Annotated,* 258–59.

27. I am referring to this character by his first, "rock" name, rather than the culminating "Farrell," usually taken to abbreviate his insanely long string of names. The Rock of Cashel is a major ecclesiastical site in Ireland.

28. David Norris suggests that "in Joyce's view, Professor Maginni was 'a flaming bloody sugar' if not actually a drag queen manqué." See his "The 'unhappy mania' and Mr. Bloom's Cigar: Homosexuality in the Works of James Joyce," *James Joyce Quarterly* 31 (spring 1994): 357–73. For a history of homosexuality in Dublin, see C. S. Andrews, *Dublin Made Me: An Autobiography* (Dublin: Mercier, 1979).

29. Virginia Woolf, *Mrs. Dalloway* (San Diego: Harcourt Brace Jovanovich, 1990), 6.

30. Bernard Benstock, *Narrative Con/Texts in "Ulysses"* (Urbana: University of Illinois Press, 1991), 165.

31. Rochford's disk machine is a narrative device; it orders the perceptions of a music hall audience, telling what act is on stage. Critics have supplied comparable mechanical numbering to order the sections and interpolations of Joyce's episode.

32. Bernard Benstock thinks that this meeting drives Stephen to his later drinking (*Narrative Con/Texts,* 56).

33. Gilligan, *In a Different Voice,* 156–57.

34. Marilyn French, *The Book as World: James Joyce's "Ulysses"* (Cambridge: Harvard University Press, 1976), 118.

POLITICAL SIRENS

1. The fullest, if most polemical, discussion of the chapter's relation to music and to musical theory can be found in David Hayman, "'Sirens' after Schonberg," *James Joyce Quarterly* 31 (summer 1994): 473–94.

2. On "Circe," in particular, see Joseph A. Boone, "Staging Sexuality: Repression, Representation, and 'Interior' States in *Ulysses*," in *Joyce: The Return of the Repressed,* ed. Susan Stanford Friedman (Ithaca: Cornell University Press, 1993), 193–205.

3. For a superb discussion of the role of synecdoche in the chapter, see Derek Attridge, "Joyce's Lipspeech: Syntax and the Subject in 'Sirens,'" in *James Joyce: The Centennial Symposium,* ed. Morris Beja, Phillip Herring, Maurice Harmon, and David Norris (Urbana: University of Illinois Press, 1986), 59–65. See also André Topia, "'Sirens': The Emblematic Vibration," in the same volume, 76–81.

4. Hugh Kenner, *Joyce's Voices* (Berkeley: University of California Press, 1979), 104.

5. Several essays in *James Joyce: The Centennial Symposium* explore the chapter's concern with orthographic and visible signs (as opposed to musical and audible ones), and with the plasticity of the signifier. See Attridge, "Joyce's Lipspeech"; Maud Ellmann, "To Sing or to Sign"; Daniel Ferrer, "Echo or Narcissus?"; Topia, "'Sirens': The Emblematic Vibration"; Jean-Michel Rabaté, "The Silence of the Sirens"; and Robert Young, "The Language of Flow." More recently, Joseph Valente has analyzed the ways in which the practices of music and text "pass into one another" throughout the chapter, in "Who Made the Tune: Becoming-Woman in 'Sirens,'" *James Joyce Quarterly* 30 (winter 1993): 191–208.

6. On the commodification of the linguistic signifier in Joyce, see Garry Leonard, "Joyce and Advertising: Advertising and Commodity Culture in Joyce's Fiction," *James Joyce Quarterly* 30/31 (summer/fall 1993): 573–92. See also Thomas Richards, *The Commodity Culture of Victorian England: Advertising and Spectacle, 1851–1914* (Stanford: Stanford University Press, 1990), 214–17.

7. Max Horkheimer and Theodor Adorno, *Dialectic of Enlightenment,* trans. John Cumming (New York: Continuum, 1987), 32–80.

8. See Franco Moretti, *Signs Taken for Wonders,* trans. Susan Fischer, David Forgacs, and David Miller (London: Verso, 1988), 191–95, 205–6; Terry Eagleton, "Nationalism: Irony and Commitment," in *Nationalism, Colonialism, and Literature,* introduction by Seamus Deane (Minneapolis: University of Minnesota Press, 1990), 30–35; and David Lloyd, *Anomalous States: Irish Writing and the Post-Colonial Moment* (Durham: Duke University Press, 1993), 104–10.

9. Adorno and Horkheimer, *Dialectic of Enlightenment,* 33.

10. For descriptions and accounts of this event, see D. G. Boyce, "'The Marginal Britons': The Irish," in *Englishness: Politics and Culture, 1880–1920,* ed. Robert Colls and Philip Dodd (London: Croom Helm, 1986), 236–37; Jeanne Sheehy, *The Rediscovery of Ireland's Past: The Celtic Revival, 1880–1930* (London: Thames and Hudson, 1980), 103–4; *"We Twa": Reminiscences of Lord and Lady Aberdeen* (London: W. Collins Sons, 1927), 248–68; Marjorie Pentland, *A Bonnie Fechter: The life of Ishbel Marjoribanks, Marchioness of Aberdeen & Temair, G.B.E., LL.D., J.P., 1857–1939* (London: Batsford, 1952), 55–65.

11. *"We Twa,"* 252–53.

12. Ibid., 251–52, emphasis added.

13. Ibid., 254, 263, 256.

14. In her brilliant discussion of the gendering of national fantasies, Lauren Berlant cautions against any attribution of agency to the national-female icon: "when the body of woman is employed symbolically to regulate or represent the field of national fantasy, her positive 'agency' lies solely in her availability to be narrativized—controlled, as de Lauretis suggests, by her circulation within a story" (*The Anatomy of National Fantasy: Hawthorne, Utopia, and Everyday Life* [Chicago: University of Chicago Press, 1991], 28).

This may remind us that Lady Aberdeen was "free" only to fashion herself in accordance with certain prescripted alternatives—ones, for instance, that did not categorically challenge the Victorian doctrine of separate spheres. I do not think that recognition of this more general constraint, however, requires us to deny the specific and limited ways in which Lady Aberdeen sought to "fashion" the viceregal image—especially if we consider the extent to which her class position enabled exceptional activity.

15. Pentland, *Bonnie Fechter,* 258–60. Compare Bloom's advertising gimmick in *Ulysses:* "I suggested to him about a transparent showcart with two smart girls sitting inside writing letters, copybooks, envelopes, blottingpaper. I bet that would have caught on. Smart girls writing something catch the eye at once. Everyone dying to know what she's writing" (8.131–35).

16. "*We Twa,*" 265–66.

17. On the increasing role of public spectacle—and particularly of royal carriage processions—in the staging of imperial British authority during precisely this period, see David Cannadine, "The Context, Performance, and Meaning of Ritual: The British Monarchy and the 'Invention of Tradition,' c. 1820–1977," in *The Invention of Tradition,* ed. Eric Hobsbawm and Terence Ranger (Cambridge: Cambridge University Press, 1983), 101–38.

18. Benedict Anderson, *Imagined Communities: Reflections on the Origin and Spread of Nationalism* (London: Verso, 1991), ch. 3, 4, 7. On the role of state processions, see also Cannadine, "The Context, Performance and Meaning of Ritual."

19. For an important discussion of the role played by *Ulysses* in negotiating among "high," "mass," and "popular" culture, and the relation of these issues to the specific colonial situation of Ireland, see Jennifer Wicke, "Modernity Must Advertise: Aura, Desire, and Decolonization in Joyce," *James Joyce Quarterly* 30/31 (summer/fall 1993): 593–613.

20. See Sheehy, *The Rediscovery of Ireland's Past,* 87.

21. Boyce, "'The Marginal Britons,'" 236–37. But compare Wicke's argument that Joyce saw the massification of Irish popular culture as a gesture beyond the colonial-imperial dyad: "this, it seems to me, is partly what Joyce thinks are the contradictions of Irish decolonization and what he writes about—that for Ireland to become a modern nation, for it to decolonize, it will need to redeploy the textures of modernity most often supplied to the society by mass cultural, and not strictly 'national,' forces" ("Modernity Must Advertise," 607).

22. It may be worth remarking here that Ireland has provided the vexing anomaly for comtemporary theories of nationalism. Benedict Anderson and E. J. Hobsbawm agree that Ireland failed to fit comfortably into the various paradigms of nineteenth-century nationalism. Unlike other nineteenth-century nationalist movements, Irish nationalism (a) made claims for actual statehood rather than simply autonomy; (b) acquired mass support *prior* to actual statehood rather than the other way around; and (c) did not possess an economy of sufficient scope to meet the viability threshold hypothesized by classical nineteenth-century political economists. Yet in an ironic way such exceptionality lies at the very heart of the nationalist project. The nation is an a posteriori attempt to instantiate norms and values which it must construct and presuppose all in the same breath. See Hobsbawm, *Nations and Nationalism since 1780: Programme, Myth, Reality* (Cambridge: Cambridge University Press, 1990), 12, 32, 37; and Benedict Anderson, *Imagined Communities,* 78–80, 90. On the economic prerequisites of nationalism, see Ernest Gellner, *Nations and Nationalism* (Ithaca: Cornell University Press, 1983), 19–62.

Thus when Franco Moretti, in his brilliant chapter on *Ulysses,* nonetheless insists that Joyce's Dublin could not possibly be the actual empirical Dublin of 1904 (which was too immature in terms of the world-historical development of capital) and that it must instead be a *figure* for the modern European metropole, we have to feel that he has both hit and missed the mark. The anomalous character of Dublin's political and social economy, attested to by Thomas Richards and Fredric Jameson in particular, makes it in many ways exemplary of twentieth-century nationalisms, which have increasingly become idiosyncratic movements of self-determination with little relation to the laws of development governing classic nineteenth- and twentieth-century state nationalisms. See Moretti, *Signs Taken for Wonders,* 190; and Fredric Jameson, "Modernism and Imperialism," in *Nationalism, Colonialism, and Literature,* 43–66.

23. Hobsbawm, *Nations and Nationalism,* 12.

24. See Ann Rosalind Jones and Peter Stallybrass, "Dismantling Irena: The Sexualizing of Ireland in Early Modern England," and Eve Kosofsky Sedgwick, "Nationalisms and Sexualities in the Age of Wilde," both in *Nationalisms and Sexualities,* ed. Andrew Parker, Mary Russo, Doris Summer, and Patricia Yaeger (New York: Routledge, 1992), 157–71, 235–45, respectively.

25. Lloyd, *Anomalous States,* 109.

26. For a fascinating Deleuzian analysis of the operations of the male gaze in the chapter, see Valente, "Who Made the Tune."

27. Ferrer observes: "An outdoor spectacle (the viceregal cavalcade) passes outside the theater (the Ormond): from within, the barmaids watch the show, but they become themselves a spectacle for a member of the viceregal party" ("Echo or Narcissus?," 74).

28. The motivating impulse of Bloom's divided strategy here is presumably his ambivalently motivated surveillance of Blazes Boylan, the project which brings him to the Ormond in the first place. Bloom is both fascinated and repelled by the thought of Boylan's and Molly's imagined impending sexual rendezvous, an ambivalence which produces his vacillating attitude toward sexual vagrancy throughout the chapter.

29. On the trajectory of synecdoche in the chapter, see Attridge, "Joyce's Lipspeech," and Topia, "'Sirens': The Emblematic Vibration."

30. Valente observes: "The institution of desire through a process of separation and exclusion that engenders (in both senses of the term) the subject-object dichotomy places women in the dual role of appropriable image or surface, a role played by the Ormond barmaids, and enigmatic alterity, a function signified by the infinitely receding voice of the sirens" ("Who Made the Tune," 197).

31. See Dympna Callaghan, "An Interview with Seamus Deane: University College, Dublin, June 1993," *Social Text* 38 (spring 1994): 41–42.

WHEN THE SAINTS COME MARCHING IN

1. I am indebted to Mark Osteen's compelling insights on "the economy of sacrifice" (and many other related issues), in his essay "Narrative Gifts: 'Cyclops' and the Economy of Excess," *Joyce Studies Annual* 1 (summer 1990): 162–96.

2. *Joyce's "Ulysses" Notesheets in the British Museum,* ed. Phillip Herring (Charlottesville: University Press of Virginia, 1972), 14.

3. For a history of Joyce's "schemes" for the novel, see Richard Ellmann's *James Joyce* (New York: Oxford University Press, 1982), 521, and *Joyce's Notes and Early Drafts for "Ulysses": Drafts from the Buffalo Collection,* ed. Phillip Herring (Charlottesville: University of Virginia Press), 121–24. Stuart Gilbert reproduces the 1921 scheme, from

which the above characterization of the "technic" of "Cyclops" is taken (*James Joyce's "Ulysses"* [New York: Vintage, 1930], 30).

4. Enda Duffy, *The Subaltern Joyce* (Minneapolis: University of Minneapolis Press, 1994), 125.

5. Osteen, "Narrative Gifts," 190.

6. Ibid., 191.

7. This reference to *High Noon,* which may seem a longshot in this context, has particular relevance because as a political allegory of the McCarthy era (itself a recessed dimension of the reception of the film), it employs woman as the fetishized other in the classic forms of saint and sinner / blonde and dark. For a discussion of this dimension of the film, see Joanna E. Rapf, "Myth, Ideology, and Feminism in *High Noon," Journal of Popular Culture* 23 (spring 1990): 75–79.

8. In the 1920 Linati schema, Joyce lists "Egocidal Terror" under the category of "Sense—Meaning." This might be interpreted to suggest that the seeming instability of the narrative accrues to or mirrors the reformation of character at the same time that it speaks to the threat evoked by the classic duel that in one sense frames the chapter. See Herring's discussion of this in *Joyce's Notes and Early Drafts for "Ulysses,"* 123–24.

9. The ballad "Father O'Flynn" is a possible source for the reference to this figure and his earlier appearance (at 8.707–13) in "Lestrygonians" (Don Gifford with Robert J. Seidman, *"Ulysses" Annotated: Notes for James Joyce's "Ulysses"* [Berkeley: University of California Press, 1988], 178).

10. See Michael Groden, *"Ulysses" in Progress* (Princeton: Princeton University Press, 1977), 116.

11. See Groden, *"Ulysses" in Progress,* 159–60, 122, for a discussion of the additions to the fair copy's list of saints, and for a list of the order of the events for the chapter.

12. In Joyce's 1907 essay, "Ireland, Island of Saints and Sages," he addresses the idea of Irish nationhood or nationality, which he suggests is probably a "convenient fiction," in terms of purity of race—an idea for which he obviously has contempt (see in particular *CW* 162, 166). See also David Lloyd's discussion of this issue: "Even where he lays claim to Irish identity ('I'm Irish; I was born here'), or where he seeks to define a nation ('The same people living in the same place'), Bloom appeals to the contingencies of merely contiguous relationships as opposed to the nationalist concern with a lineage of spirit and blood which must be kept pure. Bloom's insistence on contiguity underwrites his own figuration as a locus of contamination or hybridization as against the assimilative principles of nationalist ideology" (*Anomalous States: Irish Writing and the Post-Colonial Moment* [Durham: Duke University Press, 1993], 121–22). I develop these ideas differently in terms of Bloom's "lost tip," in "Joyce's Grand Nationals," *European Joyce Studies* 8: Feminism/Post/Colonialism (special issue edited by Ellen Carol Jones).

13. "Mixed middling" may remind one of the late-nineteenth-century term of German racial science, "*Mischling,*" referring to the offspring of a Jewish and non-Jewish parent. The term takes on both a linguistic and a sexual dimension, so that, as Sander Gilman puts it, "the Jewishness of the *Mischling* 'looks' and sounds degenerate. . . . The Jew's language reflects the corruption of the Jew and his/her discourse. It is the sign of the 'pathological early development' of the *Mischling,* who, as an adult, is unable to fulfill the promise of the member of the pure race. . . . the *Mischling* becomes the exemplary hidden Jew waiting to corrupt the body politic" (*The Jew's Body* [New York: Routledge, 1991], 102). See also my *James Joyce's Judaic Other* (Stanford University Press, 1999): ch.4.

14. In a note on this moment in the text, Gifford suggests that the Moslem rather than the Jewish tradition emphasizes the desirability of bearing male children, but I think it is safe to say that Judaism too has privileged the male child, in cultural if not strictly religious terms (*"Ulysses" Annotated,* 367).

15. Gilman takes up the issue of circumcision and the way in which it becomes "the key in marking the Jewish body as different within the perimeters of 'healthy' or 'diseased,'" and discusses Freud's "response to the label of difference" in *Moses and Monotheism* (*The Jew's Body,* 155–57). I develop the connections between circumcision, castration anxiety, and perceptions of diminished sexual capacity more thoroughly and with different conceptual aims in "Joyce's Grand Nationals."

16. For the medieval origin of the idea of *foetor Judaicus,* Jewish odor (a phrase that appears in "Circe"), and the taboo of blood, see Joshua Trachtenberg's *The Devil and the Jews: The Medieval Conception of the Jew and Its Relation to Modern Anti-Semitism* (New Haven: Yale University Press, 1943). A more recent treatment of this and related issues is Jay Geller's compelling essay, "(G)nos(e)ology: The Cultural Construction of the Other," in *People of the Body: Jews and Judaism from an Embodied Perspective,* ed. Howard Eilberg-Schwartz (Albany: State University of New York Press, 1992), 243–82. On the issue of Bloom's supposed menstruation, see Joseph A. Boone, "A New Approach to Bloom as 'Womanly Man': The Mixed Middling's Progress in *Ulysses,*" *James Joyce Quarterly* 20 (fall 1982): 67–86.

17. See Marina Warner, *Alone of All Her Sex: The Myth and Cult of the Virgin Mary* (New York: Knopf, 1976), particularly chapter 5, "Virgins and Martyrs," 75.

18. Warner, *Alone of All Her Sex,* 74. For an interesting discussion of the connections among the blood libel myth, the *foetor Judaicus,* and the Virgin Mary, see also Dympna Callaghan's "Re-reading Elizabeth Cary's *The Tragedie of Mariam, Faire Queene of Jewry,*" in *Women, "Race," and Writing in the Early Modern Period,* ed. Margo Hendricks and Patricia Parker (New York: Routledge, 1994), 163–77.

19. Gilman discusses the myths associated with Jews and syphilis and the connection to circumcision in *The Jew's Body,* 96–103. For discussion of the myth of ritual murder and the Jews, see Trachtenberg's *The Devil and the Jews,* or R. Po-Chia Hsia's *The Myth of Ritual Murder: Jews and Magic in Reformation Germany* (New Haven: Yale University Press, 1988). I discuss Joyce's use of the myth in *Ulysses* in *James Joyce's Judaic Other.* See Vicki Mahaffey's essay in this collection for her discussion of the myth of ritual murder in "Ithaca," and of the relationship between castration and circumcision in Stephen's catalog of anxieties.

20. Gilman, *The Jew's Body,* 125. See also Geller, "(G)nos(e)ology."

21. In chapter 3 of *James Joyce's Judaic Other,* I posit the novel as "textually cuckoo," informed by a poetics of Jewishness, where an idea of narrative "integrity" is displaced by a heterogeneity of forms, as we see particularly in "Cyclops." Such heterogeneity is demonstrated by the idea of "*Mauscheln,*" described as the hidden language of Jews: the German word derives from the name Moshe and characterizes the difference of Jewish speech (see *The Jew's Body,* passim).

22. I allude here to Max Nordau's idea of "muscular Jewry," from his 1903 essay, *"Muskeljudentum":* this idea sought to counteract the image of Jews as passive and bodily diseased, but, as some have argued, seemed to give credence to those stereotypes in the course of his counterargument. Certainly, Nordau promoted displaying rather than disguising the circumcised penis. Nordau's ideas provided a foundation for the Zionist figuration of Jews.

23. "Beware of false prophets who come to you in sheep's clothing but inwardly are ravenous wolves" (from the "Sermon on the Mount" in Matthew 7:15). This is also the chapter which begins with the admonition regarding judgment and vision, the beams and motes in one's eyes.

24. Certainly male saints are also mirrored in Christ's sacrifices, and it may be, as in the case of priests who become martyrs, that their human sexuality is forfeited in the service of God; but they remain distinguished from the women saints, whose sexuality in almost every instance is the key to their martyrdom.

25. E. M. Cioran, *Tears and Saints,* trans. Ilinca Zarifopol-Johnston (Chicago: University of Chicago Press, 1995), 19. This work was first written in Romanian in 1937. See also Lacan's brief address to these connections in the Bernini statue of St. Theresa, in *Feminine Sexuality: Jacques Lacan and the école freudienne,* ed. Juliet Mitchell and Jacqueline Rose (New York: Norton, 1985).

26. Cioran, *Tears and Saints,* 22.

27. I take this detail from Sean Kelly and Rosemary Rodgers's *Saints Preserve Us!* (New York: Random House, 1993), a kind of tongue-in-cheek update of the lives of saints ("Everything You Need to Know about Every Saint You'll Ever Need"). My notes on the saints are compiled from Gifford, *"Ulysses" Annotated;* the *Eleventh Britannic Encyclopedia* (Cambridge, England, 1910), a source for Joyce himself; Rev. S. Baring-Gould, *The Lives of Saints* (London: John Hodges, 1882); Donald Attwater, *The Penguin Dictionary of Saints* (Baltimore: Penguin Books, 1965); David Hugh Farmer, *The Oxford Dictionary of Saints* (Oxford: Clarendon Press, 1978); Rt. Rev. F. G. Holveck, *A Biographical Dictionary of the Saints* (St. Louis: B. Herder Book Company, 1924).

28. This detail is taken from the *Eleventh Britannica,* which quotes from Butler's *Lives of the Saints* (803).

29. For a fascinating and informative discussion of the Christian and Jewish origins of the relationship between veiling, virginity, and the male gaze/female vision, as well as classical representations of the phallus as an apotropaic device against the evil eye, in suggestively Cyclopsian form, see *Off With Her Head!: The Denial of Women's Identity in Myth, Religion and Culture,* ed. Howard Eilberg-Schwartz and Wendy Doniger (Berkeley: University of California Press, 1995), especially Mary Rose D'Angelo's "Veils, Virgins and the Tongues of Men and Angels: Women's Heads in Early Christianity," 131–64.

30. St. Barbara and St. Scholastica, while fitting generally into the scheme, here might have had particular interest to Joyce given their connections to thunderstorms. For each, a thunder noise is associated with the moment of their martyrdom. St. Barbara, yet another victim of the "excesses" of female beauty, is invoked by miners and all those who deal with explosives.

31. Cioran devotes a few pages to Rose of Lima, to her (as to all the saints') "excess love": "Rose of Lima, born in South America apparently to redeem Pizarro's crimes, is a model for all those with a vocation for suffering. Young and beautiful, she could not think of an excuse to resist her mother's wish to bring her out in society. But she finally found a compromise. Under the flowers on her head she pinned a needle that pricked her forehead incessantly. Thus she satisfied her desire to be alone in society. One conquers the temptation of the work through pain" (*Tears and Saints,* 9).

32. Margot Norris discusses Gerty's "roses" and Molly's redolence as part of her inscription of a "critical heliotropism," as she puts it, in her essay, "Joyce's Heliotrope," in *Coping With Joyce,* ed. Morris Beja and Shari Benstock (Columbus: Ohio State University Press, 1989), 3–24. In Georges Bataille's essay, "The Language of Flowers," the

emblem of the flower exposes the underside of desire, the idealized, sanitized love object: "It is evident, in fact, that if one expresses love with the aid of a flower, it is the corolla, rather than the useful organs, that becomes the sign of desire. . . . In fact the substitution of juxtaposed elements for essential elements is consistent with all we spontaneously know about the emotions that motivate us, since the object of human love is never an organ, but the person who has the organ" (in *Visions of Excess: Selected Writings, 1927–1939,* ed. Allan Soekl, with Carl Lovitt and Donald M. Leslie Jr. [Minneapolis: University of Minnesota Press, 1985], 11). One might also remember here that Molly can be no-saint because she is, at least, part Jewish; just after she begins to menstruate in "Penelope," she recalls a visit to the gynecologist where he inquires "if what I did had an offensive odour" (18.1160).

33. Bataille, "The Language of Flowers," 13.

34. Gifford, *"Ulysses" Annotated,* 39.

35. Mark Osteen also observes the similarity between Deasy's and the citizen's remarks, and comments that they are both anti-Semites ("Narrative Gifts," 172n.). And as for repeating connections, it might be worth mentioning that Eve, Helen, and "Breffni" appear in the same thought, as it were, when Stephen in "Aeolus" remembers his earlier exchange with Deasy in response to Myles Crawford's damning commentary on Deasy's wife. In other words, he seems to make a connection between mythic and personal acts of betrayal (see 7.530–39).

36. Osteen suggests that England is a "ready scapegoat" in an analysis that posits "sentimental, histrionic oratory," as a diversionary tactic from effective actions of any kind ("Narrative Gifts," 172); the reference to the English in such terms is certainly evocative of the Jewish role, the invading "stranger."

37. For a variety of reasons explained by such writers as David Lloyd and Daniel Boyarin, with particular relevance to this context, the displaced object of derision is often a projection/dejection of self. At the same time, as Lloyd has argued, resistance to the colonizer often involves, almost in an oedipal sense, a tacit identification with him (see, for example, *Nationalism and Minor Literature: James Clarence Mangan and the Emergence of Irish Cultural Nationalism* [Berkeley: University of California Press, 1987] and *Anomalous States: Irish Writing and the Post-Colonial Moment.* That is why the citizen's association of Bloom with the English ("their syphilisation" [12.1197]) and with the feminine involves both a dissociation from and identification with Bloom on his part. Boyarin would see the source of all these dissociations/identifications in the specter of Jewishness. In a marvelous review essay, he writes:

> I am suggesting that the internalized self-contempt that the colonized male comes to feel for his disempowered situation—represented in the case of Jews by the affect surrounding circumcision—is a powerful force for the production of the twin diseases of misogyny and homophobia in the postcolonial situation, precisely because their situation has been misrecognized as feminized. The intrapsychic mechanism is a kind of splitting occasioned by the "move" from one subject position—that of the colonized—to another where there is partial identification with the colonizer. The subject begins to see himself with the eyes of his oppressor and thus to wish to abject that in himself which he now identifies as contemptible by projecting it on to women and gay men. ("*Epater l'embourgeoisement:* Freud, Gender and the (De)colonized Psyche," *Diacritics* 24 [spring 1994]: 36)

Boyarin goes on to suggest through his examination of Freud's case of "Little Hans" that "hearing about circumcision is the unconscious root of misogyny, just as it is the root of anti-Semitism." In the complex of dissociations/identifications, the citizen at once berates Jews and women, and Jews as women; identifies with the ambivalent feminized image of Ireland and betrayal; and aligns, as was popular in the period, Irish history with that of the Israelites, in their quest of the promised land. The Zaretsky case, for example, which the men discuss (12.1084–110), where Jew swindles Jew, provides an analogue for the citizen's blindness to his betrayal of a fellow subaltern, both racial inferiors ("white negroes") in the eyes of the European elite and the racial discourse of the period. In all these regards, also see my "Joyce's Grand Nationals," and, in particular, chapters 1 and 3 of *James Joyce's Judaic Other.*

38. See Elizabeth Butler Cullingford, "'Thinking of Her . . . as . . . Ireland': Yeats, Pearse and Heaney," in *Textual Practice* 4 (spring 1990): 13–14.

39. This description of *The Book of Ballymote* is taken from Tim O'Neill, *The Irish Hand* (Dublin: Dolman Press, 1984). O'Neill suggests that it was a patron's book, written over time by three different scribes.

40. One can certainly look to Gilman, in *The Jew's Body* or *Freud, Race and Gender,* for discussions of and references to the specific anti-Semitic tracts on the subject of race and nationality in fin-de-siècle Europe; and one can find a discussion of the Irish analogues in these terms in, for example, David Cairns and Shaun Richards, *Writing Ireland: Colonialism, Nationalism and Culture* (Manchester: Manchester University Press, 1988), particularly in the chapter "An Essentially Feminine Race." Another recent work aligns Jews and Irish in terms of the "iconography of *domestic degeneracy* of the imperial hierarchy" (Anne McClintock, *Imperial Leather* [New York: Routledge, 1995], 53). Ethnicity provides a current corrective for the misuse of the idea of race.

41. David Hayman, "Cyclops," *James Joyce's "Ulysses": Critical Essays* (Berkeley: University of California Press, 1974), 252. Of course, Bloom seems identified with Molly here, at least racially, if not sexually, just as the citizen momentarily feels aligned with the women who have "let the strangers in." For a discussion of Bloom's masochism here and elsewhere in the text, see, for example, Frances L. Restuccia, *Joyce and the Law of the Father* (New Haven: Yale University Press, 1989).

42. Osteen, "Narrative Gifts," 179.

43. Another woman associated with Emmet in such terms is Anne Devlin, his housemaid, whose nationalist acts and subsequent imprisonment were historically represented as mediated or remediable through her love for the hero Emmet (in contradistinction to Curran, the sinner). A filmmaker like Pat Murphy, in her 1985 *Anne Devlin,* recuperates Devlin as the subject of her own story, based largely on Devlin's journals.

44. Cioran, *Tears and Saints,* 9.

45. Ibid., 45.

46. Osteen, "Narrative Gifts," 185.

47. See James Shapiro's *Shakespeare and the Jews* (New York: Columbia University Press, 1996), for a wonderful discussion of circumcision, ritual murder, and *The Merchant of Venice.* Shapiro points out Gratiano's reference to Shylock as "wolvish, bloody, starved and ravenous" (110), reminding us of the recirculations of Jewish stereotypes, the "wolf" that Bloom is.

48. It is likely that Bloom refers to the composer Felix Mendelssohn-Bartholdy, whose father was a convert to Christianity and whose grandfather, Moses, is known as the father of the Jewish Enlightenment (he is mentioned in "Ithaca"). In "Eumaeus," Bloom confuses Mercadante with the composer of *Les Huguenots,* Giacomo Meyerbeer,

who was Jewish (16.1737–38), and it is likely that he has done the same here. One can account for this in a number of ways, but here the reference to the last words of Christ seems particularly apt. Of course, there are a number of variations on what those words might be; in Matthew, which seems the relevant gospel for "Cyclops," Jesus' last words, "My God [actually repeated twice], why hast thou forsaken me," is taken by some of the bystanders to be an invocation of Elijah and therefore an announcement of the coming of the Messiah, or presumably, that Jesus is announcing himself as that messiah (Matthew 27:45–50). This is, of course, resonant with Bloom's "crucifixion" here and his ascension as ben Bloom Elijah, crying *"Abba Adonai."*

49. Susannah Heschel, "Jesus as Theological Transvestite," in *Feminist Critical Study and Judaism,* ed. Miriam Peskowitz and Laura Levitt (New York: Routledge, 1998). In this wonderful essay, Heschel goes on to demonstrate that when the Christian establishment has historically admitted Christ as Jew, they compensate for the discomfort by representing the Jewish Jesus as victim—and in that state, feminized—whose escape from Judaism makes him a man and a hero, eventually the martyr.

50. Hitler's *Mein Kampf,* of course, refers to Jews as syphilitic (see Gilman, *The Jew's Body,* 125). In a wonderful essay, Moshe Lazar begins with an epigraph from Erasmus that provides one of the profound sources of the necessary disidentification of Christians from Jews and its implications: "*Si Christianum est odissse Iudeos / hic abunde christiani sumus omnes* (If hating Jews makes one a true Christian, then we are all outstanding Christians)" ("The Lamb and the Scapegoat: The Dehumanization of the Jews in Medieval Propaganda Imagery," in *Anti-Semitism in Times of Crises,* ed. Sander L. Gilman and Steven T. Katz [New York: New York University Press, 1991], 38).

51. Heschel, "Jesus as Theological Transvestite." Let me also add here a note to Boyarin's commentary on the issue of Jewish maleness and what he sees as a rejection of performances of masculinity, which is not a sign of the "unnatural . . . but a positive cultural product" *("Epater l'embourgeoisiement,"* 39). He suggests that while Diaspora Jews felt "castrated" in cultural and national terms, the sexual or gendered attribution to the sense of dispossession was imposed from without and internalized by Jews.

52. Margot Norris tells us that "heliotrope is another name for the gem with the oxymoronic alternative name of bloodstone" ("Joyce's Heliotrope," 3).

A METAPHYSICS OF COITUS IN "NAUSICAA"

1. For an excellent, extended treatment of this complementarity, see Tony E. Jackson, "'Cyclops,' 'Nausicaa,' and Joyce's Imaginary Irish Couple," in *James Joyce Quarterly* 29 (fall 1991): 63–83.

2. Karen Lawrence, *The Odyssey of Style in James Joyce's "Ulysses"* (Princeton: Princeton University Press, 1981), 121.

3. "Between" derives from the Old English *be tweonum* (literally, "by twain") and is etymologically related to the words *twin* (O.E. *twinn*) and *twilight* (from the Middle English *twi-* and *light*), whose earliest sense seems to be "the light between." For Derrida, the French equivalent of the English "between"—the "syncategorem" *entre*—evokes all the undecidability and indefinitional lack of fixity of the "hymen, the 'between,' whether it names fusion or separation," identity or difference. See Jacques Derrida, "The Double Session," in *Dissemination,* trans. Barbara Johnson (Chicago: University of Chicago Press, 1981), especially 209–13.

4. For an excellent discussion of the manifold "twinning" in "Nausicaa"—of char-

acters, scenes, images, and themes—see Craig Smith, "Twilight in Dublin: A Look at Joyce's 'Nausicaa,'" *James Joyce Quarterly* 28 (spring 1991): 631–35.

5. See also, for example, "in in the evening" (13.132), "she knew that that would take the shine out" (13.163–64), "manly man" (13.210), "virgin of virgins" (13.289), "lowest of the low" (13.302), "two great big lovely big tears" (13.399), "even, even" (13.432), "womanly woman" (13.435), "her breath caught as she caught the expression in his eyes" (13.516), "that that little hint she gave had had the desired effect" (13.568–69), "push up the pushcart" (13.571–72), "talking about the time all the time" (13.575), "saying that that was the benediction" (13.619), "all in all" (13.671), "look, look" (13.717), and "up, up" (13.720).

6. Consider also Bloom's habit of comparatively coupling the various women and men in his life: "Martha, she [Gerty]" (13.782); "Molly and Milly" (13.785); "Mary, Martha: now as then" (13.805–6); "Molly and Josie Powell" (13.814); "Mrs Beaufoy, Purefoy" (13.959); "he, not me" (13.1239); "Was that just when he, she?" (13.848); "he gets the plums and I the plumstones" (13.1098–99); "her high notes and her low notes" (13.1011); "she an only child, I an only child" (13.1109).

7. Frank Budgen, *James Joyce and the Making of "Ulysses"* (Bloomington: Indiana University Press, 1960), 202, 211–14.

8. Margot Norris has put this best in *Joyce's Web: The Social Unraveling of Modernism* (Austin: University of Texas Press, 1992): "The voice that speaks of Gerty in 'Nausicaa' . . . makes best sense as a phantom narrator constructed by Gerty's imagination to produce the language of her desire, that is, to produce the hypothetical praises that she fears no one will ever offer, and that she equates with art. Her narration therefore represents Gerty not as she is, nor even as she is not, but as she would like to be, as she would like people to think about her, and indeed, to write about her, given the conspicuous and emphatic literariness of her narration" (169).

9. See, for example, Richard Ellmann, *Ulysses on the Liffey* (New York: Oxford University Press, 1972), 126; and Hugh Kenner, *Ulysses* (Baltimore: Johns Hopkins University Press, 1987), 101–2.

10. Don Gifford glosses "Jemina Brown" as a song about the hazards, chances, and treachery of pairing: "The speaker meets Jemina by chance, finds her attractive, and eventually goes out on a date with her; then he sees her with another man, whom she passes off as 'only brother Bill.' She gets the speaker to lend her £50 and then disappears, finally to be discovered in one more chance meeting as coproprietor (with 'brother Bill') of a grocery store in New Jersey. The speaker's £50 have, of course, purchased the store" (*"Ulysses" Annotated: Notes for James Joyce's "Ulysses"* [Berkeley: University of California Press, 1988], 397).

11. Martha's letter drifts through Bloom's mind at the following moments in "Nausicaa," more or less underlining his retrospective thoughts about Gerty: "I have such a bad headache today. Where did I put the letter? Yes, all right" (13.778–79); "Anyhow I got the best of that. Damned glad I didn't do it in the bath this morning over her silly I will punish you letter" (13.785–87); "To aid gentleman in literary" (13.835); "Did I forget to write address on that letter like the postcard I sent to Flynn?" (13.843–44); "Care of P. O. Dolphin's Barn. Are you not happy in your? Naughty darling. At Dolphin's Barn" (13.1105–6); "What is the meaning of that other world. I called you naughty boy because I do not like" (13.1262–63); "naughty Grace darling" (13.1280); and "perfume your wife" (13.1281).

12. Morgan's formula is "Pornography is the theory, rape is the practice." I wish not

to engage here in the debate as to whether or not pornography (or reading) causes violence against women, but merely to point out that far too little distinction is made in such debates between the production and consumption of pornography; my impression is that consumers of pornography are no less victims of their reading than Gerty is of hers. I have also in mind here some remarks of B. Ruby Rich, who notes, in a review of *Not a Love Story: A Motion Picture about Pornography,* that "a proper subject for the legions of feminist men" would be to "let them undertake the analysis that can tell us why men like porn (not, piously, why this or that exceptional man does *not*), why stroke books work, how oedipal formations feed the drive, and how any of it can be changed" ("Anti-Porn: Soft Issue, Hard World," *Feminist Review* 13 [spring 1983]: 66; quoted in Stephen Heath, "Male Feminism," in *Men in Feminism,* ed. Alice Jardine and Paul Smith [New York: Methuen, 1987], 2).

13. "Hysterical attacks . . . are nothing but phantasies projected and translated into motor activity and represented in pantomime," according to Sigmund Freud. In Gerty's case, of course, this motor activity would include her blushing, the rhythmic swinging of her leg, and the emotionalized sensations of excited fright and transport. Freud adds that "the common origin and normal prototype of all these phantastic creations are the so-called daydreams of adolescence. . . . These phantasies are wish-fulfillments, products of frustration and desire" ("General Remarks on Hysterical Attacks" and "Hysterical Phantasies and Their Relation to Bisexuality," in *Dora: An Analysis of a Case of Hysteria,* ed. Philip Rieff [New York: Collier Books, 1963], 153, 145–46).

14. These indications would include her recollection of Cissy Caffrey offering Tommy "the scatty heel of the loaf or brown bread with golden syrup on" (13.32–33); her recollection of Cissy joking about "jaspberry ram" after Cissy calls attention to the contents of Bloom's pants (13.272); the "compliments" that baby Boardman sends up out of "his wee fat tummy" onto his "brandnew dribbling bib" (13.610–12); the "gush[ing]" fireworks (13.736–40); and (though they are objects of perception rather than imagination) literal ejaculations like Edy Boardman's "Butter and cream" (13.65) and Cissy's "O my! Puddeny pie!" (13.613). Gerty's fantasy of how she might please a husband with her cooking in itself reads like a recipe for masturbation: her "queen Ann's pudding of delightful creaminess had won golden opinions from all . . . dredge in the fine selfraising flour and always stir in the same direction, then cream," as it says, "the milk and sugar and whisk well the white of eggs" (13.225–28). Bloom's likening of his ejaculate to "celery sauce" (13.1041)—that is, white sauce—in the second half of "Nausicaa" retrospectively sanctions these interpretations.

15. Bloom's assertion that Gerty would "sooner have me as I am than some poet chap" is belied by his fleeting memory of a phrase from the advertisement he wrote to enlist Martha's interest ("To aid gentleman in literary work"): in that situation, as in "Nausicaa," he did some "stage setting" to make himself appear, at least in his own eyes, more attractive than he actually thinks he is.

16. This sense is reinforced by a notation that Joyce made in the schema for *Ulysses* that he gave to Carlo Linati, where he designated "Nausicaa"'s significance as "The Projected Mirage." See Richard Ellmann, *Ulysses on the Liffey,* appendix.

17. Margot Norris has shrewdly noted that the three "curiosities" who occur to Bloom here are unflatteringly rendered versions of Gerty (the "nun"), Cissy Caffrey ("the dark one with the mop head and the nigger mouth" [13.898]), and Edy Boardman (the "girl with glasses"). His monologue rudely strips Gerty of its beautifications (*Joyce's Web,* 176).

18. The cock, lion, and stag suggest, of course, Boylan, Leopold, and Stephen—the prototype of the latter figured as a stag "with flashing antlers" in Joyce's early essay, "A Portrait of the Artist" (see *JJ* 176).

19. "No roses without thorns" (5.277–78), as Bloom cavalierly thinks while tossing away the pin attached to the dried flower that Martha sends with her titillating letter. The gesture suggests that real relationships, like Bloom's with Molly—and like real roses—come with pain and thorns; in fantasized relations, like those Bloom enjoys with Gerty and Martha, the thorns are conveniently detachable. A corollary retrospectively sealed by "Nausicaa" is that real relations—like real roses—yield their share of beauty and aromatic power, whereas fantasized relations, like Martha's dessicated flower, do not.

20. Bloom surmises that Gerty is "near her monthlies" early in his monologue, in part because he believes that "it makes them feel ticklish" (because, that is, he see menstruation as a trigger for Gerty's adventurous flirtatiousness), and in part because he associates her with Martha (13.777–85). Even so, his sense that there is "something in the air" (13.782)—together with his intensifying reflections on the probability that Gerty is menstruating as his monologue progresses—suggests something like the slow apprehension of her "rose" perfume over time. Joyce is, I think, trying to convey Bloom's slowly awakening olfactory perception of Gerty: "Why did I smell it only now? Took its time in coming like herself, slow but sure. Suppose it's ever so many millions of tiny grains blown across" (13.1015–17).

21. In a paradox at bottom almost as baffling as might be a meditation on the smell of the eye, Gerty's monologue is obsessed with the look of the nose, rather than with its olfactory functionality. An advertisement on "the Woman Beautiful page of the Princess Novelette" asks the question, "you have a beautiful face but your nose?"—prompting Gerty to think that "that would suit Mrs Dignam because she had a button one" (13.110–15). Reggy Wylie, by contrast, "was undeniably handsome with an exquisite nose" (13.140–41); Cissy Caffrey speaks "with a pert toss of her head and a piquant tilt of her nose" (13.168–69); and though Gerty "could not see whether [Bloom] had an aquiline nose or a slightly *retroussé*," we know that she thinks it is a nice one (13.420). The two dark blots in this parade of nasal paradigms are "the snottynosed twins" (13.529) and "the gentleman off Sandymount green that Cissy Caffrey called the man that was so like himself," of whom we learn that Gerty "would not like him for a father because he was too old or something or on account of his face . . . or his carbuncly nose with the pimples on it and his sandy moustache a bit white under the nose" (13.305–11). A note in the *Ulysses* Notebook V.A.2 clarifies the passage by specifying the "white under nostril moustach[e] [as] snots" (*Joyce's Notes and Early Drafts for "Ulysses": Selections from the Buffalo Collection,* ed. Phillip Herring [Charlottesville: University of Virginia Press, 1977], 91). The absurdity of these figurations—and of romantic fiction's conversion of the nose into an item of apparitional weight—becomes clearest when we learn that on the single occasion when Reggy Wylie gave Gerty "a half kiss (the first!) it was only the end of her nose" (13.203–4).

Obsessed as the first half of "Nausicaa" is with the "look" rather than the scenting power of the nose, a range of details evident elsewhere in Gerty's monologue suggests that perfumatory censing and deodorization—the whitewashing of the olfactory realm—might be regarded as sensory equivalents to the kinds of repression and euphemistic masking that enable her sentimental narrative to maintain its idealizations of human relations: the narrative does everything that it can to conceal not simply the indelicate, but also the malodorous. "Tommy Caffrey," for instance, "could never be got to take his castor oil unless it was Cissy Caffrey that held his nose" (13.30–31). Even more often, an awareness of the olfactory realm is not simply masked, but also overpowered by spectacle, the eye and its idealizations being made to dominate the unseemlier perceptions of the nose: "it was Gerty who tacked up on the wall of that place where she never forgot every fortnight the chlorate of lime Mr Tunney the grocer's christmas almanac, the picture of halcyon days where a young gentleman in the costume they used to wear then with a threecornered hat was offering a bunch of flowers to his ladylove with oldtime chivalry" (13.332–36). The manifold censing agents that appear throughout Gerty's monologue serve much the same function as the chlorate of lime and almanac picture here, covering over an awareness of the impure olfactory realm with a steadily maintained image of pure and idealized relations: hence the recurrent references to "the nice perfume of [Reggy Wylie's] good cigarettes" (13.144–45); Mrs. MacDowell's snuff (which was long used to mask unpleasant odors [13.328–30]); "the whiterose scent" and "alabaster pouncetbox" that Gerty keeps in "the drawer of her toilettable" (13.637–40); and the ongoing censing of the Star of the Sea chapel by Father Conroy and Canon O'Hanlon. On snuff as a deodorizing agent, and on the ongoing cultural debate about whether deodorizing perfumes are meant to enhance or mask the scents of the body, see Alain Corbin, *The Foul and the Fragrant: Odor and the French Social Imagination,* trans. Aubier Montaigne (Cambridge: Harvard University Press, 1986).

22. "Watch! Watch! See! Looked round. She smelt an onion" (13.936)—so Bloom thinks as he watches Gerty and her friends walk away from him on the beach and wonders if she will turn around to have one more look at him. The phrase "she smelt an onion," Gifford explains, derives "from a joke about a man who determined to keep himself free from any entanglement with women. In order to fulfill his determination, he ate a raw onion whenever contact with women was imminent. His scheme and his self-discipline collapsed when he met a woman who found his oniony breath extraordinarily attractive" (*"Ulysses" Annotated,* 396). As Bloom's self-conscious application of the joke to his own situation attests, it undermines the conventions of romantic and sentimental love fiction in much the same way that his own thoughts do by suggesting that you can never tell who, for what reasons, is going to find whom attractive: "As God made them he matched them" (13.976).

23. Its movement "to and fro"—"hither, thither," "Here. There"—between Gerty's and Bloom's monologues reminding us in part of their dynamic interimplication (13.752, 13.626, 13.1286), the bat also evokes the sensory extremes between which the two parts of "Nausicaa" are played out. "Blind" enough to mistake Bloom for a tree (13.1117–18)—just as Gerty mistakes Bloom for the ideal husband and "manly man" (13.210) and Bloom mistakes her for a "hot little devil" (13.776)—the bat has one of the most hyperdeveloped senses of smell in the animal kingdom: "a mother bat, entering a nursery cave where millions of mother and baby bats cling to the wall or wing through air, can find her young by calling to it or smelling a path toward it" (Diane Ackerman, *A Natural History of the Senses* [New York: Vintage, 1995], 27). Its prominence in the second half of "Nausicaa," accordingly—as it flits from Gerty's vision and the church belfry, where Bloom imagines it "hang[ing] by its heels in the odour of sanctity" (13.1121)—signifies something like the disabling of the eye and the awakening of the nose in the dark, the movement beneath vision of senses on the prowl. Its equation with Bloom is reinforced by his sympathetic identification of the animal as "a little man in a cloak . . . with tiny hands. Weeny bones" (13.1130–31), but also by the very peculiar way

in which Joyce invokes it. As a "ba" (13.1117, 13.1119, 13.1127, 13.1143), the secretively prowling bat cannot help but recall Bloom's "high grade ha" and the head it contains (4.69–70), both repositories of erotic secrets in a chapter full of erotic secrets and references to erotic secrecy.

"They're a mixed breed," Bloom moreover notes of bats: "wonder why they come out at night . . . . Birds are like hopping mice. What frightens them, light or noise?" (13.1127–29). Bloom's ruminations here lead us to see the bat not only as a cross between bird and mammal (as a generically "mixed breed" not unlike "Nausicaa" itself), but also as a creature sensorily opposite to most birds: in keeping with his eclectic encyclopedism ("Have birds no smell?" [13.1118]), Bloom seems aware that birds, unlike bats, have almost no sense of smell at all but, often enough, highly developed powers of vision ("although there are some exceptions . . . seabirds often navigate by smell" [Ackerman, *Natural History of the Senses,* 30]). In much the same way that Joyce frames his reflections on sound between exemplary figures of a deaf waiter and a blind piano tuner in "Sirens," in other words, Bloom's reflections on birds and bats—totems of the chapter's two sections—seem ultimately to amplify and frame the chapter's intricate investigations of the sensory powers of the eye and nose.

24. On "animal magnetism" and its history in relation to that of psychoanalysis, see Henri F. Ellenberger, *The Discovery of the Unconscious: The History and Evolution of Dynamic Psychotherapy* (New York: Basic Books, 1970), 53–102.

25. See, for example, Kenner, *Ulysses,* 104–5.

26. See, for instance, Fritz Senn, "Nausicaa," in *James Joyce's "Ulysses": Critical Essays,* ed. Clive Hart and David Hayman (Berkeley: University of California Press, 1974), 284–86, and Kenner, *Ulysses,* 105–6.

27. For an excellent account of Gerty's seduction by literature, see Margot Norris, "Modernism, Myth, and Desire in 'Nausicaa,'" chapter 8 of *Joyce's Web,* 164–80.

28. Students of Homer tend to see the Phaikaia (Books VI-VIII of *The Odyssey*) as a parallel to the Nostos, as an idealized version of the kind of homecoming that Odysseus might enjoy under the best and most idyllic of circumstances. Nausicaa, in this reading, emerges as the adoringly devoted child, an idealized and female version of Telemachus—just as Gerty, in ways, emerges as a female version of Stephen. Like the first half of "Nausicaa," moreover, the Phaikaian books of *The Odyssey* give a picture of Homeric life that falls somewhere halfway between myth and reality. After his voyage through a universe of gods and monsters, but before returning to the human circumstances beleaguering his family and native land, Odysseus lingers in the utopian site of Phaikaia, where, in a way, Homer provides as idealized a picture of Greek domestic life as do the sentimental novels that Gerty reads. See A. F. Garvie, "Introduction: The Phaeacian Books," in *Homer: Odyssey: Books VI-VIII,* ed. A. F. Garvie (Cambridge: Cambridge University Press, 1994), 22–25.

29. Shari Benstock and Bernard Benstock, *Who's He When He's at Home: A James Joyce Directory* (Urbana: University of Illinois Press, 1980), 30.

30. Ellmann, *Ulysses on the Liffey,* 131–32.

31. For comparably fragmented and elliptical items in Bloom's monologue in "Nausicaa," see also 13.801–2, 13.828–29, 13.844–46, 13.848, 13.860–61, 13.877–78, 13.908, 13.944–46, 13.984–85, 13.1036–37, 13.1097, 13.1108, 13.1111, 13.1212–13, and (most notoriously) 13.1258 and 13.1264.

32. The rare and precious orchid, which has delicately been transplanted from its native earth on the other side of the globe, can only be fertilized, improbably, by a bee

that happens to be carrying pollen lifted from a plant of the same species and opposite sex growing in the remote locale from which the orchid originally came. In *Cities of the Plain,* as a way of enabling Proust to comment on the uncanny ways in which homosexuals like Charlus and Jupien somehow manage to find each other, the pollen-carrying bee miraculously arrives to fertilize the orchid: there is someone for everyone. See Marcel Proust, *Remembrance of Things Past,* trans. C. K. Scott Moncrieff and Terence Kilmartin (New York: Random House, 1981), 2:535–37, 623–29, 650–56.

INTERESTING STATES

1. For a vivid partisan account of this affair see Noel Browne, *Against the Tide* (Dublin: Gill and Macmillan, 1986), 141–55.

2. For one interesting commentary on these issues written at the time they were beginning to be widely discussed in Ireland, see Rosita Sweetman, *On Our Knees* (London: Pan Books, 1978).

3. This is the reading of "Oxen of the Sun" in relation to late-colonial Irish politics, which I briefly suggest in my *The Subaltern Ulysses* (Minneapolis: University of Minnesota Press, 1994), 185.

4. Roddy Doyle, *The Snapper* (London: Penguin Books, 1992).

5. Richard Brown, *Joyce and Sexuality* (London: Cambridge University Press, 1985), 83–88.

6. Pádraig H. Pearse, *Plays Stories Poems* (Dublin: Talbot Press, 1966), 333.

7. Richard Ellmann, *Ulysses on the Liffey* (Oxford: Oxford University Press, 1979), 136–38.

8. Mary Lowe-Evans, *Crimes against Fecundity: Joyce and Population Control* (New York: Syracuse University Press, 1989), 53–74.

9. Richard Brown, *Joyce and Sexuality,* 83–88.

10. Mary Lowe-Evans, *Crimes against Fecundity,* 63, 69–70.

11. Ellen Carol Jones, "Textual Matter: Writing the Mother in Joyce," in *Joyce: The Return of the Repressed,* ed. Susan Stanford Friedman (New York: Cornell University Press, 1993), 257–83.

12. Maurizia Boscagli, *The Eye on the Flesh: Fashions of Masculinity in the Early Twentieth-Century* (Boulder: Westview Press, 1996); see particularly chapter 2, "The Hero and the Typist: Superman, Office Clerks, and the Petty Bourgeois Body," 55–91.

13. J. S. Atherton, "The Oxen of the Sun," in *James Joyce's Ulysses: Critical Essays,* ed. Clive Hart and David Hayman (Berkeley: University of California Press, 1974), 332.

14. Atherton calls these private jokes on Joyce's part ("Oxen of the Sun," 320); many of them, however, seem shamelessly public.

15. See Susan Stanford Friedman, "Creativity and the Childbirth Metaphor: Gender Differences in Literary Discourses," in *Speaking of Gender,* ed. Elaine Showalter (New York: Routledge, 1989), 71–80. Friedman notes that "the fact that Joyce partly envies the fecundity of female flesh and despairs of the sterility of male minds does not alter the fundamental sexual dualism of his complex birth metaphors. Joyce's women produce infants through the channel of the flesh, while his men produce a brainchild through the agency of language."

16. Helene Cixous notes that "Woman, if you look for her, has a strong chance of always being found in one position: in bed" ("Castration or Decapitation," *Signs* 71 [autumn 1981]: 41–55).

DISENCHANTING ENCHANTMENT

1. Homer, *The Odyssey,* trans. Robert Fitzgerald (Garden City: Doubleday, 1963), 172.

2. Lacan writes, "There is an antimony, here, that is internal to the assumption by man (*Mensch*) of his sex: why must he assume the attributes of that sex only through a threat—the threat, indeed, of their privation? In "Civilization and Its Discontents," Freud, as we know, went so far as to suggest a disturbance of human sexuality, not of a contingent, but of an essential kind" (Jacques Lacan, "The signification of the phallus," in *Ecrits: A Selection,* trans. Alan Sheridan [New York: W. W. Norton & Co., 1977], 281).

3. Michel Foucault, *The History of Sexuality,* trans. Robert Hurley (New York: Vintage Books), and Teresa de Lauretis, "The Technology of Gender," in *Technologies of Gender: Essays on Theory, Film and Fiction* (Bloomington: Indiana University Press, 1987).

4. De Lauretis, "The Technology of Gender," 4.

5. Bonnie Kime Scott, "'The Young Girl,' Jane Heap, and Trials of Gender in *Ulysses,*" in *Joycean Cultures: Culturing Joyces,* ed. Vincent C. Cheng, Kimberly J. Devlin, and Margot Norris (Newark: University of Delaware Press, 1998), 78–94.

6. See, for example, Ewa Ziarek, "'Circe': Joyce's *Argumentum ad Feminam,*" *James Joyce Quarterly* 30 (fall 1992): 51–68; Christine Froula, "Circe's Necessary Evils, or, Politico-Pornosophical Philotheology," delivered at the XIV International Joyce Conference in Seville, Spain, June 1994; Cheryl Herr, *Joyce's Anatomy of Culture* (Urbana: University of Illinois Press, 1986), ch. 4 and 5, 136–221.

7. John M. Woolsey, "The Monumental Decision of the United States District Court Rendered December 6, 1933, by Hon. John M. Woolsey Lifting the Ban on *Ulysses,*" in *Ulysses* (New York: Vintage Books, 1961), xi.

8. See Alice Jardine, "The Woman-in-Effect," in *Gynesis* (Ithaca: Cornell University Press, 1985), 31–49.

9. Kimberly J. Devlin, "Pretending in 'Penelope': Masquerade, Mimicry, and Molly Bloom," in *Molly Blooms: A Polylogue on 'Penelope' and Cultural Studies,* ed. Richard Pearce (Madison: University of Wisconsin Press, 1994), 80–102.

10. Joan Riviere, "Womanliness as a Masquerade," in *Formations of Fantasy,* ed. Victor Burgin, James Donald, and Cora Kaplan (London: Metheun, 1986), 35–44.

11. Roland Barthes, *Sade, Fourier, Loyola,* trans. Richard Miller (New York: Hill and Wang, 1976), 164.

12. Joseph A. Boone, "Staging Sexuality: Repression, Representation, and 'Interior' States in *Ulysses,*" in *Joyce: The Return of the Repressed,* ed. Susan Stanford Friedman (Ithaca: Cornell University Press, 1993), 199.

13. The illustration Bloom sees depicts the vicious discipline of indentured circus girls, as Mary Power describes it: the master's "compulsive drive for perfection leads him to beat them in the nude" ("The Discovery of Ruby," *James Joyce Quarterly* 18 [winter 1981]: 118).

14. Robert Scholes, "In the Brothel of Modernism: Picasso and Joyce," in *In Search of James Joyce* (Urbana: University of Illinois Press, 1992).

15. Karen Lawrence, *The Odyssey of Style in "Ulysses"* (Princeton: Princeton University Press, 1981), ch. 6, 146–64.

16. John Gordon, "Approaching Reality in 'Circe,'" in *James Joyce Annual 1994,* ed. Thomas F. Staley (Austin: University of Texas Press, 1994), 4.

17. Sandra M. Gilbert and Susan Gubar, *No Man's Land: The Place of the Women Writer*

in the Twentieth Century, Volume 2: Sexchanges (New Haven: Yale University Press, 1989), 332.

18. Cheryl Herr writes, "*Ulysses* argues that sexuality is sheer theater, at least on the social stage on which we dramatically construct the selves we play" (*Joyce's Anatomy of Culture,* 154).

19. Gilbert and Gubar, *No Man's Land,* 333.

20. Charles Bernheimer, *Figures of Ill Repute* (Cambridge: Harvard University Press, 1989), 3.

21. Herr, *Joyce's Anatomy of Culture,* 208.

22. Harry Blamires, *The Bloomsday Book* (London: Methuen, 1966), 185.

23. Don Gifford and Robert J. Seidman, *Notes for Joyce: An Annotation of James Joyce's "Ulysses"* (New York: Dutton, 1974), 498.

24. Woolsey, "The Monumental Decision," xi.

THE DOUBLE LIFE OF "EUMAEUS"

1. Richard Ellmann, *Ulysses on the Liffey* (New York: Oxford University Press, 1972), 154; Frank Budgen, *James Joyce and the Making of "Ulysses"* (London: Oxford University Press, 1972), 255.

2. Gerald L. Bruns, "Eumaeus," in *James Joyce's "Ulysses": Critical Essays,* ed. Clive Hart and David Hayman (Berkeley: University of California Press, 1974), 369; Hugh Kenner, *Ulysses* (Baltimore: Johns Hopkins University Press, 1987), 130.

3. Gabler's edition removed approximately six hundred of the commas that had appeared in the 1922 edition but which are not present in the Rosenbach manuscript. These commas, along with other alterations, such as the addition of quotation marks and other devices to elucidate the syntax, were likely introduced by a new typist, who typed only "Eumaeus" (*U*-G 3:1749).

4. Fritz Senn, *Inductive Scrutinies: Focus on Joyce,* ed. Christine O'Neill (Dublin: Lilliput Press, 1995), 17.

5. Karen Lawrence, *The Odyssey of Style in "Ulysses"* (Princeton: Princeton University Press, 1981), 168.

6. Bruns, "Eumaeus," 366–68, 370.

7. Ibid., 367; Lawrence, "'Beggaring Description': Politics and Style in Joyce's 'Eumaeus,'" *Modern Fiction Studies* 38 (summer 1992): 356.

8. See Jennifer Levine's excellent article, "James Joyce, Tattoo Artist: Tracing the Outlines of Homosocial Desire," *James Joyce Quarterly* 31 (spring 1994): 277–300. Levine argues that "[c]ompulsively repeating the phrase 'the other' like a nervous tic, the episode takes as a subtext the role of the homosexual Other and makes D. B. Murphy the locus of Bloom's anxiety" (295).

9. Alistair Stead, "Reflections on 'Eumaeus': Ways of Error and Glory in *Ulysses,*" *James Joyce and Modern Literature,* ed. W. J. McCormack and Alistair Stead (London: Routledge & Kegan Paul, 1982), 154–55, 145–47.

10. Barbara Stevens Heusel, "Vestiges of Truth: A Study of James Joyce's 'Eumaeus,'" *Studies in the Novel* 18 (winter 1986): 405.

11. Mark Osteen, "The Money Question at the Back of Everything: Clichés, Counterfeits and Forgeries in Joyce's 'Eumaeus,'" *Modern Fiction Studies* 38 (winter 1992): 833.

12. John Henry Raleigh, "On the Way Home to Ithaca: The Functions of the

'Eumaeus' Section in *Ulysses,*" in *Irish Studies Annual,* ed. Zack Bowen (Newark: University of Delaware Press), 2:53, 57.

13. Andrew Gibson, "'Broken Down and Fast Breaking Up': Style, Technique and Vision in the 'Eumaeus' Episode in *Ulysses,*" *Southern Review* 17 (November 1984): 263, 259, 262.

14. Lawrence, "'Beggaring Description,'" 374, 356, 366, 369, 371.

15. Ibid., 361, 363, 371–72.

16. Ibid., 374, her emphasis.

17. Levine, "Tattoo Artist," 277, 281–82.

18. Ibid., 295.

19. Derek Attridge, *Peculiar Language: Literature as Difference from the Renaissance to James Joyce* (Ithaca: Cornell University Press, 1988), 182, 183.

20. *Queer* has for centuries denoted a "strange, odd, peculiar" person "of questionable character, suspicious, dubious," used especially in Ireland and in nautical contexts; its first recorded use to refer to a homosexual person dates from 1922 (*OED*). Elaine Showalter claims that the term had homosexual connotations before the 1890s (*Sexual Anarchy* [New York: Viking, 1990], 112). The *OED* notes a later date (1935) for the homosexual designation of *gay,* although since the seventeenth century it has connoted a "loose or immoral life." *Faggot* entered the argot of Anglo-American homosexual subcultures around the turn of the century as an extension of *fag,* which referred to a British schoolboy who did menial work for an older student. Joyce's use of these terms thus stands on the boundary between their older, broader reference to persons of dissolute morals or questionable integrity and the specifically homosexual connotation that quickly attached to them in the early twentieth century, concomitant with the diffusion of sexological knowledge about homosexuality. The unusual concentration of these terms in conjunction with "the genus *homo*" in this episode suggests that Joyce was overcoding his text, implying Murphy's suspicious character and his possession of equally dubious, sexual secrets, along with Bloom's uncertain complicity in them.

21. For the etymological and cultural associations among the terms *queer, bogus, counterfeit, buggery, usury, sodomy,* and *heresy,* see Levine, "Tattoo Artist," 292, and Osteen, "The Money Question," 832.

22. Sedgwick defines the term as the endemic, fearful response of heterosexually identified men to the potential *"blackmailability"* of all male bonds "through the leverage of homophobia" (*Between Men: English Literature and Male Homosocial Desire* [New York: Columbia University Press, 1985], 89, Sedgwick's emphasis).

23. Budgen, *James Joyce and the Making of "Ulysses,"* 146.

24. Levine, "Tattoo Artist," 283.

25. According to Lawrence, the "women are 'pictured' as commodities in a system of exchanges between men" ("'Beggaring Description,'" 366), while Levine argues that "Molly lubricates Bloom's relationships with other men," suggesting that Bloom pimps for her ("Tattoo Artist," 293).

26. Don Gifford with Robert J. Seidman, *"Ulysses" Annotated: Notes for James Joyce's "Ulysses"* (Berkeley: University of California Press, 1988), 544. Gifford offers no source for this information. Stuart Gilbert associates Murphy's tattoo with the problem of signatures of identity such as that in the Tichbourne case, also alluded to in "Eumaeus" (*James Joyce's "Ulysses"* [New York: Vintage Books, 1952], 364).

27. Levine, "Tattoo Artist," 284. The Greek-artist-homosexual chain of associations

in the episode is confirmed by references to Achilles, another Greek, whose "tenderness for Patroclus, as much as his Achilles tendon, was his 'most vulnerable point'" (286).

28. Senn remarks on the association between her "black straw hat" and the "black straw sailor hat" that appears the same afternoon, thus associating the streetwalker with the traveling sailor (*Inductive Scrutinies,* 158).

29. For a discussion of the Criminal Law Amendment Act of 1885 and the link it forged between prostitution and homosexuality, see Jeffrey Weeks, "Inverts, Perverts, and Mary-Annes: Male Prostitution and the Regulation of Homosexuality in England in the Nineteenth and Early Twentieth Centuries," in *Hidden from History: Reclaiming the Gay and Lesbian Past,* ed. Martin Duberman et al. (New York: Penguin, 1989), 195–211.

30. Weldon Thornton explains Bloom's and possibly Joyce's confusion between sections 2 and 11 of the Criminal Law Amendment Act (*Allusions in "Ulysses"* [Chapel Hill: University of North Carolina Press, 1968], 447–48).

31. Among others, Susan Brienza notes that the number sixteen is "an obvious hint of self-reference to this very chapter 16," a gesture of "self-recursiveness" that, like Shem's "'indelible ink'" in the *Wake* and the "lice/lies" of both of these lowlife, perverted, artist figures or "fabricators," links Shem and Murphy, "Eumaeus" and the *Wake,* and Murphy and Joyce. In her remarkable essay, Murphy thus "appears as Jimmy Joyce wearing a Homer T-shirt" ("Murphy, Shem, Morpheus, and Murphies: 'Eumaeus' Meets the *Wake,*" in *Joycean Occasions: Essays from the Milwaukee Conference,* ed. Janet E. Dunleavy et al. [Newark: University of Delaware Press, 1987], 81–85). According to Levine, the "insistent relationship between the numbers 6, 16, and 22" in "Eumaeus" is so "overdetermined," including the relative difference between Bloom's and Stephen's ages (sixteen years), that the tattoo on Murphy's chest implicates him "both with a woman and with another man" ("Tattoo Artist," 286–87, 289).

32. Levine offers a compelling argument for an analogy between the homosexual and the Jew in this allusion; claiming that Antonio's internalized homophobia in Shakespeare's drama is linked to his anti-Semitism, she urges that "as Antonio is to Shylock, so too . . . is Bloom to Murphy—but with a twist. In the play the homosexual hates the Jew who mirrors him. In *Ulysses* the Jew hates the (projected) homosexual who mirrors him" ("Tattoo Artist," 292).

33. Among other critics, Raleigh notes that, like Joyce, Murphy has "bad eyes and an omnivorous curiosity about miscellaneous information"; moreover, the sailor remarks that "'he could read a book in the dark' . . . just as Joyce was later to write a book in the dark" ("On the Way Home to Ithaca," 107–8).

34. See, for instance, André Gide's *The Immoralist* and T. E. Lawrence's memoirs. For an analysis of the function of Burton's "Terminal Essay" in the construction of male homosexual desire in the late nineteenth century, see Sedgwick, *Between Men.*

35. Raleigh, "On the Way Home to Ithaca," 102; Brienza, "Murphy, Shem, Morpheus and Murphies," 92. Raleigh cites the fact that Murphy comes from Cork, the birthplace of John Joyce-Simon Dedalus and that he is "a wanderer, drinker," and teller of lying stories to Dubliners (105). He points out that, toward the end of *Ulysses,* Joyce began to let his characters "talk back to him," and that, in Bloom's observations regarding Murphy's yarn spinning, "Joyce appears to be allowing him to have his say about him" (109).

36. Robert Bell, quoted in Osteen, "The Money Question," 837.

37. Osteen, "The Money Question," 832. He somewhat unwillingly admits that

there is no "'essential' Bloom" in *Ulysses* but only "a series of fictions . . . or forgeries" (839).

SIDEREAL WRITING

1. That Joyce is aware of Ithaca as a rock—both a stable and disappointing destination—is apparent from his reference to the "dry rocks pages" of "Ithaca" in a letter to Harriet Shaw Weaver (*Letters I* 173).

2. Late in the chapter, the narrator stresses that return is irrational because of the "unsatisfactory equation between an exodus and return in time through reversible space and an exodus and return in space through irreversible time" (17.2025–27). I am using the term *"unheimlich"* in the sense in which Freud uses the term in his famous 1919 essay on "The 'Uncanny,'" in *On Creativity and the Unconscious: Papers on the Psychology of Art, Literature, Love, Religion,* ed. Benjamin Nelson (New York: Harper and Row, 1958), 122–61. In particular, I want to stress Freud's argument that "*heimlich* is a word the meaning of which develops towards an ambivalence, until it coincides with its opposite, *unheimlich*" (131), and his explanations of the word's two contradictory meanings: "on the one hand, it means that which is familiar and congenial, and on the other, that which is concealed and kept out of sight" (129). For an excellent account of *Finnegans Wake* as an uncanny text, see Kimberly J. Devlin, *Wandering and Return in "Finnegans Wake": An Integrative Approach to Joyce's Fictions* (Princeton: Princeton University Press, 1991).

3. See Bloom's examples of postexilic eminence: "Three seekers of the pure truth, Moses of Egypt, Moses Maimonides, author of *More Nebukim* (Guide of the Perplexed) and Moses Mendelssohn of such eminence that from Moses (of Egypt) to Moses (Mendelssohn) there arose none like Moses (Maimonides)" (17.710–14). The narrator of "Ithaca" humorously associates Bloom himself with Moses when he recalls Bloom's procession "towards the oriental edifice of the Turkish and Warm Baths, 11 Leinster street, with the light of inspiration shining in his countenance and bearing in his arms the secret of the race, graven in the language of prediction" (17.338–41, compare Exodus 34:29).

4. As Joyce explains to Frank Budgen, he wrote "Ithaca" in such a way "that the reader will know everything and know it in the baldest and coldest way" (*Letters I* 159–60).

5. Bloom's preoccupation with Eden is just one version of his hunger for a lost or unreachable promised land that haunts him throughout, whether it is figured as Zion, Agendath Netaim, or Canaan. His desire is apparent in his long fantasy of becoming a gardener (see especially 17.1582–1610), and in his construction of Molly's body as hemispheres of fruit, "plump mellow yellow smellow melons of her rump" (17.2241) that he kisses with satisfaction at the end of the day.

6. Sir Robert Ball, *The Story of the Heavens* (1886; Cassell and Company, 1900), 364.

7. Ball, *The Story of the Heavens,* 337.

8. See "God and the *Jouissance* of ~~The~~ Woman" and "A Love Letter," in *Feminine Sexuality: Jacques Lacan and the école freudienne,* ed. Juliet Mitchell and Jacqueline Rose, trans. Jacqueline Rose (New York: Norton, 1982), 137–61. Lacan's argument that "the" woman does not exist, that man only relates to the cause of his desire, which is a fantasy, helps to explain Bloom's inability to relate to his sexual partner, "the Other, except by way of mediation" (*Feminine Sexuality,* 151). I am suggesting that Joyce sought to characterize, with unusual specificity, not only Bloom's fantasy of Molly as a luminous body (which is also equivalent to mysterious writing), but also Bloom's way of mediating his

relation to her via glass—windows, lenses—which constructs her not only as desirable and fragile, but also as transparent and legible.

9. The narrator of "Ithaca" relates that both Irish and Hebrew were taught on the plain of Shinar 242 years after the flood "in the seminary instituted by Fenius Farsaigh, descendent of Noah, progenitor of Israel, and ascendant of Heber and Heremon, progenitors of Ireland" (17.748–51). Geoffrey Keating, in his seventeenth-century *The History of Ireland* (Foras Feasa ar Eirinn), traces the ancestry of Fenius Farsaigh from Japheth, son of Noah, as follows: Noah—Japheth—Magog—Baath—"Fenius Farsaidh, the ancestor of the posterity of Gaedheal"; from another of Magog's sons, Fathachto, came "Partholon [he who first occupied Ireland after the deluge] and (also) Neimhedh, son of Aghnoman, and, accordingly, the Fir Bolg and Tuatha De Danann." See Keating, *The History of Ireland,* trans. David Comyn (London: David Nutt for The Irish Texts Society, 1902), 1:227.

10. See Ruth Bauerle, *The James Joyce Songbook* (New York: Garland, 1982), 527–31.

11. *The English and Scottish Popular Ballads,* ed. Francis James Child (Boston: Houghton, Mifflin and Co., 1888, 1890), 3:235–36, 240–43. This discussion of child murder by a man named Child (which Joyce certainly consulted, since it was published in 1888 and was the most widely known and authoritative reference work on popular ballads) should be considered in relation to the Childs murder case discussed in "Oxen of the Sun" (14.958–1037), which—like "Little Harry Hughes"—might seem to be about the murder of children (especially in the context of "Oxen") but is actually about fratricide.

For a more contemporary treatment of the Hugh of Lincoln case, which occasioned the arrest in England of nearly one hundred Jews and the hanging of nineteen without a trial, see Joshua Tractenberg, *The Devil and the Jews: The Medieval Conception of the Jew and Its Relation to Modern Anti-Semitism* (New Haven: Yale University Press, 1943), 131–32. A good overview of accusations of ritual murder in Europe may be found in R. Po-Chia Hsia, *The Myth of Ritual Murder: Jews and Magic in Reformation Germany* (New Haven: Yale University Press, 1988).

12. Don Gifford says that Stephen has based his version of the ballad on the variant that Child lists as N, which refers to Little Harry Hughes and the *duke's* daughter (*"Ulysses" Annotated: Notes for James Joyce's "Ulysses"* [Berkeley: University of California Press, 1988], 579). Revealingly, though, Stephen has eliminated all of the references in the ballad to the boy's mother, changing "mother" to "master" in the lines, *"'For if my master he did hear / He'd make it a sorry ball'"* (17.819–20), and making no mention of the last eight verses listed by Child, which concern the mother's discovery of her murdered child. As he did in *Dubliners* (most notably in "Clay"), Joyce is using such changes to highlight what Stephen is repressing: here, it is the influence of his mother on his fear of young women who are quite literally "unfaithful."

13. This scene owes much to Joyce's own former interest in a Jew's daughter, Amalia Popper. See Vicki Mahaffey, "Wunderlich on Joyce and the Case against Art," *Critical Inquiry* 17 (summer 1991): 667–92, and "Fascism and Silence: The Coded History of Amalia Popper," *James Joyce Quarterly* 32 (spring/summer 1995): 501–22.

14. See Patrick McCarthy, "Joyce's Unreliable Catechist: Mathematics and the Narration of 'Ithaca,'" *ELH* 51 (fall 1984): 605–18.

15. See McCarthy's corrective that absolute zero is measured in hundreds (not thousands) of degrees below the freezing point of water ("Joyce's Unreliable Catechist," 607).

16. For the association between Molly, cloth, and obscurity, see chapter 4 of my *Reauthorizing Joyce* (Cambridge: Cambridge University Press, 1988), especially 174–82.

MOLLY'S HEAVENLY BODY AND THE ECONOMY OF THE SIGN

1. Walter Kendrick, *The Secret Museum: Pornography in Modern Culture* (New York: Viking Press, 1987).

2. *James Joyce: The Critical Heritage I,* ed. Robert H. Deming (London: Routledge, 1970), 191–93.

3. Etymologically, *pornography* means "writing about whores."

4. See also *Joyce's Notes and Early Drafts for "Ulysses": Selections from the Buffalo Collection,* ed. Phillip Herring (Charlottesville: University of Virginia Press, 1977), 63.

5. Linda Williams, *Hard Core: Power, Pleasure, and the Frenzy of the Visible* (Berkeley: University of California Press, 1989), 1.

6. Frances Restuccia speaks of the chapter as a "womb of words" (*Joyce and the Law of the Father* [New Haven: Yale University Press 1989], 94).

7. Jeri Johnson points out that "it has been a mistake to search in this ending of *Ulysses* for a recognition or, on the contrary, a censuring of feminine sexuality" ("'Beyond the Veil': *Ulysses,* Feminism, and the Figure of Woman," in *Joyce, Modernity, and Its Mediation,* ed. Christine Van Boheemen [Amsterdam: Rodopi, 1989], 207).

8. Lacan wrote his doctoral thesis on a case of psychosis significantly entitled "Aimée"; in 1933 he published an essay on the Papin sisters; and in the 1970s he devoted himself explicitly to the question Freud had deliberately stayed away from, the answer to the question, "What do women most desire?" See his *De la psychoses paranoïaque dans ses rapports avec la personalité* (Paris: Seuil, 1975).

9. Friedrich Nietzsche, *On the Genealogy of Morals and Ecce Homo,* ed. and trans. Walter Kaufmann (New York: Vintage Books), 266.

10. See Sarah Kofman, *The Enigma of Woman: Woman in Freud's Writing,* trans. Catherine Porter (Ithaca: Cornell University Press, 1985).

11. Stephen Heath, "Men in Feminism: Men and Feminist Theory," in *Men in Feminism,* ed. Alice Jardine and Paul Smith (New York: Methuen, 1987), 44.

12. See Christine Van Boheemen, *The Novel as Family Romance: Language, Gender, and Authority from Fielding to Joyce* (Ithaca: Cornell University Press, 1987).

13. Frank Budgen, *James Joyce and the Making of "Ulysses"* (Bloomington: Indiana University Press, 1960), 318. Also note the projective attribution of "woman's invisible weapon" (9.461).

14. *Joyce's "Ulysses" Notesheets in the British Museum,* ed. Phillip Herring (Charlottesville: University Press of Virginia, 1972), 494.

15. This would seem to be the position of Julia Kristeva, who takes Joyce's word for it, in "Joyce 'The Gracehoper' or the Return of Orpheus," in *James Joyce: The Augmented Ninth,* ed. Bernard Benstock (New York: Syracuse University Press, 1988), 167–81.

16. Toni Morrison, *Playing in the Dark: Whiteness and the Literary Imagination* (Cambridge: Harvard University Press, 1992), 16–17.

17. Luce Irigaray argues that "men's appropriation of the linguistic code attempts to do at least three things: 1) prove that they are fathers; 2) prove that they are more powerful than mother-women; 3) prove that they are capable of engendering the cultural domain as they have been engendered in the natural domain of the ovum, the womb,

the body of a woman" (*Je, tu, nous: Toward a Culture of Difference,* trans. Alison Martin [New York: Routledge, 1993], 69).

18. Sigmund Freud, "Inhibitions, Symptoms and Anxiety," in *The Complete Psychological Works,* trans. James Strachey (London: Hogarth Press, 1953–74), 20:128–29.

19. See also Sander L. Gilman, *Freud, Race, and Gender* (Princeton: Princeton University Press, 1993), who argues that Freud displaces his internalized Jewishness on the image of women. Apparently the *"Jud"* (the Jew) was Viennese slang for the clitoris, and there is a relationship between Freud's understanding of the clitoris as a truncated penis and the construction of circumcision as a form of castration.

20. Helene Cixous, "The Laugh of the Medusa," trans. Keith Cohen and Paula Cohen, *Signs* 1 (winter 1976): 885.

21. This is not only the name of Darantière, the printer (whose name ends the text, and whose decisiveness eventually forced Joyce to stop revising), but also of the Stanislaus character in *Stephen Hero*—the word *scrawl,* which he used to denote "Penelope" precedes shortly before (on *FW* 122).

22. *Joyce's "Ulysses" Notesheets in the British Museum,* 496.

23. See Jacques Derrida, "Ulysses Gramophone: Hear say yes in Joyce," in *James Joyce: The Augmented Ninth,* ed. Bernard Benstock (Syracuse: Syracuse University Press, 1988), 27–75.

24. In another sense, too, Bloom is already a flower of rhetoric. His father's name "Virag" (Hungarian for "flower") was somehow translated into English; but the name is the untranslatable sign outside the chain of substitution. Bloom is already a sign, not a humanistic subject. Virag is also virago without Molly's "O."

25. The protagonist of Italo Svevo's *Senilitá,* for which Joyce provided the title *As a Man Grows Older,* is only 35!

26. Both Mario Praz and Bram Dijkstra show how the image of Medusa proliferates in turn-of-the-century literature and visual art (see Praz, *The Romantic Agony,* trans. Angus Davidson [Oxford: Oxford University Press, 1970], and Dijkstra, *Idols of Perversity: Fantasies of Feminine Evil in Fin-de-Siècle Culture* [Oxford: Oxford University Press, 1986]). Praz gives a long analysis of iconographic manifestations of the phallic woman as Femme Fatale; and many of her qualities apply to Molly Bloom. I shall not pursue the theme of Molly as a bourgeois version of a Salome or Cleopatra, because that would limit my analysis to a descriptive approach of the history of representation at the beginning of the century. In my perspective the importance of Joyce, and his modernity a hundred years later, is that he moves from the iconography of Medusa (which keeps textuality and representation distinct) to invent a kind of textuality which weaves the threat of Medusa into its texture, and thus provides an antidote to it.

27. Jean Baudrillard, *America,* trans. Chris Turner (London: Verso, 1988), 5.

28. Alice A. Jardine relates inscriptions of gender to (post)modernity. The (post)modern projects its own difference from the past as its "femininity." It would seem to me that Joyce anticipates and initiates this move (*Gynesis: Configurations of Woman and Modernity* [Ithaca: Cornell University Press, 1985]).

29. Mark Shechner was probably the first such critic, in *Joyce in Nighttown: A Psychoanalytic Inquiry into "Ulysses"* (Berkeley: University of California Press, 1974); but see also Van Boheemen, *The Novel as Family Romance,* and Restuccia, *Joyce and the Law of the Father.*

30. I take the words from Freud's essay "Fetishism," in *Complete Psychological Works,* 21:154.

31. See *Joyce's Notes and Early Drafts,* 45–46. Herring notes Joyce's ambivalence. Victoria is a triumphant queen and in this connotation a fit association for the phallic Molly; but Queen Victoria is also English, and *Ulysses* also refers to her as a "dead bitch." Since Queen Victoria was dressed in black, she would seem associated with the female figures in Joyce's dreams.

32. See *Joyce's Notes and Early Drafts,* 17 or 79; and *Joyce's "Ulysses" Notesheets in the British Museum,* 494 or 504.

33. See also Philip Kuberski, "The Joycean Gaze: Lucia in the I of the Father," *Substance* 46 (1985): 49–67. Kuberski argues that "Joyce's desire for Lucia and his writing in the *Wake* are part of a refusal to segregate the energy of language and sexuality, to obstruct its libidinal exercise" (58).

34. Freud, "Character and Anal Eroticism," in *Complete Psychological Works,* 9:171.

35. Kristeva, *Revolution in Poetic Language,* trans. Margaret Waller (New York: Columbia University Press, 1984), 63.

36. See "Joyce's Sublime Body: Trauma, Textuality, and Subjectivity" in *Joycean Cultures: Culturing Joyces,* ed. Vincent C. Cheng, Kimberly J. Devlin, and Margot Norris (Newark: University of Delaware Press, 1998), 23–43.

37. Jean Baudrillard, *Symbolic Exchange and Death,* trans. Mike Gane (London: SAGE Publishers Limited, 1993), 101.

38. Jean Baudrillard, *For a Critique of the Political Economy of the Sign,* trans. Charles Levin (St. Louis: Telos Press, 1981), 95.

39. Baudrillard, *Symbolic Exchange and Death,* 102.

40. Ibid., 110.

About the Contributors

JOHN BISHOP is an associate professor of English at the University of California, Berkeley, and author of *Joyce's Book of the Dark: "Finnegans Wake"* (University of Wisconsin Press, 1986).

KIMBERLY J. DEVLIN is an associate professor of English at the University of California, Riverside. She is the author of *Wandering and Return in "Finnegans Wake"* (Princeton University Press, 1991). With Vincent J. Cheng and Margot Norris, she coedited *Joycean Cultures / Culturing Joyces* (University of Delaware Press, 1998). Her work in progress is entitled *Joycean Fraudstuff.*

ENDA DUFFY is an associate professor of English at the University of California, Santa Barbara. His book, *The Subaltern "Ulysses,"* was published by University of Minnesota Press in 1994. He is currently working on a book on speed and modernism.

MAUD ELLMANN is a university lecturer in English and a fellow of King's College, Cambridge. Her publications include *The Poetics of Impersonality: T. S. Eliot and Ezra Pound* (Harvard University Press, 1987), *The Hunger Artists: Starving, Writing, and Imprisonment* (Harvard University Press, 1993), and *Psychoanalytic Literary Criticism: A Reader* (Longman, 1994).

CHERYL HERR is a professor of English at the University of Iowa. Her books are *Joyce's Anatomy of Culture* (University of Illinois Press, 1986), *For the Land They Loved: Irish Political Melodramas, 1890–1925* (Syracuse University Press, 1996), and *Critical Regionalism and Cultural Studies* (University of Florida Press, 1996).

COLLEEN LAMOS is an associate professor of English at Rice University. Her book, *Modernism Astray: Sexual Errancy in T. S. Eliot, James Joyce and Marcel Proust,* is forthcoming from Cambridge University Press. She is coeditor of a special issue of the *European Joyce Studies Annual* on "Joycean Masculinities." Her articles on modernism and queer theory have been published in *Novel, Signs, Contemporary Literature,* the *James Joyce Quarterly,* the *National Women's Studies Association Journal, Pre/text,* the *Lesbian and Gay Studies Newsletter,* and in the collections *Joyce in Context, The Lesbian Postmodern, Lesbian Erotics, Quare Joyce, Critical Ethics,* and *Cross-Purposes.*

JULES LAW teaches as an associate professor of English at Northwestern University. He is the author of *The Rhetoric of Empiricism: Language and Perception from Locke to I. A. Richards* (Cornell University Press, 1993).

KAREN LAWRENCE is a professor of English and dean of humanities at the University of California, Irvine. She is the author of *The Odyssey of Style in "Ulysses"* (Princeton University Press, 1981) and *Penelope Voyages: Women and Travel in the British Literary Tradition* (Cornell University Press, 1994). She has also edited *Transcultural Joyce* (Cambridge University Press, 1998) and *Decolonizing Tradition: New Views of Twentieth-Century "British" Literary Canons* (Illinois University Press, 1991). She is a former president of the International James Joyce Foundation.

GARRY LEONARD is an associate professor of English at the University of Toronto. His book, *Reading "Dubliners" Again: A Lacanian Perspective,* was published by Syracuse University Press in 1993; he has also guest edited a special double issue of the *James Joyce Quarterly* on Joyce and advertising. His second book, *Joyce and Advertising: The New (Improved!) Testament* is forthcoming from University of Florida Press.

VICKI MAHAFFEY teaches as a professor of English at the University of Pennsylvania. She is the author of *Reauthorizing Joyce,* published by Cambridge University Press in 1988 (paperback edition, University of Florida Press, 1995), and *States of Desire: Wilde, Yeats, Joyce, and the Irish Experiment,* published by Oxford University Press in 1998.

PATRICK MCGEE is a professor of English at Louisiana State University. His books include *Paperspace: Style as Ideology in Joyce's "Ulysses"* (University of Nebraska Press, 1988); *Telling the Other: The Question of Value in Modern and Postcolonial Writing* (Cornell University Press, 1992); *Ismael Reed and the Ends of Race* (St. Martin's Press, 1997); and *Cinema, Theory, and Political Responsibility in Contemporary Culture* (Cambridge University Press, 1997). He is currently working on a new book manuscript, *Cultural Montage: Movies, Masculinity, and Class.*

MARGOT NORRIS is professor of English and comparative literature at the University of California, Irvine, where she teaches modern literature. She is the author of *The Decentered Universe of "Finnegans Wake"* (Johns Hopkins University Press, 1974) and *Joyce's Web* (University of Texas Press, 1992), as well as a book on modern intellectual history, *Beasts of the Modern Imagination: Darwin, Nietzsche, Kafka, Ernst, and Lawrence* (Johns Hopkins University Press, 1985). She is currently finishing a book titled *Writing War in the Twentieth Century.*

MARILYN REIZBAUM is a professor of English at Bowdoin College. She is currently at Tel Aviv University. Her book, *James Joyce's Judaic Other,* was published by Stanford University Press in 1999, and she is the author of numerous essays on Joyce. She also works in contemporary Scottish and Irish literatures and postcolonial theory, and has written on the work of Eavan Bolond, Neil Jordan, Liz Lochhead, and Irvine Welsh. Her essay, "Surviving on Cat and *Maus:* Art Spiegelman's Holocaust Tale," is forthcoming in *Theory and Criticism: An Israeli Forum.*

BONNIE KIME SCOTT is a professor of English and women's studies at the University of Delaware. She is the author of *Joyce and Feminism* (Indiana University Press, 1984), *James Joyce* (Harvester Press, 1987), and *Refiguring Modernism* (2 vols., Indiana University Press, 1995). She has edited *New Alliances in Joyce Studies* (University of Delaware, 1988) and *The Gender of Modernism: A Critical Anthology* (Indiana University Press, 1990). She has recently completed an edition of *The Selected Letters of Rebecca West* (Yale University Press, forthcoming).

CAROL SHLOSS is a professor of English at West Chester University and the author of three books: *Flannery O'Connor's Dark Comedies: The Limits of Inference* (Louisiana State University Press, 1980), *In Visible Light: Photography and the American Writer* (Oxford University Press, 1987), and *Gentlemen Photographers* (Northeastern University Press, 1987). She is currently writing a biography of Joyce's daughter, Lucia, entitled *To Dance in the Wake.*

ROBERT SPOO is the editor of the *James Joyce Quarterly* and an associate professor of English at the University of Tulsa. His book, *James Joyce and the Language of History,* was published by Oxford University Press in 1994.

JOSEPH VALENTE is an associate professor of English at the University of Illinois at Urbana-Champaign. He is author of *James Joyce and the Problem of Justice: Negotiating Sexual and Colonial Difference* (Cambridge University Press, 1995) and the editor of *Quare Joyce* (University of Michigan Press, 1998). He is also the guest editor of a special issue of the *James Joyce Quarterly* on Joyce and homosexuality. His upcoming book is entitled *Contested Territory: Ideas of Manhood in (Post)Colonial Ireland.*

CHRISTINE VAN BOHEEMEN is professor of English (chair) at the University of Amsterdam and board member of the Belle van Zuylen Institute for Women's Studies. With Fritz Senn, she edits *European Joyce Studies.* Her book, *The Novel as Family Romance: Language, Gender, and Authority from Fielding to Joyce,* was published by Cornell University Press in 1987. The essay on "Penelope" in this volume is part of a longer argument: *James Joyce and the Trauma of History: Reading, Affect and the Postcolonial Symbolic.*

Index